Purāṇa Perennis

M000305188

Purāṇa Perennis

Reciprocity and Transformation in Hindu and Jaina Texts

Edited by
Wendy Doniger

STATE UNIVERSITY OF NEW YORK PRESS

for all the Davids

Production by Ruth Fisher
Marketing by Bernadette LaManna

Published by
State University of New York Press, Albany

© 1993 State University of New York

All rights reserved

Printed in the United States of America

No part of this book may be used or reproduced in any manner whatsoever without written permission except in the case of brief quotations embodied in critical articles and reviews.

For information, address the State University of New York Press, State University Plaza, Albany, NY 12246

Library of Congress Cataloging-in-Publication Data

Doniger, Wendy.
Purana perennis : reciprocity and transformation in Hindu and Jaina texts / Wendy Doniger.
p. cm.
Includes bibliographical references and index.
ISBN 0-7914-1381-0 (alk. paper).—ISBN 0-7914-1382-9 (pbk. : alk. paper)
1. Puranas—Criticism, interpretation, etc. I. Title.
BL1140.26.D66 1993
294.5′925—dc20 92-25322
CIP

10 9 8 7 6 5 4 3 2 1

Contents

PART III. FROM HINDU TO JAINA AND BACK AGAIN

Introduction

Ezekiel saw the wheel, 'way up in the middle of the air,
Ezekiel saw the wheel, 'way up in the middle of the air.
And the little wheel ran by faith, and the big wheel ran by
the grace of God.
'Tis a wheel in a wheel, 'way up in the middle of the air.

Traditional African-American song

And when I looked, behold the four wheels by the cherubim, one wheel by one cherub, and another wheel by another cherub; and the appearance of the wheels was like the color of a beryl stone. And as for their appearances, they four had one likeness, as if a wheel had been in the midst of a wheel.

Ezekiel 10.9–10

The Hebrew Bible version of the vision of Ezekiel speaks of a wheel within a wheel; the African-American version speaks of two wheels, one of faith and the other of grace. These two texts might themselves be regarded as a wheel within a wheel, two interlocking interpretations, one written, one oral; one ancient, one modern; one Jewish, one Christian. The texts that are the subject of this volume also run on those two sets of wheels, written and oral, ancient and modern, and, in this case, Hindu and Jaina. The little wheel of faith (*śraddhā*) might stand for the so-called Great Tradition of India, to borrow Robert Redfield's seminal terminology for the pan-Indian Sanskritic tradition that self-consciously traces its lineage back to the Veda and the Epics. The big wheel of the grace of God (*bhakti*) might stand for the equally so-called Little Tradition of India, the village tradition of localized, vernacular, basically oral culture.

That the Little Tradition is the big wheel rather than the little wheel should not surprise us; the Redfield model has begun to turn upside down, or inside out. In the hands of Redfield (whom a colleague once described, unkindly, as a man who went around kicking in open doors), it began a fruitful conversation. But in later years, and in other hands, it was invoked, more often than not, to argue that vernacular myths and rituals were, in comparison with their Sanskrit counterparts, late and low (or, to use the phrase that F. Max Müller applied to myth in comparison with religion, "silly, senseless, and savage"). The paradigm was also used to draw too sharp a line between these presumably high and low cultures, ignoring the fact that a Brahmin who wrote a Sanskrit text with one hand (his right, one assumed) was also quite likely to be the author of a Tamil oral tale with the other hand (presumably the left). Or, to use A. K. Ramanujan's terminology, every Indian who had Sanskrit as his father tongue had a vernacular as his mother tongue.

Finally, in the decades since Redfield's work the most vibrant strain in Indology has concentrated on the Little Tradition, making it major in many important senses. Thus the concept of the "Great and Little Traditions" has proved to be a ladder that we used to get where we are now but must now kick out from under us, or at least modify in major ways. The wheel is within the wheel—but which is the center and which the periphery? Or would it be better to say that each is within the other?

The essays in this volume grew out of a conference on the Purāṇas at the University of Wisconsin, Madison, in August 1985, a conference organized by Velcheru Narayana Rao, generously supported by a grant from the National Endowment for the Humanities, and attended by Purāṇa scholars from India and Europe as well as America. Among the participants was Ludo Rocher, whose work on the Purāṇas has culminated not in a paper for this volume but in a volume that has immediately become the standard work on the subject, encompassing and extending the previous base established by the work of R. C. Hazra.[1] Rocher's work is cited by many of the authors in this volume and is the base from which we all implicitly proceed.[2]

The discussion at that conference ranged widely, as do the texts that inspired it, but time and again we found ourselves returning to one central theme: the relationship between the so-called Mahāpurāṇas, or "Great" Purāṇas, of the Sanskrit tradition (themselves texts that the Indologist, i.e., Sanskritic, Establishment largely ignored) and the many other sorts of Purāṇas. These latter were regarded (by those few Indologists who knew them at all) as poor cousins of the already poor Mahāpurāṇas, and included the Upapurāṇas, or "Subpurāṇas," of the Sanskrit tradition (which do not, be it noted, correspond to the Little Tradition texts); the *sthalapurāṇas* of the Dravidian Hindu traditions; and the Purāṇas of other South Asian traditions, such as the Jainas. If Vedic texts were the Brahmins of Indology, the Purāṇas were the Untouchables. We all felt that a study of these neglected traditions was long overdue, as a kind of Purāṇic affirmative action. The essays in this book represent a first step in that direction.

The readers of the manuscript (C. Mackenzie Brown, Ludo Rocher, Herman Tull, and two who preferred, like Paurāṇikas, to remain anonymous) offered many useful suggestions for improvements but basically agreed with us that such a study was badly needed. One anonymous reader rather grudgingly acknowledged:

> The literature . . . covered in this volume has attracted few Western scholars; the book covers an area of research in which there are few published monographs in English. The original texts are not found in most University libraries. The journals (mostly Indian) which contain some information on this topic are equally inaccessible. Thus the present volume fulfills a need . . . As Indian Studies progresses, scholars are giving more attention to texts which are little discussed in the standard manuals and books in the field. Indianists now are more concerned to sort out the mutual influences of the well-known pan-Indian texts and more localized or "sectarian" traditions. The book makes a contribution here . . . All the articles attempt, in different ways, to advance knowledge in the field and in some instances to re-orient scholarly thinking on this extensive body of knowledge.

And another reader said, with a bit more enthusiasm, "This is a collection of articles by leading scholars in their fields. Such a collection naturally demands our attention. Without exception the articles are intellectually stimulating, demanding, and instructive . . . The topic is very important."

C. Mackenzie Brown particularly liked "the attempt on the part of some of the authors to grapple with the problem of what the 'Purāṇic process' is, using a wide variety of examples drawn from important but relatively less well known texts, [and] the richness of insights in many of the individual essays. As a whole, they give the reader who is already somewhat familiar with Purāṇic literature a much more intimate feel of what it is like to live in a Purāṇicized world, and of what is involved in constructing and/or transforming that world from within." And Herman Tull commented, "The Purāṇas, despite all their peculiarities and pretensions, are essentially collections of stories. And the authors of the essays collected in *Purāṇa Perennis* are all superb story-tellers. They are also top-notch scholars. [The volume] is emblematic of the most important current in Indological studies in the last twenty years."

Since most of us have been one anothers' friends, colleagues, teachers, and students for decades, editing the papers felt to me more like attending a family party than chairing an academic gathering. Indeed, were it not for the presence of our two Jaina cousins, the Hindu-wallahs would have constituted an almost incestuously insular group. The authors, as well as their texts, suffer (or benefit, depending upon your point of view) from a very real sort of intertextuality. This being so, I was pleased to find that we did in fact disagree in several of our approaches to the central problems of definition and interpretation. Since most of the authors have agendas that relate to reading the Purāṇas as a whole, over and above their particular foci, they deal, often quite differently, with many of the same central issues. Thus, for example, the classical list of the "five distinguishing marks" (*pañcalakṣaṇa*) is utilized in rather different ways by Narayana Rao, Shulman, Hardy, Cort, and Jaini. The *Bhāgavata Purāṇa* also proved to be the key to several different sorts of arguments, as it was discussed in relationship to the *Devībhāgavata Purāṇa* (Doniger and Hardy), the *Mahābhāgavata Purāṇa* (Shulman), and the Jaina version of the *Bhāgavata Purāṇa* (Jaini). The *Bhāgavata Purāṇa* also served as a bridge between other issues, forming as it does a link between the Sanskrit North and the Dravidian South and between Vedic and Purāṇic Sanskrit. There are also more specific resonances between the papers: thus, for example, in addition to the more detailed resonances (even arguments) between Cort and Jaini, Ramanujan and Doniger speak of the "scrap Purāṇa" (the *Skanda*), Patton and Doniger cite different versions of the myths of Urvaśī and Utathya, Patton and Shulman discuss very different aspects of *bhakti,* and Hardy and Doniger bring out different aspects of the myths of the *liṅga* and of the sinner saved from hell. The essays in this collection constitute a kind of Venn diagram of intersecting concerns of authors attempting to trace general patterns within a set of most unruly texts.

It might at first appear that some of these essays are about ideology (political)—a contemporary (or, if you don't like it, trendy) subject, while others are about theology (religious)—a traditional (or, if you don't like it, reactionary) subject. But, as Laurie L. Patton reminds us from the start, theology *is* an ideology, and our authors explore various sorts of ideologies, Brahminic, subversive, feminist, and so forth. Patton explores the theology of the *ṛṣis*, while Narayana Rao writes about the self-definition and Brahminic ideology of the Purāṇas. Doniger and Ramanujan, through mythological and literary/semiotic analysis, respectively, draw out certain countercultural and feminist ideologies from their texts, while Shulman's text might, in other hands, be used in the service of colonial and subaltern discourse, for Rudyard Kipling's "How the Elephant Got His Nose," in his *Just-So Stories,* is surely a satire on the myth of Gajendra. Hardy charts a number of rational and rationalizing ideological strategies working within the constraints of localism. And Hardy, Jaini, and Cort trace the lineage of an agonistic interaction between Hindus and Jainas, each group encompassing the ideology of the other by laying claim to the same Purāṇic subjects. A wheel within a wheel.

The Hindu-Jaina exchange is not the only reciprocal one, however. For this whole book is about reciprocal transformations, the two-way stretch (what we call "chicken-and-egg" and Indians call "seed-and-tree") of the Great and Little Traditions, with constant cybernetic feedback between pan-Indian culture and localized culture, rather than subordination of one to the other, as has often been reductionistically supposed. These reciprocal transformations operate between Veda and Purāṇa (Patton) and among Epic, Mahāpurāṇa, and Upapurāṇa (Doniger); between North and South, in several branches: Sanskrit and Telugu (Narayana Rao), Sanskrit and Kannada (Ramanujan), Sanskrit and Tamil (Shulman), and Sanskrit, Tamil, and Prakrit (Hardy); and, finally, between Hindu and Jaina (Hardy, Jaini, and Cort).

In the hope of making the book accessible to a nonspecialist audience, I have tried to de-Sanskritize it as far as possible. This editing is the reverse of the process that M. N. Srinivas called "Sanskritization." For where castes rise in both status and power by Sanskritizing, texts fall in status but rise in (readership) power by de-Sanskritizing. (The chapter by John E. Cort, being in part a bibliographical essay, necessarily contains more Sanskrit than the other essays.) Nevertheless, there is a bare minimum of Sanskrit terminology shared by these essays that even the non-Indologist reader might be expected to learn or to ignore, as the case might be: *asura* (an anti-god), *apsaras* (a celestial nymph or courtesan), *bhakta* (a devotee), *bhakti* (devotion, passionate love of God for worshipper and worshipper for God), *brahman* (ultimate reality), *dharma* (religious law), *gandharva* (a demigod, celestial musician), *Kali Age* (the last, and worst, of the four ages), *karma* (the effects of past actions on future lives), *kāvya* (ornate poetry), *kinnara* (a mythical beast, half horse and half demigod), *līlā* (play, divine sport), *liṅga* (the erect phallus of the god Śiva), *mantra* (a hymn, particularly a Vedic hymn), *māyā* (illusion), *mokṣa* (release or liberation, especially from the wheel of rebirth), *pañcalakṣaṇa* (the five distinguishing marks of a Purāṇa), *phalaśruti* (the fruit gained by hearing a Purāṇa), *rākṣasa* (minor demon), *ṛṣi* (a seer, or sage), *saṃsāra* (the wheel of rebirth, involvement in ordinary life), *śāstra* (a science or an authoritative scientific text), *smṛti* (texts, such as the Epics, Purāṇas, and *dharmaśāstras,* created and "remembered" by humans), *śruti* (texts, such as the Vedas, created by gods and "heard" by humans), *sthalapurāṇa* (local Purāṇa), *stotra* (hymn of praise), *tapas* (inner heat produced by asceticism), and *yakṣa* (a demigod associated with magic and fertility). Further information about Sanskrit terms is provided in the Index, which Matthew Schmalz fastidiously prepared. I invite the reader, armed with this arsenal of Sanskrit terminology, to sally forth into the living jungle of texts known as Purāṇas.

I.

From Veda and Epic to Purāṇa and Upapurāṇa

1

The Transparent Text: Purāṇic Trends in the Bṛhaddevatā

Laurie L. Patton

THE QUESTION OF TRANSITIONAL TEXTS

The transition from the religious conceptions expressed in the Vedas, Brāhmaṇas and Upaniṣads to those expressed in the Purāṇas of "classical" Hinduism has always been a matter of great delicacy. How is one to account for the theological and ideological fissures among those texts that constellate (either positively or negatively) around the gods of the Vedic sacrifice and those that form around the triad of the more "popular" deities, Viṣṇu, Śiva, and Brahmā?

On the one hand, the unignorable fact is that certain large-scale transitions do occur over a discernible period. Despite his lingering magnificence,[1] Indra does take a back seat to Śiva and Viṣṇu; Sarasvatī is transformed from a sacred river to Brahmā's wife; and Viṣṇu is elevated from a triple-striding, one-act deity to a major god of colossal proportions. On the other hand, the nature and extent of these transitions are perennially open to debate, and virtually impossible to determine with any degree of certainty. Alf Hiltebeitel writes of the problem as follows:

> A period of consolidation, sometimes identified as one of "Hindu synthesis" "Brahmanic synthesis" or "orthodox synthesis"

> takes place between the time of the late Vedic *Upaniṣads* (c. 500 B.C.E.) and the period of Gupta imperial ascendancy (c. 320–467 C.E.). Discussion of this consolidation, however, is initially complicated by a lack of historiographical categories adequate to the task of integrating the diverse textual, inscriptional, and archaeological data of this long formative period. The attempt to cover as much of this span as possible with the name "epic period," because it coincides with the dates that are usually assigned to the formation and completion of the Hindu epics (particularly the *Mahābhārata*), is misleading, since so much of what transpires can hardly be labeled "epic." On the other hand, attempts to define the period in terms of heterogeneous forces operating upon Hinduism from within (assimilation of local deities and cults, geographical spread) and without (heterodox and foreign challenges) either have failed to register or have misrepresented the implications of the apparent fact that the epics were "works in progress" during the whole period.[2]

While the details of periodicization need not detain the present study, Hiltebeitel's discussion of the *Mahābhārata* raises two crucial points. First, the concept of a 'transitional period' from Vedic to classical Hinduism, of which the "epic" is the most adequate expression, is problematic. This view assumes that religious history consists of "periods" in which texts were not transitional but more "stable" in nature. From that assumption it follows that these periods were characterized by certain essential traits, which then underwent the process of change. A static perspective of religious history results. According to this schema, the transition period can be valid only if it is flanked by two stable periods; the transitional text can be valid only if there are other more "straightforward" texts before and after it.

Second, Hiltebeitel points out that the transition from Vedic to classical was mediated in a number of different ways, not all of them "epic" in character. To be sure, the *Mahābhārata* is one of the most obvious examples of a transitional text, containing Vedic material designated as "narrative" and "story" (*itihāsa* and *ākhyāna*), as well as material found in the Purāṇas of a later date, all woven around an epic rendition of the famous battle between the Pāṇḍavas and the Kauravas. However, one can also take the view that all texts are in some way transitional texts, moving between and interacting with different versions of reality. And, some texts, often characterized as awkwardly eclectic or unmanageably encyclopedic, reflect such interactions more transparently than others. Such a view opens the way toward reading works other than the Epics with an eye toward the interactions between the later Vedic worldview and that which has been deemed the more classically "Hindu" form of thought.

Wendy Doniger O'Flaherty has treated the *Jaiminīya Brāhmaṇa* in just such a fashion. The *Jaiminīya Brāhmaṇa* moves out of the Vedic sacrificial arena into other realms of human experience—of sex and violence, of human passion and royal intrigue. As she writes,

> It seems possible that the *Jaiminīya,* combining as it does the priestly and the folk traditions, the sacred and the profane, and coming as it does almost precisely half-way between the Vedic and the Epic recensions, provided a kind of stepping stone, a half-way house for the folk tradition to touch down for a moment in the Sanskrit world before leaping back into the vernacular culture that had always sustained it and would continue to do so for many centuries. Indeed, it is equally possible that the *Jaiminīya* author (or authors) did in fact invent many of the particular images and turns of phrase that make the *Jaiminīya* story different from all the others and that these bright moments then fed back into the folk tradition, enriching it in turn.[3]

The movement between the folk and the Sanskritic tradition is depicted as a interwoven process of change—so dynamic, in fact, that the distinction between "high" and "low" tradition itself becomes harder and harder to make the more one analyzes a text such as the *Jaiminīya.*

THE *BṚHADDEVATĀ*: A CASE FOR A COMPARATIVE READING

The Date of the Text

A text that has much in common with the *Jaiminīya,* the *Bṛhaddevatā* may be even more transparently interactive in nature than its *Brāhmaṇa* counterpart. Until recently, it has been classed as thoroughly and uncompromisingly Vedic. The core of the *Bṛhaddevatā* is an *anukramaṇī*—literally, a "right ordering" but perhaps more intelligibly called an "index." Its eclectic contents are gathered around a core index of Vedic deities. This index enumerates for each *mantra* (hymn) of the *Ṛg Veda* the deity that properly "belongs" to that *mantra*. Thus, by implication, the *Bṛhaddevatā* is concerned with the appropriate use of the *mantras* in Vedic ritual. The text also tells a number of *itihāsas*, or narratives, to complete the picture, detailing the circumstances in which that *mantra* was spoken to the deity. In the same Vedic vein, the basic function of the *Bṛhaddevatā*'s narratives is the explanation of *mantra* for ritual purposes. Such stories make *mantras* meaningful and thus render the sacrifice more efficacious. In this aspect, the narratives of the *Bṛhaddevatā* continue the particularly Vedic projects of the *Nirukta*[4] and *Mīmāṃsā*[5] texts of asserting the everyday meaningfulness of the Veda.[6]

Until recently, A. A. Macdonell's edition of the *Bṛhaddevatā* has been treated as the standard text. For Macdonell, it could safely be assumed that the original work was probably composed between the time of the Brāhmaṇas and that of the Sūtras. Macdonell wedges the *Bṛhaddevatā* between Yāska's etymological dictionary, the *Nirukta,* dated by Lakṣman Sarup around 500 B.C.E.,[7] and Kātyāyana's *Sarvānukramaṇī,* which, while possessing much in common with the concise style of the *Śrauta Sūtra* of the *White Yajur Veda,* still has many Vedic peculiarities that are clearly pre-Pāṇinean. For Macdonell, the *Bṛhaddevatā,* as the *Sarvānukramaṇī*'s chief source, must be placed no later than 400 B.C.E.[8] Yet Macdonell's work of dating the *Bṛhaddevatā* is complicated by the fact that there are two recensions of the text—one longer than the other by about one sixth. In order to account for these two recensions, Macdonell claims that the longer version of the *Bṛhaddevatā* was the original; this original was then later abridged to form a shorter recension.

In 1979, Muneo Tokunaga, in a Harvard dissertation and a subsequent article (1981),[9] threw all of Macdonell's editorial principles into question. Tokunaga claims that the nature of the *Bṛhaddevatā* is more complicated than Macdonell assumes. To him, none of Macdonell's arguments proves the antiquity or authenticity of the text. In an intricate philological *tour de force,* Tokunaga posits a series of three scribes who successively interpolated material onto the original "core" text. In his view, this core text was probably Śaunaka's *Devatānukramaṇī,* or "Index of Deities"—a text no longer extant, but surmised to be similar to the grammarian Śaunaka's other *anukramaṇīs* and grammatical treatises on the *Ṛg Veda*. The two recensions of the *Bṛhaddevatā* mean that the *Devatānukramaṇī* was expanded twice. Thus, Tokunaga hypothesizes that the first expansion of the *Bṛhaddevatā* was the shorter recension, composed in the early Purāṇic period between the first and fifth centuries of the common era. He believes that the later, longer version—the "second" expansion—was probably composed between the seventh and eleventh centuries of the common era. Tokunaga's idea of successive expansions also explains the title of the "*Bṛhaddevatā*"—which must originally have been the "*Bṛhaddevatānukramaṇī,*" or the "expanded *Devatānukramaṇī.*" From the perspective of dating alone, the *Bṛhaddevatā*'s expansion at the time of the formation of the early Purāṇas has important consequences for the reading and evaluation of it as an interactive text. While it is impossible to determine definitively whether the author of the text consciously drew on Purāṇic sources, a comparison with Purāṇic texts can shed some new light on its rather eclectic nature.

In addition, the *Bṛhaddevatā*'s narratives, explaining the speakers of certain dialogical (*saṃvāda*) hymns of the *Ṛg Veda,* have been deemed by some to be the source of the work's value. For Macdonell and other scholars of the nineteenth century and early twentieth century, the *Bṛhaddevatā* was thought to comprise the earliest extant collection of such explanatory legends. The text could thus shed a good deal of light on the nature of Vedic composition, Vedic interpretation, and the relationships between the Vedic and the Epic genres.

As I have demonstrated elsewhere,[10] much scholarly ink has been spilled on whether the Vedic or the Epic traditions contained the "original" or "prior" collection of narratives.[11] Because of this overemphasis upon origins, most studies comparing the *Bṛhaddevatā* with non-Vedic texts have centered upon the Epics, specifically the *Mahābhārata.*[12] There are obvious similarities in content between the two texts, such as the tales of the *ṛṣis* Lopāmudrā and Agastya, the birth and exploits of Dīrghatamas, the birth of the *ṛṣis* Agastya and Vasiṣṭha from a pot, the legend of Purūravas and Urvaśī, and others. As a result of this debate over origins,[13] however, the potentials for other kinds of comparison between the *Bṛhaddevatā* and non-Vedic texts have been ignored. The Purāṇas have been eclipsed in a flurry of motivic and text-critical analyses, and it is to these neglected comparisons that the discussion must turn.

THE *BṚHADDEVATĀ* AND THE PURĀṆAS: PARALLELS AND MODIFICATIONS

It is necessary to begin a comparison between the *Bṛhaddevatā* and the Purāṇas by a brief mention of the tales that the Purāṇas and the *Bṛhaddevatā* have in common—specifically, the well-known tale of Urvaśī and Purūravas and the equally well-known accounts of the births of the sages Aṅgiras, Bhṛgu, Atri, and Vasiṣṭha. To be sure, since these tales are common in Vedic, Epic, and Purāṇic texts, the *Bṛhaddevatā* could well be seen as doing nothing more than using famous Vedic antecedents in order to establish itself as an authentically Vedic text. While it is not my purpose to discuss each account in detail, a brief discussion of these stories will reveal that the *Bṛhaddevatā* is in fact doing more than that. As will be shown below, the *Bṛhaddevatā* adds certain emphases to these famous tales that the Brāhmaṇas lack, but that the Epics begin to incorporate, and the Purāṇas solidify and amplify. Thus, coming as it does in the later period of the formation of the Epic and the beginning period of the formation of the Purāṇas, the *Bṛhaddevatā* both reflects the changes in emphasis that the Epic makes and anticipates the further elaboration on these changes that are found in the Purāṇas.

First, the *Bṛhaddevata* adds a theological component to the tale of Purūravas and Urvaśī that the Brāhmaṇa version does not emphasize but that the Purāṇic and later accounts elaborate upon.[14] In the *Śatapatha Brāhmaṇa* version (11.5.1.1–17), the *apsaras* Urvaśī marries Purūravas with the condition that he never appear naked before her. The *gandharva*s come in one night and sneak away two lambs that were tied to her bed, and she cries out that the theft has occurred as if there were no hero or man around to stop it. Purūravas, in response to Urvaśī's cry, springs out of bed without thinking. The *gandharva*s, expecting this movement, flash lightning to expose his nakedness. As anticipated, Urvaśī disappears and Purūravas wanders until he came to a lake where there are water birds, and he thinks he recognizes Urvaśī in that form. The nymphs, also in the form of water birds, appear, and they have a conversation. The *Brāhmaṇa* mentions that Urvaśī then lies with him for one night, and the *gandharva*s give him a magic fire. Although Purūravas leaves it in the wood, he discovers the next day that it has sprouted up in the form of an *aśvattha* tree. The *gandharva*s teach him a special way to kindle and cook rice with this tree's wood, thus initiating him into becoming a *gandharva* himself.[15]

The *Bṛhaddevatā* tells the story as follows:

> Now in former times the *apsaras* Urvaśī lived with the royal *ṛṣi* Purūravas. And having made a contract together she acted according to *dharma* toward him. And the chastiser of Pāka was jealous [*asūyan*] of Purūravas's living together with her,

> his passion like that of Brahmā's and his splendor as if he were Indra. He said to the bolt at his side, with the purpose of pushing them apart, "Break up, O Bolt, the affection of these two, as you wish to be dear to me." The bolt, saying, "OK," destroyed their affection with its own *māyā;* then without her, the king wandered around as if insane. As he wandered, he saw in a lake what seemed to be the beautiful Urvaśī, surrounded by beautiful friends at her side.[16] He said to her "Come back." She said to the king in sorrow, "You cannot obtain me here and now; in heaven you will obtain me again." This conversation between two [figures] connected with an invocation, Yāska thinks is a dialogue but Śaunaka [thinks is] a story. That is the (Ṛg Vedic] *sūkta* [beginning] **"Hey wife, turn your heart and mind to me. Stay here, dangerous woman, and let us exchange words. If we do not speak out these thoughts of ours they will bring us no joy, even on the most distant day."** (*RV* 10.95.1) (*BD* 7.147cd–154)

The *Viṣṇu Purāṇa* adds the gods Mitra and Varuṇa to the story, explaining the early form of Urvaśī through a theological motif:[17] Mitra and Varuṇa produce Agastya, as they are excited by the charms of Urvaśī and spill their seed. At the same time, they curse her to descend to earth and live with a mortal. The *Bhāgavata Purāṇa*[18] and the fourteenth-century commentator Sāyaṇa, drawing on Purāṇic and other sources, further theologize the story. As Sāyaṇa tells it, Īla the king goes out hunting with the sons of Manu and comes to a place where Umā, the daughter of the mountain, is engaged in love-play with Śiva. Because he has intruded upon this scene, he is cursed to become a woman. He pleads with Śiva to make him a man again, but Śiva defers to Devī, whose judgment is to allow him to be both male and female, six months at a time. When he is female, Budha, the son of Soma, desires her and has a son by her. This son is called "Purūravas," the king of Pratiṣṭhāna. The rest of the legend follows essentially the same lines as that of the *Brāhmaṇa.*

A comparison of the three versions of the tales shows that in the *Bṛhaddevatā* it is Indra who drives the two lovers apart, and not the *gandharva* as told in the *Śatapatha Brāhmaṇa* version of the tale. The *Bṛhaddevatā* thus makes the story a function of the anger of the god Indra, one of the *Bṛhaddevatā*'s triad of Agni, Indra, Sūrya.[19] The plot of this narrative is motivated by the presence of a lustful god.

So, too, in the accounts that Sāyaṇa and the *Viṣṇu Purāṇa* give, the presence of the gods is crucial to the development of the tale. As the *Viṣṇu Purāṇa* states, the gods Mitra and Varuṇa spill their seed and curse Urvaśī to live with a mortal. Sāyaṇa adds that the god Śiva curses Īla the king to become a woman because he has interrupted the worship of a devotee. Īlā in female form becomes the mother of Purūravas, the hero of the tale. Thus, in contrast with the *Brāhmaṇa* version of the tale, both the *Bṛhaddevatā* and the Purāṇas tell an account of divine exploits, where worship of and respect for the deity become crucial to the fate of the central characters of Purūravas and Urvaśī. In both the *Bṛhaddevatā* and the Purāṇas, the theological element is stressed.

The next group of stories that share parallels with the Purāṇas also occurs in various forms in the Brāhmaṇas as well as in the Purāṇas. In *Bṛhaddevatā* 5.97–103, the births of Bhṛgu, Aṅgiras, and Atri are recounted. Vāc in bodily form appears to Ka and Prajāpati as they are sacrificing. They become excited and spill semen, scattered into the fire by Vāyu, the wind. From the coals (*aṅgareṣu*), Aṅgiras is born; from the flames, Bhṛgu is born; and Vāc then insists upon having a third son, which she is granted—Atri, the third.

As in the case of Purūravas and Urvaśī above, at first glance there is nothing unusual about the *Bṛhaddevatā*'s use of this motif. The *Brāhmanas*[20] and other Vedic texts[21] also draw upon the motif of the birth of *ṛṣis* (inspired sages) from fire, and the Purāṇas and other later works proliferate such references. Manu (1.35) mentions that Bhṛgu sprang from the fire. And the *Mahābhārata* (*Ādiparvan* 26.05) and *Vāyu Purāṇa* (1.4.100) claim that Bhṛgu was born from the heart, while the *Bhāgavata Purāṇa* (3.12.23) recounts that he was born from the skin of the creator.

However, in the *Bṛhaddevatā* the entire story is told in order to legitimate the family lineage (*gotra*) of the *ṛṣi* Bṛhaspati, who is claimed to be the descendant of Aṅgiras, and whose sons are considered to be the authors of the sixth *maṇḍala* of the *Ṛg Veda*. In the *Brāhmaṇa* accounts, the *ṛṣis* are usually created along with the donkeys, the antelopes, and others. Yet the *Bṛhaddevatā*, in contrast, is concerned only with the pedigree of the *ṛṣis* themselves. Unlike the *Brāhmaṇa* story, the *Bṛhaddevatā* portrays these *ṛṣis* not as partaking in the cosmogony but as luminous authorities in their own right, descending from powerful events and prestigious people.

Similar to the story of the birth of Bhṛgu, another *itihāsa* from the *Bṛhaddevatā* draws upon the spilling of seed, this time to account for the "pot-born" *ṛṣis*. Here, the story is even more elaborately genealogical and more explicitly concerned with a particular *gotra* than the story of the birth of Bhṛgu, Aṅgiras, and Atri:[22]

> The son of Prajāpati was Marīci, and the son of Marīci was the sage Kaśyapa. He had thirteen divine wives, the daughters of Dakṣa: Aditi, Diti, Danu, Kālā, Danāyu, Siṃhikā, Muni, Krodhā, Viśvā, Variṣṭhā, Surabhi and Vinatā, and Kadrū by name; indeed thus [Dakṣa] gave the daughters to Kaśyapa. In them the *asuras*, gods, *gandharvas*, serpents, *rākṣasas*, birds, *piśācas* and other classes were born. One of them, the goddess Aditi, gave birth to twelve sons, Bhaga, Aryaman, Aṃśa, Mitra, Varuṇa, Dhātṛ and Vidhātṛ, Vivasvat, of great brilliance, Tvaṣṭṛ, Pūṣan, Indra, and it is said that the twelfth is Viṣṇu. A pair was born of her—Mitra-Varuṇa. These two Ādityas, having seen the *apsaras* Urvaśī in the sacrificial session, spilled their seed. That [seed] fell into a jar of water that stood overnight. Therefore, at that moment, virile ascetics came into being, the two *ṛṣis* Agastya and Vasiṣṭha. When the semen had fallen in various ways—in a jar, in water, on the ground—the sage Vasiṣṭha, best of *ṛṣis*, came into being on the ground; Agastya came into being in a jar, and Matsya of great brilliance, in water. Agastya, of great glory, then arose, the measure of a stick [*śamyā*]. Because of being measured with a measure [*māna*], therefore he is here called Manya. Or because the *ṛṣi* was born from a jar [*kumbha*], by a jar also measurement is made.[23] By *kumbha* the designation of capacity is indicated. Then, when the waters were taken up, Vasiṣṭha was standing on a lotus.[24] There all the gods supported the lotus everywhere. Having arisen from the water, he then performed great *tapas* here. His name was born from his qualities; from the root *vas* [is] the expression[25] of his excellence . . . Vasiṣṭha and the Vasiṣṭhans [are] *brāhmaṇas*, in the office[26] of Brahman, thus to be given payment in all of the sacrificial rites. Therefore those who even today might be Vasiṣṭhans, present at any time, one should honor with fees; this is a *śruti* of the Bhāllavins. (*BD* 5.143–59)

As in the previous birth-story, Vedic, Epic and Purāṇic parallels to the "pot-born" (*kumbhaja*) motif abound. The birth of Agastya is referred to as early as *Ṛg Veda* 7.33.10–13, the *Nirukta* (5.13–14), and the *Mahābhārata*.[27] The *Matsya Purāṇa* (61.18–53) tells the entire story in much the same form as the *Bṛhaddevatā* account, and at least seven others Purāṇas[28] refer to this theme.

Yet more importantly for the present purposes, the *Bṛhaddevatā's* birth story is told in order to claim preeminence for the *gotra* of Vasiṣṭha. The tale underscores Vasiṣṭha's excellence and claims the primacy of all later Vasiṣṭhans in all sacrificial rites. Acting as *brāhmaṇa* priests, the Vasiṣṭhan's (and, the text implies, even those who are only suspected of being Vasiṣṭhans) are the ones who should be given payment and "honored with fees."

This emphasis upon *gotra* suggests a general similarity with both Epic and Purāṇic texts. In his work *Traditions of the Seven Ṛṣis,*[29] John Mitchiner describes the move from the first Vedic account of the seven *ṛṣis* to the addition of a second list, prominent in the Epics and expanded in the Purāṇas. With each further development, the lists of *ṛṣis* become more and more elaborate until, in the Purāṇic accounts, a group of seven *ṛṣis* appears for each of the fourteen *manvantaras*, or ages. This elaboration of the Purāṇas is achieved in part by the manipulation of *gotras*, or lineages of the *ṛṣis*.

Without discussing in elaborate detail the history of the innumerable *gotra* lists, suffice it to say that the *gotra* organization itself occurs first in the Śrauta Sūtras and is based upon the principle of tracing patrilineal descent back to a common *ṛṣi* ancestor. As Mitchiner puts it,

> The Brahmin authors of the *Śrauta Sutras* sought to bring the first main list of the Seven *Ṛṣis* more into line with what they regarded—and sought to establish—as the relative importance of each of the clans claiming descent from one or another of the *Ṛṣis*. The changes thus introduced in the *Śrauta Sūtra* lists are subsequently in turn reflected in the formulation, in the Epics and the *Purāṇas*, of the second main lists: such changes being at least partly due to the Brahmin-members of different *gotras* who traced their own descent from a particular *Ṛṣi,* and who desired—and were in a position to demand—greater recognition for their *Ṛṣi* ancestor, thereby indirectly gaining greater recognition for their own social standing.[30]

As Mitchiner notes, many of the Purāṇas contain extremely lengthy and detailed accounts of the descendants of the main groups of *ṛṣis*. The *Viṣṇu* and the *Bhāgavata Purāṇas* name the seven *ṛṣis* who constitute the list of the second, later group. In many other Purāṇas the descendants of Bhṛgu are listed with those of the other seven *ṛṣis*, the resulting list of eight being parallel to the eight "mind-born sons of Brahmā"—a group prominent in the Epics, and whose mythology is developed in many Purāṇas.

While we are not explicitly concerned with the seven *ṛṣis* as such, it is important to note that the *Bṛhaddevatā* places great emphasis upon the *ṛṣis* of the second, later list, found in the Epics and elaborated upon in the Purāṇas. Aṅgiras is one example; while he is mentioned in the Vedic texts, he is included as a founding *ṛṣi* only in the second list. However, in the *Bṛhaddevatā* he is considered the progenitor of the *ṛṣi* Bṛhaspati and has his own *gotra,* figuring as a prominent father of those who composed the sixth *maṇḍala.*

Even more strikingly, the *Bṛhaddevatā*'s story of the birth of Agastya and Vasiṣṭha places the *ṛṣi* Marīci as the father of Kaśyapa. Yet in the earlier list of seven *ṛṣis*, Kaśyapa is not Marīci's son but holds a place of prominence on his own. In these earlier lists, Marīci is not even mentioned; he appears only in the second main list. Moreover, the *gotra* of the Mārīcas appears only from the Epics onwards. And Marici, clearly of relatively late importance, comes to be termed the father of Kaśyapa in the Epics and in many different Purāṇas.[31] The *Bṛhaddevatā,* as noted above, reflects—or initiates—this later, more Purāṇic pattern.

THE IDEOLOGY OF THE *BṚHADDEVATĀ*

Up to this point, the Epic and Purāṇic parallels have gone hand in hand in this comparative study of the *Bṛhaddevatā*. An examination of the above parallels reveals that in its handling of Vedic subject matter, the *Bṛhaddevatā* also includes material more common to both Epic and Purāṇic texts. Yet it is also useful, and far less commonly done, to make a distinction between the Epic and the Purāṇic parallels to the *Bṛhaddevatā*. The usefulness of this distinction arises on the level of ideology.

While the narratives of the *Bṛhaddevatā,* the Purāṇas, and the *Mahābhārata* may be similar in content, they are used for different ideological purposes. The short example of the birth-story of the *ṛṣi* Dīrghatamas provides a good illustration. The *Bṛhaddevatā* (*BD* 4.11–16ab) uses the Dīrghatamas story in a manner similar to that seen in the birth-stories of Vasiṣṭha and Aṅgiras, discussed above. The text tells how Dīrghatamas's mother, Mamatā, curses the sexual advances of her brother-in-law Bṛhaspati. She is already with child from her lawful husband, Ucathya, and Bṛhaspati, overcome with frustration, curses the embryo with, "Let a long darkness (*dīrghatamas*) be yours!" The *Bṛhaddevatā* tells the tale to establish the *gotra* of Dīrghatamas, whose son is the famous *ṛṣi* Kakṣīvat. In contrast, the *Mahābhārata* tells the same tale to highlight particularly pious individuals who embody the principle of *dharma,* religious and social duty. In the *Mahābhārata,* Ucathya, a Brahmin of virtue, fathers a child on his wife Mamatā. When Mamatā protests at Bṛhaspati's violation of her already implanted seed, she shows herself to be a lover of *dharma.*[32] Thus, the *Mahābhārata* uses the Dīrghatamas story as an occasion to remark upon the bravery of women who protest any interference with dharmic reproduction. Other parallels between the *Mahābhārata* and the *Bṛhaddevatā* reveal this same difference in emphasis.[33]

The *Bṛhaddevatā* possesses an ideological perspective of its own—neither purely Vedic nor purely Epic in style. While the sacrifice remains the focal point in the Vedic perspectives of the *Brāhmaṇas,* and *dharma* remains the focal point for the *Mahābhārata,* both sacrifice and *dharma* are relegated to the background in the *Bṛhaddevatā*'s narratives. Instead, Vedic deity and *mantra* come into the foreground. Because in its core form the *Bṛhaddevatā* is an index of Vedic deities, once the text is expanded its focus is naturally upon the relationship between *ṛṣi* and deity—not *dharma* or sacrifice. The *Bṛhaddevatā* thus shares the theological focus of the Purāṇas.

From an ideological as well as a chronological perspective, then, the *Bṛhaddevatā*'s emphasis upon deities suggests comparison with the Purāṇas as well as the *Brāhmaṇa*s or the *Mahābhārata.*[34] Much of the text can be read with an eye toward the different values and uses of such narratives within the changing landscape of Ṛg Vedic interpretive tradition during the period of emergence of the first Purāṇas. More specifically, one can read these narratives with a view toward their portrayal of the relationship between humans and gods.[35] Indeed, one might well say that the *Bṛhaddevatā* provides a view into the interaction between Vedic and Purāṇic perspectives: while its specific theological content remains Vedic, its forms of thought have much in common with Purāṇic points of view.

THE POWERS OF PERSUASION: ṚṢIS AND GODS

The first of these Purāṇic tendencies is the *Bṛhaddevatā*'s portrayal of the alliances between *ṛṣi*s and gods. These relationships are oddly devotional; they do not fit any of the categories with which one usually thinks about Vedic mythology. Wendy O'Flaherty, in her *Origins of Evil in Hindu Mythology,* divides the relationship among gods, men, and demons into three categories, which revolve around three distinct religious activities: Vedic, which revolves around sacrifice; post-Vedic, which revolves around asceticism; and devotional, which revolves around *bhakti.* As she puts it,

> one is referring not to three discrete strata of texts but rather to three attitudes, each one a reaction to the one preceding it and thus "later" in an ideological sense, though not necessarily in a chronological sense. The Vedic period includes the *Ṛg Veda* and many *Brāhmaṇa*s and *Upaniṣad*s, but the Vedic attitude also persists in many parts of the *Mahābhārata*, the *Rāmāyaṇa,* and the *Purāṇa*s. The post-Vedic stage includes some later *Brāhmaṇa*s and *Upaniṣad*s, though it is mainly composed of Epic and Purāṇic texts, as is the prevalent, "orthodox" attitude. . . . The *bhakti* myths appear in many of these same texts (though not in the *dharmaśāstra*s) and in some *Tantra*s as well.[36]

While it is not necessary to discuss her theories in elaborate detail, some further discussion is enlightening for the present purposes. O'Flaherty describes these groups as ringing various changes on the relationships described above. In the first, Vedic attitude, gods and demons are opposed to one another, and gods unite with men against the demons. When gods were thought to live on sacrifice provided by devout men, the gods wished men to be virtuous, for then they would continue to offer sacrifices. The demons, on the other hand, wished to weaken the gods; occasionally this action may have accidentally corrupted mankind. Demons would try to kill men unless they were protected by gods who had had their fill of sacrificial offerings.[37]

In the later attitude, when sacrificial power came into competition with ascetic and meditative power, the tone of narratives was also changed. As Brahmins came to regard themselves as more important to cosmic order than to the gods themselves, the gods became jealous and treated both men and demons as potential threats to their authority. In fact, according to this perspective, ascetic demons were more dangerous than "demonic" demons. The antagonism between gods and men derived from two facts: (1) the belief within ritual tradition that men alone, by performing the sacrifice, could obtain the achievement of their goals—wealth, offspring, and so forth; and (2) from the Upaniṣads, the belief that without participation in ritual, a man could, through his own individual efforts, achieve a kind of immortality equal or superior to the gods. Thus, priests came to mediate between the gods and their twofold challengers—men and demons—who, without the priests, could be destroyed or corrupted by the gods.[38]

The third attitude, that of *bhakti,* reacted in turn against this antagonism between men and gods. Here, the Vedic concept of dependence upon the gods is reintroduced, and devoted men and demons are protected by the gods, who encourage virtue in both. Against the elitist, establishment view, the *bhakti* texts set the alternative that the priests had previously obscured, that the gods might be willing to make good men or demons into gods. This view eliminates the need for any priests at all, for men and gods are now joined in a mutual dependence that is direct and personal, unlike the Vedic dependence, which relied on priestly mediation. Thus *bhakti* mythology displays an increasingly cynical attitude to the "now logically superfluous but nevertheless persistent figure" of the priest of the demons or the gods.[39]

The *Bṛhaddevatā* is a curious combination of all of these attitudes. As mentioned above, the most likely probability is that it existed as the *Devatānukramaṇī,* a core text that indexed the deities for the hymns. As it was expanded or enlarged, becoming the *Bṛhaddevatā[nukramaṇī]*, various pieces were added on to underscore the validity of the Vedic *mantra*s: narratives and pieces of philosophy, which were probably extant in various ways from the Brāhmaṇas and Epic sources, were added to further legitimate the Vedic way of knowing. The general tone of these stories begins with a Brāhmaṇa-like perspective characteristic of the second stage; there is some tension between gods and men, usually with the *ṛṣi*s, which needs to be righted—the jealousy of a god, or the attempt by a *ṛṣi* to get help for a gargantuan sacrifice that would make him a rival of the gods. There also remains the underlying Vedic tension between gods and demons; many of the *ṛṣi*s are battered by demons disguised as *ṛṣi*s or demons without disguise (*asura*s).

The Vedic theme of the mutual dependence of men and gods is also present, though recast in a fashion reminiscent of the *bhakti* perspective, whereby the utterance of *mantra,* and not the sacrifice, is almost always the pivotal point of the narrative. There is an important difference, however: the utterers of *mantra*—the priestly *ṛṣi*s—do not become superfluous or the objects of cynicism, as they do in *bhakti*. Because the text is concerned with the legitimation of *mantra,* the *Bṛhaddevatā* must show that *mantra*s work. Therefore, perhaps at times even inadvertently, the seers of *mantra*s become the agents of intervention in equal status to the gods, like those mortal sacrificers who were a potential threat to the gods. Yet, unlike those sacrificers, the seers in the *Bṛhaddevatā* have no punishment or antagonism toward men, but its contrary. The result of the right *mantra* at the right time is a *bhakti*-like harmony between the two parties. Thus, ironically, in an attempt to legitimate Vedic *mantra,* the *Bṛhaddevatā* reverses the usual order of the more orthodox tale. When the *ṛṣi* becomes powerful, he does not incur the antagonism of and perhaps punishment by the gods, as in the second stage, but achieves friendship or parity with the gods, as in the third stage.

While at first glance, this pattern does not fit neatly into any of the above types of relationship between gods and humans in Indian texts, it is consistent in the light of the portrayal of *ṛṣis* in certain Purāṇic stories. First, *ṛṣis* are far more aligned with the gods than are other humans in the Purāṇas, often portrayed as allies and as offspring. As mentioned above, in earlier Purāṇas, the *ṛṣis* are called "mind-born sons" and are seen as the offspring of Brahmā. Indeed, they, and not the deity, are primarily responsible for creation. In the *Matsya Purāṇa* (3.30–41), Brahmā loses his creative powers of *tapas* (inner ascetic heat) because of his lust for Savitrī, and thus his sons, the *ṛṣis*, carry on the work of creation. In the *Liṅga Purāṇa* 2.85.12, Brahmā is said to be unable to carry on the creation of the three worlds without help and for that reason created his mind-born sons, the *ṛṣis*. They themselves are called Brahmās (*sapta brahmāṇaḥ*). In addition, the Purāṇas also designate them as Prajāpatis, underscoring their function as creators and sustainers of the three worlds.

The *Ṛṣi* Worshipped by Indra

Several particular examples from the *Bṛhaddevatā* can illustrate the similarities between the *Bṛhaddevatā*'s and the Purāṇas' portrayals of the *bhakti*-like alliance between *ṛṣi* and god. Like the origin story of Dīrghatamas, discussed above, the following narrative addresses two issues at once—the power of the seer Gṛtsamada and the origin of his name. Here, the *Bṛhaddevatā* touches upon the theme of the "being like Indra" and the resulting complications. Elsewhere, I have treated this story as an illustration of Vedic authority, of the power of saying the right Vedic *mantra* at the right time.[40] (The citations in bold are those *mantras* of the *Ṛg Veda* referred to in the story.) Most importantly for the present purposes, the story provides a good example of how the alliance between a devotee and a god can be established.

> Having yoked himself to *tapas* he, with a body like Indra's, suddenly appeared in the sky and on earth. Now the two terrifyingly powerful Daityas, Dhuni and Cumuri, thinking him to be Indra, fell upon him with weapons. The *ṛṣi,* having recognizing the nature of the two who desired evil, with the *sūkta* **"Who when born"** (*RV* 2.12.1), proclaimed the actions of Indra. When the actions of Indra had been spoken, fright quickly

entered the two. Now, Indra, saying, "This is the occasion," struck the two down. Having struck them down, Śakra spoke to the *ṛṣi* Gṛtsamada. "Regard me, friend, in the manner of a loved one, for you have become dear to me. Ask a boon from me; and let your *tapas* be imperishable." Bowing, the seer answered back, "For us, O lord of speakers, let there be safety of our bodies and speech that enlivens the heart. Let there be the possession of heroes and wealth; O Indra we think of you. And you, O Indra, we can become aware of in each birth; my state of mind (*bhāva*) has gone to you; don't go away. You are the better charioteer." This boon (*varya*) is explained by the last verse, **"O Indra, the best"** (*RV* 2.21.6); he chose all this as a boon. When the Lord of Śacī, the Swift Conqueror,[41] heard that, he said, "OK," and grabbed [him] by the right hand, and the *ṛṣi,* through his friendship, touched his hand.[42] Thus they went together to the great dwelling of Indra. There the Destroyer of Forts himself honored him [Gṛtsamada] with love and honored the *ṛṣi* with the prescribed ceremony. Again from friendship the Lord of Bays spoke to him: "Since you, O best of *ṛṣi*s, delight us, praising [*gṛṇan mādayase*], therefore you will become Gṛtsamada, son of Śunahotra." Then with twelve *sūkta*s, beginning **"Hear the call, Indra; do not be neglectful. May we be yours for the giving of treasures. These oblations for wealth increase your strength like flowing rivers"** (*RV* 2.11.1), the *ṛṣi* praised Indra. Right when he was praising, there he saw Brahmaṇaspati. He praised Brahmaṇaspati with those [verses] in which his sign is apparent. He also praised him with the four following this one. (*BD* 4.66–80)

Gṛtsamada begins his encounter with the Daityas in a rather risky position. Like Kutsa, who looks exactly like Indra in the *Jaiminīya Brāhmaṇa,*[43] through Gṛtsamada's own powerful *tapas* he has attained the status and likeness of a god. He is also like Kutsa insofar as his likeness to Indra gets him into trouble. As Kutsa incurs the wrath of Indra when he attempts to seduce Indra's wife, so too Gṛtsamada's divine shape prompts the Daityas to mistake him for their enemy Indra and to attempt to kill him. But here, Gṛtsamada's praise in *mantra*s is more powerful than the result of his *tapas,* because Indra, instead of being angry at Gṛtsamada, comes to rescue him as the result of his praise. The first *mantra* that

Gṛtsamada speaks, praising the actions of Indra, serves a double function—it instills fear into the demons Dhuni and Cumuri, so that they are immobilized, and it also invokes the god Indra, so that he can strike the final blow. The seer is all the more powerful because the effect of his praise is eternal friendship with Indra. Indra then bestows upon him his name—Gṛtsamada—honors him in due ceremony, and invites him to dwell with him in his own home.

This kind of alliance has a multitude of parallels in Purāṇic texts. Certainly, hearing the right words at the right time is behind the larger principle of *phalaśruti,* the "fruits of hearing," claimed even by earlier Vedic and Upaniṣadic texts. Because Indra hears the right words at the right time, he rescues the *ṛṣi* and makes him his companion in heaven. In their *bhakti*-like views on *phalaśruti,* the Purāṇas emphasize the same kind of heavenly camaraderie that the *Bṛhaddevatā* does. Thus, Devarāja the notorious sinner goes to heaven, protected by Śiva's retinue, simply because he heard the *Śiva Purāṇa* during the hours of his feverish death (*Śiva Purāṇa* 1.2.15–40).

More specifically, however, one must remember that the story of Gṛtsamada is a tale about the fruits of speaking as well as hearing. Just as Gṛtsamada is rewarded in particular ways for his well-placed *mantra,* the Purāṇic stories make quite specific and elaborate claims as to what the rewards of particular words will be. The *Vāmana Purāṇa* (15–16), for instance, tells the story of Sukeśin, the *rākṣasa* (demon) who taught so much *dharma* to his fellow demons that their lustre overcame the light of the sun and moon. The sun, in anger, burned the city up, and Sukeśin, seeing his city falling, cried "Honor to Śiva!" Upon hearing this, Śiva caused the sun to fall and rescued the city. After propitiation from his devotes, Śiva restored the sun to the sky and took Sukeśin with him to heaven. Thus, the worlds of the *Bṛhaddevatā* and the worlds of the earlier Purāṇas are not so far apart; the right words at the right time gain eternal friendship in heaven with a god.

Moreover, it should be noted that, while in many of the *Brāhmaṇa*s the *ṛṣi*s gain heaven primarily through *tapas,* in the Purāṇas the emphasis is quite different.[44] In the *Aitareya Brāhmaṇa* and other Vedic texts, Vasiṣṭha and Viśvāmitra attain the realm of Indra through *tapas.* Yet in the Purāṇas, heaven is far more frequently attained through the summoning of the presence of that deity on earth, so that the god, being pleased with the *ṛṣi,* appears before him and grants him a desire.[45] So too in the *Bṛhaddevatā*'s story of Gṛtsamada, the devotional *mantra* of praise actually replaces Vedic *tapas* as the means of attaining the realm of Indra.

Seeing through the God

In the next story, shape-changing Indra, ever hungry for praise, disguises himself in order to "test" the *ṛṣi*. In this story too, the identity of Indra is in question; only this time it is not the seer but the god who is in another form.

> Indra, desiring praise again, having become a partridge, settling himself on the right part of the *ṛṣi,* who was about to set out, uttered a cry. Having recognized him with a *ṛṣi*'s eye as being in the form of a bird, he praised [him] with the following two verses, **"With repeated cry, foretelling what will come, he directs** [his] **voice as a helmsman** [directs] **a boat. Be ominous of good fortune and may no misfortune happen to you from any side."** (*RV* 2.42.1) (*BD* 4.93–94)

This small story shows the degree of the god's dependence upon the seer, as well as the seer's dependence upon the god. Unlike the Brāhmaṇas, however, which demonstrate that a god who has not been praised sufficiently may wreak havoc upon the sacrifice and upon the universe, here the problem is neatly solved by the shrewdness of the *ṛṣi*'s eye, which can discern Indra's trick immediately.[46] This ability to see through apparent reality is amply attested in the Purāṇas; *ṛṣis* are often credited with the ability to see beyond the present into the future and past and to recognize gods in disguise.

Helping Indra Appear

Unlike the previous two stories, where the *ṛṣi*'s *mantra* is motivated by fear of the demons or catching onto a trick, this narrative directly connects the power of the *ṛṣi* to his fervent devotion. The *ṛṣi* literally "speaks" the god into existence.

> With the triplet, **"I will go here before you with my son; the all-gods follow after me; Indra, if you keep wealth for me, then put forward your strength for me. I offer the beverage of the intoxicating drink first to you; let**

> **the pressed, delightful Soma be placed first in you; be a friend on my right hand; then we two will kill many enemies. Offer praise to Indra, those who go to war, if he indeed exists. Nema (many a one) says, 'Indeed there is no Indra.' Who has ever seen him? Whom shall we praise?"** [*RV* 8.100.1–3] Nema, son of Bhṛgu, praised[47] Indra without seeing him. And then Indra [answered] in the couplet, **"Here I am; see me, O *ṛṣi*! See me here. I overpower all creatures with my power; the instructors of order strengthen me with their praises; I the shatterer of worlds."** [4,5] For Nema, being alone, while praising, had said, "There is no Indra." After hearing that, Indra praised himself with two verses and appeared. The *ṛṣi,* having seen him, was quite pleased, and with the couplet [beginning] **"All of these deeds of yours are to be proclaimed for the one who presses** [Soma] **in the sacrifices,"** [6,7] he recited various actions and the gift of Indra. [*BD* 6.117-20ab]

Some would simply explain away this *itihāsa* by calling it the result of a misunderstanding of two words, *na* and *ima* ("many a one," literally, "not a few"), which are combined in the third verse to make "Nema." Thus one could read the verse without positing a *ṛṣi* Nema, son of Bhṛgu at all.[48] Yet if one does posit the *ṛṣi* Nema, as the *Bṛhaddevatā* does, an intriguing story is created in which a *mantra* is used to praise a god without seeing him, either in animal or in human form. What is more, the effect of this unusual praise without seeing is nothing less than the appearance of the god himself. Indra first praises himself and then makes himself known to the *ṛṣi,* who, in a classical exchange of *mantra*s, pays for the god's appearance with further praise.

So too the Purāṇas abound with accounts of devotional prayer and worship that achieve what is elsewhere achieved by *tapas.* As the *Brahmavaivarta Purāṇa* (4.46.45) recounts, when the *ṛṣi*s Gautama and Viśvāmitra have lost their wives, they regain them by praying to Śiva. In the *Agni Purāṇa* (218.1–2), Vasiṣṭha becomes a great *yogin* by devotion to the Śiva *liṅga* and recitation of the Vedic Gāyatrī *mantra.*

The Vedic Power of Speech Expanded

The stories above show that in the *Bṛhaddevatā,* the *ṛṣi*s act as eloquent savior-figures, intervening at the right time with the right *mantra.* More examples could be cited from the text: the *ṛṣi*

Medhāthiti saves King Āsaṅga from the curse of being a woman and turns her back into a man (*BD* 6.40–41). So too the *ṛṣi* Sobhari saves the sacrifice from being devoured by rats through using the right form of praise (*BD* 6.58–62). In the Purāṇas this same function of the *ṛṣis* is elaborated. The *Brahmā* (13.9–11), the *Liṅga* (1.63.71–73), and the *Skanda Purāṇa*s (7.1.20,42–44) all narrate the story whereby Atri, merely by uttering the words, "May all be well with you," stops the sun from falling from the sky. In a similar manner, Vasiṣṭha performs a series of rescuing functions in the *Bhāgavata Purāṇa* (9.18–42). Merely by uttering praise to Puruṣa, the *ṛṣi* both effects a sex change and saves a sacrifice, as Medhāthiti and Sobhari do in the *Bṛhaddevatā:*

> Before Manu had children, his lordly priest Vasiṣṭha, it is told, performed an oblation to Mitra and Varuṇa in order to secure offspring for him. Manu's wife Śraddhā, who was keeping a milking vow, approaching the *hotṛ,* prostrated herself and begged for a daughter. When summoned by the *adhvaryu* for the recitation, the *hotṛ* had her plea so heavily on his mind that he made a mistake in pronouncing the demand-for-the-oblation. Because of the *hotṛ*'s mistake a girl by the name of Ilā was born. When he saw the girl, Manu said to his guru not too cheerfully, "Honored one, how has this ritual of you Brahmins, who are supposed to know the *brahman,* come to be perverted? Ah, woe! There should not have been any distortion of the rite. You know the *mantra*s, you have *tapas,* your evil has been burnt away—how then could a falsifying perversion of the intention of the rite have occurred among you who are like gods?" The blessed great-grandfather had been aware of the *hotṛ*'s error, and upon hearing Manu's words he replied, "The distortion of the intention is due to an error by your *hotṛ*. Nevertheless I shall take measures, under my own power, to ensure that you have good offspring." Thus resolved, the famous priest gave praise to the Puruṣa, in order to change Ilā into a man. The blessed lord Hari was satisfied and gave a boon, and it was because of that boon that Ilā became the man Sudyumna.[49]

Unlike the more sacrificially circumscribed Brāhmaṇas, in both the *Bṛhaddevatā* and the Purāṇas, *ṛṣis* often clean up the messes of everyday religious life—performing cures, fixing ceremonies that have erred, and the like.

The *ṛṣis* work these wonders through speech—the praise and response mechanism illustrated by Vasiṣṭha's and Hari's exchange above. As Mitchiner notes, in the Purāṇas "the *ṛṣis* come to be seen as a kind of oracle, an infallible speaker whose speech alone literally carries power and authority—a fiery utterance from a receptacle of fire and *tapas*."[50] In a sense, the *Bṛhaddevatā*'s emphasis upon the *ṛṣis*' speech, while embedded in the task of the legitimation of Vedic *mantra,* also anticipates the powers of speech that the *ṛṣis* enjoy in the Purāṇas.

Moreover, while the Purāṇas view *mantra* with less reverence than the explicitly Vedic texts such as the *Bṛhaddevatā* do, *mantra*s still do function as forms of exchange and honor in the Purāṇas. The well-known story of the Destruction of Dakṣa's Sacrifice from the *Kūrma Purāṇa* (1.14.4–97) provides a good example. When the sage Dadhīci notices that King Dakṣa has gathered all beings except Śiva together for a sacrifice, he asks Dakṣa why he has omitted Śiva. The king replies that "In all the sacrifices there is no share assigned to him, nor are there any *mantra*s to be offered to Śankara and his wife!" Dadhīci counters that Śiva is declared to be the true object of the *mantra*s, "That god of a thousand rays who is praised by the *hotṛ, sāman,* and *adhvaryu* priests." When Śiva hears from his wife that Dakṣa's sacrifice is nonetheless continuing, the god sends his *gaṇa* (troop), led by their chief—all manner of beasts—to the sacrifice. Upon entering, they proclaim, "We are all the servants of Śarva of infinite splendor. We have come out of desire for our shares of the sacrifice. Give us the portions we want! Or else tell us who gave the order that you are to receive the shares and not we, so that we may know who he is!" The story goes on:

> The gods led by Prajāpati said to the Lord, "There are no *mantra*s prescribing your share of the sacrifice!" And when they heard this, those gods whose minds were obscured by illusion still ignored the lord, so the *mantra*s went to their home. Then the Lord Rudra touched the divine sage Dadhīci with his hand and, in the company of his wife and his troops, addressed the deities: "You are arrogant with power, refusing as you do the authority of the *mantra*s. Because of this I shall humble you and destroy your conceit!"[51]

And the troops and hordes go on to destroy the sacrifice.

Notice here that it is not the *mantra* that changes but the object of the *mantra*. In a rather *Bṛhaddevatā*-like manner, the sage Dadhīci emphasizes that while the *mantra* may have been the same, the sages and gods did not know which deity they were praising! Moreover, the *mantra*s have the power, almost like small creatures, to abandon the gods and "go to their own home." And it is not only the insult of being ignored in the sacrifice, but the ignorance of the *mantras* that is the final accusation hurled against the gods by Śiva. Thus, even while the *Purāṇa* is co-opting Vedic imagery and cosmogony for Śaivite purposes, the *Bṛhaddevatā* pattern of an alliance between god (Śiva) and *ṛṣi* (Dadhīci), established over the correct use of the *mantras*, remains the same.

In the Purāṇas, however, there is one important change in the treatment of *mantra* itself. In these later texts, the *mantra* is usually not quoted but simply mentioned. The mere reference to the *mantra* is what matters. The *mantras* become icons for power, yet the inner mechanisms of their power are not explicated, as they are in the Brāhmaṇas. One could almost trace the movement from the Vedas to the Purāṇas in terms of the gradual abstraction of *mantra,* where concern for the actual contents of the *mantra* gives way to the attitude that the *mantra* is an attribute of a powerful deity or *ṛṣi,* almost like Viṣṇu's discus or conch shell. In the *Bṛhaddevatā,* the *mantra* is the vehicle of the relationship between deity and *ṛṣi,* whereas in the *Purāṇa,* the *mantra,* while powerful, is one among many vehicles in such a relationship.[52]

TRIADS IN THE PURĀṆAS AND THE *BṚHADDEVATĀ*

In addition to its depiction of loving alliances between human and divine, there is one final aspect of the *Bṛhaddevatā* that makes it a curiously Purāṇic kind of text. The *Bṛhaddevatā* has a pronounced and unmistakable tendency to create triadic conceptions of deities. To be sure, this tendency is nothing new. As Gonda notes, the tendency to distinguish several triads of divine powers, so explicit in the Purāṇas, is present even in the earliest era of Indian religious thought.[53] Both the *Ṛg Veda* and the *Atharva Veda* describe three groups of eleven gods, who conduct their affairs on earth, heaven, and the remaining part of the world.[54] The Brāhmaṇas[55] view Agni, Indra, and Sūrya as superior deities. Most Ṛg Vedic commentatorial texts maintain that in reality there are three deities only: Agni, Vāyu or Indra, and Sūrya.[56] Gonda comments,

> The division into the three classes of the terrestrial Vasus, the aerial Rudra, and the celestial Ādityas distinguished by the poets of the *saṃhitās* as well as the compilers of the *brāhmaṇas* and surviving as the constituent groups of the thirty-three

gods in epic times, may probably be considered to have eventually paved the way for the constitution of the classical triad of high gods.[57]

In addition, the Purāṇic concept of *trimūrti*—one god whose nature is manifested in a threefold manner—has its origins in Vedic thought.[58] As is well known, the Brāhmaṇas' creator god Prajāpati, identified with *brahman,* also has a threefold character and is often identified with other gods such as Vāyu, Puruṣa, and Agni.[59] It is also well known that in the Upaniṣads there are several references to the threefold nature of *brahman*—as that from which creatures are born, by which they live, and into which, when departing, they enter.[60]

It must be admitted that, in many ways, the *Bṛhaddevatā* follows these earlier, Vedic texts:

> Some know the sun alone as the one origin and dissolution of all this [universe] moving and still, and of the present, past, and future. Prajāpati is the source of this being and nonbeing—he who is the syllable and that which is to be spoken is thus the eternal *brahman.* For he, having made himself threefold, abides in these worlds, making all the gods enter into his rays in the right order. (*BD* 1.61–63)

Moreover, the *Bṛhaddevatā* mirrors the basic Vedic pattern of classifying the deities according to three categories.

Yet there is an important difference. In its adept use of word derivations, the *Bṛhaddevatā* tightens its cosmology into a stricter threefold schema. Some explanation of the process of word derivation is in order at this point. Like the etymological text, the *Nirukta,* which precedes it, the *Bṛhaddevatā* uses word derivations to list the names for a single god, all of these names derived from a particularly characteristic action of the deity in question. To take a simple example, *Bṛhaddevatā* 2.24 describes Agni's name in terms of his essential activities:

> Because he was born at the head [*ag-re*] of creatures, and because he is an initiator [*agra-ṇi*] at the sacrifice, or because he brings together the body [*aṅgaṃ saṃ-ni*], he is praised by sages as Agni.

The *Bṛhaddevatā* does not stop at simply listing derivations, however. The text uses these word derivations explicitly to subordinate other deities' functions to the actions of the deities of the triad. Its emphasis upon the triad is far stricter than that of the *Nirukta* or any of the earlier texts; all Vedic characters—divine or otherwise—fit into the *Bṛhaddevatā*'s threefold schema. The text's treatment of the character of Purūravas is a good example. He is clearly an autonomous figure in the Ṛg Vedic hymn as well as in later legends. However, in the *Bṛhaddevatā* Purūravas is subordinated to become merely a form of Indra, who "roars" (*ruvan*) in the sky. In contrast, while the *Nirukta* (10.46) gives a similar, and rather humorous, derivation (Purūravas is so called because "he cries too much" [*purūrava bahudhā rorūyate*]), its definition is not in any way related to the threefold cosmology that was introduced earlier in the text. Numerous other examples of this kind of looseness of definition in earlier Vedic texts could be cited.[61] The *Bṛhaddevatā*'s theological meticulousness implies a trend toward a tighter cosmology.

This pattern of thought is parallel to the Purāṇas' attempts to subordinate all deities to their own triad of very different deities—Śiva, Viṣṇu, and Brahmā.[62] A story from the *Kūrma Purāṇa* provides an illustration. In the heated exchange between the sage Dadhīci and Dakṣa, which we have seen, the more specific question comes up as to whether the Ādityas, formerly divine beings in their own right, are to be subordinated to Rudra (Śiva) or not:

> [Dadhīci said:] "This fiery Rudra, the great god who carries a skull, whose neck is blue, the ruddy Hara, is the blessed Āditya the Sun, that god of a thousand rays who is to be praised by the *sāman, adhvaryu* and *hotṛ* priests! Witness this god who has fashioned the universe, whose form is Rudra, purpose of the three Vedas!" Dakṣa answered, "These twelve Ādityas who have come for their shares of the sacrifice are the only known suns. There is no other sun."[63]

Like the *Bṛhaddevatā,* the earlier Purāṇas manipulate theology. In his argument with Dakṣa, Dadhīci attempts to make the Ādityas a function of Rudra's brilliance, as the *Bṛhaddevatā* makes Purūravas a function of Indra's roaring in the sky.

It should be noted here as well that the Purāṇas also use word derivations to do theology, as do the earlier, Vedic texts; the Purāṇas are continuous with the Vedic purposes in that they describe the essential activity of a deity. For example, the *Kūrma Purāṇa* also tells a name-derivation story of Rudra, the howler. Brahmā scolds the dying Rudra, "Stop your howling!" The story goes on:

> [Brahmā says] "Because of your howling [*rud*] you will be known in the world as Rudra, the howler!" And the grandfather of the world gave him seven other names, along with eight wives, eight immortal sons and eight forms. Bhava, Śarva, Īśāna, Paśupati, Bhīma, Ugra and Mahādeva are his seven names.[64]

Again, these name-story examples could be multiplied endlessly. The point here is that, like the *Bṛhaddevatā,* the Purāṇas highlight the multiplicity of divine names in order to underscore the multitude of divine activities, which are in turn organized under the aegis of one primary deity who is part of a triad.

Moreover, the *Bṛhaddevatā* also provides a stepping stone for the hypostatization of the three gods into parts of one deity, a concept that achieves its full doctrinal expression in the Purāṇas,[65] where the triad of Śiva, Viṣṇu, and Brahmā is a single, mutually interlocking entity. While the Vedic texts allude to such an interlocking cosmology, they mention it only in the context of a very Vedic concern—that of clarifying confusion about the myriad names of gods used in ritual. For instance, while the *Nirukta* (7.5) mentions that the many diverse gods are "the individual limbs of a single self," its explanation for this interlocking cosmology is based on the idea of ritual praise; the text goes on to explain that, "*ṛṣi*s praise objects according to the multiplicities of their original nature, as well as from their universality."

To be sure, in the *Bṛhaddevatā,* typically Vedic ideas about power and ritual praise are echoed:

> Because of their greatness, different names are found [for each]; it (the diversity of names) appears here and there, according to the distinction between [their] abodes. For their power [inheres in the fact] that their names are many. In the *mantra*s poets speak of their origin one from another. (*BD* 1.70–71)

However, the *Bṛhaddevatā*'s ideas take on a fuller force as an independent cosmological description. Indeed, praise is virtually subordinated to the larger question of their nature as divinities:

> It is not possible to explain [fully] their coming into being, their power, their abode or their birth; for the whole universe is pervaded by them. For Agni is inherent in Vaiśvānara and Vaiśvānara is inherent in Agni; Jātavedas is in these two; in

> the same way they are in Jātavedas. The divinity of each of them is from the pervasiveness of their energy, from their sharing one birth and from their sharing one world; yet they appear separately praised. (*BD* 1.96–98)

In the *Vāyu Purāṇa* (5.17) the description of a threefold interlocking cosmology is entirely independent from the context of ritual praise: "They exist through each other and uphold each other; they are twin parts of one another; they subsist through one another; they are not for a moment separated; they never abandon one another."

Finally, the *Bṛhaddevatā* places an unusual emphasis on the forms of Vāc. In *Bṛhaddevatā* 2.72–84, she is treated as a single, separate goddess with a multitude of forms, as the goddess is in the Purāṇas. Unlike the *Nirukta,* where goddesses are incorporated into the cosmogony miscellaneously, a few for each sphere, the *Bṛhaddevatā* treats Vāc with special status as the fourth, together with the three great gods Agni, Indra/Vāyu, and Sūrya. Like the great gods of the triad, she is the overarching divine category under whom all other deities are subordinated, and she maintains her own celestial, atmospheric, and terrestrial forms (*BD* 2.73). She also has a list of Ṛg Vedic hymns and names, enumerated according to these forms. Although it uses the vocabulary of Vedic deities, the *Bṛhaddevatā* mirrors the Purāṇic pattern far more closely than earlier Vedic texts.

CONCLUSION

The recent redating of the *Bṛhaddevatā* to the time of the early Purāṇas is more than suggestive. An actual comparison between the *Bṛhaddevatā* and the Purāṇas reveals it to be a transparently "interactive" text indeed. Neither Vedic nor Purāṇic views rule, but both are mixed in a medley of different themes and motifs. While the characters might have remained Vedic, the forms of thought are clearly drifting in a different direction, consonant with Purāṇic tales. The *ṛṣis* are portrayed as far more independent characters, aiding and abetting the gods of their own accord. Through the strategy of word derivation, the Vedic pantheon becomes more and more tightly consolidated into a tripartite system, accompanied by a single goddess who takes many different forms.

Thus, while the *Bṛhaddevatā* shares with many Indian texts a reluctance to reveal the particulars of its sociohistorical moment, the text does reveal new aspects of the movement between Vedic and

Purāṇic forms of thought. Like the *Mahābhārata,* the *Bṛhaddevatā* too is a "work in progress," echoing the Vedas and anticipating the Purāṇas. Just as Indra must be recognized by the *ṛṣi* as one whose shape is constantly changing, so too the *Bṛhaddevatā* must be viewed as a "shape-changing" text; its very nature is to shift and mix religious registers.

2

Echoes of the Mahābhārata: *Why is a Parrot the Narrator of the* Bhāgavata Purāṇa *and the* Devībhāgavata Purāṇa?

Wendy Doniger

When we hear a story that claims to be true, our skepticism often leads us to ask, Where did you hear that story? Who told you that? This impulse is reflected in the tradition of Indian storytelling, too, which requires that its important stories be framed in a line of transmission, a *paraṃ-parā,* "from one to another," tracing its descent from the original storyteller to the author of the present text. And the choice of that author tells us a great deal about the text's image of itself; the nature of the author is appropriate to the nature of the text. Where we might raise the question of author intentionality, or try to construct a psychobiography, the ancient Hindus tried to place the author of a text in the context of previous authors, in particular, of authors who were characters in earlier works that we would call "mythological." The authors of the two great Sanskrit Epics, the *Mahābhārata* and the *Rāmāyaṇa,* are actors in their own stories: Vyāsa fathers the fathers of the Pāṇḍavas and the Kauravas, the two warring families; and Vālmīki raises the abandoned children of the hero, Rāma. Their personalities tell us much about the character of the two Epics; but that is another story.[1]

In this essay, I want to look at the frame, and the author, of a great Sanskrit text closely related to the *Mahābhārata:* the

Bhāgavata Purāṇa. And I want to ask why this text has chosen as its narrator the sage Śuka, whose name means "the parrot." The answer to this question will be found by searching, not only within the *Bhāgavata Purāṇa*[2] itself, but within the two texts that provide its textual context: the *Mahābhārata* (composed a few centuries before the *Bhāgavata*),[3] which the *Bhāgavata* self-consciously quotes and echoes, and the *Devībhāgavata Purāṇa,*[4] which self-consciously quotes and echoes the *Bhāgavata Purāṇa.*

Tracing the saga of Śuka from the *Mahābhārata* to the *Bhāgavata* to the *Devībhāgavata* affords us a splendid working example of the process of transformation of traditional texts through what A. K. Ramanujan has called "intertextuality," the way in which Indian texts engage in conversation with one another. For the *Devībhāgavata,* which is usually regarded as an Upapurāṇa, was composed several centuries after the *Bhāgavata.* One can hardly imagine a more forceful statement of, simultaneously, lineage and deviation, than is made by adding the name of the Goddess (Devī) to the title of the great classic Mahāpurāṇa of Kṛṣṇa-*bhakti.* A play entitled "Queen Lear" would provide but a pale parallel.

THE *BHĀGAVATA*

Let us begin by looking at the beginning of the *Bhāgavata Purāṇa* for clues about its purported author. The very first words tell us about him; immediately after the initial verse of invocation and meditation, the text goes on to say: "This *Bhāgavata Purāṇa* composed by the great sage . . . is the ripe fruit from the wishing-tree of the Veda, dropped from the mouth of Śuka; it is full of the immortal juice; drink it now" (*BP* 1.1.2–3). The claim that an important Hindu text is the fruit of the Vedas (here expressed through the metaphor of the magic tree that produces whatever you wish for) is a common one.[5] Where Vedic scripture, or *śruti,* grounds itself in the claim of divine revelation, which is by nature secret,[6] Epic and Purāṇic tradition (*smṛti*) defines itself by the chain of human memory, displaying each link as publicly as possible. The *Bhāgavata* in particular goes out of its way to ground itself in the archaic tradition;[7] but, as we shall see, it cares more to establish its link with the *Mahābhārata* than with the Veda.

The Vedic "wishing-tree" is thus the lineage of the text into the past; the lineage of its transmission into the future begins with the fate of the fruit, "dropped from the mouth of Śuka" as a fruit might be dropped by a parrot. And Śuka remains the narrator of most of the Purāṇa. But the situation is confused by the presence of several other narrators, who stand on both sides of Śuka, telling about him and being told about by him. From the story in the *Mahābhārata,* as we shall see, the transmission clearly passes from Viṣṇu to Nārada to Vyāsa to Śuka, and this is the basic structure of the *Bhāgavata* transmission as well.

The first of these supplementary narrators, the god Viṣṇu, is identified by most commentators on this text, including the most famous, Śrīdhara, as the "great sage" in the second verse.[8] Thus Śrīdhara's commentary unpacks the verse: "This fruit called the *Bhāgavata* [*Purāṇa*] was found on Vaikuṇṭha [the sacred mountain of Viṣṇu] and brought to me [Vyāsa] by [the divine sage] Nārada. I placed it in the mouth of Śuka. And from his mouth that [book] fell on the earth, and by the chain of transmission from pupil to pupil it eventually descended intact."

This verse also implicitly introduces the second narrator, Vyāsa. For "me" in Śrīdhara's gloss must be Vyāsa, who thus situates himself within the story (between Nārada and Śuka). Śrīdhara, like most editors, places this verse in the mouth of Vyāsa, assuming that the entire Purāṇa, including these first verses, is narrated by Vyāsa. The phrase "Vyāsa said" is inserted at the beginning of chapter 2 and again at the start of chapter 4; "Vyāsa said" continues to introduce the text until Śuka takes over. Thus Vyāsa encompasses the professional bard who is telling about the transmission of the text. Though in chapter 2 Vyāsa has not yet been introduced as a narrator, the editor, like Śrīdhara, simply *assumes* that Vyāsa narrates this as he narrates so many Purāṇas. Thus in addition to playing an important part within the story, Vyāsa is also situated on the outermost frame (telling about Nārada and Śuka). (This ambiguous position is equally characteristic of Vyāsa's role in the *Mahābhārata.*)

The *Bhāgavata* prologue then identifies Vyāsa as a storyteller, though not specifically as a narrator of this text. But first it introduces the professional bard, who is always called the "Sūta" ("charioteer"). It is significant that *sūta* also means "one who has been born," more precisely a male child, which in this context constitutes an extended pun, since Vyāsa's bard (Sūta) is also his son (*sūta,* Śuka):

> In the Naimiṣa Forest, Śaunaka and the other sages were holding a sacrifice for a thousand years in order to attain the world of heaven. One day when the sages had performed their morning oblations, they said to the Sūta who was seated there,

"Whatever that best of Veda-knowers, the lord Vyāsa, and the other sages know, O Sūta, you know all that." (*BP* 1.1.4–8)

And they ask him to tell them about Viṣṇu. Chapter 2 then begins with the insertion, "Vyāsa said," and procedes:

The Sūta[9] was pleased with the question of the Brahmins and began like this: "I bow to the silent sage [Śuka], the one whom the Island-born [Vyāsa] summoned back, when [Śuka] was setting forth from home to be a renouncer, though he had not yet received his initiatory thread. Overcome by the sadness of separation, [Vyāsa] cried out, 'My son!' and the trees, because they were made of him [i.e., of Śuka] who had entered the hearts of all creatures, answered him [Vyāsa]." (*BP* 1.2.2)

This is a highly concentrated and obscure verse; Śuka is still not named, and Vyāsa is referred to only by his place of birth (the island). And though Vyāsa is identified as the father of Śuka, neither Vyāsa nor Śuka is associated with the narration of this text. Moreover, how, precisely, do the trees respond? Eric A. Huberman has mused upon this question: "Is it their rustling upon absorbing Śuka, or their vast silence? What response, finally, can be given in face of inevitable loss? . . . On the one hand, there is *viraha,* separation from the father, and on the other hand, there is a suggestion of total union/identification."[10] The Sanskrit commentaries, too, offer some help. Śrīdhara says merely that Śuka gave his answer in the form of the trees, but Visvanatha Cakravarty says that the trees' answer was an echo (*pratidhvani*), which Huberman regards as "echoing Vyāsa's misapprehension. If Vyasa cries out 'O son,' and the trees respond in the exact same manner, 'O son,' then Śuka is indirectly saying, 'If I am the son, who are you? Who is son and who is father?' For, having become one with all beings, he no longer lives by such distinctions." In fact, the verse alludes to a story in the *Mahābhārata* that is the key to the role of Śuka as the narrator of the *Bhāgavata Purāṇa,* a story that incorporates both the idea of nature echoing human grief and the problem of a son who becomes his father's father. We will soon consider that story in detail.

Still within the *Bhāgavata,* no further reference is made to the episode of the talking trees; instead, the Sūta goes on to clarify the further details of the line of the transmission, now at last identifying Vyāsa not only as the father of the narrator Śuka but as a narrator in his own right:

> I seek refuge with the guru of sages, the son of Vyāsa, who out of his compassion . . . narrated the secret Purāṇa . . . The revered sage [Vyāsa] compiled this Purāṇa named the *Bhāgavata,* the essence of all the Vedas, and then he caused his own son to receive it. He [Śuka] told it to King Parikṣit when he was dying beside the Ganges, surrounded by all the sages. While they were listening to it, I came there and listened to it too, by his favor. And I will tell it to you. (*BP* 1.2.3, 1.3.40–44).

This is a most interesting move. It extends the original cluster of transmissions from Vyāsa to Śuka and then closes it by connecting it with the present narrator, the Sūta. But it does far more than this. It inserts the telling of the text within the framework of the *Mahābhārata.* Now, the events described in the *Bhāgavata Purāṇa* are directly connected with those of the *Mahābhārata;* the Purāṇa extracts from the Epic the events that concern Kṛṣṇa and expands upon them. It thus behooves the Purāṇa to situate itself within the Epic itself, which it accomplishes with the reference to Parikṣit. For in the *Mahābhārata,* the entire story is told in the course of a snake sacrifice performed by Janamejaya, the son of Parikṣit, in order to avenge Parikṣit's death; the frame story of the Epic narrates in some detail the conditions leading to that death.[11] But in the Epic, Parikṣit dies in just a couple of lines; no one narrates anything to him at all, let alone the entire *Bhāgavata Purāṇa.* The *Bhāgavata* thus mimics (parrots, one might say) the Epic by projecting its own frame into an episode (the death of Parikṣit) immediately adjacent to the episode (Janamejaya's sacrifice) in which the Epic frames itself, expanding that episode to allow for the telling of its own text. There is a further irony in this maneuver. For the one person in the *Mahābhārata* who dies as slowly as Parikṣit dies in the *Bhāgavata* and who, like a long-winded character in an opera, narrates the longest book of the *Mahābhārata* (the "Śānti Parvan") from his deathbed, is Bhīṣma, the witness of the entire holocaust. And it is in the course of this narrative that Bhīṣma tells the story of Vyāsa and Śuka and the speaking trees, the story alluded to in the second, cryptic verse of the *Bhāgavata.*

During the rest of the first book of the *Bhāgavata,* the Sūta tells the sages the story of Parikṣit at some length, with no essential divergences from the *Mahābhārata* version. In chapter 7, the Sūta says, "Now I will tell you the birth, works, and death of King Parikṣit, as it gives rise to the story of Kṛṣṇa" (*BP* 1.7.12). He then tells how Kṛṣṇa saved Parikṣit at birth.[12] But the sages say, "By means of the knowledge that Śuka gave him, Parikṣit reached the feet of

Viṣṇu. Tell us what was told to Parikṣit (by Śuka)" (*BP* 1.18.16). The Sūta then tells how, when Parikṣit was dying of a fatal snake bite, "By chance, the son of Vyāsa happened to come there, wandering around with no goal, with no sign to distinguish him, surrounded by women and children, and wearing the garb of a social outcaste" (*BP* 1.19.25).[13] When Parikṣit asked Śuka to tell him what a dying man needs to know, "The glorious son of Vyāsa began to speak to King Parikṣit in reply" (*BP* 1.19.40). Śuka's reply consists of the rest of the *Bhāgavata Purāṇa* (beginning with the second book, which starts here), at the end of which Śuka says to the king, "Do you want to hear anything else?" to which Parikṣit replies, "No, thank you," and dies, and Śuka departs.[14]

THE *DEVĪBHĀGAVATA*

None of this explains why Śuka rather than Vyāsa is the narrator. The Purāṇa enhances Śuka's reputation by insinuating him retrospectively into the frame story of the *Mahābhārata;* but nothing in that original frame would lead one to select Śuka as a narrator. This awkwardness is avoided in the *Devībhāgavata Purāṇa,* where the Sūta, instead of overhearing Śuka tell the story to Parikṣit (an incident that does not occur at all in that text), overhears Vyāsa telling it to Śuka. The Sūta there says:

> Then when Vyāsa had made this surpassingly beautiful Purāṇa [the *Devībhāgavata*], he read it to his noble son, Śuka, who was born of the fire-sticks, when he realized that he was devoid of passion. I heard it there from the mouth of Vyāsa, and took it in with its meanings, the secret of the Purāṇa, all of it, by the grace of the guru. When he was questioned by his son [*sūta!*] who was born of no womb and who had a marvellous mind, Vyāsa of the Island told the whole thing, the secret of the Purāṇa, and I heard it there. (*DBP* 1.3.36–38)

The connection with the *Mahābhārata* is then made by the *Devībhāgavata* in an entirely different way. After telling the story of Vyāsa's sadness on being separated from Śuka (*DBP* 1.20, a story that we will soon examine in detail), the text states that Vyāsa was still so unhappy that he went back to the Ganges to find his mother, Satyavatī. At this point we pick up the thread of the first book of the *Mahābhārata:* Vyāsa learned that his mother had married Śantanu, that her son Vicitravīrya had died, and that her other son,

Bhīṣma, had taken a vow never to beget children; Vyāsa then engendered Pāṇḍu and Dhṛtarāṣṭra in Vicitravīrya's widows. In other words, the text tells us that the other, more famous sons of Vyāsa—the heroes of the Epic—were born only after (and perhaps to compensate for) the loss of his first son, Śuka.

Book 2 of the *Devībhāgavata* then retells the rest of the story of the *Mahābhārata,* and after a great deal of other material (mostly about the goddess), the final book, book 12, reverts to the Epic frame. There we find King Janamejaya listening to the whole story from Vyāsa; there is not a word about Śuka:

> Vyāsa said, "Thus, O King [Janamejaya], I have told you what you asked, what Viṣṇu told Nārada. Anyone who hears this Purāṇa of the Great Goddess [Devī] becomes dear to the Devī. But since you are distressed, knowing the bad way that your father [Parikṣit] has gone, lift up your father by performing a sacrifice to the Mother."
>
> The Sūta said:
>
> Hearing this, the tiger among kings. . . . had Brahmins recite the *Devībhāgavata Purāṇa.* And just as he was completing the sacrifice, Nārada came there from the sky, sounding his lute. Hastily the king arose when he saw Nārada and asked him why he had come there. Nārada said, "Today, great king, I saw a great miracle in the world of the gods, and I came here to tell you about it. Your father went a bad way, because of the ripening of his own *karma.* But that very man has now taken on a heavenly form and is praised by the gods and surrounded by celestial nymphs (*apsaras*es). Mounting a jeweled chariot, he has gone to the Island of Jewels, because of the fruit of hearing the *Devībhāgavata Purāṇa.*" Janamejaya rejoiced and thanked Vyāsa, and Vyāsa departed. (*DBP* 12.13)

Thus the *Devībhāgavata* inserts the description of the way that it was told into the very spot occupied by the description of the telling of the *Mahābhārata* in the *Mahābhārata:* into the interstices of the snake sacrifice performed by Janamejaya to avenge the death of his father, Parikṣit. But more than that: the *Devībhāgavata* substitutes for the snake sacrifice a sacrifice to the Devī, and indeed it is not that sacrifice at all but the actual telling of the Purāṇa that avenges—and, beyond that, saves—Parikṣit. This greatly exalts the Purāṇa, but it also incidentally produces an awkward doubling of the telling of the Purāṇa: the Sūta tells us how Vyāsa told the Purāṇa to Janamejaya for the sake of Parikṣit (as the *Bhāgavata* tells us that the Sūta heard Śuka tell it to Parikṣit himself), but we are also left with the statement that the Sūta heard the Purāṇa when Vyāsa told it to Śuka, for reasons that we will soon examine. In any case, Vyāsa, not Śuka, is the narrator of the *Devībhāgavata;* the Sūta recites a long list of the twenty-eight different Vyāsas who composed all the Purāṇas, ending with the *Bhāgavata,* before he composed the best of all, the *Devībhāgavata* (*DBP* 1.3.1–35).

And the frame of the *Bhāgavata* goes on to tell us more about Vyāsa's involvement with the text than about Śuka's. The Sūta, repeating a well-known statement from the *Mahābhārata* itself, tells how Vyāsa, knowing that people were no longer able to comprehend the Vedas in the present Kali Age, divided the Vedas. But since he knew that women and Śūdras and low people could not use the Vedas, he went on to compose the *Mahābhārata* (BP 1.4.14). One day, when he was still worried, the divine sage Nārada came to him and, smiling a little, said "Now are you fully satisfied?" (BP 1.4.32). When Vyāsa said that he wasn't, Nārada told him all about Kṛṣṇa, and, when Nārada left, Vyāsa composed the *Bhāgavata Purāṇa* for ignorant people (*BP* 1.7.6). He then taught it to his son Śuka, who had renounced all passions (BP 1.7.8).

Śuka's renunciation raises questions in the mind of Śaunaka, the most articulate of the sages in the Naimiṣa Forest listening to the Sūta. He asks the Sūta, "Since the sage [Śuka] had renounced all passion, for whose sake [or for what cause] did he learn this great big [book]?" (*BP* 1.7.9; cf. also *DBP* 1.4.3: "Śuka was formerly famous for being a yogi even in the womb; how then did he study this very long Purāṇa?"). And the Sūta replies, "Even sages who delight in the Soul and who have no ties [or no books: two meanings of *nirgrantha*], even they indulge for no reason in devotion to the wide-striding [Viṣṇu] who has such qualities. His mind fascinated by the virtues of Viṣṇu, the venerable one descended from Vyāsa [Śuka] learned this great story" (BP 1.7.10–11). The *Mahābhārata* had already presented Śuka as more elitist than Vyāsa in the transmission of its own text: "Vyāsa taught the *Mahābhārata* to his own son Śuka and, later, to other students. Nārada recited it to the gods, Asita Devala to the Ancestors, and Śuka taught it to demigods and demons (*gandharva*s, *yakṣa*s, and *rākṣasa*s)" (*M* 1.1.63–64) This formula is repeated, with a slight variation, at the end of the *Mahābhārata:* "Nārada recited it to the gods, and Asita Devala, to the Ancestors. Śuka taught it to the *rākṣasa*s and *yakṣa*s, and Vaisampāyana told it to mortals" (*M* 18.5.42).

These are the supernatural creatures with whom Śuka generally prefers to hobnob, both in the Epics and in the Purāṇas. In the

Mahābhārata, too, Vyāsa's other sons are warrior kings who are involved as actors in the central action. In the *Bhāgavata Purāṇa,* by contrast, it is Vyāsa's intellectual son, the detached Brahmin, who plays a crucial role, though still not one that involves him in any activity other than storytelling.

Vyāsa creates his story because of his compassion for and involvement with inadequate humans; the dispassionate Śuka learns the story out of love for God, even as the dispassionate God becomes involved in the world out of unmotivated play (*līlā*) or, later, out of his compassion for humans.

But Śuka's complete detachment and renunciation is what finally qualifies him to narrate the *Bhāgavata Purāṇa.* There are, as we have said, episodes in the *Mahābhārata* that provide us with information about Śuka that explains why he is better suited than Vyāsa to narrate the *Bhāgavata.* And there are within the *Bhāgavata* frame story, beyond that one cryptic verse, clearer allusions to these Epic escapades of Śuka.

At the beginning of chapter 4 (introduced, again, by the unjustified phrase, "Vyāsa said"), Śaunaka asks,

> How was Śuka recognized by the city-dwellers when he arrived at the country of the Kurus and Jangalas, as he wandered around in the Elephant City [Hastināpura] like a mad, mute, idiot? Vyāsa's son, who is a great and single-minded yogi, appears to be a stupid fool. When the goddesses saw the sage [Vyāsa] going along after his son, they were ashamed, even though he was not naked, and they put on their clothes, but they did not do this for his son [Śuka, who was naked]. When the sage [Vyāsa] saw this and asked them why, they said, "In your mind there is a distinction between men and women, but your son's gaze does not discriminate in that way." (BP 1.4.3–6)

Śrīdhara adds some details to this brief vignette: the women are water nymphs (*apsaras*es), playing in the water, and Śuka encounters them when he is going forth to renounce.

ŚUKA'S BIRTH

To understand this episode, which is part of the same story alluded to in the verse about the talking trees, we must consult the long series of passages in the *Mahābhārata* (some dozen chapters of the "Mokṣadharma" section of the "Śānti Parvan") that tells the story of Śuka and Vyāsa. For the *paraṃ-parā* of the Purāṇa is from father to son, like the *paraṃ-parā* of life itself, and the *Mahābhārata* explains how the son surpassed the father, even as the *Bhāgavata Purāṇa* claims to surpass the text that is its father, the *Mahābhārata*.[15]

The Epic text begins, appropriately, with Śuka's birth (never described in the *Bhāgavata Purāṇa*), which is abnormal. Yudhiṣṭhira asks: "How was Śuka born the son of Vyāsa, and how did he achieve his highest success? Tell me. In what woman did Vyāsa beget Śuka? For I don't know his mother" (*M* 12.310.1). Bhīṣma replies:

> Once upon a time, on a peak of Meru, Śiva was sporting with his terrifying troops, and Pārvatī was with him. Vyāsa was performing fierce acts of asceticism in order to obtain a son, thinking, "Let me have a son who will equal, in his manliness (*vīrya*), fire, earth, water, wind, and sky." With this intention he asked Śiva for a boon. Markaṇḍeya told me this story; he was there doing some errand for the gods. Śiva was pleased by this asceticism and said, smiling, "You will have a son of just that sort, who will be just like fire, just like wind, just like earth, just like water, and just like sky—just as pure as they are. He will be of that essence, of that intelligence, of that soul, of that recourse. And he will be famous throughout the three worlds."
>
> Having obtained this boon from Śiva, (Vyāsa) the son of Satyavatī took the fire stick and twirled it in order to make a fire. Then the sage Vyāsa saw the beautiful nymph named Ghṛtācī, and he was deluded by lust. When she had agitated Vyāsa's mind with lust, Ghṛtācī became a female parrot [*śukī*] and approached him. And when he saw that the nymph had taken on another form, though his every limb was pervaded by lust, the sage made a great effort to control himself. But Vyāsa was not able to restrain his heart that had gone forth, as he was enchanted by the form of Ghṛtācī. And as he strained to control himself, in his desire to make a fire, he shed his seed suddenly right on the fire stick. Calmly the Brahmin sage churned the stick just like that, and Śuka was born in it. While the seed [*śukra*] was being churned, Śuka of great ascetic power was born, the great yogi whose womb was the fire stick. And as soon as he was born, the Vedas came to dwell in him, as they dwelt in his father. (*M* 12.310.11–29 and 12.311.1–22)

Let us pause to note a few features that will recur in subsequent episodes. Vyāsa is worldly; he wants a manly son, and he is vulnerable to nymphs; he is a fire-maker, a hot character, a sacrificer rather than a renouncer. His fire stick (a feminine noun, in Sanskrit, and often used as a metaphor for a mother) receives the seed that he sheds in response to a nymph whose name means "Sacrificial Ladle full of Clarified Butter," a fine metaphor for a womb fit to receive the clarified seed of a great Vedic sage. This conjunction of sacrificial implements, female fire sticks and concave ladles, provides a womb for a child connected with a parrot, even as Śiva himself fathers a child (Skanda) born through the intervention of the god of fire himself, Agni, who takes the form of a parrot.[16] And the pun on the name of the child further connects him with Śiva: the child, named Śuka, is born of Vyāsa's seed (*śukra*) even as Śukra, the priest of the demons, is so called because he comes out of Śiva's penis (*M* 12.278.1–38).[17]

Śiva knows all about Vyāsa's worldly intentions and plays a trick on him; he smiles as he grants his boon—twisting it subtly so that Vyāsa's son excels in purity rather than in manliness, in detachment rather than in attachment. The trick will eventually become even trickier: Vyāsa's son will actually *become* the elements to which Vyāsa intends merely to liken him metaphorically. The son is as good as his father—the Vedas that his father struggled to divide come to him right away—and he will soon be even better than his father. It is also interesting to note, in passing, that Bhīṣma takes pains to declare his own source for this story—the sage Markaṇḍeya.

When the story of Śuka's birth is retold in the *Devībhāgavata Purāṇa,* the text clearly borrows its basic structure from the *Mahābhārata,* but it also makes several significance innovations. The story is told in response to a casual reference to Śuka that prompts the usual question: The sages said, "In what wife of Vyāsa was Śuka born, and how? You said that Śuka was born from no womb, that he was born of fire sticks. There is a lot of doubt about this. Tell us" (*DBP* 1.4.1–2; also 1.10.1–3). The Sūta then begins by telling the story of Vyāsa and the two sparrows and their child (which we will analyze below), an episode which makes him want to have a son of his own:

> As he was worrying in this way, [Vyāsa] the son of Satyavatī sighed and became depressed. Then he decided to perform asceticism on a peak of Mount Meru. As he was wondering which god to ask for a boon, Nārada came to him by chance, lute in

hand. . . . Nārada advised him to ask Devī for his boon. . . . On a lovely peak of Meru, Vyāsa the son of Satyavatī continued to perform his asceticism to obtain a son, muttering a one-syllable seed *mantra* that he had learnt from Nārada, meditating on the great Māyā [the Power of Illusion incarnate in the Goddess], thinking: "Let me have a son equal in manliness to fire, earth, wind, and space."

When Indra saw that the universe was pervaded with Vyāsa's great fiery glory, he became afraid. When Śiva asked him why he was afraid, Indra told him about Vyāsa, and Śiva said, "Parāśara's son Vyāsa is doing this to get a son. I will go there and give him a son." Then Śiva went to the sage and said, "Get up; you will have a fine son. He will be made of all fiery glory, wise, famous, dear to all people always, filled with all the virtues." Hearing this speech, Vyāsa bowed to Śiva and went back to his own hermitage, and after tormenting himself for many years he became exhausted. He churned the secret fire stick, desiring to make a fire, and as he did it there appeared in his mind the strong desire for a son: "Just as fire arises from the churning that comes from the union of the churning stick and the fire stick, how will happiness arise for me? For I do not have the woman who is known as 'Fire stick for a son,' a young, beautiful woman born of a good family, chaste, a woman clever at bringing forth sons, and dwelling in chastity. But how can I make her my beloved, to be a chain for my two feet? . . . Even Śiva is bound to his woman; how then can I become a householder?"

As he was thinking in this way, the beautiful Ghṛtācī came within his line of sight as she went through the sky. Seeing that ultimate nymph, his body was pervaded by lust, and he thought, "What shall I do now in this difficulty? If I take possession of this woman, the noble ascetics will all laugh at me. Now, I don't care how much I am blamed, as long as I am completely happy. And the wise say that the householder stage gives happiness, gives a son, gives heaven, and gives release. But surely I won't get that with this heavenly woman. For once in the past I heard a little story from Nārada about how King Purūravas fell into the clutches of Urvaśī and was overcome by her." (*DBP* 1.4.21–24, 1.4.65, and 1.10.4–20)

In addition to the obvious changes occasioned by making the Goddess the supreme deity (an awkward adjustment, since it is still Śiva who grants Vyāsa the boon, though perhaps the Goddess may be regarded as expanding the bit part played by Pārvatī in the Epic), there are a number of small but significant alterations. Śiva no longer changes "manliness" to "purity" in granting the boon, but his statement that the child would be "made of all fiery glory" (*sarvatejomaya*) may reflect and foreshadow the statement that when Śuka leaves his body he will be "made of all elements" (*sarvabhūtamaya*). The detailed portrayal of Vyāsa's ambivalence about becoming a householder will soon be mirrored, with even greater intensity, in the ambivalence of his son Śuka.[18]

But it is in the relationship with nymphs that this Purāṇa is particularly innovative. Vyāsa has already set the scene for his abnormal method of procreation by referring to the ideal wife as a "Fire stick for a son." At this point we expect a nymph to enter, and in fact one does appear, but not Ghṛtācī. In response to the statement that Vyāsa remembered the story of Urvaśī (told, significantly, by the omnipresent Nārada), the sages ask the Sūta all about Urvaśī and Purūravas, and he tells them the story (*DBP* 1.11–13), ending with "Now I have told you the whole story of Urvaśī" (*DBP* 1.13.34). This is the only appearance that Urvaśī makes in this version of the story; she plays a far more important role in the story of Śuka in the *Mahābhārata*.

The Sūta then resumes the story of Vyāsa:

> Seeing the dark eyed lady, Vyāsa got worried and thought, "What should I do? This divine maiden, this nymph, is not appropriate." Seeing that Vyāsa was thinking in this way, the nymph began to fear: "This man will curse me." And so she took the form of a female parrot and flew away in terror. Vyāsa was amazed when he saw her in the sky as a bird, but, just from seeing her, lust entered his body, and his heart became agitated. The sage made a great effort to control himself, but he could not restrain his heart that had gone out to Ghṛtācī, enchanted by her, because of what was fated to be. As he was churning with a desire to produce fire, suddenly he dropped his seed right on the female fire stick. He didn't notice that it had fallen, and went on churning the fire stick. From that Śuka was born, charming with the form of Vyāsa. At first Vyāsa was amazed to see his son, and wondered, "What is this?" Then he realized that this was the result of the boon of Śiva. (*DBP* 1.14.1)

The main contribution of this text is to explain what remains unexplained in the *Mahābhārata* version, the fact that the nymph took the form of a parrot: where in the Epic she becomes a parrot to approach Vyāsa, which seems strange, here she does it to get away from Vyāsa.

CHERCHEZ LA NYMPH

Nymphs continue to play an important role in the story of Vyāsa and Śuka; in particular, the superiority of Śuka over Vyāsa is demonstrated by the dramatic contrast between Śuka's imperviousness to nymphs and Vyāsa's perviousness. The next two episodes in the *Mahābhārata* version depict this superiority:

> When Vyāsa realized that his son was talented in the knowledge of release [*mokṣa*], he said "Go to Janaka the king of Mithilā. He will talk to you about release in all its details. But go by the normal human path, without performing any miracles; don't go by the path of your magic powers, through the air. Go by the straight path, not by the path where you can look for pleasures to which you might become attached. And don't manifest egotism toward the king, who is my sacrificial patron; put yourself in his power and he will dispel your doubts. He knows a lot about *dharma* and about release; whatever my sacrificial patron tells you to do, do it."
>
> As his father commanded, Śuka went to Janaka of Mithilā. Though he was capable of going through the air, he went on earth, on his own two feet. He went past mountains and rivers . . . He arrived at Mithilā and was not tired or hungry or thirsty or hot. He was ushered into three rooms of the palaces; in the third was the harem, like the heavenly garden of Indra. He was surrounded by young women as beautiful as nymphs, with lovely clothes and good hips, good to look at, good at the ways of love, clever at murmuring, dancing, singing, and smiling. They gave him water to wash his feet, and played and laughed and sang to him. But he who had conquered his senses neither rejoiced nor became angry. The women gave him a magnificent bed. Śuka washed his feet and said his twilight prayer and lay down and went to sleep properly. Then he got up and washed and meditated, surrounded by the women. And that is how he spent the night in the king's palace.
>
> The next day Janaka received him and taught him about release. Then he went away to the north, to the icy mountains. (*M* 12.312.1–46)

By sending his son to king Janaka for his spiritual education, Vyāsa is anchoring himself in the Vedic tradition by doing a very Vedantic thing: he is mimicking the action of several sages in the Upaniṣads.[19] And by forbidding Śuka to fly, he is doing a very Buddhist thing: the early Buddhist scriptures warned the monks not to demonstrate their miraculous powers, particularly not to fly.[20] But in this context, Vyāsa may have other motives as well; he may be jealous of his son's superior powers, and he may dimly foresee that Śuka will finally fly away from him entirely. This possibility is supported by what does happen to Śuka on this journey: he is miraculously untouched by his long travels, and he resists the women in the harem (another quasi-Buddhist motif[21]), who are like the nymphs that his father could not resist.

In the *Devībhāgavata,* when Vyāsa urges Śuka to take a wife and Śuka criticizes the householder's life (*DBP* 1.15.1), Vyāsa starts to cry, and Śuka marvels that even his father, who had divided the Vedas, was deluded by the power of Māyā. This is the first of many indications that Śuka has more control over his emotions than Vyāsa has. Thereupon, here as in the *Mahābhārata,* Vyāsa sends Śuka to Janaka:

> Seeing that his son wanted to go, Vyāsa embraced him firmly and said, "Be well, Śuka, and live long, my son. But promise me before you go: Say that you will come back to my hermitage and will never again go away anywhere. My son, I am happy when I see your lotus face; but if I do not see you I become very unhappy; you are my very life's breath. When you have seen Janaka and dispelled your doubts, come back here and stay here, happily studying the Vedas." Thus addressed, Śuka bowed to his noble father and circumambulated him, and then he moved off as fast as an arrow shot from a bow. (*DBP* 1.17.6–12)

Vyāsa here does not forbid Śuka literally to fly, but he forbids him to flee in the broader sense. Though Śuka departs in dramatic haste, he obeys the unspoken literal command (he walks the whole way, which is described in detail similar to that of the Epic), and he does return, but only to go away forever. First, however, this text further exploits the meeting with the courtesans:

> The minister brought Śuka into a second inner room, with a lovely flowering forest. Beautiful women in the service of the king, skilled at singing and playing, and clever at the science of erotic love [*kāmaśāstra*], were instructed by the minister to

> serve Śuka. The women were overcome by lust when they saw the handsome Śuka, who was like a second Kāma himself, but realizing that Śuka had conquered his senses, they served him, and he, the son of a fire-stick, regarded them with the emotion due to a mother. He went to bed and arose again. (*DBP* 1.17.54)

One wonders whether he regarded them with the emotion due to *his* mother (the fire-stick), but perhaps this is a more general statement of lustlessness. Though Śuka remains impervious to pleasure, he is not impervious to a good argument: Janaka persuades him that the Vedas are good (Śuka had said it was evil to kill animals) and that it is also good to marry. Śuka returns to Vyāsa:

> Seeing his son come there, Vyāsa was very happy, and embraced him and smelled his head and asked how he was. And Śuka stayed in his father's hermitage, at his side, studying the Vedas and all the learned traditions [*śāstra*s]. Then Śuka married a girl named Pīvarī, even though he was still on the path of yoga. In her he begat four sons—Kṛṣṇa, Gauraprabha, Bhūri, and Devaśruta—and a daughter named Kīrti, whom he gave in marriage to Anuha. Kīrti and Anuha had a son, Brahmadatta, who became a great king. (*DBP* 1.19.42)

This is a truly major innovation: Śuka has sons, and even a most worldly grandson! Yet he goes on to renounce them all, thus demonstrating, perhaps even more vividly than in texts in which he never marries, his rejection of all passion.

The rejection of women, more precisely nymphs, is the key to the final series of episodes in the *Mahābhārata:*

> One day Nārada came to Śuka and talked to him about release. When Śuka had heard the words of Nārada he made a firm resolution: "Sons and wives are a great obstacle to knowledge. I want to reach the highest level. Through yoga, I will abandon this house-corpse; I will become wind and enter the sun. For the sun does not perish like the moon with the gods. (When one enters the moon) he is shaken loose and falls to the earth and enters again upon the wheel of rebirth. The moon constantly wanes and is filled up again. But the sun heats the worlds with its rays and its disk never diminishes. I will go to the sun and live there, discarding this body. I will enter into all the elements in the world." He asked Nārada for permission to depart, which Nārada granted; and then he went to his father. He

> bowed to Vyāsa and asked him [for permission to do yoga]. Hearing Śuka's speech, the great sage was pleased and said to him, "Hello [*bho*], my son! Stay here for a while today, so that I can feast my eyes on you." But Śuka, who had no attachments and no affection, who had loosened all his bonds, having set his heart on release, determined to go. And abandoning his father, he went. (*M* 12.318.46–63)

Nārada is often instrumental in turning sons into renouncers against the wishes of their more worldly fathers.[22] In the *Devībhāgavata,* Śuka's desire to renounce the world is not at first attributed to a visit by Nārada; it is simply natural to him. But later there is a brief reference to the effects of Nārada upon Śuka after his return from Janaka:

> After a long time, as a result of the teaching of Nārada, he attained the highest knowledge and the highest path of yoga, and installing his son in the kingdom he went to the Bāḍarikā hermitage. By means of the seed syllable of Māyā, and by the grace of Nārada, the knowledge of the highest reality [*brahman*] that gives liberation arose in him. Śuka abandoned his connection with his father and meditated on a lovely peak of Kailāsa, averse to all connections. (DBP 1.19.43–46)

ŚUKA'S RELEASE

In the *Mahābhārata,* Nārada inspires Śuka in a manner that is once again Vedantic: Śuka's meditation is a reference to the famous doctrine of the two paths, one to the sun and the other to the moon, in the Upaniṣads.[23] But in addition to merging with the sun, Śuka wishes to go still further and to merge with all the elements in the world. This is a concretized extension of Vyāsa's original wish for him: that he be "just like" the five elements. In order to achieve this, Śuka then sets out on his final journey:

> Climbing a mountain peak, the son of Vyāsa sat down in a deserted spot. He engaged in yoga; and he laughed when he saw the sun. Then he left Mount Kailāsa and flew to the sky. All the sages were amazed: "Who is this who moves in the intermediate space [*antarīkṣa*], who has achieved success through his asceticism? Body down, head up, he is carried along by his eyes." All the flocks of nymphs, seeing him coming

along suddenly, were flustered and highly amazed, and they stared at him. Then he went to Mount Malaya, the haunt of the nymph Urvaśī. She was amazed to see the son of the Brahmin sage and she said, "By serving his father he has achieved the highest success. Devoted to his father, the dear son of his father, how has he separated himself from his father who has no one but him in his heart?" When he heard Urvaśī say this, Śuka, who knew all about *dharma,* said to the gods, "If my father should follow me, crying out, 'Śuka!' then answer him, all of you together. If you love me, promise me this." Hearing Śuka's words, the cardinal directions, forests, oceans, rivers, and mountains all together replied to him: "As you command, Brahmin, even so will it be. When the sage speaks, we will all answer."

Then Śuka abandoned the four sorts of worlds. He gave up the three strands that compose all matter:[24] the eight forms of darkness, the five forms of energy, and goodness. Free of the strands of matter, dwelling in ultimate reality,[25] he was like a blazing fire without any smoke. Showers of meteors fell. Now, there were two divine peaks of Himālaya and Meru very close together, a hundred leagues wide and high, one white and one gold. Going toward the north, Śuka saw them and calmly flew into them; immediately the two peaks split into two, an unprecedented marvel. And when everyone saw the mountains split in two they said, "Bravo, bravo!"

Śuka then saw the heavenly river Ganges, in which flocks of nymphs were bathing and playing. Though they had no clothes on, they looked upon Śuka as one who had emptied his own form (inside). His father, knowing that he had gone forth, was filled with affection for him and went on the highest path, following after him. But Śuka went beyond the wind and into the intermediate space, and demonstrating his own supernatural power he became a part of all the elements.

Then Vyāsa used his own great yoga, for he had great ascetic power too, and in the blink of an eye he went after Śuka. He saw where Śuka had split the mountain peak in two, and all the sages praised his son's deeds to him. Then the father cried out, "Śuka!" in a long cry, in his own voice, loudly, making the three worlds resound. Śuka, who had gone into everything, who was the soul of everything and had everything as his mouth, answered, "Hello!" (*bho*), making the word resound in answer. That one syllable was picked up and echoed by everything in the universe, moving or still. And from that time forth, even today, Śuka causes loud individual sounds to echo on the slopes and caves of mountains. And Śuka, invisible, displaying his supernatural power, having abandoned all qualities including sounds, went on the highest path.

Seeing the greatness of his own son, Vyāsa sat down on the mountain, thinking about his son. Then a flock of nymphs, playing on the banks of the celestial Ganges, saw the sage and became flustered and, indeed, hysterical; some of them dove into the water, some hid in clumps of grass, and some put on their clothes when they saw the sage. Then the sage realized that his son was free and that he himself was attached, and this made him both pleased and ashamed.

At that moment, Śiva came to Vyāsa to comfort him as he mourned with grief for his son. Śiva said to him, "In the past you chose to have a son who would be, in his manliness, like fire, earth, water, wind, and sky. That is the kind of son that was born to you because of your asceticism. Now he has gone to the highest path that is hard to attain for people who have not conquered their senses. Why do you mourn for him? As long as the mountains stand and the oceans remain, so long will the fame of your son be undying. But I will do you a favor: you will see a shadow [*chāyā*] that looks just like your son and that will never go away in this world." Thus Vyāsa was reconciled by the lord Śiva, and when he saw the shadow he was filled with the highest joy.

Thus I have told you, in detail, the birth and the final end of Śuka, as you asked. Once upon a time the divine sage Nārada told it to me, and so did Vyāsa the great yogi, in a series of conversations, line by line. (*M* 12.319.1–29, 320.1–40)

Thus, at the end, the *Mahābhārata* establishes a double line of transmission, from Nārada *and* from Vyāsa, which the *Bhāgavata* will condense into a single line: Nārada inspired Vyāsa to tell the story of Kṛṣṇa, and Vyāsa told it to Śuka, who told it to Parikṣit and the Sūta. But Nārada, like Vyāsa in the *Mahābhārata,* is instrumental not only in the telling of the story but in the action itself: it is he who inspires Śuka to renounce the world.

That renunciation takes several overlapping forms, all involving doubles. First, let us note the importance of mountains. Even though Śuka has shed his physical form, he is able to act upon matter so effectively that he makes the conjoined peak of two mountains into *two separate* peaks, a violent metaphor for his own separation from his father. And at the end, it is in the mountains that his auditory echoes lodge, and it is the endurance of mountains that Śiva uses as a metaphor for the endurance of the fame of Śuka in the absence of his material body. (It is interesting to note that the *Mahābhārata* does not single out the trees as the source of the echo that replies to Vyāsa's call, as the cryptic verse in the *Bhāgavata* does; here it is the entire universe, including trees, that replies).

Next follow the mirror episodes of the encounters with the nymphs, who do not fear Śuka but fear his father; this produces in Vyāsa an explicit ambivalence, making him "both pleased [that his son was so great] and ashamed [that he himself was not]." Śuka then becomes diffused into the world in general, but out of compassion for his father he returns as a double set of doubles: first Śuka himself becomes an echo, an auditory double, and then Śiva produces a shadow, a visual double. Both of these serve to comfort the one person who is attached to him, his father. It is perhaps ironic that the nymph Urvaśī is the one who chides him for abandoning his father, for she herself is notorious in Hindu mythology for having abandoned her own husband and son,[26] a story whose telling is, as we have seen, an explicit factor in the life of Śuka and Vyāsa as it is told in the *Devībhāgavata Purāṇa*.

That text has its own version of Śuka's apotheosis, too, still closely based upon the Epic narrative but this time somewhat shorter than the Epic. Again Śuka splits the mountain peak in two, though there are no encounters with naked nymphs. Then:

> Vyāsa, tormented by separation, crying out "My son, my son," over and over again, came to the mountain peak where Śuka had stayed. Then, seeing that Vyāsa was so wretched and exhausted, and seeing him crying out, he [Śuka] who had gone into all elements, the witness, gave an answering sound. And even today, on the peak of the mountain, an answering sound echoes. Seeing Vyāsa crying and destroyed by sorrow, hearing him say, "My son, my son," as he was flooded with the pain of separation, Śiva came there to enlighten Vyāsa the son of Parāśara. He said, "Vyāsa, do not sorrow for your son, who is a supreme yogi. He has gone the highest way. You have gotten great fame from your son."[27] Vyāsa replied, "My sorrow does not go away. What shall I do? My two eyes have not been sated, but still long to look at my son." Śiva said, "You will see an enchanting shadow of your son staying by your side. Look at it, tiger among sages, and give up your sorrow." Then Vyāsa saw the shadow of his son, and when Śiva had given him this boon he vanished. But when Vyāsa went back to his own hermitage,

> he still grieved because of his separation from Śuka; he was still terribly unhappy. (DBP 1.19.48–60)

In this version, Vyāsa merely cries out, "My son," as in the single verse in the *Bhāgavata Purāṇa,* instead of calling Śuka's name, as in the Epic. The echo is created in a much more straightforward way (there being no encounter with Urvaśī or nymphs to set it up), but here it is less effective. Vyāsa specifically demands a visual echo as well, and gets it. This, too, is regarded as inadequate in this text, as in other stories: when Saraṇyū abandons her husband, the sun, and leaves in her place a shadow, Chāyā, the surrogate proves unsatisfactory, and the sun goes in search of his true wife.[28] Vyāsa then goes on to beget his *Mahābhārata* sons, real sons, to take the place of Śuka.

ECHOES AND ANIMALS

The combined auditory and visual reflections in this final episode are reminiscent of a similar double metamorphosis in a myth told by Ovid:

> Narcissus was born when the River god Cephisus raped the blue nymph Leiriope. The seer Teiresias told Leiriope, "Narcissus will live a long time, as long as he does not know himself." He was so beautiful that many people fell in love with him, but he rejected them all, for he was too proud of his own beauty. One person who fell in love with him was the nymph Echo, who could use her voice only to repeat what someone else said. [This was a punishment for having told long stories to keep Hera's attention while Zeus's mistresses, the mountain nymphs, escaped from her.] When Echo tried to embrace Narcissus he repelled her, and she spent the rest of her life pining for him until only her voice remained.[29] Finally, Artemis caused Narcissus to fall in love with his own reflection in a clear spring. Unable to possess the image, he lay gazing helplessly into the pool. Echo stayed beside him and echoed his cries as he plunged a dagger into his breast and died. Out of his blood there grew the narcissus plant.[30]

In addition to certain familiar motifs, such as the birth from nymphs and the ambiguous prophecy of the fate of the unborn child, there are more important resonances between the two texts. The conjunction of auditory and visual echoes is the same, and to a certain extent a similar point is made. For the Latin myth demonstrates the devastating reflexivity of perverse *erotic* love; while the Hindu myth, too, clearly denounces the charms of the nymphs and exalts, relatively, the love of a father for a son. Yet even that love is regarded as an all too human weakness, which makes necessary the creation of empty reflections of sound and sight.

In this context, it is interesting to recall another Hindu myth about erotic love, the myth of the destruction of the god of sexual love and desire incarnate, Kāma: Śiva burnt him to ashes, but this merely released Kāma's power into the world, where he continues to pervade all creatures and to exert his power over them even more effectively as the Disembodied One (Ananga).[31] And the animal in which this disembodied god (and his consort, Rati the goddess of sexual pleasure) is carried in the world is the parrot. Thus we may read the story of Śuka, in which Śiva plays such a similar role, as the mirror image of the story of Kāma: it is Śuka's freedom from lust that diffuses him into the world, whereas it is Kāma's essence of lust that diffuses him into all creatures. Both lust and the rejection of lust are "parrots": they appear only in forms that mimic them. Or perhaps it would be better to say that both lust and the rejection of lust always mimic something else.

The connection between birds and lust, or birds and procreation, is further reflected in the version of the birth of Śuka told in the *Devībhāgavata Purāṇa:*

> Once upon a time, in his hermitage on the banks of the Sarasvatī, Vyāsa the son of Satyavatī saw two *kalavinka* birds (sparrows), and he was astonished when he saw how lovingly they cared for their newborn child, rubbing his body with their bodies, feeding him, kissing his mouth with great love and great joy. Seeing this marvel of the love (*prema*) of the two sparrows for their child, Vyāsa's mind was disturbed, and he conceived a desire in his heart to have a son of his own. (DBP 1.4.4–9)

And it is this that inspires him to perform asceticism for Śiva. This episode may have been inspired by the role of the female parrot in the *Mahābhārata* version of Śuka's birth.

But there is another episode from another Epic that may well resonate in the story of Vyāsa and Śuka. Vyāsa's cry, expressing the grief of separation from someone that he loves, inspire's Śuka's answering echo that brings echoes into the world at large. The frame story told at the very beginning of the *Rāmāyaṇa* of Vālmīki contains a similar tale:

> The sage Vālmīki asked the sage Nārada, "Is there in the world a man of perfect virtue?" and Nārada replied by telling Vālmīki about Rāma. Then Nārada departed, and Vālmīki went to bathe by a river. There he saw a pair of curlews[32] mating; suddenly a hunter killed the male, and when the hen grieved Vālmīki cried out, "Hunter, since you killed one of these birds at the height of its passion, you will not live very long." Then Vālmīki realized that he had instinctively uttered this curse in verse, in a meter that he called the *śloka,* because it was uttered in sorrow (*śoka*). (*R* 1.1–2)[33]

And this is the meter in which he begins to tell story of Rāma, the *Rāmāyaṇa.*

The sorrowful separation in Vālmīki's vignette is between a sexual couple, as in the Latin myth of Echo and Narcissus, and as in the *Mahābhārata,* where Pāṇḍu, the father of the Pāṇḍavas, kills a sage mating with a wife (they had taken the form of a stag and a doe to do this) and is cursed to die in the embrace of his own wife (*M* 1.109). Within the *Rāmāyaṇa,* too, this theme is echoed in the separation of Rāma and his wife Sītā. But the story of Vālmīki and the birds also carries overtones of a separation between father and son, as in the story of Śuka and Vyāsa: for within the Epic that Vālmīki will tell in his *śloka*s, Rāma's father accidentally kills the only son of an old man (mistaking him for an elephant, as Pāṇḍu mistakes the sage for a stag), who curses him to be separated from his own son, Rāma (*R* 2.57–58). And there is yet another story in the *Rāmāyaṇa* that connects the language of birds, the interruption of sexuality, and a curse of separation from someone beloved:

> Kaikeyī's father had been granted a boon, which enabled him to understand the speech of animals, but he was warned that he must not tell anyone about it. Once when he overheard what a bird was saying he laughed out loud. His wife, lying in bed with him and thinking that he was laughing at her, demanded to know the reason for his laughter. The king replied that, were he to tell her, he would immediately die [for breaking the condition of the boon]. His wife persisted in her demand, regardless of whether he might live or die. The king then related the incident to the sage who had granted him the boon. The sage cautioned the king against telling, whatever his wife might do.

> Thereupon the king divorced his wife, "and enjoyed himself like Kubera." (This passage is rejected by the critical edition at 2.32, app. 1, 14, 21–54.)[34]

Thus Daśaratha's father-in-law hears a bird talking when he is in a sexual situation, and laughs, which exposes the hearer to the danger of death and separates him from his mate; while Vālmīki sees a bird who is in a sexual situation and is then killed and separated from his mate, which makes the viewer cry.

And there is another central episode of a person mistaken for an animal in the *Rāmāyaṇa*. When Rāvaṇa plots to capture Sītā, he gets the demon Marīca to take the form of a marvelous golden deer, with horns studded with jewels and hoofs like emeralds. Though Lakṣmaṇa sees through the disguise and warns Sītā that it is just the demon Marīca in disguise, Sītā is captivated by the deer and urges Rāma to pursue it for her. The deer leads Rāma far away from Sītā, and, when Rāma kills it, the deer assumes its true form as Marīca. Rāma then realizes that he has been tricked and has thereby lost Sītā. Thus, once again, the killing of a human (here, a demon) in animal form causes the hunter to suffer the curse of separation from his sexual partner (*R* 3.41–44).

These stories form a corpus in which we can read the story of Śuka and Vyāsa: stories in which the emotion of separation from someone beloved is a direct source of the poetic medium in which that separation is expressed. They also form a corpus that links together the themes of mistaking a human for an animal and killing the "animal" (a theme that culminates, in the *Mahābhārata,* with the death of Kṛṣṇa, whom a hunter mistakes for a deer and kills by shooting him accidentally in the sole of his foot), killing someone's son by mistake, interrupting the sexual act (by killing one or both of the partners), understanding the language of animals, and discovering the origin of poetic language. Here we can see the connection between sexual substitution (the animal acting as the surrogate for the human) and the creation of special, indirect forms of speech. If we were to be so foolish as to attempt to construct a logical message given by the corpus as a whole, we would list a chain of theorems: (1) human sexual activity is dangerous; (2) humans have (human) language; (3) some humans become animals when they become sexual; (4) some humans understand the language of animals, particularly when the humans, the animals, or both are involved in sexual situations; (5) sexual activity kills the animals and/or the humans; (6) this combination of sexual activity, animal language, death, and sorrow results in poetry.

THE AUTHOR AS PARROT

In both the story of Śuka and the story of the curlews, Nārada begins the entire process by telling the story of the avatar of Viṣṇu (Kṛṣṇa or Rāma) and then going away; the story is later transformed into a text when the author is moved by sorrow and/or compassion. The *Rāmāyaṇa* story of the invention of the *śloka* is reflected in transformation in the *Devībhāgavata,* where it is said that the Goddess herself (corresponding to Viṣṇu, the first author of the *Bhāgavata*) first composed the *Devībhāgavata* in the form of a half-*śloka,* which she gave to Viṣṇu when he was lying on a banyan leaf, in the form of a child:[35]

> [Vyāsa said,] "Viṣṇu muttered this half *sloka* over and over . . . Viṣṇu said, 'In the Third Age that half-*śloka* will become expanded.' When Brahmā was born of the lotus in Viṣṇu's navel he received [that half-*śloka*]. And he told it to Nārada, his son, and then the sage Nārada gave it to me, once upon a time, and I made it into this full twelve books." (*DBP* 1.15.49–52, 1.16.29)

This is the story of the expansion of the Purāṇa from a single half-*śloka* to the full twelve books. But Vyāsa is more famous as a condenser than as an expander, and at the end of the *Devībhāgavata* another version of the transmission casts him in this more familiar role:

> The Sūta said, "The *Devībhāgavata* whose essence was a half-*śloka* that came out of the mouth of the Devī, the culmination of the Vedas, was taught to Viṣṇu when he was still dwelling on the leaf of the banyan tree. Then Brahmā made it into a work of a hundred million *śloka*s. Putting the essence of that into one place, Vyāsa, for the sake of Śuka, made it into eighteen thousand *śloka*s, in twelve books. And it was written down as the Purāṇa named the *Devībhāgavata.* But even today, in the world of the gods, the longer version still exists." (*DBP* 12.14.1–4)

Instead of expanding the Purāṇa from a half-*śloka* to twelve books, Vyāsa now reduces it from the newly postulated intermediate stage of a hundred million *śloka*s to the mere eighteen thousand that we have in the extant twelve books. In the *Bhāgavata Purāṇa,* as we have noted, the sages wonder why a dispassionate sage like

Śuka bothered to learn such a big book. Perhaps this is why Vyāsa condensed it: because the dispassionate Śuka has no time for a really long book. In the *Mahābhārata,* it was the shortcomings of men during the Kali Age that justified the condensation; in this passage of the *Devībhāgavata* the text is condensed because the listener is too good (too great a yogi), not too bad, to read a long book.

Indeed, there is another episode in the *Devībhāgavata* that turns on its head the problem of Śuka's interest in any *Purāṇa.* Vyāsa's first attempt to dissuade Śuka from renouncing takes a most interesting tack: "Vyāsa, seeing that Śuka wanted to become a renouncer, said to him, 'My son, read this *Bhāgavata Purāṇa* that I have made. It is beautiful and not too long, a Purāṇa that is the equal of the Veda'" (*DBP* 1.15.47). Vyāsa then tells Śuka the story of the origin of the Purāṇa from the half-*śloka* given by the Goddess, whereupon the Sūta remarks, "Thus he spoke, and he told it to his son and to me, and I grasped the whole Purāṇa, though it was very long. Śuka studied the Purāṇa and remained in the lovely *āśrama* of Vyāsa, but he did not find peace there" (*DBP* 1.16.39). Vyāsa hopes to use the Purāṇa to enchant Śuka into remaining with him; his plan fails, however, perhaps because his statement that the Purāṇa is "not too long" is merely wishful thinking: though he apparently tries to reduce it for the sake of Śuka's limited attention span for things worldly, the Sūta still thinks it is very long, and perhaps Śuka thought it was too long.

In the *Bhāgavata,* as in the *Mahābhārata,* manifestations of Śiva frame the Vaiṣṇava avatar: Śiva grants Vyāsa the son in the first place and sets the stage for his disappearance; and he returns in the end to grant Vyāsa the shadow of his vanished son. Śiva is also present as an echo in the parrot that suggests the stories of Śiva and Kāma and Śiva/Agni and Skanda. The appropriateness of a parrot to tell the story of Kṛṣṇa may also be supported by yet another Upaniṣadic image, the image of the two birds, one of whom eats the fruit while the other does not;[36] one bird is said to be dark blue, like Kṛṣṇa, and the other green with red eyes, surely a parrot.[37] This parrot (doubled in the pair of sparrows) is to Vyāsa's poetry what the curlews are to Vālmīki's poetry: the curlews give Vālmīki his sweet sound of sorrow, and the parrot (and sparrows) provide Vyāsa with a disciple who can "echo" his work in the presence of the dying king.[38] The parrot and the echo in the cave together provide a brilliant paradigm for the Purāṇa that is an echo of the Epic. Yet we must not forget that the Purāṇa (anachronisticly, we would say) regards itself as the original, of which the Epic is but an echo.

Vyāsa is fertile in body as well as in mind; he is receptive to any number of nymphs besides Ghṛtācī and produces a significant percentage of the cast of characters in any drama that he narrates. Śuka is sterile in body; indeed, he deconstructs his body altogether. But his purity of spirit is entirely appropriate to the spiritual burden of the *Bhāgavata.* Moreover, by becoming disembodied, Śuka *disperses* himself into all creatures pervasively, just like Kāma, the god of lust that he rejects. This is a fine metaphor for the process of proselytization. This need to proselytize is characteristic, not of a martial Epic like the *Mahābhārata,* but of a work of devotion and renunciation like the *Bhāgavata Purāṇa.*

A propos of this story of Śuka and Vyāsa, P. C. Roy, the translator/publisher of the *Mahābhārata,* observed (and Sorensen says that he "rightly remarks"[39]): "It is evident from this that the Śuka who recited the *Śrimad Bhāgavata* to Parikṣit, the grandson of Yudhiṣṭhira, could not possibly be the Śuka who was Vyāsa's son. Orthodoxy would be staggered at this; the prevailing impression is that it was Vyāsa's son Śuka who recited the *Bhāgavata* to Parikṣit."[40] The logic behind this argument seems to be that since Śuka no longer existed on earth, he could not have lived to talk to Parikṣit. This need not be so, however; Śuka could certainly have told the *Bhāgavata* to Parikṣit *before* his final departure from earth.

But in any case it is madness to argue with such flat-footed logic about the number of nymphs dancing on the head of this mythical transmission. How could the *Mahābhārata* tell us when Śuka narrated the *Bhāgavata* to Parikṣit, when the *Bhāgavata* was not to be composed for another millennium? More to the point, surely a sage who was born through the combined forces of a female parrot named Sacrificial Ladle, an uncontrolled meditating sage, and a fire-stick, a sage who becomes an echo and a shadow, who is diffused throughout the universe, and who, finally, metaphysically surpasses his father, the author of the great Epic, *must* be the narrator of the *Bhāgavata Purāṇa.*

3

The Scrapbook of Undeserved Salvation: The Kedāra Khaṇḍa *of the* Skanda Purāṇa

Wendy Doniger

THE SCRAP PURĀṆA

Western Indologists often assume that the Purāṇas were made, like camels in the old joke, by a noncommunicating committee, or that, like the elephants in another old joke, they continued to be perceived blindly by different members of the tradition as a composite of several distinct, noncommunicating sorts of texts, to which anyone was entitled to add a snake here (the trunk, a hymn of praise), a rope there (the tail, a local folktale), and so forth. And indeed there is some truth in this, as in most wrong ideas. Certainly the authors of the Purāṇas did not share our respect for the integrity of an inherited written script. For one thing, they worked as often from oral as from written texts, and, for another, their tradition was one that encouraged improvisation.[1]

In this world of ever-shifting Purāṇic sands, the *Skanda Purāṇa* is surely the shiftiest, or perhaps the sandiest, of all. The longest and most sprawling of all the Purāṇas, though it was usually grouped with the Mahā- rather than the Upāpurāṇas it was regarded even by the native Indian tradition as a "scrap-bag;" its name forms a pun to this effect in Tamil, where it is the "scrap" Purāṇa (*Kantal-Purāṇam*). Its open-endedness has proved most useful to Indian authors through the ages; whenever a Paurāṇika came upon a story that seemed to be, or ought to be, old, but did not seem to have any known provenance, he could remark, without fear of contradiction, "It's in the *Skanda Purāṇa,*" just as family members assure one another, when looking for a misplaced object, "It's probably in that old closet in the attic." Many a naive Indologist (myself included) has wasted days searching in the extant editions of the *Skanda Purāṇa* for stories said to be there, but not there now. I got my own back once, however, by resorting to this ploy myself when, having misplaced the source of a quotation that I distinctly remembered copying out of some now irretrievable Purāṇic text, I finally decided to use it anyway and to attribute it to the *Skanda Purāṇa.*[2]

Certainly, different parts of the *Skanda Purāṇa* were added at different periods (even the formidable Ludo Rocher despairs of dating this text[3]), and divergent traditions, composed in increments over several centuries, were brought together in the present redactions. The text often betrays its checkered past, despite its constant attempts to integrate each new view. But this is its strength, not its weakness. The *Skanda Purāṇa* is, in a very real sense, a *living* Purāṇa, one of the few living Purāṇas still extant in Sanskrit, and certainly one of the most popular.[4] Why has it survived where other Purāṇas have become literary dinosaurs? Clearly, it has served someone's purposes, perhaps even several conflicting purposes. On the one hand, it has proved a means whereby the Sanskrit tradition could encompass rival traditions, could "kill by embracing" as the saying goes. Or, to look at it from the other standpoint, it has been a door through which the local, vernacular Purāṇas could enter into the *soi-distant* mainstream tradition. It has enabled the vernacular tradition to legitimate itself by claiming to be a part of an infinitely expansible Sanskrit text.

It has been noted that the *Bhāgavata Purāṇa* represents a revolution in Purāṇas, establishing *bhakti* over ritualism as a means to salvation. And I have argued elsewhere in this volume that, within the post-revolutionary *bhakti paraṃparā* of Kṛṣṇa worship, the *Bhāgavata* made a successful claim to have encompassed the *Mahābhārata,* with Śuka surpassing Vyāsa (author of the *Mahābhārata*) as the author first of the *Bhāgavata* and then of the further-encompassing *Devībhāgavata.* But V. Narayana Rao has shown us ways in which the *Bhāgavata* is, in turn, rejected in Telugu epics by those who no longer share its ideology.[5] Here I wish to argue that the *Skanda Purāṇa,* like the Telugu tradition, goes one step further than the *Bhāgavata* and surpasses *bhakti* itself. In this, the *Skanda* is a counterrevolutionary text, which undoes *bhakti* (or deconstructs it, to use the trendy word) by reabsorbing the *sthalapurāṇa* traditions into the conservative ritualist tradition of the *Mahābhārata,* or, if you prefer, revalidates Epic ritualism through a consistent reformulation of traditional Purāṇic myths. It also introduces into many traditional myths a cynical and feminist point of view that is, in its own quiet way, subversive.

PAURĀṆIKAS AND INDOLOGISTS

We must not, therefore, follow most Sanskritists in regarding the *Skanda Purāṇa* as not only authorless (as Michel Foucault tells us all texts are) but mindless (like Paul Griffith's Buddhists). The scraps were not thrown into the scrap bag without any consideration of their relevance to what was already in the bag. The divergent traditions were synthesized and arranged in a new plan devised by the compiler of this one text.[6]

We generally believe, and not without reason, that the mission of Indologists is rather different from the mission of the authors of the texts that they study. Indologists comb through the texts of ancient India in search of pieces of a new puzzle that they hope to construct (and, perhaps, to solve) from the fragments of the rather different, often insoluble, puzzles posed by the texts themselves. And so we go about, snipping a few pieces from the *Ṛg Veda,* a few from the *Mahābhārata,* and so forth, in order to produce our new Purāṇa, our own monograph on "Horses in Ancient India" or, more narrowly, "Evidence for the Use of the Stirrup in Ancient India." Naturally, our agendas are different from theirs; most basically, of course, they were usually composing texts related to worship, while we compose texts related to academic tenure or the narcissism of publication. But there are also a number of less obvious, more intellectual agendas that we as Indologists may very well share with the authors of the texts that we study.

THE "KEDĀRA KHAṆḌA"

In particular, the redactor of the "Kedāra Khaṇḍa" (the first book of the first section, the "Maheśvara Khaṇḍa," of the *Skanda Purāṇa*) seems to me to have had an agenda very like that of many Indologists.[7] That is, he sifted through the texts of his own tradition and selected those myths that seemed to him to have certain themes in common. And then, in retelling them, he added bits and pieces of his own interpretation to make their inherent correspondences more blatantly apparent and, in some cases, to use them in entirely new ways. This process could well stand as a mirror for the academic discipline of Indology. True, the author's plan is colored by a devotional agenda—he is setting out to magnify his god, Śiva—but there, too, I wonder how far he is from the spirit of those anthropologists who regard the people among whom they do their fieldwork as "their" tribe.

Other Purāṇas, of course, have unifying themes, though these are often of a more traditional character. For instance, many Purāṇas weave their stories around the central theme of the place in which they were composed: all the great events of the mythical past are said to have taken place *here*.[8] Or there may be a theme of pilgrimage: as the author moves through a sacred geography, he tells us what happened in each special place along the way.[9] Or there may be a genealogy: stories are told about each of the ancestors in a long line.[10] Or, finally, there may be episodes in the biography of a single god. This last technique works best for gods who have quasi-human lives, like Kṛṣṇa, but it is also done for other gods, including Viṣṇu and Śiva, whose life-cycles, however supernatural, nevertheless touch down at many of the human rites of passage (birth, marriage, the occasional adultery, and, in some texts, even a kind of temporary death).

What is unusual about the first book of the *Skanda Purāṇa* is that it seems to organize its stories about abstract themes, rather than a concrete person or a place; it has an intellectual agenda. The principle of organization is neither spatial (geographic) nor temporal (the lifestory narrative), but thematic. One might have expected, from the title, some kind of geographical focus upon the temple of Kedāranātha in the Himālayas, said to be "the highest . . . and coldest of the holy places."[11] But this is not the case; the scope of the text, both in its sources and in its claims, is pan-Indian and often Vedic. Thus, instead of producing yet another local, self-aggrandizing *sthalapurāṇa,* this text does what we always thought only Indologists did: it looks at its own mythological tradition, selects from it, rearranges it, and restructures it into a thematic essay.[12]

It does this in two ways: it winds a set of old stories together into a new text, adding just enough to each story to make its point, and it adds new stories that are not found elsewhere. The text puts a particular spin on each tale that it retells, and that spin, picking up the impetus already present within the older story, like a good judo player, throws the separate stories together into an orchestrated constellation of new movement. The new stories add up to make a statement that will go on to be echoed in many vernacular texts: the grace granted to the "accidental devotee" or "immoral or undeserving devotee" through the worship of the *liṅga,* the erect penis of the god Śiva. And the old stories are retold in a satirical and quasi-feminist vein. Both of these new projects involve major reversals of conventional moral expectations, positioning marginal figures (sinners, women) at the center of the grace of God. Let us consider the two projects one by one.

THE UNDESERVING DEVOTEE OF THE *LIṄGA*

The theme of the "undeserving devotee" or "accidental devotee" is not unique to the "Kedāra Khaṇḍa." It appears in the *Padma Purāṇa*[13] and in the appended prologue to the *Śiva Purāṇa,* in the story of Devarāja.[14] (Indeed, the Devarāja story is a bit more self-referential: it is by hearing the *Śiva Purāṇa,* accidentally and without paying any attention to it, that Devarāja is saved from the consequences of his sins). And it is common in non-Sanskritic texts, particularly in South India. But where most of the other texts tell just one story, often as a kind of extreme *phalaśruti* (advertisement for the benefits of reading/hearing the work in question), the "Kedāra Khaṇḍa" tells a number of interrelated stories of this genre and even uses it as a kind of armature on which to build the text as a whole.

The theme of the undeserving devotee implicitly repositions ritualism, apparently "mindless" ritualism, over *bhakti.* It argues that feelings, emotions, intentions, do not count at all; that certain actions are efficacious in themselves in procuring salvation for the unwitting devotee. In this it mirrors another sort of *bhakti,* one that is, significantly, characteristic of the Śaiva Siddhānta of South India: the *bhakti* of the kitten, who goes limp to let God the mother cat pick him up by the scruff of the neck, in contrast with the *bhakti* of the baby monkey, who holds on tight to God the mother monkey.

But the accidental devotion of the "Kedāra Khaṇḍa" is far from a return to Vedic ritualism. For knowledge (an essential criterion of Vedic ritualism) does not count any more than emotion, in this line of argument; you don't even have to know how to do the ritual, but you do it "naturally," almost like the natural (*sahaja*) acts of Tantric ritual. In this sense, at least, this is a Tantric argument for the efficacy of a text useful for sinners in the Kali Age.[15]

The particular inflection of this motif that is presented in the "Kedāra Khaṇḍa," the theme of "great sinners who were saved from hell by an accidental act of *liṅga* worship," incorporates (and reverses) an old story, told elsewhere, not of a sinner, but of a *good* man, a devotee of Śiva, who is saved from death (Yama or Kāla) by Śiva in the form of Yamāntaka ("the ender of Yama") or Kālāntaka ("the ender of Kāla"). The *Bhāgavata Purāṇa* calls him "Markaṇḍeya," and depicts him worshipping the *liṅga,* from which Śiva emerges, as he does in the classical story of Brahmā and Viṣṇu and the flame-*liṅga.*[16] Other Purāṇas call him Śveta and depict him, too, as worshipping the *liṅga,* from which Śiva emerges to destroy Kāla.[17] In yet other texts, however, Śveta is not worshipping the *liṅga* at the critical moment, though he is still rescued by Śiva,[18] and this is also true of the "Kedāra Khaṇḍa" version:

> King Śveta was, from birth, a virtuous king and a devotee of Śiva; he told the truth and ruled with *dharma,* and everyone in his kingdom was happy. No one grieved for the death of a son, and there was no disrespect and no murder, nor any poverty. Yama and Kāla (here regarded as the master of Yama) came to take him one day when he was worshipping Śiva. Then Śiva, the Destroyer of Kāla, saw Kāla, and he looked at Kāla with his third eye and burnt him to ashes in order to protect his devotee. Śveta awoke from his meditation to see Kāla burnt in front of him. He praised Śiva and asked him what had happened, and Śiva told him, "Kāla eats all creatures, and he came here to eat you in my presence and so I burnt him. You and I will kill evil men who violate *dharma,* heretics who wish to destroy people." But Śveta said, "This world behaves properly because of Kāla, who protects and creates by destroying creatures. If you are devoted to creation, you should revive Kāla, for without him there will be nothing." Śiva did as his devotee suggested; he laughed and revived Kāla with the form he had had. Then Kāla praised Śiva the Destroyer of Kāla, he who made Kāma disembodied and destroyed the sacrifice of Dakṣa, and who pervades the universe with the form of the *liṅga.* And Kāla told his messengers, "The devotees of Śiva, with their matted hair and rosaries and Śaiva names, wear the garb of Śiva. Even if they are parasites who terrify people, even if they are evil and do bad things, you must not bring them to my world" (32.4–96)

Despite its general advocacy of *liṅga* worship, the "Kedāra Khaṇḍa" does not specify what sort of worship Śveta is engaged in at the moment when death comes for him. Instead, this text assimilates the killing of Yama to the burning and revival of Kāma, which it has just narrated ("Kedāra Khaṇḍa" 21.68–126; see below). This not a tale of grace given to a sinner. On the contrary, it shares the old *bhakti* assumption (itself based upon the older Vedic assumption) that if you love God and serve him he will love you and serve you.[19] But within the text we can note a crucial shift in the attitude to the virtue, or lack of it, of the devotee who is to be saved. At first, the criterion (which Śveta embodies) is a combination of virtue and Śiva-*bhakti*. Midway, however, the criterion shifts to virtue, with no reference to sectarian orientation, when Śiva proposes that, usurping the task of the now-defunct god of the dead, he and Śveta should punish evildoers and heretics (even, supposedly, evildoers who are also Śiva worshippers). But in the end Kāla exempts from death all Śiva worshippers, *even if they are evildoers* (and, indeed, evil-thinkers: even heretics and liars go to heaven if they worship Śiva [5.101]). Thus, the paradigmatic story of virtue rewarded is subtly twisted into a tale of (possibly virtueless) devotion rewarded.

The paradigm of the good *bhakta,* already shadowed by the possibility of the evil *bhakta* in the story of Śveta, is then transformed, in other episodes, into the paradigm of the evil man who is not even consciously a *bhakta:*

> A thief, who killed Brahmins, drank wine, stole gold, and corrupted other men's wives, lost everything in a game of dice. That night, he climbed on the head of a Śiva-*liṅga* and took away the bell [inadvertently ringing it]. At that moment, Śiva sent his servants from Kailāsa to that temple. When the thief saw them, he wanted to run away from the head of the *liṅga,* but Vīrabhadra said, "You fool, what are you afraid of? Śiva is pleased with you today." And they put him in the heavenly car and brought him to Kailāsa and made him a servant of Śiva. (8.1–13).

The thief himself is unaware of the theological twist that makes him, as Śiva tells his servants, "the best of all my devotees" (8.8). But the god saves him despite himself.

Three variants on this theme are collected together in a single chapter of the "Kedāra Khaṇḍa." The first story in the series is the tale of Indrasena:

> Indrasena was a king who was crazy about hunting, a cruel man who nourished his own life's breaths by the life's breaths of others. He was a thief and an adulterer, a drunkard and Brahminicide, seducer of his guru's wife. When he died, Yama's

> messengers bound him and brought him to Yama, but then Yama rose, bowed his head to Śiva, reviled his own messengers, and set Indrasena free from his bonds. He promised to send him to glorious worlds, saying, "For you are a great devotee of Śiva." Indrasena said, "I don't know Śiva. I've always been addicted to hunting." Then Yama said, "You always used to say (when hunting), 'Get that! [*āhara*]. Strike him! [*praharasva*]' [phrases containing Hara, the name of Śiva]. And by the ripening of that *karma* you have been purified." Then Yama's messengers took Indrasena to Śiva, who embraced him and made him his servant, named Caṇḍa. (5.64–85)

Directly after this story we are told another brief vignette of accidental grace:

> An evil thief was killed by the king's men. A dog came to eat him, and accidentally, unconsciously [*caitanyena vinā*], the dog's nails made the mark of Śiva's trident on the man's forehead. As a result, Rudra's messengers took him to Kailāsa. (5.92–95)

The bard then tells another, longer story:

> A Kirāṭa [a mountaineer and hunter, regarded as a member of an Untouchable caste], addicted to hunting, devoid of discrimination, harming living creatures, one day came upon a *liṅga* in the forest when he was parched with thirst. He worshipped the *liṅga* by spitting cheekfuls of water onto it and placing the flesh of wild animals on it with his left hand, and vowed to devote himself to heaven from that day forth. He, too, was translated to heaven, even before his death. There he took on the same form as Śiva, and the Goddess laughed and said, "He is certainly just like you, with your own form and movement and laughable qualities. But you are the only one that I serve." When the Kirāṭa heard what the Goddess said, he immediately turned away his face, while Śiva was watching, and said, "Forgive me, Śiva, and make me your doorkeeper." And Śiva did. (5.111–97)

This story makes a new point: the Kirāṭa is not unconscious of his act of worship, but he is unconscious of the normal rules of worship. The gifts that he offers are hideously unclean from the traditional point of view, but Śiva accepts them in the spirit in which they are offered. The character of the Kirāṭa resonates with one of the earliest and most famous myths of Śiva, the *Mahābhārata* story of the combat between Arjuna and Śiva, when Śiva took the form of a Kirāṭa, vanquished Arjuna, and then revealed himself and gave Arjuna the magic weapons that he sought.[20] This identification alerts us to one of the implications of the theme of accidental devotion: that, since the god himself is an outsider, violent and iconoclastic, he is partial to worshippers who are, as the Goddess mockingly remarks, like him.

The laughter of the Goddess at Śiva's expense is a theme that we will encounter often in this text; here she mocks the traditional translation of the devotee into the image of Śiva and implies, perhaps, that this identity might bring about an inappropriate intimacy between her and the devotee.[21] Blushing at this implication, the Kirāṭa volunteers to *prevent* others from becoming too intimate with her (or Śiva) by guarding the door. This is a theme closely connected with incest; it is Gaṇeśa, in particular, who is given the task of guarding the door to protect the Goddess from Śiva and who is punished by Śiva for his intimacy with the Goddess.[22] A brief version of this episode is alluded to elsewhere in our text:

> Gaṇeśa was born of Nature [*prakṛti*, the Goddess] and looked exactly like Śiva, with the very same form. A battle took place between him and Śiva, because, being born of Nature, he did not know Śiva [and did not let him past the door]. Śiva cut him down with his trident, together with the elephant that he was mounted on, but when the supreme Śakti praised Śiva he offered her a boon, and she said, "This person that you have killed is my son. The fool did not know you, because he was born of a portion of Nature. Please make him live." Śiva laughed and revived the illusory son and gave him a red face and an elephant's head. (10.28–35)

Pārvatī's implicit inability to distinguish Gaṇeśa from Śiva (which is the cause of the problem in other texts) is here cleverly transformed into Gaṇeśa's inability to distinguish Śiva from an intruder. But the result is the same: Śiva kills Gaṇeśa. And now a further twist is given when the Kirāṭa, facing the same problem of identical form, volunteers to guard the door just as Gaṇeśa does, explicitly in other variants of this story and implicitly here as well.

Another undeserving devotee appears in the "Kedāra Khaṇḍa"'s version of the *Vaiṣṇava* story of the generous demon, Bali. The transformation is achieved, not by making Bali, the arch Viṣṇu worshipper, a Śiva worshipper, but by giving him a former life as a Śiva worshipper. Thus Bali's tale is supplemented by the tale of Kiṭava, which forms a bridge between our basic theme, great sinners who were saved from hell by an accidental act of Śiva worship, and a closely related theme, demons who worshipped Śiva's *liṅga* and usurped Indra's throne, of which two variants are narrated in this text.[23] Conflating the categories of "(human) sinner" and "demon," Kiṭava both gets saved and usurps, and does one of them (the usurping) twice, once as the human sinner Kiṭava and once when he becomes reincarnate as the demon Bali. Here is the new episode, the episode of Kiṭava:

> In a former life Bali had been Kiṭava (rogue), and one day when he was bringing flowers and betel and sandalwood and so forth to his whore, running to her house, he had stumbled and fallen on the ground and passed out for a moment. An idea occurred to him as he regained consciousness, as a result of his former *karma* and his great pain and misery: "Let the perfume and flowers and so forth that fell on the ground be given to Śiva." And as a result of that good deed, after his death when Yama's minions took him to hell, he won the place of Indra for a brief period, while Indra, suffering from Brahminicide, was in hiding.
>
> Indra and the other gods were miserable, but Kiṭava and his servants, delighting in the worship of Śiva, were very happy. Then Nārada said to Kiṭava, "Bring Indrāṇī here." But Kiṭava, the darling of Śiva, laughed and said, "I should not speak to Indrāṇī, or have anything to do with her, honored sir." And then he started to give things away; he gave Indra's elephant Airāvata and the other things to Agastya and the other sages. But when the brief period allotted to him in heaven was over, the former master, Indra, returned to heaven, and Indrāṇī rejoiced.
>
> Then the fool, Indra, said to Indrāṇī, "Did Kiṭava make love with you? Tell me truly." The guiltless woman laughed and said to Indra, "You think everyone else is just like you. Kiṭava is a noble person, free of passion, by the grace of Śiva." When Indra heard her words he was ashamed and silent. But when he saw that Kiṭava had given away all his things, he went down to Yama and complained against him.
>
> Yama said to Kiṭava, "Giving is prescribed on earth, where actions bear fruit. But no one is supposed to give anything to anyone in heaven, you fool, and so you should be punished,

> because you have not behaved according to the textbooks." But Yama's servant argued that all of Kiṭava's evil deeds had been burnt to ashes by the grace of Śiva and that, because of the greatness of his giving, Kiṭava did not belong in hell, and Indra returned in embarrassment to heaven. (18.52–116)

This story may be read as an embellishment of the story of Nahuṣa that has just been told (15.61–89), for Nahuṣa falls from the position of Indra when he lusts after Indrāṇī, Indra's wife. But it may also be a satire on the notorious *Rāmāyaṇa* episode of the rejection of Sītā by Rāma, who is swayed by public rumor that she had succumbed to the demon Rāvaṇa.

Most directly, the tale of Kiṭava is an expansion of the story of Bali, a demon who is punished for his excessive giving, a famous story that has just been alluded to (18.41–44). Here, Kiṭava is not punished for his excessive giving; on the contrary, Yama's servant expressly says that Kiṭava obtained his position through giving, and Kiṭava merely withdraws when his term in office is up. Though Kiṭava never actually worships the *liṅga,* the flowers and incense that he "dedicates" to Śiva on the doorstep of the brothel (the literal *limen,* like the liminal door of the temple) would normally be placed on the *liṅga*. And *bhakti,* even accidental *bhakti,* renders all conventional power struggles irrelevant.

The objections that Yama makes elsewhere to the emptiness of hell as a consequence of the democratization of *bhakti* are not only not addressed here but inverted: it is Yama who persuades Indra that Kiṭava should not go to hell. Yama's objections are explicitly stated, and answered, in a later part of the text, where what amounts to accidental *bhakti* poses a problem that is then inverted to make it not the problem but the solution:

> When sinners merely looked at Skanda they became purified, even if they were the most evil dog-cookers. Yama took Brahmā and Viṣṇu and went to Śiva and praised him and said, "By the greatness of the sight of Skanda all people are going to heaven, even if they are evil. What should I do about distinguishing between what should and should not be done? For those who are truthful and peaceful, free of lust and anger, virtuous sacrificers, are going to the same place that all the dog cookers and violators of *dharma* are going to. They have all left my place; what is there for me to do now?" Śiva replied, "People who have evil within them often do meritorious deeds, and their purification takes place in the mind-and-heart. Women and fools

> and Śūdras and the lowest dog cookers are born in evil wombs because of their previous lives, but nevertheless, by fate and their former deeds, they become purified human beings. Do not be amazed at this. . ." And Yama became enlightened. (31.2–77)

Looked at from the point of view not of the worshipper but of the god of hell, universal salvation *is* a problem.[24] Here, Yama is simply talked out of it. But, as if unsatisfied by this pat solution, the author is then, finally, inspired to tell the story that is the granddaddy of the genre of the devotee saved from hell, the story of Śveta, the *virtuous* devotee, with which we began this analysis. The text then immediately reverts to the sinful and accidental devotee, and tells the final, and by far the most elaborate, story in this series, the penultimate story in the whole book:

> Once upon a time there was a certain Kirāṭa named Caṇḍa [Fierce], a man of cruel addictions. He killed fish with a net and various wild animals with arrows, and in his fury he killed birds, and Brahmins, too,[25] and his wife was just like him. One night, on the dark fourteenth of Māgha, on the great Night of Śiva [*śivarātrī*], he was hunting a hog. He hadn't caught anything all day, and at night he was up in a sacred *bilva* tree, awake without blinking an eye.[26] In order to get a better view of his prey, he cut off many *bilva* leaves and thus, unknowingly, effortlessly, even though he was angry, he did *pūjā* [worship] to a Śiva-*liṅga* that was under the *bilva* tree. And he spat mouthfuls of water, which chanced to fall on that Śiva-*liṅga,* and by the force of fate, that too became a Śiva *pūjā,* by bathing the *liṅga.* Then he got down from the tree and went to the water to fish.
>
> His wife stayed up all night worrying about him, and then she followed his tracks, for she was afraid that he had been killed. At dawn she went to bring him food, and saw him by the river. They both bathed, but just as they came out a dog arrived and ate all the food.[27] She got mad and started to kill the dog, saying [to her husband], "This evil one has eaten our food, yours and mine. You fool, what will you eat? Tomorrow you will be hungry." Then Caṇḍa, dear to Śiva, said to her, "I am satisfied by knowing that the dog has eaten the food. What use is this body, anyway? Stop being angry." So she was enlightened by him.
>
> Then Śiva sent his messengers with a heavenly chariot. His servants said that they had come to take the Kirāṭa to the

> world of Śiva, with his wife, because he had worshipped the *liṅga* on the Night of Śiva. But the Kirāṭa said, "I am a violent hunter, a sinner. How can I go to heaven? How did I worship the Śiva-*linga?*" They said, "Śiva is pleased with you." Then they told him how on the Night of Śiva he had cut the *bilva* leaves and put them on the head of the *liṅga,* and stayed awake (as had his wife), and they had both fasted. They brought the couple to heaven, with great celebration. (33.1–64)

This is truly a story of amazing grace. It recapitulates and integrates the three stories that we have encountered in a single chapter: *liṅga* worship by mouthfuls of water from a Kirāṭa, inadvertent worship by a hunter named Caṇḍa, and salvation for a man touched by a dog. It also includes the man's wife in the process of his salvation. Let us therefore turn to the theme of women in the "Kedāra Khaṇḍa."

THE FEMINIZATION OF VIṢṆU

The very first triad of stories about undeserving devotees introduces the corollary to the theorem of Śiva worship that will be the basis of the rest of the book: that it is the worship of the *liṅga,* rather than any other form of Śiva worship, that opens all doors and rights all wrongs. Implicit in this assertion is another dogma that the "Kedāra Khaṇḍa" shares with many other Śaiva Purāṇas: that Śiva subsumes Viṣṇu within him. But here the "Kedāra Khaṇḍa" begins to weave its own secondary agenda, a quasi-feminist agenda. As a result of lying about having seen the top of the *liṅga,* Brahmā is cursed never to be worshipped again; this is also said in other Purāṇas. But Viṣṇu, who did not lie, is also subjected to a change in worship status:

> When the *liṅga* raged out of control, Brahmā and the sages praised Śiva, and he, pacified, told them to ask Viṣṇu for help. They praised Viṣṇu, and he laughed and said, "In the past I saved you from demons, but I can't save you from this *liṅga.*" Then a voice in space, reassuring the gods, said to Viṣṇu, "Envelop this *liṅga,* Viṣṇu, become the base [*piṇḍa*], and save everyone that moves and that is still." And the lord assented to this in his mind. (7.1–21)

Since, in other versions of this story, it is the Goddess, or Śiva's Śakti, who is called in to support and control the *liṅga* by taking the form of the *piṇḍa* base (also called the *yoni,* "vagina," or *pīṭha,* "seat"), the assignment of this role to Viṣṇu in this text amounts to the feminizing of Viṣṇu, the subordination of Viṣṇu to Śiva, through the incorporation of Viṣṇu into the Goddess's role in the worship of the *liṅga*.

And the text goes on to tell us that the whole universe is made of Śiva and Śakti; the clear proof of this is the fact that all men have the *liṅga,* and all women the *piṇḍa* (8.18–19). This affords incidental support to the argument about the "naturalness" (and hence the possibility of accidental performance) of *liṅga* worship: every human being is walking around with the essential materials for worship. Moreover, the lack of vertical distinction between the male god and human males, on the one hand, and the female goddess and human females, on the other, is then given a horizontal counterpart: there is no distinction between Śiva (the male part of the *liṅga*) and Viṣṇu (its female base, the *piṇḍa*).

A similar feminization takes place in the telling of the story of the churning of the ocean, which follows the standard plot until the moment when the devastating *halāhalā* poison appears. Then the text continues:

> Viṣṇu and Brahmā and the others, pervaded by the poison, sought the help of Heramba (Gaṇeśa), who propitiated Śiva until the supreme Śakti appeared in the form of the *yoni.* Gaṇeśa praised Śiva united with Śakti, and the *liṅga,* pleased by Heramba's praise, swallowed the poison. (10.7–11, 39–56)

This episode does not appear in the extant Sanskrit *Mahābhārata* version of the churning of the ocean (where Śiva in his anthropomorphic form, rather than as the *liṅga,* swallows the poison), but it resonantes with another Epic episode that is subsequently related by the "Kedāra Khaṇḍa":

> When the Soma appeared from the churning, the demon Vṛṣaparvan stole it and carried it down to the underworld. At the behest of the gods, Viṣṇu took the form of Mohiṇī, a beautiful enchantress, bewitched the demons, took back the Soma, and gave it to the gods. (12.1–74)

Where the *Mahābhārata* describes the feminization of Viṣṇu as Mohiṇī in just two verses,[28] and later Purāṇas add an episode in which Śiva is enchanted by this enchantress and embraces her (giving birth to Hariharaputra—"the son of Viṣṇu and Śiva"),[29] the "Kedāra

Khaṇḍa" inserts into the story a wonderfully cynical conversation between Mohiṇī and Bali, king of the demons:

> Bali said to Mohiṇī, "You must distribute the elixir right away." She smiled and said to Bali, "A smart man shouldn't trust in women. Lies, violence, deception, stupidity, excessive greed, impurity, and cruelty are the natural flaws of women. Like sadistic jackals among beasts of prey, like crows among birds, and like swindlers among men—that's how women should be recognized by wise men. How can I make friends with you? Consider who you are, and who I am. Therefore you should think about what should and should not be done. . ." Bali replied, "The women you have been talking about are common women, whom common men like. But you do not belong among those women you have been talking about. No more talk; do what we ask. Distribute the elixir; we will take what you give us, I promise you." (12.18–28)

The self-hating misogyny of Mohiṇī's speech repeats the serious statements of many other texts, beginning with the *Ṛg Veda,* which puts similar words into the mouth of Urvaśī ("There are no friendships with women; they have the hearts of jackals"[30]), and Manu ("The bed and the seat, jewelry, lust, anger, crookedness, a malicious nature, and bad conduct are what Manu assigned to women."[31]) But in the "Kedāra Khaṇḍa," this can only be a satire on Hindu misogyny, as becomes apparent from a survey of the subversive role of women in this text.

PRIMITIVE FEMINISM IN THE "KEDĀRA KHAṆḌA"

It is worth noting the strong human women in this text, women like Caṇḍa's wife. When the gods murder Dadhīca to take his body to make their weapons, his wife, Suvarcā, curses the gods and does not mince her words: "O you gods, you're worse than anyone, impotent and greedy. Therefore you gods who dwell in heaven will have no progeny". . . So, too, when the dwarf (Viṣṇu) has taken only two steps and has had Garuḍa bind Bali with the nooses of Varuṇa, Bali's wife, Vindhyāvalī, goes into action. She goes to the dwarf and asks him to step on the heads of her child, herself, and Bali; he does so and sets Bali free to live in Sutala, where he promises that he, Viṣṇu, will dwell as Bali's doorkeeper (a significant reversal of the Śaiva pattern, where the devotee becomes the doorkeeper) (17.7–14, 19.32–58).

But it is the Goddesses Indrāṇī and Pārvatī who best express the powers of women; after all, they are *called* "power," Śacī and Śakti. We have already seen some instances of the text's quasi-feminism in the Goddess's mocking remarks about the resemblance between Śiva and his devotees and Indrāṇī's mockery of Indra. Other stories are also told about the Goddess and Indrāṇī, in other traditional episodes that become, through the strength of character attributed to the women, much less traditional. Thus, whereas in the *Mahābhārata,* when Nahuṣa usurps the throne of Indra, Indrāṇī weeps and seeks the help of Bṛhaspati and Indra, who tell her how to trick Nahuṣa so that he loses the throne and is cursed to become a snake,[32] in the "Kedāra Khaṇḍa" she dries her tears and thinks up the plot all by herself:

> When Nārada urged the gods to install Nahuṣa on the throne of Indra (who was once again recuperating from Brahminicide), Śacī, hearing the words from the mouth of Nārada, burst into tears and retired into the inner apartments of the palace. The gods installed Nahuṣa as king of the gods, and he summoned Indrāṇī to come to him. Indrāṇī laughed and said, "If he lusts for me, another man's wife, let him come to get me in a nonvehicular vehicle." When Nahuṣa, deluded with lust for Indrāṇī, heard what she had said, he considered what might be nonvehicular and decided that it was Brahmins rich in asceticism. So he harnessed two of them to his palanquin, and as he drove them on he shouted, "Go! Go!" [*sarpa sarpa*], and so Agastya, one of the sages drawing the palanquin, cursed him to become a serpent [*ajagara,* also known as a *sarpa*].
>
> Śacī then sent the gods to search for Indra, and she cursed Bṛhaspati: "Because you brought two surrogates to me [Nahuṣa and Yayāti, Nahuṣa's son] while Indra was still alive, someone else will do what you should do while you are alive; he will have your marital luck and beget a famous son in your 'field' [i.e., your wife]. Go and look for Indra with the rest of the gods; if you don't, I'll give you another curse." When he heard what Śacī said, Bṛhaspati went with the other gods. (15.62–89, 16.1–10)

Indrāṇī's curse refers to the well-known ancient story of the adultery of Tārā, Bṛhaspati's wife, with Candra (the moon), resulting in the birth of Budha, the great king. To my knowledge, no other text suggests that this affair took place as the result of a curse of vengeance for Bṛhaspati's role in pandering for Indra's surrogates with

Indrāṇī. (Indeed, the *Mahābhārata,* following the *Bṛhaddevatā,* tells of a more direct possible cause for Bṛhaspati's cuckolding: Bṛhaspati raped the wife of his brother, Utathya.[33] This, too, the "Kedāra Khaṇḍa" ignores in favor of its own set of connections.[34])

Pārvatī, however, is the great heroine of the "Kedāra Khaṇḍa," and she is assisted by Rati, the wife of Kāma and goddess of sexual pleasure, after Śiva has burnt Kāma to ashes:

> As Pārvatī wondered how she could get Śiva into her power, Rati said to her, "Do not despair, Pārvatī; *I* will revive Kāma." And having consoled Pārvatī in this way, Rati began to engage in asceticism. Nārada then came to Rati and asked whose she was. Furious, Rati said, "I know you, Nārada, you're a virgin boy, for sure. Go back wherever you came from, and don't delay. You don't know anything, and all you do is make quarrels. You are the first among lovers of other men's wives, rakes, and low adulterers, people who do not work, parasites.'
>
> When Rati had reviled him in this way, Nārada went and told the demon Sambara to abduct Rati. Sambara, deluded by lust for Rati, asked her to come with him, and wanted to grab her by the hand, but she said, "If you touch me, you will be burnt." He took her to his house and put her in charge of the kitchen, where she was known as Māyāvatī. (21.100–25)

Now, several texts say that, after the death of Kāma, Rati was reborn as Māyāvatī.[35] And one says that, after Rati had become Māyāvatī, Nārada visited her and told her, to her benefit, what she was to do.[36] But the "Kedāra Khaṇḍa" alone blames Nārada for the degradation of Rati, inflicted in revenge for her spirited denunciation of him (which manages somehow to imply simultaneously that he is sexually innocent and lascivious).

THE DECONSTRUCTION OF ŚIVA

Pārvatī herself takes complex revenge against Śiva in the final myth told in the "Kedāra Khaṇḍa," right after the tale of the Kirāṭa, a myth that not only recapitulates all the myths of *liṅga*-worship that recur in this text but goes on to satirize them. (And we might see in Pārvatī's masquerade as a mountain woman, a Śabarī, a variant of the theme of the mountaineer who worshipped the *liṅga.*) The story begins as a variant on the well-known, though not particularly early, theme of the dice-game quarrel of Śiva and Pārvatī:

One day the sage Nārada came to visit Śiva and Pārvatī on Kailāsa and said, "There would be greater pleasure for the two of you in playing dice than in making love." They began to play dice and began to argue, and, as the hosts of Śiva joined in the quarrel, Śiva's servant, Bhṛngi, reminded Pārvatī of the time when Śiva had burnt Kāma, and the time when Śiva had been reviled at the sacrifice of Dakṣa and Satī committed suicide. Then Pārvatī got mad and said to Bhṛngi, "You're always trying to come between us. But how can there be any separation between us two? I will give you a curse: be without flesh."

Then, in fury, she put her hand on the serpent Vasuki and took it down from Śiva's neck, and [then she took] many other things, ornaments, and the crescent moon, and elephant skin, and then, laughing, she took even his loincloth. When all the troops of Śiva averted their faces in modesty, Śiva said, "All the sages are laughing at this joke, and Brahmā and Viṣṇu. How can you, born in a good family, do this? If you have won, then at least give me back my loincloth." Then she laughed and said, "Why do you need a loincloth, you hermit? You were naked enough when you went into the Pine Forest, begging for alms and seducing the sages' wives. The sages made your 'loincloth' fall down there. And that's why I took it from you in the game of dice."

Hearing that, Śiva was angry and looked at her in fury with his third eye. Everyone was terrified, but she laughed and said, "Why are you looking at me with that third eye? I'm not Kāla or Kāma, nor am I Dakṣa's sacrifice. I'm not the triple city, or Andhaka. You're wasting your time with that third eye on me." She said a lot of things like this to him, and he set his heart on going to a deserted spot in the forest.

When Śiva had gone to the forest, Pārvatī was tormented by longing in separation. Still, she laughed and said, "I beat him and reduced him to poverty. What can't I do? Without me he is ugly; I made him beautiful. Watch me play a new game with him now." And with that, she set out to go to Śiva, taking the form of a magnificent mountain woman [Śabarī], dark and slender, with lips like bimba fruits, and she went where Śiva was meditating. He woke up and saw her and was filled with lust. He took her by the hand, but as soon as he touched her, she vanished. Then he, who was the destroyer of mistaken perceptions, himself was enveloped in a mistaken perception. Unable to see her, he was tormented by longing in separation.

But then he saw her again, and he asked who she was and

she said, teasing him, "I am seeking my/a husband,[37] a man who is omniscient, independent, unchanging, and the best lord of the universe." He replied, "I am a suitable husband for you, but no one else is." She smiled and said, "You are indeed the husband that I seek. But let me tell you something. You are devoid of virtue.[38] For a woman chose you before and won you by her great inner ascetic heat, and you abandoned her in the wilderness." Śiva denied that he had abandoned a woman with great inner ascetic heat. When he continued to insist that she marry him, she said he must ask her father, Himālaya.

She took him to her father, stood with him at the door, and said, "This is my father. Ask. Don't be ashamed. He will give me, there is no doubt about that. Don't hesitate." Śiva bowed to Himālaya and said, "Best of mountains, give your daughter to me today." Hearing this pitiful speech, Himālaya stood up and said to Śiva, "What kind of a joke is this? It doesn't befit you. You're the one who gives everything in the universe." Just then Nārada arrived, laughed, and said, "Contact with women always leads to the deception [*viḍamba*] of men. You are the lord of the universe. You should speak as befits you." Thus enlightened by Nārada, Śiva woke up and laughed and said, "You spoke the truth, Nārada. Mere contact with women is the downfall of men. Today she deluded me and brought me here; this act was like [a rape] by a ghoul. Therefore I won't stay near this mountain; I'll go to another part of the forest." Then Śiva vanished, but they all praised him, and he came back. Drums sounded, and all the gods, Indra and the others, sent a rain of flowers, and the great Śiva reigned there with Pārvatī. (34.20–153, 35.1–58)

The arguments about the supremacy of Śiva versus Śakti recapitulate arguments that have been made throughout this book about Śiva versus Viṣṇu and Viṣṇu as Śakti, beginning with the reviling of Śiva at the sacrifice of Dakṣa. Indeed, this episode refers explicitly to the Dakṣa episode several times, linking this final episode with the first episode in the "Kedāra Khaṇḍa," the story of Dakṣa's sacrifice, in which Satī, as usual, defends Śiva with great spirit and reminds her parents and the gods of his great deeds:

> Once upon a time, Brahmā, you became five-headed in your pride, and Śiva made you four-headed—do you remember? Once upon a time, he wandered begging in the Pine Forest, and you cursed him, and his mere limb filled the whole universe,

> which became a *liṅga* at that moment. How can you have forgotten? (3.10–14)

Her words predict several myths that will be told, seriously, later in the book; but she refers to the same myths in this final episode only to mock them, turning the text itself on its head in the end.

Pārvatī argues, against Bhṛngi, that Śiva and Śakti are one, despite their quarrels (just as, we have seen, Śiva and Viṣṇu are one, despite the quarrels of their devotees). In this way, the myth of Bhṛngi, which is not narrated in detail here, is evoked: Bhṛngi had wanted to worship Śiva without worshipping Pārvatī, and in punishment for his disrespect for the female side of God, she deprived him of the female side of every person: the flesh.[39] By reviving the quarrel with Bhṛngi at this point, the text implicitly analogizes it not only to the old myth of the sacrifice of Dakṣa but to the new myth, created by the "Kedāra Khaṇḍa," of the integration of Śiva with the feminine, both with Śakti and with the feminized Viṣṇu.

There are also several different sorts of references here to Śiva's burning of Kāma and of Kāla/Yama; these references bring out a parallelism between the two incidents that is reflected in two parallel epithets of Śiva (Kāmāntaka and Yamāntaka, or Kālāntaka) but is seldom explicitly remarked upon in Sanskrit texts. The myth of Kāma is also recapitulated in the episode of the Śabarī as a whole, which is a satire on the well-known myth that we have already heard in this text, the episode in which Pārvatī, having been rejected by Śiva as a lovely young girl, returns to him in another form, as an ascetic woman, when he is meditating, inspires him with love, and causes him to ask her father for permission to marry her.

One particular argument of the "Kedāra Khaṇḍa" version of that episode is particularly relevant here:

> When Pārvatī asked permission to serve Śiva while he mediated, he said to Himālaya, "This slender young girl with her terrific hips and her sweet smile must not come into my presence." But Pārvatī laughed and replied, "You should consider who you are, and who Nature [*prakṛti*] is." When he retorted, "I will destroy Nature with my ultimate inner ascetic heat, and I will stay here without Nature," she said, "How could you transcend Nature? What you hear, what you eat, what you see—it's all Nature. How could you be beyond Nature? You are enveloped in Nature, even though you don't know it. But if you are, in fact, beyond Nature, then what do you have to fear from me?" Śiva laughed and let her stay. (20.15–26)

So, too, in the final episode, Pārvatī reminds him that he literally cannot exist without her.

And, finally, when Pārvatī teases Śiva, she deconstructs the whole mythology of the "Kedāra Khaṇḍa" and even myths that are not told here, other myths of the third eye such as the ancient myth of the burning of the triple city and the later myth of the impalement of the demon Andhaka. Best of all, by forcing Śiva to play what amounts to a game of strip poker, Pārvatī offers a superb satire on the central myth in this book, the story of the falling of Śiva's *liṅga* in the Pine Forest. In her mockery of her husband, Pārvatī equates the loincloth with the *liṅga,* teasing him about the time the sages caused his "loincloth" to fall. In fact, the sages caused his erect penis to fall; does this mean, therefore, that when she takes his loincloth she castrates him, too? Śiva himself implicitly mocks and feminizes himself, when he says that he has been treated like the victim of a marriage of the ghouls, which Manu defines thus: "The lowest and most evil of marriages, known as that of the ghouls, takes place when a man secretly has sex with a girl who is asleep, drunk, or out of her mind."[40] Śiva seems to be saying that he was out of his mind (presumably with a combination of ordinary lust and the extraordinary illusory powers of the Goddess) when the Śabarī seduced him. Where Pārvatī is at first said to be "tormented by longing in separation," she turns the tables until he himself is "tormented by longing in separation."

This is more than a play on words. The Śakti demonstrates that she, too, can play the otiose trick—now you see me, now you don't—just as Śiva did in the stories of Dakṣa's sacrifice and the Pine Forest. In doing this, she is usurping the top place, just as he had done to Viṣṇu. By giving the upper hand to Pārvatī, the text is parodying the basic, assumed paradigm of the worshipper as female and the god as male (a reversal that we may also see in the feminizing of Viṣṇu). So, too, by making Śiva the fool who, despite his delusion, "accidentally" wins his own wife (his own deity), the text reverses the conventional roles of god and worshipper. As David Shulman has put it, "The god, too, ends up acting out the logic of reversal no less than his human counterparts."[41]

When Śiva, too, becomes otiose again near the end of the story, ludicrously embarrassed by his public humiliation in proposing to his own wife, just as Indra had been embarrassed (and separated from his wife) by the more serious sin of Brahminicide, the gods bring him back with praise. That praise that brings god back to us, the husband to his wife, the wife to the husband, is the *raison d'être* of the "Kedāra Khaṇḍa" of the *Skanda Purāṇa,* as it is of all Purāṇas: "The people who recite with supreme faith this marvellous glorification of Śiva, this Śiva text that Śiva loves, and the people who listen to it with devotion and delight, they go to the ultimate level of existence" (35.64, the final verse of the "Kedāra Khaṇḍa").

But the "Kedāra Khaṇḍa" differs from other Purāṇas in its inclusive attitude to "the people" who listen and recite the Purāṇa. By granting the grace of god to unregenerate sinners and to women, the "Kedāra Khaṇḍa" is salvaging two human groups that more conventional Purāṇas have marginalized and excluded: women and (male) sinners who do not consciously worship at all. The justification for including both is the same: the worship of the *liṅga* and *yoni* is so "natural" (because we are all carrying around the materials for the liturgy) that it can be carried out mindlessly, by people who do not know what they are doing when they worship god. So, too, women in this text represent "Nature" (*prakṛti*) in opposition to "culture" (the elaborate ritualism of other Purāṇas, from which women are excluded). This is, as we have seen, the argument by which Pārvatī gains access to Śiva so that she can ultimately conquer him: he cannot live without Nature. This being so, it is through natural acts of worship that sinners and women find their way to him.

In salvaging these discarded pieces of society, the "Kedāra Khaṇḍa" also salvages discarded pieces of Purāṇic lore, off-beat stories, precious scraps, bottom-fished from the great ocean of Indian story. We, the readers, thus participate in a double salvation when we read the "Kedāra Khaṇḍa": of ourselves (women and sinners) and of the scraps of stories.

Appendix: The Contents of the "Kedāra Khaṇḍa"

This is how Ludo Rocher describes the entire contents of the "Kedāra Khaṇḍa":

> The Kedārakhaṇḍa (1.1) begins with the destruction of Dakṣa's sacrifice. It devotes several chapters to the churning of the ocean, and proceeds to describe the birth and activities of Pārvatī, up to her marriage with Śiva. The description of Kārttikeya's birth is followed by that of his successful fight with the demon Tāraka. The *khaṇḍa* ends with the story in which Śiva loses everything to Pārvatī in a game of dice, their temporary separation, and their reunion.[42]

42. Ludo Rocher, *The Purāṇas,* Vol. 2, fasc. 3 of *A History of Indian Literature,* ed. Jan Gonda (Wiesbaden: Otto Harrassowitz, 1986), 230.

This is, more precisely, a summary of those parts of its contents that are known from other Sanskrit texts as well, and it forms a consecutive narrative sequence, an integrated story. But it does not provide us with an armature on which to build all the rest of the book. For there is more, far, far more. Here, in brief, is what is in the "Kedāra Khaṇḍa":

1.1.1. Introduction: the sages in the Naimiṣa Forest question Lomaśa about Śiva.

1.1.1–4 Śiva destroys Dakṣa's sacrifice.

1.1.5 Indrasena, a very evil man, says "Hara" unconsciously and is saved from hell. A Kirāṭa (mountaineer and hunter) is taken to Śiva's heaven.

1.1.6 The Pine Forest sages cause Śiva's *liṅga* to fall.

1.1.7 The *liṅgodbhava:* the flame *liṅga* appears to Viṣṇu and Brahmā.

1.1.8 A man steals a bell and is saved from hell. Rāvaṇa worships Śiva and Viṣṇu becomes incarnate as Rāma.

1.1.9 The demon Bali takes Indra's throne. The gods and demons churn the ocean.

1.1.10 Viṣṇu and Brahmā and the others, pervaded by the poison, seek help from Gaṇeśa, the supreme Śakti in the form of the *yoni,* and the *liṅga* form, which swallows the poison.

1.1.11–14 Viṣṇu appears as Mohiṇī, and the gods get the Soma.

1.1.15 Indra kills Viśvarūpa and suffers from Brahminicide. Nahuṣa takes Indra's throne but is undone by his lust for Indra's wife.

1.1.16–17. His Brahminicide dispelled, Indra kills Vṛtra and incurs Brahminicide again.

1.1.18 Kiṭava (Bali in a former life) is saved from hell and takes Indra's throne.

1.1.19 Indra wins his throne back from Bali, with Viṣṇu's help.

1.1.20–31 Śiva burns Kāma, marries Pārvatī, and begets Skanda.

1.1.32 Śveta, the devotee of Śiva, is saved from hell.

1.1.33 A Kirāṭa is saved from hell.

1.1.34 The Goddess tricks Śiva at dice and in adultery, becoming a mountain woman (Śabarī).

II.

From South to North and Back Again

4

Purāṇa as Brahminic Ideology

Velcheru Narayana Rao

During Labor Day weekend in 1985 I attended a meeting of Telugu people in the United States held in Los Angeles, where a singer of *harikathā* ("Tales of Viṣṇu") gave a performance. *Harikathā* singing is relatively new in Andhra; evidence suggests that Ajjada Adibhatla Narayana Dasu (1864–1945) was the originator of this tradition. A learned Sanskrit scholar and a wonderful musician, Narayana Dasu brought a new popularity to the recitation of Purāṇic stories, which he had composed in a musical style, interspersed with entertaining prose commentaries. This new genre acquired wide popularity and has been adopted by hundreds of learned singers. Along with its popularity came a respectable history of the genre. At the beginning of every *harikathā* performance, the singer spoke, as a part of his performance, about the antiquity of his profession. The singer whom I heard in Los Angeles did the same. To paraphrase his statement, he said:

> The first *harikathā* singer was Nārada, the celestial singer who sang for the god Viṣṇu. Then came Kuśa and Lava, the twin sons of Rāma, who sang the *Rāmāyaṇa* for him. (He abridged the list and stopped with only two because he was singing in Los Angeles and not in India.) And then in the Kali Age (the last of the four Ages) the great guru Narayana Dasu was born to popularize *harikathā* on the earth.

Let me narrate another anecdote concerning similar connections to mythology. On October 31, 1854, a Brahmin village land owner, Maciraju Venkatrayudu, sent an appeal to the British governor of Bengal. His land was occupied by the local Kāpu, a non-Brahmin peasant. His complaints to the lower officers of the administration did not help. The Brahmin felt that the lower officers were working hand in glove with the Kāpu peasant. Therefore he thought that the highest authority of the land should be informed of this injustice. Venkatrayudu wrote: "During the time of the kings who ruled this country in the past, King Śrīrāma, the sixteen great emperors beginning with Hariścandra, King Bali and King Vikramārka, Brahmins suffered no poverty. In your government, however, you treat all human beings equally and you are not respecting the code of *varṇa* and *āśrama* [class and stage of life]." Then the Brahmin went on to quote from a Sanskrit text showing how King Nala treated the Brahmins. Finally he appealed to the governor-general to restore his land to him.[1]

Going a few centuries back to the period of King Kṛṣṇadevarāya (sixteenth century), I would like to quote one more illustration of the use of mythology. This relates to the genealogy that Peddanna, the court poet, provides for his royal patron. Peddanna writes in his *Manucaritra:*

> First there was the moon. His son was Budha.
> To him was born Purūrava, and he, in turn,
> generated Ayuvu, and to Ayuvu,
> Yayāti the king was born.
>
> Yadu and Turvasu were born as his sons
> killers of the enemies and connoisseurs of the arts
> and of these two, Turvasu, a vessel
> of virtue, acquired illustrious fame.
>
> His family became the dynasty of Tuluvas
> to which many kings were born, filling the world
> in its entirety with their surging and eternal
> fame. Then in that family, Timma was born.[2]

Yadu and Turvasu, as is well known, are mythical descendants of Budha, who was the son of the moon god, whereas the Tuluvas are historical, as is Timma of this dynasty.

What is common to all the three cases I have mentioned above is that all of them begin with what we call "myth" and move into what we call "history," with no dividing line between them. This is one continuous line of events. I intend to show in the early part of this paper that this continuity is what the Purāṇic worldview promotes, and that it results from the ideological frame of Purāṇas. Later in the paper I shall attempt to explore the nature of Purāṇas as conceptually organized texts whose meanings are best perceived by what they say about themselves as well as by what they do not say.

THE FIVE DISTINGUISHING MARKS

Again and again we are told that Purāṇas have five *lakṣaṇa*s, or distinguishing marks.[3] These components of a Purāṇa are primary creation or cosmogony (*sarga*), secondary creation, or the destruction and renovation of worlds, including chronology (*pratisarga*), the genealogy of gods and patriarchs (*vaṃśa*), the reigns of the Manus (*manvantarāṇi*), and history, "or such particulars as have been preserved of the princes of the solar and lunar races, and of their descendants to modern times (*vaṃśānucarita*)."[4]

Earlier scholars who discussed the five *lakṣaṇa*s accepted them as constituting the definition of a Purāṇa. But many Purāṇas do not conform to this definition. Therefore the conclusion was that the Purāṇas that now exist are not the old versions of the Purāṇas and that much of the older version has been lost.

Scholars also thought that the five features constituted the subjects or the contents of the Purāṇas. Again there was a problem, because the information regarding the five *lakṣaṇa*s was very minimal in most of the Purāṇas. To quote Vans Kennedy, "Though these topics are certainly treated of at greater or less length in most of the Purāṇas, they still by no means form the principal subject of the study"[5] As Ludo Rocher has stated, "The fact that the *Purāṇas* contain relatively little *pañcalakṣaṇa* materials has been noticed repeatedly in the scholarly literature."[6] According to Kane's calculation, the five topics occupy less than three per cent of the extant Mahāpurāṇas.[7]

Then why does *pañcalakṣaṇa* continue to be considered important for distinguishing a Purāṇa from other genres? Setting aside suggestions that *pañcalakṣaṇa* is a literary myth,[8] or explanations that our understanding of this compound word is erroneous and that it means something else,[9] I would like to suggest and try to demonstrate that *pañcalakṣaṇa* is the ideological frame that transforms whatever content is incorporated into that frame. Since the ideas of *pañcalakṣaṇa* are tacitly assumed in the Brahminic worldview, they do not even appear in every Purāṇa and do not constitute a sizeable length of the text even when thy appear.

I shall not concern myself with the texts that describe the *pañcalakṣaṇa* for identifying the oldest strata of the Purāṇas. My interest is not text-historical. I am interested, rather, in the nature of text as an ideological product. The strategy here is to listen to what the texts say and what they do not say. It is analogous to the question Nietzsche asked: What is man saying? What is he hiding when he says what he says? By asking these questions, I believe, one can see the ideology of text production, which, in the words of Macherray is "silently inscribed" within the text.[10]

All civilizations make their own past to make sense of the present, to control the present. When a new power emerges, the first thing it does to is to reject the old past and to create a new one in its place. This is done not just by altering the "facts" of the past but by creating a new way of perceiving the "facts." An extreme instance of creating a new way of perceiving facts is evidenced when the very concepts of time and space in which events take place are changed.

Such a change in the concepts of time and space was made when Western civilization via the British colonial power came to dominate India. An earlier concept of time and space is that of Brahminic civilization, which coexists with what might be called, for want of a better name, a "folk concept" of time and space. Thus, India has had three different ways of conceptualizing time and space, all of which are still at work in the lives of Indian people. The low-caste, nonliterate people have a folk concept of time/space, uppercaste Sanskrit-educated Brahmins have a Purāṇic concept of time/space, and Westernized educated Indians have a modern concept of time/space. My low-caste milkmaid has great difficulty in understanding how I calculate the first day of the month (according to the Gregorian calendar, when I get my salary and she gets paid for the milk she had supplied to me all the month) without the aid of the moon. I have a similar difficulty in reckoning without the aid of my family priest the death anniversary of my father, which is to be observed according to the Brahminic *pañcāngam* calendar.

Folk time is repetitive and regenerative. It shares some of the features of a cyclic view of time, such as the return of similar events like seasons, phases of the moon, and so on; but it does not deteriorate and therefore does not spiral downward. Folk time is analogous with agricultural seasons: the rainy season, which brings growing crops, then a season of harvesting, and then summer, when the earth is dried up followed by a rains and new life.

Purāṇic time, however, deteriorates. Each of the four Ages (*yugas*) is inferior to the previous one until the final dissolution (*pralaya*) completes the cycle and starts a new one. Thus it spirals downward until a new cycle begins. In keeping with this view, the Purāṇas say that the texts themselves deteriorate. The *Matsya Purāṇa* says that originally the Purāṇas were one Purāṇa, which belonged to the world of the gods (*devaloka*) and was a hundred million verses long (*śatakoṭipravistara*). For the benefit of human beings, who have an inferior intellect, Hari took the form of Vyāsa and reduced the huge text into eighteen texts with a total of four hundred thousand *ślokas*. This story repeats itself. Vyāsa is born in every third *yuga*. Kṛṣṇadvaipāyana is the Vyāsa in the twenty-eighth third *yuga* of the eon of the White Boar.

It is in this context that I propose to examine the *pañcalakṣaṇa* of the Purāṇas. *Lakṣaṇa* is not a definition; nor do the five *lakṣaṇas* inform us of the contents of a Purāṇa. *Lakṣaṇa,* as the dictionary tells us, is a distinguishing mark. Further more, *lakṣaṇas* are not necessarily objective, empirically observed facts; they could be perceived "facts." If Brahmin scholars say that Purāṇas have the five *lakṣaṇas*, they have them. The question, for me, is not locating, textually, where they exist and then examining their relative length in words as determinants of their importance or antiquity. The question rather is why Brahmin scholars call them distinguishing marks. There is plenty of evidence that a Purāṇa is viewed as having the five *lakṣaṇas*. Not only does an early text like *Nāmalingānuśāsana* identify Purāṇas with *pañcalakṣaṇa,* and a number of Purāṇas themselves speak of the five distinguishing marks, but as late a text as *Śukranīti* says, describing a Paurāṇika (a Purāṇa performer/scholar), "One who is a scholar of literary theory, who is knowledgeable in music, has a good voice, and knows the five *lakṣaṇas*, creation and the others, such a man is known as a Paurāṇika."[11]

The five *lakṣaṇas* order the events of the Purāṇa. They provide the listeners with a view of time and space in which the events narrated in the Purāṇas occur. In other words, the *pañcalakṣaṇas* create a world and a worldview.

PURĀṆIZING THE FOLK TRADITION

Any event placed in the frame of the *lakṣaṇas* will have a specific meaning for anyone who lives in this particular world. If I say that I wrote my paper on July 25, 1985 of the common era, in

Visakahpatnam, South India, that date and place constitute only a small part of the text of my paper. For all of us who participate in the ideology of dating things on the linear scale of time, it does not even appear to be significant. But then, it is not the same thing as saying that I wrote my paper in the first quarter (*prathama pāda*) of the fourth Age (the Kali Age) of the reign (*manvantara*) of Manu Vaivāsvata, in the eon (*kalpa*) of the white boar (*svetavarāha*), sitting in a place located in the southern part of the land (*dakṣiṇa digbhāga*) with reference to Mount Meru. Locating an event in time and place appears nominal, if you participate in the specific ideology that gives you those concepts of time and space. The contrast is striking if you do not participate in that ideology. For example, questions regarding when Vyāsa was born and when the Purāṇas were composed would have two completely different answers in these two different systems of belief.

To illustrate the nature of ideological change that a folk story undergoes when it is Purāṇized, let me cite a story of the Komaṭi caste of Andhra. Komaṭis are a caste of merchants who were at one time considered a left-handed caste. Now their status has moved up and they are included in the Vaiśya class, the third class in the four *varṇa* system. The story of the Komaṭis centers on their caste goddess Kanyakā, whose name means "a virgin." The story is set in Penugonda, the city of the Komaṭis in West Godavari district. There the wealthy Komaṭi leader Kusumaśreṣṭi lives with his daughter Kanyakā, the most beautiful woman in the world. One day, the king of the area visits the city and the Komaṭis receive him with honor; Kanyakā welcomes him with a flame offering. When the king sees her, he desires her and sends word to her father that he wishes to marry her; if the father refuses, he will invade the city and abduct her.

For the Komaṭis this is a serious problem. It would be loss of caste purity to give a woman from their caste to a non-Komaṭi man. And not to be able to protect themselves when they are forced to surrender would be humiliating. The Komaṭi elders meet to discuss the crisis, but cannot find any solution. They conclude that they are powerless to fight and some even suggest a surrender so that they can gain favors from the king.

Now Kanyakā evaluates the situation. She sends word to the king that her father agrees to the marriage but needs time to prepare for it. The king is to wait outside the city, behind the hills surrounding it. Meanwhile, Kanyakā assembles the elders and informs them of her intention to immolate herself. She asks which caste families will be willing to die with her; among the 102 families (*gotras*) who agree to die with her, she selects only the wives and husbands, leaving the yet unmarried young men and women to continue the caste line. All other families are ordered out of the caste.

She then orders a deep pit to be dug and a fire kindled in it. When the king sends some soldiers to see what is causing the delay, they learn of Kanyakā's plans and decide to serve her instead of the king. When the soldiers do not return, the king grows suspicious and invades the city, but it is too late; Kanyakā and the others have died in the fire. Before that, however, Kanyakā has sanctioned a code of conduct for the caste. Cross-cousin marriage is never to be avoided, even when the boy or girl is poor, sick, or deformed; all Komaṭi girls are to be given her name. All Komaṭi girls, moreover, are to be born ugly so that no man will desire them. She also ordains that the king who caused this calamity will die instantly when he enters the city. Penugonda is to become a pilgrimage center for Komaṭis with Kanyakā as its goddess, and an annual ritual is to be celebrated there in her honor.

This is the summary of the folk version of the story, which I gathered in Andhra Pradesh from interviews with the folk singers called "Mailārlu."

In the *Vāsava Kanyakā Purāṇa,* a Sanskrit text that claims to be a part of the *Sanatsujātiya Khaṇḍa* of the *Skanda Purāṇa,* the story remains faithful to the outlines given above, but becomes Purāṇized.

First, the story is set in the Naimiṣa Forest. Sūta is the narrator. Śaunaka and other sages ask him to tell them a story of the Vaisyas. This story is narrated to Dharmanandana (Yudhiṣṭhira) by Ādiśeṣa, the ancient snake. Being set in a Purāṇic context, the story elaborately narrates how it first takes place in the world of gods (*devaloka*). A *gandharva* (demigod) there falls in love with a Vaiśya girl, but the Vaiśya elders reject his proposal to marry her. The *gandharva* curses the Vaiśyas to fall from the world of gods onto the earth, where they will all burn in fire and perish. In return, the Vaiśyas curse the *gandharva* to take a miserable human birth and die a horrible death. The Vaiśyas are reluctant to go to the earthly world of sin, but the gods insist that they are needed there to restore order and trade and to uplift the human beings. And in the end they will return to the world of Śiva through their death by fire. After the *gandharva* is born as the king and the girl as Kanyakā, the story is reenacted on earth.[12]

It is obvious that these changes in the story are not neutral. Placing the story in the Purāṇic context transforms the nature of the events. To make a quick note of such transformations, the merchant-caste Komaṭis are now Vaiśyas with a status in the four-class system. They are here in the human world for a purpose; they are no ordinary profit seekers. The events of the story are reenactments of a predetermined script, and the Vaiśyas are part of a divine scheme. In the folk version, Kanyakā is the chief player, who makes decisions for herself as well as for the caste. In the Sanskrit version, the decision-making role is played by the Brahmin priest Bhāskarācārya, who is obeyed by all the Vaiśyas. Kanyakā, in this version, is a chaste woman, obeying the commands of the family and the priest.

Vast bodies of folk/regional stories, events, legends, and histories have been incorporated into the Purāṇas along with prescriptive codes of behavior appropriate to people of different stations of life. Such incorporation has made a Brahminic interpretation of the material possible without necessarily erasing local color and regional flavor.

The ideological import of the Purāṇas is not limited to the *pañcalakṣaṇa* frame; it is inscribed in the concepts that surround the Purāṇa texts. We have a tendency to look at the Purāṇas as disparate texts, each neatly bound in identifiable volumes. But the texts do not work in isolation; they are part of a totality of a text tradition with intertextual relationships and commentorial contexts. One could make sense of any of these texts only by listening to the texts as a part of this tradition.

PURĀṆA: WHAT IT IS AND WHAT IT IS NOT

One way to conceptualize the Purāṇas is to compare them with texts that are not Purāṇas. Such a contrast is made by means of two variables, sound (*śabda*) and meaning (*artha*), the two technically inseparable components of a word. Mammaṭa, the twelfth-century writer on poetics, tells us that the Veda is sound-primary (*śabdapradhāna*), and Purāṇa is meaning-primary (*arthapradhāna*), while ornate poetry (*kāvya*) accords equal importance to sound and meaning (*śabdārthapradhāna*). This aphorism is worth exploring. If the Veda is important for its sound, it is unalterable. Every nuance of this sound has to be reproduced without change. It cannot be written down, because a graphic representation of the sound does not guarantee its accurate reproduction; nor can it be translated into another language, paraphrased, or summarized, because any such effort changes its sound. If, then, the sound is fixed, its context is also fixed and unalterable. The fact that it is orally reproduced does not make it an oral text. It is more fixed than any written text; it is inscribed in sound.

We know that in practice, many who recite the Veda do not even know its meaning, nor are they expected to know. On the other hand, those who know the meaning may not often chant the Veda; they have not learned the chanting well enough to reproduce the sound correctly. Vedic sound-text is preserved in complex chanting styles with terrible taboos invoked against any mispronunciation. The Vedic text is preserved in India as a mummy is preserved in an Egyptian tomb. Nothing can be added to it, and nothing can be transformed by it.

An unalterable, fixed text, by itself, is incapable of serving as an active vehicle of ideology. For that you need a text flexible in content but fixed in its ideological apparatus. *Purāṇa* and *itihāsa,* which are often combined to make one compound word, are such texts, which serve as correlates to the Veda. Vatsyana says in the *Nyāyabhāṣya:* the subject matter of *itihāsapurāṇa* is the events of the world.[13] It is also stated that the Veda speaks like a king, a Purāṇa like a friend, and a *kāvya* like a beloved woman (*prabhusammita, mitrasammita,* and *kāntāsammita*).[14] The contrast, the tradition wants us to believe, is not in the essential meaning but only in the style. And there is a difference not only in style but also in status.

Elsewhere I have argued that authorship of a text, in the Indian tradition, is not intended to inform us about the actual producer of the text, to offer biographical data about him, but has a semiotic function of conveying the status of the text.[15] The texts of the highest authority are above human authorship. The Veda comes under this classification. Texts of the next level of authority are composed by a superhuman, and therefore infallible, person, Vyāsa. The texts of the next level of authority are the *kāvya*s, made by human poets, who have creative abilities given by Sarasvatī, the goddess of arts, but who are still human and therefore fallible. You could find errors in a Kālidāsa, but not in a Vyāsa, and certainly not in the Veda.

If Purāṇa is valued for its meaning, it is also stated that it is not the meaning we get from its words; it is the meaning known to the *ṛṣi,* the one who sees. A popular statement about Śrīdhara, who wrote a commentary on the *Bhāgavata Purāṇa,* says, "Vyāsa knows, Śuka knows; whether the king [Parikṣit] knows or not, Śrīdhara knows everything, because of the blessing of the Man-lion god."[16]

The person who knows the meaning of the Purāṇa is in a class by himself; he belongs to the status of Vyāsa, Śuka, and the commentator Śrīdhara. This is knowledge beyond logic (*na hantavyāni hetubhiḥ*). It is recognized that Purāṇas differ in status among themselves.[17] But those differences do not lead to a contradiction in meaning. A *Mahābhārata* aphorism reconciles the apparent problem:

> The revealed texts conflict with each other as
> the remembered texts do.
> And there is no seer whose words are the authority.
> The essence of *dharma* lies hidden from view.
> So, follow the path of great men.[18]

The great men, *mahājana,* are the commentators, the knowers of the meaning.

THE AUTHOR/SPEAKER OF THE PURĀṆAS

Like that of the Veda, the origin of the Purāṇa is beyond humans. Brahmā spoke the Purāṇas, from all four of his mouths. According to the *Nāradīyapūraṇa,* the Purāṇas came first and then the Veda.[19] The *Mārkaṇḍeya Purāṇa* says that as soon as Brahmā was born, both the Purāṇa and the Veda came out of his mouth; the seven *ṛṣis* took the Veda and the *munis* took the Purāṇa.[20] Vyāsa, as we have seen, was only the compiler and editor of the texts in an abridged form.

Then there are different speakers of the Purāṇas for different listeners. Each Purāṇa has a specific speaker. However, it is important to note that no speaker ever directly narrates. All the Purāṇa narratives are reported narratives. Each speaker has an earlier speaker. Each listener has an earlier listener. They look inward and backward drawing us into an ideologically closed environment. But if the Purāṇas are ideologically closed texts, they are functionally open texts: they have accepted into their fold events, stories, legends, and occurrences of many regions and communities, transforming them to confirm to a fixed ideology.

PURĀṆA AND ORALITY

Purāṇas are available as written texts, and we know that as such they cause the worst possible headaches to scholars who work on critical editions. One reason suggested for the state of Purāṇic texts is that they were originally oral and were later put into writing. Continuing our position of looking into the text for what it says and for what it does not say, we find that inside the text Purāṇas do not furnish evidence that they were written texts, except for the story of Gaṇeśa as Vyāsa's scribe, which occurs in the *Mahābhārata*. In fact, in Purāṇic literature the Sanskrit verb *likh,* "to write," was never used to mean "to compose." Purāṇa texts are spoken. Writing was known in India from a very early period, at least the third century B.C.E., but its use was limited to preserving a text rather than producing it or communicating it. Scribes were a different group of people in India, who, like modern day typists, specialized in a technical skill. There are many instances, even as late as the nineteenth century, of scholars who could not "write." They composed the texts mentally and recited them orally, and then the scribe wrote them down. But the Purāṇa scholar who did not write was not illiterate. Sanskrit has a syllabic organization independent of the graphic form of the letters. The *varṇa,* the basic unit of Sanskrit syllabary, is a sound unit roughly equivalent to a phoneme. Sanskrit grammarians syllabified the language and developed a sophisticated morphological analysis but felt no compelling need to write it down. This situation is different from that of the Western languages, where "letter" indicates a graphic form, with a name of its own, distinct from the several phonemic values that it represents. In the West, to be literate in a language inevitably means to be able to write, but in India there is also a kind of oral literacy, as it were. The Purāṇa scholar had all the sophistication of the language scholar, with a complete awareness of grammatical organization. Therefore, he set himself apart from the illiterate oral poet who not only could not write but also lacked any awareness of the grammar of his language.

Thus, while the internal evidence in the texts of the Purāṇas shows that they were originally oral, it is important for us to note that their orality is different from the orality of the folk narratives. The orality of the Purāṇas is literate orality. These are scholars who are oral in performing the Purāṇas, and probably even in composing some of them, but who are very proud of their knowledge of grammar and their ability to possess a written text of what they perform orally. Therefore we meet with an interesting contradiction. The texts say they were oral, Brahmā uttered them, Vyāsa spoke them, and a number of his disciples narrated them. But outside the text you can see that every Paurāṇika values the written tradition by carrying a book with him. An oral narrative of the illiterate low castes is derisively called in Telugu a *pukkiṭipurāṇa,* an "oral Purāṇa," referring to the fact that it does not have a written text to authenticate it. In summary, a Purāṇa without a written text that says in writing that it is not a written text but a text spoken by a great God, is not an authentic Purāṇa.

WHAT THE PURĀṆAS SAY

At this point it will be useful to summarize what the Purāṇas say about themselves so that we can go on to the next step, to examine what they do not say.

1. Brahmā originally uttered the Purāṇas; in their original form they are one hundred million.
2. Vyāsa in every *manvantara* organizes the Purāṇas into eighteen texts by abridging them for the benefit of the inferior humans, whose intelligence, over the course of generations, gradually deteriorates until the end of the Kali Age.
3. A Purāṇa has five features, features that are valued as definitive marks of the genre. Together these five features provide a concept of time and space to the audience of the Purāṇa.
4. Purāṇas speak like a friend, whereas the Veda speaks like a master, but they say the same thing.
5. Purāṇas are oral.
6. In the Purāṇa tradition, the earlier and mythical narrators are more authoritative than the later human narratives.
7. A Purāṇa is valued for its meaning, a meaning that is known only to the sage or sage-like commentator.

WHAT PURĀṆAS DO NOT SAY

Texts come into writing when someone records what he has heard earlier or when he composes the text himself. The vast body of written materials of the Purāṇas obviously came into existence because a host of scholars wrote them. But the Purāṇas do not say who wrote them. A large body like the Purāṇa literature, which clearly received materials from different sources, including folk sources, contains a host of self-contradictions. But the Purāṇas maintain that such contradictions are only apparent and that, underneath, they are all one, with a unified meaning that is in conformity with *śruti,* the Veda. Purāṇas do not inform us where the different narratives and other received elements were borrowed from, nor do they give us any understanding of how such materials are transformed by being incorporated into the Purāṇas. Finally, the Purāṇas do not inform us why it is said that there are eighteen Mahāpurāṇas and eighteen Upapurāṇas, while the textual evidence shows that the actual number is greater. Nor are we told what precise reasons generated the difference between the Upa- and Mahāpurāṇas.

Anyone acquainted with Hindu society with its hierarchy and differences in status, religious oppositions, and divisions of caste knows that it presents an intense scene of conflicts and tensions. At the same time the dominant ideology of the society presents a homogeneous view of a well-ordered society. But despite the best efforts of the dominant ideology to present a homogeneous picture, we can still detect the ideological tensions both within the texts and outside the texts. I shall present some evidence to show that such tensions exist between the Vaidikas and the Paurāṇikas, between the Paurāṇikas and the Ālankārikas (scholars of ornate poetry), between one group of Purāṇas and another group, and finally between the literate Paurāṇikas and the illiterate low-caste oral-epic singers.

The great respect that a reciter of the Veda receives in Hindu society is well known. But what is less well known is that he is also slighted as a *vedajaḍa,* a moron whose mind is dulled by constant repetition of the Veda. *Chandas* in Sanskrit means a "Veda verse." A *chāndasa* therefore means one who is well versed in the Veda. But in popular Sanskrit, a *chāndasa* is a disrespectful term that refers to a stupid ritualist, who does not understand the way of the world as a Paurāṇika or a *kāvya* poet does. Connoisseurs of *kāvya* give Vyāsa the nickname *cakārakukṣi,* "one who has *ca* syllables in his belly." A *śloka* in Purāṇic Sanskrit contains a number of filler syllables, *ca*s, as in *sargaś ca pratisargaś ca vaṃśo manvantarāṇi ca.* For a *kāvya* poet who values a tightly composed style, this is poor Sanskrit. The statement by Cornelia Dimmitt and J. A. B. van Buitenen that the Purāṇas are "composed in Sanskrit of a mediocre quality" reflects a *kāvya* bias.[21] There is also another bias, often heard from grammarians and other *śāstra* experts, that Purāṇas are popular literature, meant for the ordinary folk. The implication is that they are not good *śāstra.*

It is well known that the Purāṇas are classified according to the system of three *guṇas*, or strands that together constitute matter: lucidity, or goodness (*sattva*); energy, or passion (*rajas*); and torpor, or darkness (*tamas*). Thus there are Purāṇas characterized by lucidity (*sāttvika*), Purāṇas characterized by energy (*rājasika*), and Purāṇas characterized by torpor (*tāmasika*). The *Parāśarya Upapurāṇa* even states that the Purāṇas of torpor are unworthy of reading. The dispute as to whether a particular Purāṇa is a *Mahāpurāṇa* or an *Upapurāṇa* also belongs in this category. The *Brahmavaivarta Purāṇa* states that the five *lakṣaṇas* apply only to *Upapurāṇas* and that Purāṇas that have more than ten *lakṣaṇas* are known as *Mahāpurāṇas*. If one were to pursue this logic further, the *Matsya, Vāyu,* and *Brahma Purāṇas* would have to lose their status and be classified as *Upapurāṇas*.

THE CHANGE IN THE NATURE OF THE PURĀṆAS

Like all the aspects of Brahminic Hinduism, Purāṇas have also undergone a major shift as result of *bhakti*. The devotional mode of relationship between the deity and the devotee, and between one devotee and other devotees, has a profound influence on the Purāṇas. The mode of Purāṇa composition has changed significantly; the *Bhāgavata Purāṇa* marks that shift more definitively than any other Purāṇa.

While it is not easy to demonstrate the shift in any detail in the span of this paper, I shall refer to one prominent feature of the *Bhāgavata Purāṇa* here. Let me quote from the Telugu version of this Purāṇa, where Parikṣit asks Śuka for the story of Kṛṣṇa's birth.[22]

> He is the form of Time and Being. He is inside and outside of people in this world. He gives life and death, bondage and liberation. Pray, narrate his story in full.
> You said that (Bala) Rāma was the son of Rohinī. Then why was he in the womb of Devakī? How did the lotus-eyed lord leave his parents to live with the cowherds? Where did he live? What did he do, and why did he kill his uncle Kaṃsa? How long did he live as a man on earth? How many wives did he take? And what else did he do? Tell me everything of the life of Mādhava.
>
> And further he said: The more I hear you, the more I drink

> the nectar of Kṛṣṇa's stories that flows from your mouth,
> my body grows livelier; my grief is gone; I feel neither
> hunger nor thirst, my heart is pleased.
>
> When Parikṣit had said this, the son of Vyāsa replied to him: Viṣṇu's stories purify the man who enjoys them and the man who asks for them, like water from the river which flows from Viṣṇu's foot.

Parikṣit's request is to be informed of the story of Kṛṣṇa's birth; but a closer look will reveal that he actually asks to listen to a story he already knows, for the joy of listening to Kṛṣṇa's story another time, for the mere joy of hearing. The earlier Purāṇas have informed their listeners about creation, mythology, history, and a host of other subjects, instructed them in the essential religious modes of behavior, sermonized on codes of conduct, and legitimized local gods and goddesses. The *bhakti* Purāṇas now essentially create an atmosphere of participation in religious ecstasy. The emphasis is not on information but rather on a renewed opportunity to experience the divine. It is not communication but communion.

While this shift in the aesthetics of the Purāṇa sets the *bhakti* Purāṇas in a class by themselves, the Paurāṇika tradition indicates this by a change in the number of *lakṣaṇa*s that this Purāṇa contains: instead of the usual five *lakṣaṇa*s, the *Bhāgavata Purāṇa* has ten. This numerical adjustment is an effort on the part of the Brahminic ideology to signify two things: one, the incorporation of *bhakti* into its fold and, two, Purāṇic approval of *bhakti*. But still the enhancement in the number of *lakṣaṇa*s leads to a small-scale controversy regarding the relative status of Purāṇa texts. *Bhakti* Purāṇas now claim far higher status than pre-*bhakti* Purāṇas. But in Hindu society, this is no more problematic than a caste that is normally classed low but claims a higher status in society and justifies its claim to an enhanced self-image because of a greater devotion to a deity than other castes or because of some such merit.

Sociologists study texts as models for societies; they study societies as texts. I am suggesting the reverse. We should look at texts in India as a society. Sanskrit texts are organized just as Brahminic society is organized, in four *varṇa*s: Brāhmaṇas, Kṣatriyas, Vaiśyas, and Śūdras. We know that, in reality, we find hundreds of different castes, and we do not find the neat classification of the four *varṇa*s. I am afraid that we in Purāṇa studies are like the early empirical anthropologists who found a bewildering variety of *jāti*s and were at a loss to understand why Brahmins spoke of only four. They later knew that the *varṇa* is an ideological system that organizes the *jāti*s into a Sanskritic conceptual scheme. I suggest that if we are to understand Purāṇas, their status in Brahminic textual traditions, and their role in Brahminic culture, we get little help from a empirical study of the Purāṇic texts themselves. We have to listen to what the tradition says and what it does not say, to consider the totality of the Brahminic textual tradition as an ideological system.

5

On Folk Mythologies and Folk Purāṇas

A. K. Ramanujan

Among the narrative genres of oral folk traditions, I'd like to include one that may be called "folk mythologies," to be distinguished from folk epics, ballads, the various types of folktales, and so forth. When these folk mythologies are related to a local cult, caste, with its own origin myths, sacred calendar, and sacred geography, they tend to crystallize around a god-figure into long narratives that may be called "folk Purāṇas." The best known of these are *sthalapurāṇas* of the kind that David Shulman has studied for Tamil Nadu.[1] Whatever their oral sources, they tend to get written and elaborated by named poets. U. Ve. Caminatiar, in his autobiography[2] speaks of his guru in the nineteenth century being commissioned to write these "temple myths."

Folk mythologies of the kind I'm talking about haven't been written or written down except by folklorists in the last few decades—here I confine myself to the Kannada region where I've done my field studies. About five of them are well known in different districts of that area. In the latter part of this paper, I shall speak in detail of only one and present a section of it—the *Maleya Mādēśvara* narrative of about twenty-five thousand lines, some fifteen hundred pages in print, collated (and unfortunately conflated) by P. K. Rajasekhara in 1973.[3] It tells the story of Mādappa, a god/hero/saint of the Southern Mysore hills, his arrival from the north, traveling from place to place in search of parents (as a form of Śiva, he has none and has to acquire suitable ones), then in pursuit of an evil Bali-like demon king (who has imprisoned all the celestials and set even Pārvatī to menial tasks), and then in search of devotees. In these searches, he ruthlessly tricks and destroys wicked men and women who refuse him oil for his bath or food for his begging bowl; and he brings his devotees wealth, children, and power. Each of these episodes is set in a Mysore location that acquires a name from the incident described. His trail and his enemies and supporters make the geography sacred and mythic. Rivers, valleys, stones, hills, and plants are revalorized in this process. For instance, villagers show visitors a protrusion in a rock that commemorates the demon trying to embrace Pārvatī: but she disappears and leaves a rock in his arms. But his phallus penetrates and goes through the rock—leaving to this day a visible protrusion.

In the interests of placing folk Purāṇas in perspective, I shall digress a little and talk about the ambience of these mostly uncollected but pervasive folk mythologies out of which the Purāṇas are made.

One could speak of several kinds of relations between the Sanskritic (which for me include works in Sanskrit as well as in the standard, literary, especially poetic, dialects of our mother tongues) and the folk mythologies that exist in the substandard, not necessarily rural, nonliterate dialects, those motherliest of mother-tongue dialects. If we may call the motifs, characters like Rāma or Sūrya, and episodes like those between Śiva and Pārvatī or between Pārvatī and the demon, *signifiers* and call the meanings they carry for the natives their *signified,* I'd like to propose at least four different, rather obvious, relations between the Sanskritic and the folk mythologies. Epics and Purāṇas are not distinguished here.

Examples for 1 in table 5.1 are the major avatars that both the Sanskritic texts and the folk texts share; for 2, the figures of Śiva and Pārvatī who appear in both texts, but with different functions, episodes, and so forth, or in new avatars not found in the Sanskritic texts; for 3, Mādappa's journey as narrated above, which shares neither signifier nor signified (though abstracted patterns may be similar); for 4, Madappa's killing the demon king, where the signifier is new but the signified is shared with many of the myths of Śiva and Viṣṇu.

Folk mythologies relate to Sanskritic ones in all four ways. They also relate in a fifth way, that is, they garble what they retell, a process that goes both ways, in both kinds of texts, to delight and frustrate scholars, giving rise both to new myths and to new scholarly papers.

Table 5.1 Relations between Sanskritic and Folk Elements

	SIGNIFIERS	SIGNIFIED
1	same	same
2	same	different
3	different	different
4	different	same

In taking the same gods and heroes as in the Sanskritic Epics and Purāṇas and making them do, say, and mean different things in a local milieu, the folk myths *domesticate* them, *incorporate* them in bodies that sweat, stink, defecate, and menstruate (which their Purāṇic counterparts usually don't, with a few notable exceptions, like Pārvatī making Gaṇeśa out of her body dirt), *localize* them, and often *contemporize* them. As I've written of these processes elsewhere,[4] I shall cite just one example.

Rāmanāthapūra is a place in Hassan district, Karnataka. People tell the following story about it: when Rāma and Lakṣmaṇa wandered in the southern forests in the hot season, they couldn't find any water to bathe in. They were covered with dirt and Rāma positively stank to high heaven. When they came near this place, the villagers said, "O, that Rāma, he really stinks!" But they also showed him their little stream, in which Rāma bathed and came out clean, even fragrant. He left all his stench in the stream. So that place was called "Śrirāmanāthapūra." In Sanskrit, it means, "the town of Rāma's lord," but in Kannada it means, "the town of Rāma's stink." In Kannada, *nātha* means "stink, (bad) smell." In this bilingual pun, we see the way the Rāma story is localized, de-Sanskritized, made earthy and corporeal.

Folk myths also extend the common stock of well-known Purāṇic incidents in hundreds of ways. To give just one example: after the Churning of the Ocean, the sweat and dirt of the laboring gods and anti-gods muddied the waters and made it dark and salty. The dismayed Lord of Oceans came to Viṣṇu with a complaint. Viṣṇu gave him a boon—that sea water would look dark only at a distance and would be crystal clear in the hand. Such a story connects a daily perception with a mythic incident—as the Sanskritic Purāṇas themselves do very often. Such etiological myths that explain why something is what it is—why dogs copulate in public and get teased for it, why cats hide their faeces, why the chipmunk has three stripes, why the sky is so high (all because of mythic events)—give us a pervasive mythology of ordinary life. This process is the obverse of domesticating the Purāṇic myths, but the result is the same—connecting a myth set in the past with a mundane event in the present. Such connections are made in all three semiotic modes: the symbolic, the iconic, and the indexical, in Charles Peirce's terms. Localizations as in the Rāmanāthapūra story make an *indexical* connection, for the place is the context for the incident. An example of the *iconic* would be why the onion is taboo for Vaiṣṇavas: because one cross section of an onion is like the conch of Viṣṇu and another cross section is like his discus. Another charming story illustrates the *symbolic:* Draupadī didn't want her husband Bhīma ever to forget her sorrow when they lived incognito in Virāṭa's court. So she prayed to Kṛṣṇa who created onions and threw them into Bhīma's kitchen. Every time he peeled an onion, he would remember Draupadī; his eyes would burn and keep his revenge alive. Folk or false etymologies (false from the point of linguistic inquiry), again a favorite feature of Sanskritic myths, connect a language item or a place name to a mythic event, for example, the etymology for Rāmanāthapūra.

In many of the features, the folk myths are similar to the Sanskritic or "classical" Purāṇic myths—except that we see them not in texts but in everyday speech, in a collective yet diachronic process, the stories being varied, reworked, etymologized, informed, or garbled by successive tellers—not really different, indeed, from the variant Purāṇic texts themselves, except that in the latter the variation is not as variable and the process is arrested by the fixation of texts.

Out of such shifting materials, such *sañcāri* (changing) motifs, a *sthāyi* (relatively stable) folk Purāṇa crystallizes around a charismatic figure, a combination of hero, saint, and god, who claims miracles, collects devotees, asserts power over evil, becomes the center of a cult in a locale. Purāṇas, whether Sanskritic or folk, differ from other texts. They've been called "mosaics" (Bonazzoli). To know a work of Kālidāsa is to know his exact words. But few Hindus, if any, know a Purāṇa as a whole text; they just know the stories. They fit Lévi-Strauss's description of myths as stories that survive translation (unlike poetry which, according to Frost, is what gets lost). Like most Hindus, for instance, I know the details of the avatars of Viṣṇu, but I do not know the *Viṣṇu Purāṇa*. (I've argued elsewhere[5] that the Epics are similarly held in Hindu memories, though parts of mother-tongue texts tend to be remembered verbatim, especially if they are considered sacred, like Tulasi's *Rāmacaritamānasa*.

Among the Purāṇas, the *Bhāgavata* may be among the exceptions.) In spite of repeated efforts to impose schemes and canons on them from time to time, Purāṇas are open systems. In Tamil, the *Kanta Purāṇam* is called "*kantal purāṇam,*" meaning a Purāṇa of *kante* or *kantal,* of rags, of "shreds and patches." I recently found references to Christ, Moses, the Messiah, Noah, and Queen Victoria in the appropriately up-to-date *Bhaviṣya Purāṇa. Purā navam bhavati,* says an old *Nirukta* commentary—the old becomes new, exactly like any folk text. One may go further and say that in such texts as the Purāṇas (as suggested above, the difference in range of variation between Sanskritic written ones and the oral folk Purāṇas is only a matter of degree) we see clearly and in extreme forms the nature of all texts, particularly Indian texts. We have been reminded in the last few years by text theory that

> any text is a new tissue of past citations. Bits of codes, formulae, rhythmic models, fragments of social languages, etc., pass into the text and are redistributed within it, and there is always language before and around the text. Intertextuality, the condition of any text whatsoever, cannot of course be reduced to a problem of sources or influences; the intertext is a general field of anonymous formulae whose origin can scarcely ever be located; of unconscious or automatic quotations, given without quotation marks.[6]

Folk texts, especially, never let you forget the intertextual nature of all texts. It also helps to see the many narrative genres of a cultural unit (family, caste, village, and so forth) in relation to each other in a kind of ecological array of genres: folktales and folk myths, texts in mother tongues and in Sanskrit (and other father tongues), oral and written in their fixed and fluid forms (for both oral and written have both), and so on. Furthermore, motifs, structures, and whole narratives may move through different genres and acquire different properties and meanings according to the ambience of each genre. Contrary to one of the early principles of transformational grammar, we need to assert that meaning is *not* constant under transformations. Each text has to be read for itself and in context to get its meanings. Texts cannot predict contexts, structures cannot predict functions, nor motifs and types meanings. Archetypes are empty unless cultures, by which I mean subcultures, fill them.

In the light of all these remarks, I'd like briefly to characterize folk-Purāṇas and present a section from *Maleya Mādēśvara.*

Folk Purāṇas in Kannada are distinguished from other folk narratives by the following characteristics:

1. They are sung, maintained, and learned according to certain ritual prescriptions by a group of specialists devoted to a specific god and initiated by, and raised to perform, special observances.

2. A musical instrument symbolic (or iconic or indexical) of the god is used in the singing/chanting/reciting of the Purāṇa, usually in a group with foreground (*mummēḷa*) and background (*himmēḷa*) performers. When not in use, these instruments are worshipped at the god's altar.

3. These Purāṇas are performed on special days (pilgrimages and occasions) and in places sacred to the god.

4. These narratives are long, several nights long. They contain chanted prose, verse, song, and refrains. They are segmented in *sālu* or line, and *kava(ṭ)lu* or branch (section). *Sālu* represents a night's or two nights' worth of narrative; *kavalu* is a substory, a shorter narrative within the main one, not a unit of time. No single teller (to our knowledge) sings all of them, though he may know of them. Of the fourteen *sālu*s of *Mādēśvara,* collected by P. K. Rājaśēkhara from nearly twenty singers in 1973, few singers knew more than a couple. In a sense the entire folk Purāṇa is known in detail only to a folklorist, who is a modern Vyāsa. Folklore in its natural state has Sūtas or reciters, but no Vyāsas or editors.

5. Like the Sanskritic Purāṇas, the story begins with a creation myth (certainly the two major Kannada Purāṇas do)—though one can find them also without such creation myths. They also contain a series of "etiological" episodes that explain the names and epithets of the god/hero/saint (for he is all three), the holy places he visited, destroyed, blessed, or cursed. The crisscross wanderings of the hero thus map his country, inscribing telltale traces of his miracles, wars, stratagems, and so forth on places, many of them ending in the conversion of unwilling or arrogant people into devotees.[7]

6. One last point: in terms of Sanskritic Epics and Purāṇas, folklore in general, and folk Purāṇas in particular, present an alternative world; they are what we may call "counter-texts" to their better-known "classical" analogues. They may use (see earlier discussion of table 5.1) many of the same characters, motifs, and so on (as Purāṇa experts will immediately recognize) but counter and invert them and give them new meanings. I shall present the opening creation myth from *Mādēśvara,* to convey the style and tone of the Purāṇa. Then I shall suggest a few ways in which the folk Purāṇa uses and inverts classical motifs.

A Creation Myth in a Folk Purāṇa

Ādiśakti came into being
three days before earth, heaven,
and the netherworld
came into being,

three days before Brahmā, Viṣṇu,
and Śiva.

As time passed, she attained puberty.
She looked at the sky
and said, "Ahha, nothing in sight
to satisfy my passion,
to please my youth.
I've to (be)get one myself,"

and gave birth
to Brahmā.

When Brahmā was born,
four faces and eight hands,
she said to him: "My boy, do you know
why I've brought you into the world?
I'm young and need a man
to satisfy me.
Look at me and be my husband.
I'll give you all my arts
and the world will be yours."

Brahmā heard what his mother said
and let out four sighs.
"Mother, you bring me into the world
and ask me to be your
husband.
Would that be right? You are my mother."

"Ché, idiot," she said.
"Is it for this I got you?
Burn then
for your disobedience."
So saying,
she placed her hand on his head.

Her hand had an eye of fire
and it burned him to ashes.

"I created this four-faced creature
to take care of my youth, but he wouldn't.
We'll have to get a new one," said she,
and on the second day
she (be)got Ma'Isnu (Mahāviṣṇu).

He looked beautiful to her, even better
than the four-faced one.
Her youth overflowed and she giggled
and giggled with pleasure.

Ma'Isnu asked her,
"Mother, why do you laugh like that?"
She sat him next to her
and said lovingly, looking at his face:
"My man, do you know
why I've got you here?
I got one yesterday, but he wouldn't do
what I asked him to do.
I asked him to be my husband and satisfy me,
quench my youth's passion.
Let's live as if we are on the ocean
of milk, I said.
But he wouldn't look at me,
he talked back.
So I burned him to ashes.
I want you to look at me, be my husband
and quench my passion," said the Great Mother.

The hair on Ma'Isnu's body stood on end.
"What kind of new talk
is this?" he said. "Is this *dharma?*
You give birth to me and ask
me to look at you and be your husband.
In the world yet to come,
in that arrangement of things,
would the children born to the mother
go to the mother?"

The Great Mother said,

"Son, shouldn't a son go to the mother?"
Ma'Isnu knew all about this.
He said, "Children go to the mother
to drink her milk, to give her happiness.
Would they satisfy the passion of the mother
who bore them? Why did you beget me?
I can't look at you," he said.

She listened to Isnu.
Her youth makes her prance. Her eyes are full.
Her body is filling out like a bright yellow lemon.
She was now in a rage.
"Look, I got this fellow but he won't satisfy me.
Why should I let him live?
I'll burn him down
just like the other one," she said
and turned him to ashes.
All she had to do was to place her hand
with its eye of fire on his head and he went up
in flames.

By the third day,
brimming with youth
she couldn't bear it any more.
She thought, "Let's get a three-eyed one
for the third day.
What does it matter if he does not satisfy me?
Let's get a fellow
who will bring light to the world."

Saying that, with her *māyā* [power of illusion]
she (be)got Śiva.

"My boy," she said,
"I got you here to satisfy my youth,
to quench my passion.
I'll be yours, you be mine.
Be my husband
and give me pleasure."

"Mother, you didn't wait long
to say such good words, did you?
Do sons and mothers ever get together like that?

That's not right.
If that's right, *dharma* will be in ruins,
karma will increase.
No, mother,
this won't do.
I won't raise my eyes and look at you,"
said Mādēśvara [Śiva].

Ādiśakti replied,
"If you and I don't live together
as husband and wife, the world will not sprout,
the dark that's around will not
clear up, and how will the world see light?
Where will children come
from and family life begin?
Don't talk like a coward now and ruin yourself.
Just listen to me and become my husband."

"I can't. I can't be your husband, mother,
and I don't want you
to be my wife.
If we live as husband and wife,
the Wishing Cow will give no milk,
mother earth will be stunted,
clouds won't gather and pour down rain,
the fire goddess will turn away,
the Ganges will vanish.
In the Kali Age yet to come,
those who say Śiva will forget Śiva,
those who say Hara will not know Hara.
Liṅga-less heretics will rule the world,
darkness will shroud the world,
dharma will be in ruins, *karma* will swell. No, no,
I'll not look at you."

"*Shabāsh,* my son. You are young,
but your talk is neat.
You are clever, smooth; your words have color.
But don't you know I'm Ādiśakti?
All three gods are in my hands.
Fire, Ganges, gods, antigods,
the human race, are in these hands.
The world is entirely inside my heart.

Who's greater than me?
My hands have the power to create
worlds, and the power to burn them down.
Look at me,
and satisfy me, cover my youth."

"Mother, are you the eldest, the greatest, in the world?"
"Yes, son, I'm Ādiśakti."
"Mother, if I don't become your husband, what will you do to me?"
"I'll burn you down in a minute."
"Really?"
"Really. I got two more like you before you.
They refused to satisfy me,
said like you
that they wouldn't do that to me, their mother.
So I thought, Why should they grow up?
and I burned them to ashes."
He listened carefully.
He was born with long matted hair;
it cascaded down his forehead.
He gathered it up and tied it over his head.
The Great Mother's youth brimmed over.
He asked, "Mother, where are these fellows you burned down?"
"Not far from you. Turn around."

Mādēva turned around and saw
two heaps of ash.
The hair on his body stood on end.
"She'll do the same to me," he thought,
and became wary.

"Mother, you are the greatest.
You got me so that I could be your husband.
Right? Don't you want to see me grow up
and become bigger than you?
Don't you think
the husband should be stronger than the wife?"

She agreed, made a pavilion for him
to grow up in and saw him grow.
Then she said, "My boy, I've helped you grow

from a little man to a big one.
You now look taller than me. Come now, satisfy me."

"Wait, wait a little, mother.
You've waited this long,
can't you wait just a little bit more?"

She was happy.
She thought, "Ahha, he will satisfy me."
She asked him, "What else do you want?"
"Mother, if you want me to be your husband,
shouldn't I the husband be stronger than the wife?
Teach me all your arts," said Mādēva.

"*Shabāsh,* my son. I'll teach you all my arts
and make you powerful.
What do you want?
I can give birth, burn, create things."

"Mother, you give birth. You burn.
You make, you break.
If I have
to be your husband,
I must have at least a feather's worth more
than your powers."

She was amazed at his words.
She looked at the sky and then she said,
"But why do you want these powers?"
"Mother, if you want me to be your husband,
you must fill me with your energy
and enterprise.
I must light up the world.
I must darken the lighted world.
I must give birth to celestials, rear humans,
create goddesses like Mārī, Durgī, and Chauḍī,
three hundred million gods,
*gandharva*s, *yakṣa*s, *kinnara*s, Kāli Mākālīs,
create earth, heaven,
and the netherworlds,
ten directions all around, sun and moon,
Indra and Nārada, birds, demons, men,

and three crores of creatures—
teach me to do all that."

"My boy, I've this ring on my hand.
All my power is in it.
If I take it off and lay it on the ground,
I'll not have the strength
to take a step.
And if I lose the eye of fire in my palm,
I'll have no life at all.
Let me keep my eye of fire.
Here, take my ring,
wear it, you'll see the universe
in this diamond," said she,
full of love and infatuation.

Śiva learned all her arts from her,
Mādēśvara, lord with the eye
of fire.
He felt like laughing, but the mother didn't understand
his tricks.

"What else do you want to learn?" she asked.

"Amma, I'm expert in all the arts now.
I want to ask you something.
I have your *māyā,* your arts, your powers.
Now who's greater, you or me?"

"My child, what does it matter
how many arts you've learned?
I'm the one who brought you forth, am I not
the one who gave you all
your powers?"

As she said it, he laughed aloud.

"You haven't lost
your high and mighty ways, mother.
Am I not greater than you now?
All your powers are in my hands."

"But my son, I am Ādiśakti, the source
of all those arts.

"Am I not then greater than you, my child?"

"Amma, then let's do something," said Mādēva, our father.

"What's that?"

"Let's not argue. Let's see who is greater.
Let's dance," said he.
"If you and I face each other and dance,
your passion will increase.
When you overflow with it,
I'll be your mate."

"How will you do that?"

"Let's dance.
If you defeat me, if you win,
I'll be your husband."

"*Shabāsh,* that's my boy. Let's dance, as you wish."

"Let's get ready then, mother," said Mādēva
and began to dance.

When he stamped his foot, so did she.
When he lifted a leg, so did she.
She did not see through
Mādēśvara's stratagem.
She danced
better than Mādēva, harder and harder.
All she wanted was to defeat him.
Streams of sweat ran down her body.
Her hair longer than two arms came loose
like a haystack.
She had no care even for her modesty.
She danced and danced.

Then, as he was getting tired,
our father the wizard placed his own right hand
on his head.

She too forgetfully
placed her right hand on her head, and at once
she went up in flames, did the Great Mother.

Even as she burned, she came towards him saying,
"My son, I brought you forth,
but you are greater than me.
Take my eye of fire."
And she wanted to give him the Eye, but he thought,
"Ādiśakti will burn me down," and vanished,
Maker of Seven
Hills, the solitary one.

Ādiśakti was full of grief.
"*Ayyo!* With whom can I share
this sorrow?
O eye of fire, you go now
to my son's forehead and become his third eye,"
she cried.

Then, even as she turned to ash,
she cursed Śiva:
"He refused a woman, so
may his body be stuck
with the very kind of female he refused."

Who knows what's first?
The seed, or is it the tree?
Only Mādappa, Śiva who is Ādiśakti,
only he knows.

In the next section or *kavaṭḷu* (branch), Śiva makes Brahmā and Viṣṇu rise from their ashes and tells them what he has done, how he has burned down Ādiśakti, and he shows them the heap of ash. They praise him as the first god of the world and embrace his feet.

Then Mādēva said,
"We three are Brahmā, Viṣṇu, and Īśvara,
the Three Gods of the world.
We have to create three million worlds,
three million gods, human beings, demons,
kinnaras, *yakṣas*, Indras and Nāradas,
eighty million beings, plants and trees
and tubers, and also the oceans.

If all this is to be done,
we need women.
We must marry and rule our wives.
Kailāsa, Vaikuṇṭha, and Brahmaloka
are yet to be created.
Let's not throw
away the ashes of our mother,
but share it."

The three of them went and stood
before the ashes, now divided
into three heaps.
Śiva held out the ring
that the Great Mother had given him
and placed it once on each of the heaps.

Out of them
rose three women:
Pārvatī who is Isnu's sister, Sarasvatī
who is Śiva's sister, Lakṣmī
who is Brahmā's sister.
Śiva married
the first,
Brahmā married the second, and Isnu the third.

Then each said to the other,
"I've given my sister in marriage to you,
and married your sister.
We are brothers-in-law to each other
in more ways than one.
Let's create the worlds."

Then Śiva created heaven and three paradises,
Vaikuṇṭha, Brahmaloka, and Kailāsa
—the first for Isnu and Lakṣmī,
the second for Brahmā and Sarasvatī,
the third for Śiva and Pārvatī.

In heaven, he created eighty(?) million beings, gods, men,
demons, birds, ants, chameleons, lizards, snakes, scorpions,
bushes, reeds, trees, plants, tubers.

Then our father the wizard

Mādēva called all living beings and said to them,
"Children, you will not suffer
old age or death, you will not suffer hunger
or thirst.
One thing but: you should not eat the plants,
break the trees or pluck the fruit.
If you do, you'll be in trouble."

All the eighty
million creatures listened to him,
shook their heads in assent
and said,
"We'll do as you wish.
You are the lord of the world."

Among these eighty million,
there were cats and hens as well.
One day, when the hen laid an egg,
the snake looked at it
and wanted to eat it.

But he knew
that Śiva had asked them to eat nothing.
"But I want to eat that egg," he said to himself
and went to the gods.
He tried to persuade them
to eat the grain, the plants and trees
and become strong.
But they were angry with him.
They drove him
away, saying, "This black snake
will not only ruin himself, he
will destroy all of us."

Then he went to where the demons
and humans were sitting around.
He called out to them. "People,
this is not fair:
We don't have the strength
that the gods have. If
we can eat the grain
and the leaves and the fruits here, we will
become strong.

That's why Śiva has ordered us not to eat anything.
This is not good for us.
If we want more strength we must eat.
Śiva too deceives.
Let's go against what he said,
and eat food."

The demons and men felt the desire to eat.
They began to pull off
and eat seeds, twigs, leaves, bark, and all.
The serpent devoured the egg.
They all made a mess of heaven.
It stank of dirt and shit.

Mādēva became aware of the way
men and demons had become low beings.
He cursed them: "You widows' sons,
I gave you
no thirst, no hunger.
You went against my orders
and you have made heaven a dirty
stinking place.
You are not fit to live there."

He summoned Brahmā and said,
"These demons and men have spoiled
heaven,
they have ravaged the plants and eaten them.
Let us move
them from there.
Create the earth and cast them down there."

The *rākṣasa*s and human beings heard this
and came running.
They fell on his feet and pleaded.
"Lord, why do you want to throw us
out? It is not our fault.
It is all the fault of that snake
that's lying there."

Mādēva said to Brahmā, "Create a netherworld
and send that snake there."
Then the snake woke up and pleaded.

"Why are you sending me to
the netherworld?
I talked to them but they listened.
They are the ones who ate everything, and now
they are carrying tales against me."

Mādēva said, "You can't escape punishment.
You can't say it isn't
your fault.
And I can't take back my curse.
I'll let you be in two
places,
in the netherworld and also round my neck."

Brahmā created the earth and sent demons and humans
and many other beings there.
When the demons and humans grieved and cried
aloud, Śiva said,
"People, if you remember me with devotion, and
behave yourselves, I'll protect you in times of trouble."

At the very end, a line of ants came to Śiva.
"You are sending us
also to the earth.
All the other creatures are so big, but we are
so small.
What sin have we committed?
You must be fair, show us
the way."
Śiva said, "Dear ants, that's what's given to you.
Don't ask for more. Ask for something else."
They said, "Lord,
the big creatures kill us
because we are so small.
Give our bodies
some poison.
Let there be a death every time we bite."
Śiva got angry. "You sinners,
if I fill you with poison, will you
spare my world?
You've asked quite a boon.

All right, whenever you

bite anything, there will be a death,
yours!"

Inversions. In the Vedas and elsewhere, Brahmā the creator lusts after his daughter. But here, the creator deity is female and she lusts after her sons. While in the other Purāṇas, the gods give their powers and weapons to the goddess, here it is the goddess who gives her powers and her eye of fire to Śiva. (In other versions, e.g., in Telugu, she gives all three major gods their insignia.)

In the story of Mohiṇī and Bhasmāsura, Viṣṇu appears as a female dancer and tricks a demon into putting his own hand on his head, which act destroys him by his own power: he has received a boon from Śiva that enables him to burn down anything by placing his hand on it. Here the genders are reversed: Śiva plays the same trick on his mother.

In the Vedic Indraśatru story, Vṛtra gets literally the boon he asks for and destroys himself. Vṛtra wants to kill Indraśatru, which means "Indra the enemy" or "Indra's enemy," depending on the accent (the latter being himself); he puts the accent on the wrong syllable and is promptly destroyed. Here a very similar motif is employed to teach the ants a lesson.

One may go on, but I think I've said enough to suggest the way the folk Purāṇa reworks motifs from the Purāṇic pool. The myth here, like other women-centered folk materials, also suggests a very feminine (even a feminist) view of the Hindu pantheon: the source of all creation was a woman, who is tricked out of her powers by her son, destroyed, divided, and domesticated into three lesser, docile, consort goddesses for the three gods, Viṣṇu, Śiva and Brahmā. Though they refuse to sleep with their mother, refusing to break the incest taboo when she asks them to, they marry fragments of her once her powers are transferred to Śiva and she herself is reduced to ashes. Out of her ashes, they remake three manageable wives. They marry their mother, but only after fragmenting her.

Lastly, one may note a Genesis-like story of a paradise lost through the cunning and disobedience of a snake—though, here, characteristically, there is no taboo on sex. Biblical motifs (spread, no doubt, by local missionaries preaching in the mother tongues) no less than the Purāṇic ones are part of the intertextual weave.

6

Remaking a Purāṇa: The Rescue of Gajendra in Potana's Telugu Mahābhāgavatamu

David Shulman

Most famous, perhaps, of all South Indian Vaiṣṇava *bhakti* texts, the *Bhāgavata Purāṇa* (ninth century?) embodies the mythology of Viṣṇu as seen in medieval Tamil Nadu in deliberately classical, Sanskritic form. This Purāṇa, whose roots have been shown to lie, in part, in the emotional *bhakti* of the Tamil Āḻvār poets, became one of the major vehicles by which this religious movement transcended its immediate historical environment and reached out to other areas of the subcontinent. Various aspects of the process that produced the *Bhāgavata* and that involved transposing the Tamil theistic devotion of the Āḻvārs into a somewhat archaic Sanskrit, replete with Vedic resonances, as well as into a Vedantic philosophical idiom, are by now relatively well known.[1] But the peculiar vision of the *Bhāgavata Purāṇa* went on developing in South India beyond the confines of even this most influential parent text. Later generations produced new versions of the *Bhāgavata* in the regional languages, thus completing a historical circle: what began, with the Āḻvārs, in the Tamil vernacular (a popular Tamil at that, as opposed to the baroque *kāvya*-style Tamil of the Jainas from the period) eventually returned to the vernaculars in various altered forms, after a "detour" through the rarefied and prestigious medium of Sanskrit.[2] One of the most beautiful and beloved of these later versions is the fifteenth-century Telugu *Bhāgavatamu* of Bammĕra Potana, rightly considered one of the classic achievements of medieval Andhra civilization.

We may observe something of Potana's stature and importance in stories told about his poem: when Potana refused to dedicate his work to a local king, Sarvajña Siṅgama Nāyuḍu, the latter took it from the author by force and buried it in the ground; the god Rāma appeared in a dream to the king's wife and revealed that her family would be destroyed if the book were not returned; but when the palm leaves were dug up, portions of the text were found to have been ruined. Another version says that Potana hid the text himself in the shrine where he worshiped; only on his deathbed did he reveal its hiding place to his son, who again, on recovering the text, discovered large parts missing (destroyed by white ants).[3] These stories seek to explain the fact that Potana's composition, as we have it, is incomplete; various sections are attributed to Vĕligandala Nāraya and others, who are said to have filled in the missing portions after Potana's death. But the stories also bring the Telugu *Bhāgavatamu* into line with the very widespread theme of the sacred text that is lost, damaged, and—usually only partially—recovered.[4] Such a career, indeed, appears to be a necessary attribute of sacred knowledge in South India; Potana thus becomes, in the eyes of the Telugu tradition, a member of a series of poets whose works bear the unmistakable imprint of the divine. One should also note the tension evident in the first story between the *bhakti*-poet and the king. Another well-known tale, built around a popular verse, relates that Sarasvatī herself, the goddess of arts and learning, appeared to Potana and begged him, with tears in her eyes, not to sell her to a king in exchange for gold and land. As Velcheru Narayana Rao has suggested, we have here the traces of an important typological division in medieval Telugu between the "court poets" and the "temple poets," who chose to isolate themselves from royal patronage and all the consequences of contact with political power.[5] Potana clearly belongs in the latter category; the invocatory verses at the beginning of each book (*skandha*) address his chosen deity, Rāma, rather than any human king.[6]

We know only a few details about Potana himself. He was a Niyogi Brahmin, son of Kesana and Lakkamamba, brought up in an atmosphere of Śaiva devotion. *Vīrabhadravijayamu,* a poetic reworking of an important Śaiva myth, is also attributed to him. He ascribes his transition to a Vaiṣṇava poetic vocation to merit accumulated in his former births (1.13). His precise dates and place of birth are still the subject of heated debate. The Telugu literary tradition, with a fine intuition, makes him a contemporary of the great peripatetic poet Śrīnātha (early fifteenth century); we shall explore this linkage. We may also note that during the fourteenth and fifteenth centuries Andhra witnessed intensive Vaiṣṇava activity both in the great temple centers such as Ahobilam and Simhacalam[7] and outside them; although far too little is known about this phenomenon, this clearly formative period for Andhra Vaiṣṇava institutions and intellectual development may have provided the essential context for Potana's work.

Traditional scholarship on Potana has often focused on two issues: (1) the narrative changes, elaborations, and occasional deletions the Telugu poet has made from his Sanskrit prototype and (2) Potana's occasional deviations from the strict classical norms of Telugu prosody.[8] The latter issue need not concern us here, though we may note in passing that its resolution lies in Potana's close relation to the oral poetics of the folk tradition, which has left its impact on his diction and syntax and on the formal structure of many verses.[9] But the first problem is based on an all-too-prevalent misunderstanding of the interrelationships of texts such as these, that is, a classical Sanskrit model and a "translation" or adaptation into one of the regional languages. Narrative innovations alone are often the least impressive transformations we find in studying these works. In fact, in Potana's case actual changes in the narrative structure, including the detailed progression of most individual narrative episodes, are relatively minimal; in retelling the stories, he has, on the whole, stuck closely to his Sanskrit text, often to the point of quoting whole phrases verbatim in the form of long Sanskrit compounds transposed, with the sole addition of a Telugu ending, to the Telugu verses. Such a practice is, indeed, normal in medieval Telugu. Nevertheless, despite this close verbal correspondence and even, on occasion, identity, Potana's verses breathe a rather different spirit from that of the Sanskrit original—the spirit, no doubt, of fifteenth-century Andhra as well as of the idiosyncratic inner world of this particular poet. This is the miracle of transmutation, which we encounter regularly in Telugu versions of Sanskrit classics and which is particularly salient and powerful in the case of Potana. Minor changes on the level of plot are of little help in elucidating this process. Clearly, we need a more rigorous and wide-ranging approach to the problem, one based on more careful and sensitive readings of the relevant texts. The following pages attempt to develop such an approach with reference to a single episode, "releasing the elephant" (*gajendra-mokṣa*)—one of the most popular in Potana's *Bhāgavatamu*—and, at the same time, to relate the issue of textual transformation to the more general one of Purāṇa making in late medieval South India.

THE SANSKRIT *BHĀGAVATA*: AN ANOMALOUS PURĀṆA

One part of our thesis may be stated briefly at the outset. Despite the formal features that align this text with the Purāṇa corpus, despite its use of a conventional Purāṇa-style framework, and despite its own declared intention and self-vision, the Sanskrit *Bhāgavata Purāṇa* can only with some difficulty be fitted into the category of Purāṇa, with its genre-specific norms. At best, it is a most atypical and unusual specimen of this class. Potana's Telugu work, on the other hand, for all its pronounced formal affinities with ornate poetic composition (*kāvya*), is in fact a Purāṇa of a particular, late medieval, South Indian type. It is customary to imagine a process by which, over the centuries, many individual Sanskrit Purāṇic passages or, indeed, whole books were transformed into Telugu *kāvya*s or *prabandha*s, each with its author, its patron, its adoption of the elevated *prabandha* style.[10] But here we have a reverse instance: Potana has, in effect, created a Purāṇa from a Sanskrit original of a rather different nature. To understand this process, we need to characterize the Sanskrit *Bhāgavata* at least in its broad outlines.

Purāṇas are habitually defined by their contents: the *purāṇa-pañcalakṣaṇa,* that is, the five main topics of primary creation (*sarga*), secondary creation (*pratisarga*), the genealogies of gods and sages (*vaṃśa*), history of the cosmic ages associated with the Manus (*manvantarāṇi*), and the dynasties of human kings (*vaṃśānucarita*). In short, Purāṇas deal with the past, with old traditions (as the name *Purāṇa* itself indicates) of what we would call "myth," and with a rather specific vision of what should, in fact, be called "history," however much it differs from traditional Western notions of what constitutes historical awareness. Though the material is always felt to be ancient, the Purāṇa reformulates it in a new way: "What, though from long ago, becomes new—that is a Purāṇa" (*purāpi navam bhavati purāṇam*). This saying contains an important insight into the nature of the Purāṇic process, which is always a dynamic and transformative one; still, the traditional definitions do not suffice to illuminate the workings of the genre. Other formal features are generally present—for example, the use of a frame in which one speaker, the Sūta or, at times, a sage, answers the questions of his audience (usually the sages in the Naimiṣa Forest). The dialogue—which transpires on more than one axis, between speaker and listener but also frequently between different voices emerging, as it were, from within the main narrator—follows certain conventional patterns.[11] Early Purāṇas, especially the so-called Mahāpurāṇas or Great Purāṇas, are also fairly heterogeneous, "agglutinative,"[12] inclusive of an extremely wide range of materials—although much of it is assimilated to the specific semantic forms required by the genre.[13] An overall drive toward ordering, arranging, integrating, and, especially, ranking and stabilizing values, ideas, and experience, is conspicuous in many exemplary works of the genre. Stylistically, Purāṇas tend to be couched in a relatively simple Sanskrit akin to that of the Epic and prefer the Epic *śloka* meter, although here, too, there is room for considerable variation.

Where does the *Bhāgavata* stand in the light of these few, selected traits? It does present us with a great deal of traditional Purāṇic materials (including those of the *pañcalakṣaṇa* categories), and it definitely makes use of the dialogic frame: most of the text is narrated by the sage Śuka, Vyāsa's "lunatic" son, to King Parikṣit as the latter sits by the Ganges and prepares for the death by snakebite that he knows to be his destiny.[14] But already this dramatic, indeed melodramatic frame may suggest that we are dealing with a text with somewhat different emphases and goals than those of other Purāṇas. The "audience" here is literally situated between life and death, and the ultimate seriousness of the narrator's message is thereby powerfully heightened: his teaching constitutes the last words that Parikṣit will hear, and the king's last hope to achieve salvation. Śuka's teaching is also strikingly uniform in its effect: the give and take so typical of other Purāṇic dialogues has been largely replaced by a programmatic explication of the mythic materials in terms of a specific metaphysical reading of Vaiṣṇava *bhakti*. We can define this orientation, at least in general terms, as a kind of theistic Advaita with strong yogic components.[15] The stories presented by the text thus tend to be "explained" to us by the narrator as Viṣṇu's "amusements" (*līlā*) reflected in the distorting and illusionary mirror of *māyā,* which is ultimately no different from the great god's true being, at rest in itself. As one might imagine, this metaphysical standpoint can create interesting tensions of its own in juxtaposition with the various mythic narratives that it seeks to elucidate; F. Hardy has aptly remarked: "It is difficult to imagine what kind of a person the author could have been, maintaining in himself this incredible tension between intense emotionalism and monistic and theistic illusionism. But however incongrous this enormous edifice may appear to us, it contains stimuli and inspiration which remained operative for the following thousand years."[16] We will observe something of the dynamics of this peculiar combination, worked out in a striking and rather self-conscious manner, in the episode discussed below; and it should also be instructive to see how the Telugu version handles the apparent "incongruity" of its textual source.

The *Bhāgavata* also stands apart from the rest of Sanskrit Purāṇic literature by virtue of its unique diction and style. As many scholars have noted,[17] the *Bhāgavata* was composed in a strangely archaic Sanskrit, filled with Vedic vocabulary, verbal formulas and direct quotations from the Veda, and even obsolete Vedic morphemes; these features are integrated into an elevated and often somewhat difficult style that is, moreover, uniformly distributed throughout the text. The difference from the more usual Purāṇic Sanskrit is immediately apparent to anyone who reads even a few lines; the *Bhāgavata* fails to justify the conventional literary bias against Purāṇas (*kavitvahīnāḥ purāṇabhaṭṭāḥ,* "those devoid of poetic talent become composers of Purāṇas," in the words of a well-known verse).[18] Hardy has also remarked on the relatively high distribution of classical lyric meters in this text (as opposed to the Epic *śloka*); he concludes that it is "beyond doubt that the BhP wants to be more than a simple epic narrative, viz. a *kāvya*."[19] Indeed, in many ways—both in individual passages and on the level of its general plan and tone—the *Bhāgavata* seems closer to *kāvya* than to Purāṇa, and the striking unity of the text together with its unusual style would suggest that behind it lurks the figure of a single author (or, at most, a very small group of poets working together at a single historical time and place). Again, the contrast with the Sanskrit Mahāpurāṇas is plain. Van Buitenen, in a seminal article,[20] offered an explanation for the text's patently anachronistic, Vedicizing discourse in terms of its author's wish to secure Vedic, that is, orthodox legitimacy for the still insecure Vaiṣṇava sectarian movement in the Tamil area.[21] A similar motivation may underlie the attempt to translate Tamil *bhakti* religion into a somewhat alien Advaitic discourse.[22] These strategies are also suited to the stage in the evolution of Tamil Śrīvaiṣṇavism represented by the *Bhāgavata,* a stage of far-reaching Brahminization and Sanskritization (from approximately the ninth century onward) that eventually crystallized in the systematic work of Nāthamuni and the school of Yāmuna.[23]

All of this adds up to a picture of the *Bhāgavata,* historically one of the most popular of all Purāṇas, as, ironically, slightly out of place. Its striking homogeneity, its programmatic drive, its strained containment of the Purāṇic dialogic structure, its *kāvya*-like style, pace, and lyricism, the sense it conveys of a single hand at work in singular ways—all set the *Bhāgavata* apart from other Sanskrit Purāṇas. But the purpose of this compressed discussion, which naturally fails to do justice to the complexities of the *Bhāgavata*'s poetics, is not to take issue with the Indian tradition's classification of what is, after all, a major text. Rather, our concern is to highlight the transformation that Potana has achieved and to analyze its main features by exploring the microcosm of one short but typical episode.

THE STORY OF GAJENDRA: *BHĀGAVATA PURĀṆA* 8.2–4

The story itself is an extremely simple one, so simple that one hesitates to dignify it with the name of myth—it appears, in fact, to be only one step removed from a gnomic animal fable. It tells of the elephant Gajendra's long, losing battle with a crocodile, Gajendra's despair and plea for help, and Viṣṇu's sudden appearance in the nick of time to save the elephant by slaying the crocodile. In strict narrative terms, that is all there is to it, although, as we shall see, the potential for a more complicated reading of the tale does exist. In any case, simplicity hardly precludes popularity: this is a deeply loved tale, whose explicit moral, if one is needed, is that of Viṣṇu's easy accessibility (*saulabhya*) to his devotees in the hour of their need. Reciting the story is said to be an effective antidote to nightmares.[24]

It is also much older than the *Bhāgavata Purāṇa,* though not represented in earlier Vaiṣṇava texts such as the *Viṣṇu Purāṇa* and the *Harivaṃśa;*[25] the Āḻvārs cite it in their hymns.[26] One hesitates to ascribe a date; there is a possible early iconographic representation on a carved pillar from Mathura (400–415 C.E.),[27] and we must note the most famous of all such depictions, the Gupta panel from the early sixth century at Deogarh.[28] This lovely relief shows Viṣṇu appearing on Garuḍa to save Gajendra from the clutches of his tormentor, here somewhat surprisingly portrayed as a Nāga (half-cobra deity) rising from the waters in devotional pose (no doubt as a result of the god's intervention). The story underwent continuous development in Vaiṣṇava traditions: the *Brahmavaivarta Purāṇa* makes Gajendra the source, through the action of Viṣṇu, of Gaṇeśa's elephant's head![29] The major Tamil Vaiṣṇava shrine of Varadarājasvāmin at Kancipuram assimilated the story to its local tradition, identifying Varadarāja as Gajendra's savior.[30] Various medieval authors expanded upon the tale, particularly in South India: Raghunātha Nāyaka of Tanjore (1614–33), the great poet-king, composed a Telugu dance-drama (*yakṣagāna*) on this theme.[31] We may also note the prevalence of the general motif of the devouring crocodile, often identified with Death or Time, in South Indian literature—most notably, perhaps, in the story of Cuntaramūrttināyaṉār's successful resuscitation of a Brahmin boy swallowed (two years earlier!) by a crocodile at Avināci in the Konku region.[32]

Since our primary concern is with Potana, we will limit our discussion of the Sanskrit versions to that of *Bhāgavata Purāṇa* 8.2–4. This version may conveniently be divided into seven main segments:

1. Preliminary: linkage with the frame (8.1.27–33)
2. Setting the scene: the Trikūṭa Mountain and the elephants' play (8.2.1–26)
3. Gajendra's struggle with the crocodile (8.2.27–33)
4. Gajendra's impersonal prayer (8.3.1–29)
5. Viṣṇu's intervention (8.3.30–8.4.2)
6. The karmic prehistory of the story (8.4.3–13)
7. *Phalaśruti:* the rewards promised to those who hear or recite the tale (8.4.14–26)

Of the above, segments 2–5 provide the main field for Potana's development of the text. As will become evident, in some cases the Telugu poet elaborates a single Sanskrit verse or set of verses; we may thus delay close scrutiny of certain elements of the Sanskrit text to our next section, where they can be seen in conjunction with the Telugu material. At this point, let us briefly review the Sanskrit prototype as a whole.

The Frame

The eighth book (*skandha*) opens with a cosmo-historical sketch, suitably revised to incorporate the tones of Vaiṣṇava yoga, of the first four Manus and their corresponding *manvantaras* (ages). Viṣṇu/Hari was born during the fourth *manvantara* to Harimedhas and his wife Hariṇī; it was this Hari—so Śuka informs Parikṣit—who saved the elephant Gajendra from the crocodile (*graha*). Parikṣit, as usual, asks Śuka to tell him the story he has just mentioned—a story that is itself a form of merit and blessing (*sumahat puṇyaṃ dhanyaṃ svastyāyanam śubham*)—at greater length.

Setting the Scene

Śuka begins by describing a mountain—Trikūṭa Mountain, with its three peaks of silver, iron, and gold, the radiance of its jewels, its luxurious trees and noisy waterfalls and pellucid pools. The rather prolix description, in *śloka* meter but bordering on an embellished *kāvya* style, includes a lengthy list of the trees and creepers that graced one of the mountain valleys and of the birds at home in one of its clear lakes—an oral-poetic survival in this elevated and Sanskritized milieu.[33] A somewhat pallid erotic tinge, derived from stereotypical landscape descriptions in the Sanskrit courtly *kāvya* (e.g., canto 1 of *Kumārasambhava*), emerges in one or two verses: *kinnaras* and their *apsaras* lovers play in the mountain caves; breezes carry the fragrance of the streams in which divine women are bathing (2.8). In this wondrous setting, a great elephant in rut, the leader of a herd, roams about with his wives and children. There is a violent aspect to his appearance: the first verse to mention him (in *vaṃśastha* meter, carried through in *vaṃśamālā* until the end of the chapter) depicts him crashing against trees and trampling clumps of reeds and bamboo (2.20); he is, moreover, a terror to all the terrifying jungle animals—lions, other elephants, tigers, rhinoceros, great serpents, and so forth, who flee when they smell his presence. On the other hand, smaller animals—wolves, boars, monkeys, hares, and others—live peacefully and without fear beside him, because of his merciful nature (*anugraha*). We see something of this softer side of Gajendra as we watch him enter a pool fragrant with the pollen of golden lotuses and water lilies; after quenching his thirst and spraying himself with water, he gently and compassionately bathes his cows and children and brings them water to drink from his trunk. None of this may seem particularly pertinent to the main themes of the story, and one might even be tempted to dismiss it as so much extraneous "filling," were it not for the integral use that Potana makes of these initial scenes.

The Struggle

Gajendra, intoxicated by rut and under the sway of the Lord's befuddling *māyā,* is unaware of approaching danger: a crocodile impelled by fate seizes his foot. Gajendra strives valiantly to free himself, while his wives cry out piteously and the other male elephants vainly attempt to extricate him. Thus a thousand years go by, as the crocodile pulls the elephant deeper into the water, while Gajendra struggles back toward the bank. But the elephant's powers eventually begin to wane, and the crocodile, who is in his element, continues strong. At this point Gajendra, clearly an intelligent elephant, perceives the hopelessness of the struggle and the imminent danger to his life; he sums up the situation in two eloquent and important verses:

> These other elephants, my relatives, are unable to save me in my misery—how much less so can my wives! Caught in destiny's snare embodied by this monster, I shall take refuge with the Supreme. There must be some god who protects a frightened person who turns to him from powerful Death, running after him like a vicious serpent—I seek refuge with that god, whom Death himself flees in fear. (2.33–4)

Gajendra's words are heavy with familiar associations: the crocodile has become the snare (*pāśa*) of fate and the terrible serpent, Death; the elephant turns for refuge (*prapatti*)[34] to the supreme god, who inspires even Death with fear. As Śrīdhara, most famous of the commentators on the *Bhāgavata,* notes, this last attribute brings to mind Upaniṣadic statements about the Absolute (citing Taittirīya Upaniṣad 2.8.1.)—as we might well expect from the *Bhāgavata*'s program. The signal feature of this crucial moment of transition is, however, the impersonality of the god whose help Gajendra seeks: he is "some god" (*kaścaneśo*), the supreme goal (*paraṃ parāyaṇam*), by no means identified yet by name or other attribute with the *Bhāgavata*'s primary deity. This sets the stage for the *stotra,* the praise-poem to this impersonal Absolute, that now follows as the single largest unit of this episode.

The Prayer

As is so often the case in the *Bhāgavata* (and, indeed, in other Purāṇas as well), this *stotra* seems at first to be only loosely linked to the narrative. We have an apparently autonomous segment of the text, guided by its own drives and concerns, embedded in a timeless moment within a story unfolding, as stories must, in time. On closer inspection, we can observe an essential semantic linkage that also helps to explain the relative length of this section and its function at this juncture of the story. We shall see this element clearly at the conclusion of the *stotra,* that is, at the second seam uniting it to the narrative context.

I must confess that I have been unable to discover any organizing structure to the *stotra* as a unit. Thematically, it offers a reworking of largely Sānkhya-Yoga terms and concepts, couched in pseudo-Vedic language, in the direction of what Hardy has called "intellectual *bhakti*."[35] Still, the impersonality of the deity addressed is carefully preserved throughout. Underlying the Sānkhya terminology we detect the "extreme idealistic monism"[36] ascribed to the *Bhāgavata* by Dasgupta, although it is somewhat less clearly articulated here. In short, this is a *stotra* to the primary divine principle that subsumes all, conceived in relatively abstract and universal terms and described in stereotypical phrases drawn from Veda, Upaniṣads, and Sānkhya-Yoga. To convey something of the poem's flavor, let us cite a few typical passages:

> 3.2. I pay homage to that Lord who is the source of the universe imbued with consciousness (*yata etad cidātmakam*); to Puruṣa, the primal seed (Śrīdhara: = *prakṛti*), the supreme lord: thus I meditate (*abhidhīmahi,* echoing the Gāyatrī *mantra, RV* 3.62.10!).[37]
>
> 3.5. When, through the power of time, all the worlds disappeared together with their guardians and all causes, there was (only) profound darkness (*tamas tadāsīd gahanaṃ gabhīram;* cf. *RV* 10.129.1); he is the lord (*vibhu*) who reigned, shining, beyond it.
>
> 3.6. Gods and sages cannot discover his true place; his way is inscrutable, like that of an actor who moves through constantly changing forms.
>
> 3.8. He is without birth, *karma,* name and form, attributes or flaws, but he assumes all of these, at the proper time, through his *māyā* in order to destroy and to create the world.

He is the Witness (3.10), lord of complete detachment, the joyful experience of *nirvāṇa* (3.11), master of the field, root of the *ātman* (3.13), true being reflected in the false images of form and matter (3.14), ocean of all Veda and Āgama (3.15), release itself, compassionate, free, "capable of freeing from their fetters souls like me who turn to him" (3.17). He cannot be attained by those who remain attached to themselves, their children, friends, houses, wealth, or other people (3.18). Those who concentrate solely on him, who have turned to the lord, joyfully sing his amazing and auspicious story

(3.20—an isolated hint in this context of the other active pole of the *Bhāgavata*'s devotional world). He is the supreme, imperishable *brahman,* unmanifest (*avyakta;* = *prakṛti?*), reached through yoga, beyond the senses, very subtle, very remote, infinite (3.21). He is not god or demon, human or animal, not male, female, or eunuch, neither existent nor nonexistent (*sat/asat*); he is what is left when all else is denied (3.25).

And so on—the consistent tenor of the hymn should be clear. We will return to individual statements below in connection with Potana's reworking. But we must conclude this précis with the verse carrying the main thrust of Gajendra's plea to the remote and hidden Absolute that he has just described: "I have no wish to live this life, born from an elephant's womb, shrouded from within and from without; I seek release from all that veils the light of the spirit and that cannot be removed just by the passing of time" (3.25). It is a beautiful request, beautifully stated, and it immediately lifts Gajendra out of his helpless struggle with the crocodile into an entirely new plane of feeling: his concern is no longer with one, violent, imminent death in the pool but with the whole unhappy round of existence. More than any other, perhaps, this verse justifies the common title given this episode by the tradition—*Gajendramokṣa* (Gajendra's Release). All the more striking, then, is the fact that it has no parallel in the Telugu version.

The Intervention

This is the turning point of the story: Viṣṇu appears in response to Gajendra's prayer, on Garuḍa, with the discus in his hand. But the transition here is most telling: "When Brahmā and the other gods, completely identified each with his distinct, individual traits (*vividhaliṅgabhidābhimānāḥ*), failed to come toward Gajendra, who had just described God as without any specific characteristics, then Hari, who comprises within him all the other deities, revealed himself—for he is the inner being of all" (3.30). This verse links the *stotra* to the continuation of the narrative, and one sees at once how it turns the impersonality of the hymn to good effect, using it to illuminate one of the central messages of the *Bhāgavata.* The hymn and Viṣṇu's response now demonstrate this Purāṇa's program: Gajendra, not knowing which god to address by name and attribute, sings to the unqualified and nameless Absolute, which—or, rather, "who"—flies to his aid in the form of that one god who, alone, is that Absolute. The moral is stated unambiguously and self-consciously. Brahmā and the other gods belong to another, lower level of being, a level of obsession with ego-identities that enslave and delude them; Viṣṇu is All, Being itself, but Being uniquely embodied in this singular, visionary form. Moreover, as such, hearing himself addressed as such, he arrives to save the helpless victim who has called to him anonymously. Like the *Bhāgavata* poet, Viṣṇu knows himself as the Absolute; knows, too, and accepts the devotee's demand for help from this absolute source. The long *stotra* leads into a metaphysical statement of direct relevance to the story's development. Yet this seam between the two segments of the story we are studying retains a certain tension, bordering on paradox, that informs the explicit message—for the move from the abstract claims of the *stotra* to the god's dramatic intervention in his standard iconic or mythic form is a progression from a somewhat detached monistic illusionism to a context of concrete emotional immediacy. Viṣṇu, in confirming his ultimate identity as *brahman,* seems almost to leap beyond the Advaitic premises of this equation into a world that is all too real, all too saturated with terror.

In any case, upon his arrival, Gajendra can now identify his savior by name: "Nārāyaṇa, universal guru, Lord," he cries in recognition, raising his trunk toward the god; the latter lifts both elephant and crocodile out of the pond and beheads the crocodile with his discus. "Thus Hari delivered Gajendra before the eyes of the gods" (3.33). The usual precipitation of heavenly flowers follows on schedule.

The Prehistory

What Purāṇic story is limited to a single lifetime? Both crocodile and elephant were living out their past. The crocodile had once been a *gandharva* named Hūhū, who was cursed by the sage Devala to assume this form. Released from the curse by being slain by Viṣṇu, he bows and returns to his own world. Gajendra, for his part, had been Indradyumna, the Pāṇḍya king and ruler of the Draviḍa land,[38] a great devotee of Viṣṇu whose very devotion had caused him trouble. Once the sage Agastya had visited the king while the latter was immersed in worshiping the deity and vowed to silence; since Indradyumna failed thus to honor the sage, Agastya cursed him to suffer darkness (in the form of an elephant, stubborn as he was—thus Śrīdhara). Although birth as an elephant normally destroys memory, Gajendra, by virtue of worshiping Hari, retained his (4.12).[39] Now, at the touch of the lord's hand, Gajendra is freed—not simply from the crocodile, but from the fetters of ignorance (4.6); he acquires the form of Viṣṇu, with golden garments and four arms, and joins the god's retinue.

One might imagine that the text is articulating an interesting conflict in this karmic excursus. After all, the Pāṇḍya king was only following the constantly reiterated recommendation of the *Bhāgavata* itself—to give oneself over to unrelenting *bhakti* that largely closes off the rest of the world—yet his devotion was rewarded by Agastya's curse, a seemingly clear-cut case of undeserved suffering. In fact, the text pays no attention whatsoever to this conflict. Its vision is directed toward the final, happy ending, which makes it all seem worthwhile: even a thousand years of battling a crocodile, to say nothing of the general state of becoming an elephant, are a small price to pay for what Gajendra eventually achieves. Passages such as this can easily convey the impression that the *Bhāgavata* presents us with a world without evil, since in the end every figure in the text is related to the god in a devotional pose of one type or another (including, of course, the by no means ineffective hostile relationships)—and that is what counts.[40] This view has much to commend it. Nevertheless, the *Bhāgavata* does have its own theory of evil as well as a sensitivity and empathy for intense suffering, as one can see, for example, in the horrific book 11. This is not the place to pursue this problem in detail; what emerges from the present example is a certain tendency to smooth the edges of potential conflict of this type, a tendency linked here to the suggestive theme of redemptive memory triumphing over the potential disaster of forgetting—for Gajendra, we are told earlier, carried the knowledge of his *stotra* over from his prior birth (3.1).

The Reward

The *phalaśruti* has two parts, joined awkwardly together. First Śuka, the narrator of the frame, assures Parikṣit that this story brings divine splendor, an end to the evils of the Kali Age, and release from nightmares to all who hear it. Then Viṣṇu magically reappears to announce to Gajendra that whoever remembers him, that is, Viṣṇu, or Gajendra, or the mountain or pool where this story took place, or a long list of other sacred items, will be freed from all evil; those who praise the god with this story will receive pure knowledge from him at the moment of their death. Note, once again, the emphasis on memory and its saving power.

Such are the essentials of the Gajendra story in this Sanskrit version. The actual narrative events are few and related with surprising economy; large parts of the text are taken up by the landscape description, the concluding *phalaśruti,* and the *stotra* that both forms its central core and helps to structure its key message. Let us now see how Potana works with this rich classical inheritance.

THE TELUGU GAJENDRA: BRINGING THE STORY HOME

As mentioned earlier, Potana follows his Sanskrit prototype very closely both in the basic units of the narrative structure and, to some extent, in verbal reproduction of elements drawn from the Sanskrit. We thus find the same progression of seven narrative segments that we have seen in the preceding section. Let us take them one by one.

The Frame

Śuka begins with the fourth *manvantara,* in which Hari, that ocean of compassion (18),[41] saved Gajendra from mortal fear. Parikṣit wants to hear more: any story in which Hari is mentioned is auspicious, to be listened to joyfully (21). This formulaic verse, repeated by the Sūta to the sages, leads immediately to the opening description of Trikūṭa Mountain.

The Scene

Here we observe a considerable expansion: lyrical description of the story's setting and of the elephants' play takes up twenty-eight verses (23–50), including a long prose passage, as befits Potana's *campū* style, which imitates the list of trees and aquatic fauna in the Sanskrit text. But this is no mechanical reproduction of the model. The setting has come alive in a new manner closely linked to the semantic burdens of the text. First, the stature and energy of the elephants, especially Gajendra, are magnified through a string of hyperboles that enhance the dimensions of the dramatic struggle about to unfold: the elephants issue from the mountain caves like all the darkness of the world, emerging at nightfall after hiding all day from the sun's light (27); the young elephant calves playing on the hills are fearless, unwilling to give way before lions, mountains, even thunderbolts (28); the powerful movements of the elephants' trunks and rut-filled temples turn mountains upside down and cause the universe to tremble (36). Gajendra, spraying himself with water, scatters crocodiles and crabs from the pool into the heavens, where they join the stars of the zodiac (47). The specificity of the natural setting is opened up and extended toward the limits of the Purāṇic mytho-cosmic map. But even more striking is the way in which the wilderness landscape is itself vitalized, eroticized, made sensually present with an immediacy never achieved by the Sanskrit text. If, as Parikṣit assures us in the frame-introduction, this is a story about God, then the primary feature that captures our attention as we move into the story through these early verses is the sensual profusion of the setting the Telugu poet has created for his narrative. Viṣṇu acts in the Telugu *Bhāgavatamu* in a world that enchants and fascinates the senses:

The body came alive
  at the touch of cool and gentle breezes,
  soaked with lotus scent;
the wild geese who live on lotus fibers
  murmured their perfect speech,
  a celebration for the ears;
the flowering water lilies and lotuses gave delight
  with their perfume
while parched tongues revived
  with drops of limpid water
  sprayed from the waves;
eyes rejoiced
  in a pristine radiance, new to the three worlds—

forgetting
  the daily working
  of all five senses,
that herd of elephants in rut
went down to the pond. (44)

Characteristically for Potana, still vitally connected to an oral-poetic medium, this verse is neatly and symmetrically divided, with a line for each of the senses; and, although the series is crowned with luminous vision, the more generalized sensations made present in the poem are olfactory and tactile, as we might expect—especially given the existential potency of smells in medieval South Indian culture.[42] This sensual quality is sustained throughout the entire episode, as we shall see.

And not without incorporating a strong erotic component (much more vivid and effective than in the isolated hints in the Sanskrit text): the bees—so often markers of eroticism in Indian poetry—drunk on the scent of the rut, which they are sipping with avid desire, vie with one another in bringing this delicacy to their female lovers (31); or the males nobly renounce their portion so that the females can enjoy it (33). The animal world is one of passion and, somewhat surprisingly, of mutual caring; it is also repeatedly and systematically correlated to female beauty. The grace of the elephants' walk exceeds that of young women; the full breasts of beautiful women hide within their saris, "shamed" by the round fullness of the elephants' temples; women veil their thighs after noticing the superior charm of the elephants' trunks, and so on (40).[43] More explicit still is a prose passage that, in fact, concludes this entire, descriptive section, summarizing its overall tenor in a series of paronomastically phrased images: the splendor of that pool, disturbed by Gajendra's entry, was like that of a woman whose ornaments have been violently disordered by her passionate and skillful lover; the bees that are her dark curls have been scattered, her lotus-face is drained of nectar, the lovebirds that are her two round breasts have been shaken from their place, the sands that are her hips have been trodden in desire (50). The picture, in short, is of a beautiful woman exhausted after making love. Enter, into this eroticized and sensually vibrant setting, the brutal crocodile.

Before we turn to the battle section, however, we may draw out certain of the implications of the transformation we have witnessed so far. First, there are striking continuities with a much older South Indian tradition, one that affected the Sanskrit *Bhāgavata* as well—that of classical Tamil love poetry, known as the "inner" category, *akam*. To see something of the connection, observe the following verses:

> Tenderly, the great elephant offered grass from the pool or newly flowering branches, still bright with buds, to his wives, dear to him as his very life; with his huge ears, cool from the flowing rut, he stood and fanned them, dried their sweat; softly, with love, he caressed their delicate necks with his trunk.

This, of course, is still Potana (39); verbally and thematically, the verse adumbrates a later one, to which we shall come in due course. Here (also in v. 49) the poet is elaborating upon the far more condensed Sanskrit statement:

> The compassionate elephant, like a householder, bathed his cows and the young calves and gave them water to drink which he drew up for them with his trunk; but, intoxicated by rut,

> deluded by the *māyā* of the lord, he failed to see the approaching danger. (2.26)

We have already cited the end of this verse—and it is, perhaps, significant that the transition to the next, violent scene is embedded in the same context of the elephant's family idyll. The Tamil author of the Sanskrit *Bhāgavata* may conceivably have drawn the image he uses from the corpus of classical love poetry, from examples such as the following:

> Tusks red and reeking
> from the tigers he has fought,
> pearls rustling at their base,
> an elephant caresses his mate and their calf
> with his long trunk,
> feeding them great mouthfuls of golden flowers
> from the honey-soaked, broken branches
> of the *veṅkai* tree on the hill,
> whose trunk he has smashed,
>
> here, in your father's
> wilderness,
> my love . . .[44]

As with Potana, the motif of the caring elephant nurturing his wife and child belongs to the wilderness landscape of Tamil poetry; indeed, the wild setting clearly provides an effective contrast to the gentle solidarity displayed within the elephants' nuclear family.[45] This is not the place to analyze the Tamil poem at length, although we may note in passing the striking combination of violent and gentle images. What does need to be emphasized is that Potana has not simply assimilated a familiar motif, which he then develops, on the basis of a single verse of his model, far beyond what we find in the latter text. The more important continuity is on the level of poetic technique. Consciously or not, Potana has refashioned the introductory descriptive section of the story in a manner reminiscent of the central principle of classical Tamil *akam* poetry—that of the suggestive correspondence of external, landscape features to an inner world of feeling and emotion.[46] The lyrical and sensual portrayal of the Trikūṭa Mountain and its pool now points directly toward the mood and themes of the central narrative segments of the text. Gajendra's struggle transpires within a world of luxuriant, overpowering beauty, in a landscape of passion and, perhaps most markedly, of loving tenderness. Liquid and mellifluous tones predominate both on the level of language and in the images the poet has selected. If something of this atmosphere already exists, *in nuce,* in the Sanskrit version, Potana has definitely given it far more vigorous and systematic expression. Moreover, we may suspect that the features we have outlined will be linked in the coming sections to the poet's underlying conceptions of divine modes of being and acting in the world.

The Struggle

I will not attempt to reproduce here the graphic and phonoaesthetic qualities of the battle scene. Suffice it to say that Potana again exceeds his prototype in both visual hyperboles and the powerful auditory effects he achieves. A long prose passage (55) shows us the two enemies struggling through their thousand-year contest, without food or sleep, alternating blows as night follows day—like two lions or two mountains entangled in hopeless conflict. We might pursue, for a moment, the leonine metaphor, which recurs in verse 62:

> He [the crocodile] leapt toward his temples
> like a lion,
> snarling, slashing at his feet,
> biting his neck, his back,
> snapping at his tail
> as if in play,
> pulverizing Gajendra's body,
> cracking his bones, his tusks,
> then falling back, only to strike again—
>
> while waiting, always waiting
> for the right moment
> for the kill.

One cannot help wondering if the choice of words conveys a designated irony—*hari,* the lion (both here and in v. 55) is also, of course, Viṣṇu's name celebrated at the opening of the episode (21; see above). As if to sustain this possible double entendre, verse 65, at the very climax of the struggle, presents a further ambiguity:

> Like a mighty yogi
> who plants his feet on the ground,

controls his breath,
subdues the madness of his five senses
and playfully, holding only to the power of the Supreme
without sorrow,
brings the creeping vine of wisdom
to bloom—
the crocodile stood firm, holding fast
to the elephant's foot.

The image of the lion, wholly absorbed by the crocodile in verse 62, seems to lead into other specifically Vaiṣṇava associations: the crocodile now stands before us (*vikramiñcĕn*), somewhat surprisingly, like the yogi who triumphs over his body and the world. The verb is suggestive, a derivative of Viṣṇu's classic root *vi-kram,* used to describe the god's ascent through the cosmos in the *Ṛg Veda* and his famous three steps (*vikrama*) as Vāmana-Trivikrama in the Purāṇic myth of Bali and the Dwarf avatar.[47] Note that in the Sanskrit version of our episode, it is Gajendra who attracts this verb (*so 'tibalo vicakrame,* 2.27; cited above)—a more natural association, perhaps, of the hero of the story with the deity who is to save him. In the Telugu text the root appears yet another time in the prose statement (64) immediately preceding the verse just quoted: the crocodile, fighting with immense power (*nirvakravikramambunan*), is like the darkness of delusion that extinguishes the lamp of understanding in the hearts of fools. So the yogic imagery works both ways, with the crocodile compared both to the successful and heroic ascetic and to the darkness that the yogi strives against—and also perhaps, implicitly, to the yogi's god, celebrated by this Purāṇa. In the hands of a more sophisticated and complex poet, these correspondences might take on a more significant load of suggestion: Viṣṇu's relations with the crocodile, indeed with death and violence generally, could create the basis for a rather different mythic reading of the tale. It is almost as if the poet were recalling the Vedic description of Viṣṇu as the "frightful beast wandering over the mountain, in whose three great steps all beings dwell" (*RV* 1.154.2). Were this the case, Viṣṇu would appropriately be seen not simply as Gajendra's rescuer but also as the source of the mortal danger from which he needs to be rescued! Such a view would certainly be possible in other South Indian Vaiṣṇava contexts—one thinks of Kampan's Tamil *Rāmāyaṇa,* for example[48]—but in Potana's text we have no more than playful hints in this direction, hints neither sustained nor developed to any degree by the poet.

The yogic imagery recurs at the end of the battle scene; Potana, taking up a single word from the Sanskrit text—*dehi,* the "living, embodied" elephant, seeing the danger to his life (8.2.31)—gives it a metaphysical turn: the flagging Gajendra fights on "like the soul (*dehi kriya*), a prey to doubt, unable to release itself from the entangling creeper of delusion wound around its feet" (67). Note the theme of doubt, which finds still stronger expression in the *stotra.* We might expect from this image, which bridges the transition to the hymn, that the yoga-style "intellectual" *bhakti* so evident in the Sanskrit text will be repeated with only minor deviations in Potana's account. But it is precisely here that the Telugu text presents us with its most unexpected surprises.

The Prayer

First, listen to Gajendra's decision to call for help:

> Why hang on to false hopes? I can never fight this crocodile on equal terms. . . What deity should I imagine? To whom shall I call? Who might intervene for me and stop this crocodile? Are there no auspicious gods, aware of all that happens, who could hear the cry of the distressed? To such a god I bow. For a long time I was the honored leader of herds of elephants, lord to thousands of elephant-cows; why did I have to come here to this pool, instead of resting in the shade of sandal trees watered by my rut? What will be with this fear of mine, O lord? (70–72)

One is immediately struck by the utterly personal and familiar quality of this inner monologue, in obvious contrast to Gajendra's rather formal speech in the Sanskrit version. Potana has followed the Sanskrit's pointed reference to the existence of "some god" (*kaś-caneśo,* discussed above) who could help; but this has become a negative rhetorical question, couched in colloquial syntax: "Are there no auspicious gods?"[49] Gajendra's entire existential stance vis-à-vis this important question is radically different from what we have seen in the Sanskrit *Bhāgavata,* as the further progression of the hymn will show. It is also difficult not to smile at the tone of exasperation and mild self-reproach that this so very human elephant adopts at this critical moment—why, after all, did he have to pick this particular pool? And then, at the very end of the verse, a real cry from the heart: "Lord, I am afraid." He is invoking a deity whom he desperately needs to be present—not an abstract principle remembered from the learning of a former birth, as in the Sanskrit model (although Potana also tells us in v. 70 that Gajendra is calling upon the divine wisdom that is the fruit of earlier merits).

After this personal and engaging beginning, Gajendra can now "revert" to the impersonal characterization of the god that we have seen to be the hallmark of his Sanskrit *stotra*. Many of the epithets he uses are lifted directly from the Sanskrit text: Gajendra bows to the god who externalizes the universe and reabsorbs it in himself, the flawless Witness, the *ātman* (74), playfully embodied, like an actor in many forms (76) but without birth, flaws, forms, deeds, epithets, or attributes, beyond words, knowledge, and thought (78), quiescent, conscious of the bliss of release, lord of *nirvāṇa,* the field-knower, ocean of compassion, the root of nature and the root of the *ātman* (79), visualized by those who have burned their *karma* in the fire of yoga (80) but unattainable by those who remain attached to their sons, cattle, houses, and wives (81)—and the god capable of suppressing the evil "of souls like me who have no other refuge" (81). All this and more is familiar to us from the Sanskrit source. But the most striking aspect of the Telugu version of the *stotra*—the element that makes it into a critical node of transformation—is the fact that these tones cannot be sustained beyond a certain point. As if determined from within by the poet's most profound intuition, another voice makes itself heard in the midst of this high-flown metaphysical rhetoric. This is a voice that speaks softly, intimately, with flowing feeling; that coaxes, teases, taunts; that comes alive only in a personalized relational mode.

> They say he exists
> wherever someone is in pain.
> They say he exists
> near all the greatest yogis.
> They say he exists
> everywhere in space.
>
> This one they say exists—
> is he really there
> or not?
>
> He who has neither being nor nonbeing,
> whom I doubt—
> won't he be there for me?
> He who acts to save good people
>   suffering from the wicked—
> won't he act for me?

He who sees those who see him
   without using their eyes—
won't he see the trouble I'm in?
He who hides himself,
   but who knows when even fools cry to him—
won't he hear my cry?

All forms are in his form,
without beginning, middle, or end.
He is near to his devotees
   and to those who are in pain.
Won't he hear me,
see me,
think of me,
won't he come
right away? (86–87)

It is difficult to convey in English the intimate pathos of the Telugu negatives: *vinaḍĕ, cūḍaḍĕ, talapaḍĕ, vega rāḍĕ*. Gajendra is speaking to someone close and beloved, someone he needs but whom he can also taunt with the simultaneously playful and pathetic notes of skepticism that suddenly emerge in these verses. This skeptical theme, which borders on a kind of emotional blackmail, intensifies as the passage progresses:

Everyone knows you hear what people say,
that you will go to the most inaccessible places
   to help them,
that, if they call to you,
you'll call back: "I'm on my way!"—
everyone knows you see everything there is to see.
Only I
now have my doubts,
great ocean of mercy! (91)

This verse follows a plaintive description of Gajendra's state: "My strength is failing, my courage gone, my body faint and weary; I know no one but you; shouldn't you forgive those who are in trouble?" (90). Clearly, the elephant knows whom he is addressing—indeed, one has the distinct impression that he has known him all along, long before producing the impersonal string of attributes at the start of the *stotra*. He has, in fact, visualized the god in his mind (89) and can now, in the final verse of the *stotra*, easily and naturally call to him by name: "O Kamalākṣa,[50] O Varada." And again, in conclusion, the sweetly intimate imperatives: "Won't you come now, have compassion; won't you remember me and save me?" (*rāve, karuṇimpave, talapave, śaranārthini nannū gāvave,* 92).

The hymn has taken a rather different course from that "prescribed" for it by the Sanskrit original. Despite the wholesale borrowing of epithets and terms, we hardly recognize the model in its Telugu reproduction—especially as the poem of praise reaches its culmination. The entire atmosphere has been transformed: Gajendra now appears to have been praying from the start to a close, familiar, wholly personal, and concrete divinity, a divinity whom he knows by name and whom he identifies without apparent difficulty or dissonance with the abstract epithets of the Vedantic absolute. His use of Viṣṇu's names—which would have been impossible in the Sanskrit *stotra,* given its investment in the impersonality of the elephant's address—merely symbolizes and finalizes a process that has been implicitly present from the opening words of the hymn. In the Telugu text, Gajendra's god is anything but remote; he is here at hand, a specific, named presence both accessible and intimately known. Such, in any case, is the sense conveyed as we move through the *stotra* to its conclusion, which most patently illuminates the essential transformation Potana has achieved. For corresponding to this basic change in the poem's orientation is a palpable distinction in the poetic tones that Potana employs: the "borrowed," Advaita-laden verses are, in effect, poetic failures, a withered root somewhat artificially transplanted into the Telugu text from its model; the poem is quickened back to life only when Gajendra moves into the intimate mode of query and personal demand.

Thus, although the "moral" of the Sanskrit juxtaposition of impersonal stotra and concrete personal revelation is retained in the Telugu version—verse 94 tells us that Brahmā and the other gods remained impassive in the face of the elephant's call, since they "do not comprise all," whereas Viṣṇu, who is all, responded—its point has, in effect, been superseded by the whole thrust and tenor of the passage. The hymn has already "personalized" itself to an extreme degree. There is no shock of recognition, on Gajendra's part or that of the reader/listener, when Viṣṇu appears on the scene; he, and only he, has been expected all along. In this way Potana smooths the problematic transition from *stotra* back to story and heals and harmonizes the disjunction that is so conspicuous (and so laden with meaning) in the Sanskrit original; at the same time, in failing to maintain the pretense of impersonality, with its consequent tensions, to the end of the hymn, he significantly reduces the role of the

Bhāgavata's Advaita metaphysics in the episode as a whole. Or, more precisely: the disjunction that largely generates the power of the Sanskrit hymn has here been transposed onto a different axis, suggestive of a different configuration of meanings. As we shall see, the atrophy of the Advaitic rationale is only one part of the change.

One should also note what is missing from the Telugu *stotra*. We have cited the verse that crowns the Sanskrit text, in which Gajendra suddenly shows himself to be primarily interested in release (*mokṣa*) and speaks contemptuously of his elephant's birth (8.3.25). There is no real parallel to this statement in the Telugu text. If anything, we feel that Gajendra wants to go on being an elephant, that what he fears is not the endless cycle of *saṃsāra* but the tangible, immediate danger of the crocodile's teeth. This omission is consistent with the general transformation of the *stotra* in the direction noted, away from monistic illusionism and toward the familiar, the sensual, the concrete.

But the most interesting aspect of this transformation—the aspect that, in my view, lies at the very heart of the Telugu Purāṇa's cognitive program—remains to be defined. It is not merely a question of blunting the force of the Sanskrit text's Advaitic ideology, or of softening the transition evident there between the story and its metaphysical moral. The gap between these two existing elements has not simply disappeared without trace. Rather, out of the intimacy and personal familiarity of the Telugu prayer, a new and unexpected chasm has opened up. Gajendra, in his "pathetic" skeptical mode, delineates the edges of this no-man's-land: Is Viṣṇu really there at all? Will he materialize in order to help his servant? Perhaps it is all a fantasy, this talk of rescue, a quixotic attempt on the part of the devotees to comfort themselves with a reassuring but unreliable promise of release from pain. Perhaps only the latter is truly "real." Not surprisingly, these questions and doubts, which Gajendra explicitly formulates, will have the effect of forcing the issue, moving the god to an action that will bridge the glaring gap. We may see them as a kind of riddling, reminiscent of the Vedic *brahmodya,* with Gajendra in the unlikely role of the doubting (and motivating) Nāstika. A new dynamism enters the poem at this point: the string of lifeless Advaitic epithets has ended up in a tantalizing empty space, an open gulf between devotee and deity that articulates, by its mere existence, an urgent demand. Movement is generated not out of certainty—the rationalizing metaphysics of the Sanskrit *stotra*—but out of the blackmail and pathos of personal doubt.

That we stand here at a significant point of transition was

clearly recognized by the Telugu folk tradition, which tells us that Potana, having composed the verses quoted above, suddenly became stuck. Unable to proceed, he left his house for a walk. While he was out, Viṣṇu himself took Potana's form, entered the house, and, before the eyes of Potana's daughter, completed the next verse himself. When the poet returned and, to his shock, found the new verse completed, his daughter asked him why he was surprised—had he not composed it himself in her presence? The poet, realizing what had happened, marveled at this gift to his child, who had seen with her eyes the deity whom he, the poet, had served all his life.[51] The folktale sensitively reenacts the textual dynamics at this crucial juncture: as in the case of Gajendra, so with the poet, it is now up to the god to act in order to fill in the gap. The very conditions of intimacy, in both cases, have produced an open "nowhere" space riddled with uncertainty; this is the real space that the god inhabits and out of which he can, perhaps, be coaxed or driven to appear. Where the Sanskrit *Bhāgavata* offers a clear-cut lesson, rationally defined and then enacted (but a lesson whose poetic force derives from a powerful disjunction), Potana, working in a mode of emotional and intuitive immediacy, restores something of the divine mystery and provides a technique for entering into it—by letting Gajendra challenge the god with his doubt, in the tenderly sarcastic tones of the riddle.

The Intervention

The verse allegedly completed by Viṣṇu takes us at once to the other side of the chasm—to the god in his heaven, Vaikuṇṭha, where he is busy arguing with, and also making love to, his wife Śrī. From this point on, the story, moving to its conclusion, assumes the form of an endearing, subtly comical, divine coitus interruptus:

> He didn't say a word to Śrī,
> didn't reach for his conch and discus,
> didn't call to his retainers
> or harness his bird,
> didn't straighten the long hair that fell wildly about his
>   ears,
> didn't even let go
>   of the end of his wife's sari
>   that he had pulled from her breasts;
> he simply rushed out, racing
>   to save that elephant's life. (96)

A prose passage characterizes the frenzied deity further:

> Thus Nārāyaṇa, always intent on saving his devotees, who resides within the lotus-heart of every living being, hearing the elephant's piteous cries, restrained his passion for his lover, Lakṣmī; agitated, he scanned the four quarters of space (in search of Gajendra), since saving him was now his one overriding goal. (97)

Note the insistence on the god's indwelling in every creature in the context of his arrival, as it were from outside, to help his devotee. We now have a picturesque parade as the various inhabitants of Viṣṇu's heaven—first Śrī, followed by the other women of the harem, Garuḍa, the god's personified weapons (the bow, Kaumodakī-club, conch, and discus), Nārada, Viṣvaksena, and then everyone else, from children to cowherds (98)—come rushing after him in disarray. But the poet's attention focuses on Śrī, alluring, disheveled, awkwardly abandoned *in medias res,* her sari still dangling from the hand of her husband as he hastens away; her earrings are madly dancing, her hair hangs loose around her shoulders, her full and heavy breasts are exposed, the auspicious dot on her forehead has been smudged (102), and—intensifying these images of charming deshabille—she is both curious and confused:

> He didn't even say where he was going—
> did he hear some helpless women cry?
> Have thieves made off with the Vedas?
> Has the army of the demons invaded heaven?
> Have evil people in mockery
> asked his devotees, "Show us your Discus-bearing god!"? (100)

She hesitates to question her husband—in any case, he probably would not answer (103). But her various hypotheses have the effect of elevating Gajendra's story to the level of several well-known mythic situations—Somaka's theft of the Vedas, the recurring danger of demonic attack upon the gods, and, most suggestively, Hiraṇyakaśipu's brutal and skeptical interrogation of his son, the devoted demon Prahlāda. The latter reference is particularly striking, a kind of "internal framing"[52] of the tale, since the story of Prahlāda and the Man-Lion avatar appears elsewhere in our text as one of its most powerful and elaborate episodes.[53] The beautiful goddess, in her alarm, thus effectively transports the story beyond its immediate context, situating it on a continuum of self-consciously connected vignettes of the deity in his relations with the world (or with the dispersed parts of his self); she also unwittingly makes an important point for the audience, listening outside the story, a point never fully articulated in the Sanskrit prototype: Viṣṇu will rush to the side of any devotee in distress with the same impetuous concern that he manifests in moments of crisis on a cosmic scale.

All of this is new, as are the tones of rich erotic commotion coloring the scene and the sensuous texture of the language used to describe the god's departure. Eroticism continues to inform the poet's imagery as Viṣṇu arrives at the pool and throws his discus at the crocodile: the fiery discus plunges into the water as if it were the Sun, intent on making love to the Lotus Lady hidden in that lotus pond (111). This metaphorical Death-in-Love is instantaneously effected: the crocodile, still suffering illusions of victory, is instantly beheaded; Gajendra is saved, "like the mind of someone without desire and thus detached from the misery of *saṃsāra*" (115)—a rather mild recurrence, though at a climactic moment, of the yogic ideology more explicitly realized in the Sanskrit.

And, literally, a final touch: the god himself lifts the elephant up with his long arms and gently fondles him, wipes away the streaks of rut on his body, removes his sorrow. At the touch of Śrī Hari's hand, all of Gajendra's pain disappears (118–19); and this moment of moving, tactile connection, almost palpably conveyed in the Telugu, continues for another verse, which gently concludes this section (and, in effect, the story as a whole) with a last, harmonious, tender scene harking back to the introductory lyric:

> Lovingly, the cows caressed him,
> alive by Hari's gift,
> drawing near to him
> to intertwine their trunks
> once more
> with his. (120)[54]

We are back in the domestic atmosphere of verse 39, discussed above with reference to the single Sanskrit verse from which it departs and the still earlier Tamil *Caṅkam* motif of the jungle elephants' family solidarity. Verbally, too, the later verse echoes the earlier one; the initial harmonies of the Trikūṭa landscape, temporarily rent apart by the crocodile's attack, have been restored, the trauma healed, the hero returned to the bosom of his loving wives—by an equally loving deity. Not by accident, the tale proper ends with a double caress.

The Prehistory and the Reward

The remaining verses (sections 6 and 7 of our division) follow the Sanskrit text with little variation. We learn the karmic conditions that helped to produce the story and the gifts to be gained by reciting it. There is a slight revision of the theme of memory, which we saw to be important to the Sanskrit text: in a short dialogue with Śrī, who has arrived breathless on the scene, the god declares that he forgets those who forget him, but remembers those who never forget this truth, and who call to him in their need (130). He asks his wife why she followed him—was it just to recover her sari? She answers in two beautiful verses:

Lord, what can I say?
My only task is to hold your feet
firmly in my heart . . .
It is only right that you
should hear the cry of the suffering,
that you should save them
and bless them,
for you, great god,
are in their power! (132–33)

The goddess offers another "moral," of a very different cast from what we saw in the Sanskrit version of the story: Viṣṇu, the divine hero of the text, is not only close to his devotees, wholly familiar to them and accessible at any time—he is also actually within their power. The devotee, as we know from other South Indian traditions, can control the deity of his devotion; in offering love, the *bhakta* puts the recipient at a certain disadvantage (as is generally the case in the South Indian theory of the gift).[55] Here this notion is extended a step farther, so that it is the weak, the suffering, the distressed who activate this power over their god; he cannot but respond to their call. But Potana, unlike the Śaiva poets, for example, shows no interest in developing this theme beyond the suggestive epithet he has chosen. His story is over: Viṣṇu, appropriately, embraces the impassioned, bedraggled goddess and takes her home (134).

CONCLUSION: A SOOTHING AND SENSUAL *BHAKTI*

It is time for us to sum up the major points of difference that have emerged from our comparison of the two texts. Ostensibly, the

Telugu text has reproduced its model with striking fidelity on many levels; in reality, we have been subtly but systematically transported into a rather different inner world. The means of transformation are primarily linked neither to the narrative itself nor to the explicit metaphysics that it conveys by literal, discursive statement; rather, they are embedded in the texture of the telling. The process is linguistic and stylistic, permeating the poet's choices—both lexical and syntactic—and consistently pushing him in a particular, characteristic direction. Let us try to define Potana's technique, with its specific semantics, linked to a specific vision of the divine in the world, by outlining a (somewhat abstracted) series of general features in relation to the Sanskrit "shadow"-text serving as model.

1. Potana's version of the Gajendra episode is softer, sweeter, more lyrical and liquid than the Sanskrit original. There is, so to speak, a significant semantic investment in the mellifluous. To some extent, this feature is, no doubt, an innate property of Telugu itself; but then there are Telugu poets (Tikkana, for example) about whom one could not make such a claim. Here gentle, flowing language embodies scenes of natural tenderness, both in the introductory landscape-lyric and in the climax of the story (the *stotra* and Viṣṇu's intervention). For all the terror of the central battle scene, the overriding tones of the text are gently reassuring.

2. The language of the Telugu version is also far simpler and more accessible than the arcane Sanskrit of the *Bhāgavata Purāṇa*. No traces remain of the anachronistic Vedicism of the latter work. Potana's poem may be seen as a prime example of Telugu Purāṇic style—at least as popular and easily intelligible as Purāṇic Sanskrit—as we find it from the fourteenth century on.

3. The enveloping atmosphere, embodied with astonishing consistency in the poet's language, has changed in the direction of the sensual and the physically immediate and concrete—and, of the senses involved, one feels the heightened role of the tactile. The story has acquired a near-tangible presence: the listener, no less than Gajendra himself, experiences the caressing touch of the god. In itself this effect represents a considerable triumph for the poet. Its roots lie, no doubt, in the Sanskrit original, with its introductory description of the luxuriant Trikūṭa setting; but Potana has maintained a sensual liveliness throughout the episode, including even the seemingly abstract and "intellectual" section of the *stotra*. Moreover, this quality intensifies as the *stotra* reaches its culmination and Viṣṇu enters the scene. The story transpires in a world made present to us, as the everyday world is, through our senses; the poet, far from apologizing for such a world, enhances the immediacy of its impact with all the devices he has at hand.

4. A further step in this direction is the gentle eroticizing of the narration. Here Potana clearly transcends his source. We have seen this tendency in the initial landscape (suggestively employed to create a new sense of the dynamics of the episode as a whole) as well as in its most dramatic expression in the section dealing with the rescue (Śrī's pursuit of her vanished lover; the erotic overtones of the crocodile's demise). Indeed, the effect lingers on even after the god's intervention, in the verse that reunites Gajendra with his wives. Note that this is, on the whole, a rather domestic eroticism, alive within the nuclear family (whether of the elephants or of Viṣṇu and Śrī). We are still a long way removed from the erotic immersion of, say, the Nāyaka period poet Kṣetrayya in the *kṛṣṇalīlā*. Potana's poetic eroticism is couched in a gentler mode, endowed with slightly comic touches, which does, however, presage the development of Telugu Vaiṣṇava *bhakti* in Annamācārya and Kṣetrayya.

5. The above features, together, have the conspicuous effect of healing the disjunction that gives the Sanskrit version something of its peculiar power. In general, the texture of the Telugu text seems to empty the Advaita metaphysics that it inherited of most of their force. In the context of so much sensual energy, it becomes harder and harder to maintain the seriousness of the *Bhāgavata*'s illusionistic message—unless we are to imagine a kind of tactile Vedānta, not alienated from everyday physical sensation and thus opposed to the classic ideology of yoga (if not, perhaps, to certain Upaniṣadic presentations of *brahman*). One hesitates to go so far as to assert that Potana merely pays lip service to the Advaitic explication so prominent in his source; but the strange incongruities of the Sanskrit *Bhāgavata,* mentioned at the beginning of this essay, are definitely harmonized and reduced in its Telugu descendant. The tension which so enlivens the Sanskrit original, and which depends on the poetic and intellectual vitality of its metaphysical sections, has been defused in the Telugu poem; and the apparent unity which the Sanskrit text affirms by consistently "translating" its stories into a rational explanatory ideology is achieved in Potana on the level of texture, through the tactile, familiar language of his *bhakti*. The development we observed within the Telugu *stotra,* where abstract and impersonal perceptions give way, without dissonance, to more concrete and familiar tones, is a cogent indication of the direction of change. On the level of verbal technique, we have seen how Potana fuses the elements of his narrative, removing the visible seams of the prototype. More generally, we might see the harmonious softness of Potana's work as smoothing the problematic transition—or the rift—between outside and inside.

6. Thematically, there are obvious consequences to this transformation. The explicit moral that we isolated in the Sanskrit—Viṣṇu's identification, at first unknown to Gajendra, with the Vedantic impersonal absolute—is exchanged in the Telugu text for a formulation of a different order entirely, one concerned with the god's dependence upon the suffering devotees who cry out to him. Similarly, the theme of release (*mokṣa*)—Gajendra's ultimate release—has lost something of its urgency; even if, in the end, the elephant acquires Viṣṇu's form, this result is achieved not by a turning away from the world or by the god's gracious willingness to demonstrate his unique identification with *brahman* but by the endearing skeptical taunts with which Gajendra badgers him. There is no question any longer of the elephant's miraculous retention of his pre-elephantine memory, which offers unexpected hope for his release; now it is the god, very much alive in the world, who either remembers or deliberately forgets. On the whole, the ironies of disjunction that infuse the thematics of the Sanskrit Purāṇa are either diminished or displaced (to the somewhat playful axis of the devotee and his god).

7. This process depends on a wider one of "bringing the story home." Perhaps the most signal new feature of the Telugu text is the familiarity and intimacy it establishes between Gajendra and Viṣṇu (and also, to some extent, between Gajendra and the listener—for the elephant has come alive to us in a new way that allows for empathy and identification). Gajendra speaks to the god with the knowledge of closeness, in tones appropriate for intimates, teasing him, prodding him, coaxing him to appear. Similarly, we hear the great goddess Śrī adopt the speech and inner dialogue of a young bride, embarrassingly deserted by her husband in the midst of their passion. The figures of sacred tale stand before us as breathing, essentially human realities (whether incarnate as elephant or god). Potana strives for the very opposite of a Brechtian *Verfremdung* or Shklovskian *priyom ostraneniya;* he endows a grandiose, semi-mythic situation with familiar flesh, bones, and feeling.[56] Admittedly, this process is taken only to a certain point, by no means as far as in the South Indian folktale transformations of mythic or epic themes, of which A. K. Ramanujan and Stuart Blackburn have written.[57] Potana's text is not a folk Purāṇa. Rather, it is a Brahminic, regional adaptation of a classical Sanskrit text, which, as such, seeks to domesticate its materials in one specific, generally harmonious mode. This type of "domestication" is not, as we shall see in a moment, the vernacular poet's only option.

8. Finally, perhaps underlying all the above features, there is a somewhat elusive and more intangible quality that pervades this text. We are clearly dealing not with a mere surface or formal transformation but with the emergence of a remarkably distinct and coherent universe of feeling. The change reflects a persistent quality that I shall call, with some hesitation, "innerness," and that corresponds precisely to what is perhaps the major message of this episode. We can sense this force in many ways—in the gentle, flowing tones so evident throughout; in the intimacy of the discourse, especially at the critical node when Gajendra addresses his god; in the soft sensuality that ultimately replaces abstract and impersonal metaphysics; in the explicit emphasis, at the very moment of Viṣṇu's appearance before Gajendra, on the god's existence within the living soul; in the harmonization of outer and inner realms of which we have spoken, and which contrasts with the apparent discontinuities of discourse in the Sanskrit *Bhāgavata;* in the domestic "at-homeness" of the story, and its draining away of tension; in the use of the external landscape scenes, at the outset of this episode, to suggest an inner world of emotion, as in classical Tamil *akam* poetics. If, following A. K. Ramanujan, we transpose the ancient Tamil opposition of inner (*akam*) and outer (*puṟam*) to the textual continuum of a later period,[58] then Potana has moved away from *puṟam* toward an *akam* mode very much his own, in which the inner quality is specifically correlated to the other features we have mentioned (softening, harmonizing, domesticating, sensual expressivity, and so on). Perhaps the most striking element in this move is the fact that the essential message of the text—that of the god's proximity, familiarity, immediate availability, his being, as it were, as close to us as our innermost, most intimately sensed reality—is, in fact, enacted by the texture, the entire linguistic creation, of the narration. Potana's language is to us as Potana's god is to Gajendra. It is not only syntax that contains, reflects, and effects the representation of reality, as Auerbach has shown in his classic study;[59] the Telugu text of the *Bhāgavatamu* realizes a coherent, specific vision through its texture.

How does this considerable transformation relate to the issue of composing a Purāṇa in fifteenth-century Andhra?

Before answering this question, it is important to observe that we are dealing with a distinct type of *bhakti*—distinct not only from that of the Sanskrit *Bhāgavata* but also to some extent from what we see in the Tamil Āḻvārs and Nāyaṉmārs. Potana depicts a relation between the devotee and his god that is ultimately harmonious, soothing, realized through sensual media, dependably close and constant—in short, devoid of tension and alienation. It may include skeptical tones, it certainly does not preclude suffering; but, all in all, it suggests a relationship nicely stated by the Tamil Nāyaṉār, Tiruñāṉacampantar:

> Whenever my heart is peaceful [literally, "cool"],
> I turn to you in joy.[60]

Of course, the Nāyaṉār's heart is by no means always "cool"; Tamil *bhakti* from the early, formative period (seventh century to ninth century) is filled with harsh, conflicted tones. One of the Tamil Śaiva poets, Cuntaramūrtti, even specializes in just such an angry, anguished, often alienated mode. Others, too, such as Nammāḻvār, feel tormented by their god's absence (*viraha*), to which they respond with urgent longing.[61] And this is precisely the contrast with Potana's *bhakti* as seen in the Gajendra episode, which celebrates, above all, the god's closeness and palpable presence. The Sanskrit *Bhāgavata* alleviates the agonies of *viraha* by measured doses of Advaita illusionism: thus, in the tenth book (the heart of this Purāṇa, describing Kṛṣṇa's birth and youth), Kṛṣṇa reassures the lovelorn *gopīs* through the mouth of Uddhava: "As the inner soul of all, I am never truly separated from you. . . I am removed from your sight only in order to bring your hearts near to me through meditation; women dwell more on an absent than a present lover" (10.47.29, 34–35). Amazingly, the *gopīs* are even said to be convinced and comforted by this reasoning (10.47.53)! Some of it, as we have seen, is retained in the Telugu text, but there the more profound development takes place on another level. The Advaita preachings are subordinated to the familiar and sensual re-presentation of the deity, whose absence has thereby lost much of its sting. Thus even one of the most famous *viraha* passages of the tenth book, the "Bee Songs" (*bhramara gītalu*) modeled on 10.47.12–21,[62] although couched in language clearly dependent on the Sanskrit verses, no longer conveys the same intense hopelessness at the god's unpredictable games of hide-and-seek with his lovers. The passage has become, as the poet states, a playful figure of speech (10.14.53). This illustration follows the general pattern we have been observing—two texts sharing, in part, the same words, with the same literal meaning; only a relatively minor adjustment, in several of the verses, of order and syntax—and yet, in the end, two different worlds. But Potana's reworking of the Kṛṣṇa story in book 10 is the subject for a separate and longer study.

In short, Potana presents us with a kind of *bhakti* that, in contrast with the early Tamil sources, is at once "emotional," open to the senses, but not rooted in separation. There is, however, an even stronger contrast, closer to home, from within the Telugu tradition itself. Potana's Purāṇa belongs to a period of Brahminic reaction against the militant *bhakti* of the Vīraśaiva poets such as Pālkuṟiki Somanātha, author of the twelfth-century *Basavapurāṇamu*. The *Basavapurāṇamu* is a violent and angry work,[63] and much of the violence in which it delights emerges out of the complex relations between the devotees and their deity. Here it is not unusual for the fanatical devotee to excommunicate his own god, or to abuse him verbally, or to vow never to let Śiva win against him, even in a dream! And yet this text, too, often "domesticates" the deity, brings him into the realm of the familiar, of the household and family relations. There is, for example, Bĕjjamahādevi, who decides to become Śiva's mother (and thus to cure him of his unkempt appearance and extravagant habits); she is stubborn enough to force the god in his temple image to accept her decision and to nurse at her breast.[64] This is only one example out of many. But one can sense even from this simple summary that the Vīraśaiva experiments with "domestication" follow a different logic from Potana's, a logic of ironic intimacy, rich in subtle tensions (between god, symbol, devotee). A large gap divides this antinomian, heterodox Vīraśaiva Purāṇa from the symbolic and semantic universe of the fifteenth-century Brahminic Purāṇic texts.

Thus when Śrīnātha, Potana's contemporary in the eyes of the tradition, composed his *Haravilāsamu*—a Brahminized and Purāṇicized version of Śaiva materials drawn, in part, from the *Basavapurāṇamu*—he followed a path similar to Potana's. The story of Ciruttŏṇḍanambi (Tamil Ciṟuttŏṇṭar)—one of the most gruesome of South Indian Śaiva myths, in which the devotee is made to kill and cook his own son for Śiva's dinner[65]—appears in the *Basavapurāṇamu* in appropriately lurid form; Śrīnātha, even while verbally appropriating parts of that text (as Potana does from the *Bhāgavata*), manages to refashion the story in a shockingly calm and harmonious direction. We are familiar by now with this kind of transformation, which is even more extreme in Śrīnātha's case. The tradition rightly associates these two fifteenth-century poets; for all their differences, which are substantial, both are part of a more general process of Purāṇa making in Andhra. In both cases we can see mechanisms of adaptation and assimilation that bring diverse materials into conformity with the late medieval, vernacular Purāṇic structure. Moreover, this Purāṇa making is itself one of the major diagnostic signs of a wider process of rearticulating the Brahminic order in post-Kākatīya Andhra. This wider process is still poorly understood, although we can see certain important features—the redrawing of the cultural boundaries by deliberately excluding challengers such as the Vīraśaivas, a process always accompanied by the assimilation of texts and concepts and by their transformation; the political situation of diffusion and fragmentation, pressure from the Muslim power of the Deccan, and a concomitant cultural shift toward the paddy-growing centers of coastal Andhra, with their Brahmin settlements (*agrahāras*)—although Potana himself belongs to Telangana; the creation of a new, regional sacred geography structured around the great Brahminic shrines, which now produce Telugu Purāṇas giving classical form to their local mythology and cult (here again we find Śrīnātha active as the author of the *Bhīmeśvarapurāṇamu,* on Dakṣārāma); the internalization, both institutional and intellectual, of the Tamil *bhakti* inheritance (both Tĕṉkaḷai and Vaṭakaḷai Vaiṣṇavism were vigorously propagated in Andhra from the late fourteenth century) and the production of a new theological literature of *bhakti* in Sanskrit (Vallabhācārya, fifteenth century). Clearly, in this essay we have been looking at the tip of the iceberg—at the refraction of a much more profound movement of social and intellectual reorganization in the tonality and semantics of a single prominent text. This movement remains to be studied in detail; for now, we may complete our analysis of one microcosmic epitome by summarizing those features of textual transformation in Potana that are directly relevant to the crystallization of the fifteenth-century Brahminic Telugu Purāṇa.[66]

Unlike the Sanskrit *Bhāgavata,* and utterly unlike the Vīraśaiva hagiography, Potana's Purāṇa harmonizes, unifies, defuses tension and disjunction (while still allowing for their presence on some level, e.g., in the survival of illusionist rhetoric in the context of sensual and emotional *bhakti*);[67] it domesticates and makes familiar, though in a manner distinct from that of the Śaiva poets; it simplifies language, softens contours, soothes us with its particular brand of devotion to a present, accessible deity; it absorbs the listener into the text through identification with the audience within the dialogic frame (thus making the story immediately present and also wreaking havoc with the listener's everyday orientation in time);[68] it reduces irony and dissonance, integrating and assimilating diverse voices within a single subsuming order; and it ranks and hierarchizes the elements it thus incorporates and that it seeks throughout to organize and arrange—in this case with reference to the poet's primary vision of a personal and intimately experienced god. The apparent incongruity of Advaita Absolute and concrete mythic embodiment gives way in Potana to a hierarchy that "rises" inwards, stabilizing the perceived universe from this projected inner center, which is identified with the wholly personalized and present god. The drive to order and define in this manner fits well into the general Purāṇic pattern (in Sanskrit as well as the regional languages); the striking difference here is that the poet has produced this Purāṇic order not out of folk or other disparate materials—as is more often the case in this period—but rather from a classical Sanskrit text that purports to be, despite its unusual character, a "Great Purāṇa" itself.

7

Information and Transformation—Two Faces of the Purāṇas

Friedhelm Hardy

One of the lesser known Jesuit missionaries who worked in South India during the late sixteenth century and early seventeenth century was the Portuguese Gonçalo Fernandes Trancoso (1541–1621). In a period of intense interest in "adaptation," namely, evolving a life-style in conformity with Brahmin values, he composed (during 1616 in Maturai) a treatise on "Hinduism" as a contribution to this discussion. Naturally the emphasis is initially on how Brahmins are supposed to behave; but eventually he does turn to matters of belief: "the things Brahmins are obliged to confess and to profess about the creator of the universe."[1] Without much ado he provides under this heading an account of "two Purāṇas of Sūta,"[2] and in the subsequent section he tells us "what about the same matter is said in the Purāṇa which they call *Brahmāṇḍa Purāṇa,* in its first chapter."[3] Obviously a religious life without definite views on the creation of the world, and its creator, is unthinkable to our Jesuit missionary. We can imagine him, during his many years in South India, importuning his Brahmin informants with these matters so central to his native view of religion. When he then provides altogether four[4] different accounts of the Hindu creator and of creation, as the outcome of his researches, we may well sense a feeling of frustration at this apparent lack of interest in a fixed doctrinal system. But for the moment I would like to draw attention to the social setting: here is a man interested in religious matters who asks the learned men of South Indian society: who created the universe? And they reply:

> When all the *ṛṣis* were performing a sacrifice which lasted for twelve years, a disciple of the *ṛṣi* Vyāsa arrived, whom they called Romaharṣaṇa (which is to say: a man who by means of the extraordinary ancient stories he narrates causes the hair to stand on end)... And all the *ṛṣis* gathered around the said Sūta Romaharṣaṇa with intense desire to listen to many stories, surrounding him on all sides... Then they spoke to him: "You have heard from the mouth of the sage Vyāsa the ancient stories about the gods, due to which you know everything... Please tell us some ancient stories about the gods."[5]

While the Jesuit missionary asks a theological question, he is given passages from the Purāṇas in reply. Not only that: the Purāṇas themselves duplicate the question-and-answer situation, with the *ṛṣis* consulting Sūta.

> These *ṛṣis* spoke to him [when he had narrated various ancient stories]: "Those Purāṇas speak equally about Brahmā, Viṣṇu, Rudra, the Sun, the Moon, the Fire and the Wind. This being so—about whom among them should we say that he is the creator of the world? For were we to say that all of them are the creators of the world, nothing could be created and nothing could be done, since one will always oppose another and each will want to create different things—and we do see that the things of this world derive from one single design..." To this Sūta replied...[6]

Thus not just the external situation of question and answer is duplicated but also the great variety of possible answers. It is precisely this variety that puzzled the *ṛṣis*, just as it must have confused Father Fernandes. Now in the answer that Sūta provides we hear:

> He who is regarded as universal lord must possess a very cheerful appearance and must be splendid like the sun and the moon; he must not be born and must not die. Finding himself without a world, he created it, and in conformity with [their] merits and demerits created the noble and ignoble castes [*castas*] and made all other things: he abides in the heart of all—such a one will be the lord of the universe.[7]

This now introduces a rational element into the seemingly random narration of the "ancient stories": somewhere it all has to make sense, and criteria for this making sense are provided. And this is obviously what our missionary wants: a rational basis for discussion.

That such a view of the Purāṇas is not self-evident can be shown from the writings of another missionary. The oft-quoted Abbé Dubois states:

> To Vyasa is also attributed the authorship of the eighteen Puranas. These are eighteen poems, all equally futile, containing most minute accounts of Hindu mythology with its gods and heroes. The fables contained in them are responsible for the gross forms of idolatry practised by the Hindus.[8]

No wonder then that the same author, when talking about beliefs, ignores the puranic discussion and makes up his own theology around the concept of the *trimūrti*.[9]

> In short, we find in the Hindu books [Purāṇas] a mere tissue of contradictions relating to the *Trimurti,* and the absurd details which are related in connexion with each are even more inconsistent. The point on which they agree to a certain extent is that which relates to the excesses and abominable amours of the three divinities composing it.[10]

What has been my purpose in exploring these perceptions of the Purāṇas presented by two missionaries? My intention has been to extricate from all this a conceptual framework, with the help of which it might be possible to attempt something like a global exploration of this literary genre. The points I would like to abstract from the observations made so far are as follows. First, the "ancient stories" are not random products of some over-fertile imagination; they function in a specific social context—the question-answer situation—as providers of information desired by a particular kind of intellectual curiosity. Second, an element of critical self-awareness, coupled with a decidedly rational approach, appears in the stories themselves. Taking both points together, one could venture a characterisation of the Purāṇas as providing, through a rational interpretation of past events, information (and that is the same as meaning or significance) for a present situation in the form of stories.

So what is novel or useful in this? For example—to mention here first a random minor detail—this kind of characterization allows us to solve a formal dilemma, something that has given a bad headache to the text-historical scholars. When we open a book that presents itself as the *x-Purāṇa,* for many pages we encounter people asking someone about that same *x-Purāṇa.* And only when, say, two cantos' worth of episodes have been told, does the actual "text" begin. But in view of the program suggested here, these introductory two books need not be discarded as "later interpolations." They can in fact be regarded as information about a particular social context that acts as the intellectual constraint upon the ancient stories as told in later portions of the text. This frame and all the subsequent interruptions in the narration are essential for the self-understanding of the Purāṇas as traditionally handed down discussions.

Much more important than such a formal matter is the problem of interpreting the stories themselves. The program suggested here would not treat them in isolation (or line up similar ones for comparative purposes) but would explore the significance of such a story individually in relation to a specific intellectual (that is, rational) discussion—our question-answer situation.

To link the interpretation of Purāṇic material with some external constraint is nothing new. For instance Rösel, in a very idiosyncratic and provocative piece, reflects on the local myths he collected in Puri.[11]

> My servant reported that every time when he met a different priest at the Rohini-Well, he was told a different story about its sanctity. Length and ornamentation of the individual story varied according to the amount of Dakhina paid. This last remark I consider the really decisive one. In the following analysis of the stories, the reader must constantly keep in mind the situational aspect. To tell stories is one of the most essential services provided by the Pandas [temple priests in Puri]. The form of the story told by them now depends on two things: the wish of the priest to provide as much entertainment as possible, and not to allow his colleagues and rivals to find out about his version of the story.

It is clear from my previous remarks on intellectual context that I would prefer to trace a less cynical line of constraints on Purāṇic storytelling than Rösel does. But when he remarks, obviously with reference specifically to the situation in the temple of Puri, that "stories are not literary objects, but social processes" and that "the individual temple, shrine or tree becomes valuable to the pilgrim only through a meaning-imbuing story,"[12] this is in full agreement with the conceptual framework pursued here. By now we are clearly moving away from an understanding of the Purāṇas as definite literary works, in the direction of situationally controlled oral processes and their individual literary expression.[13]

This kind of story is thus not an objective, fixed entity: it is an element in a live event. Consisting of innumerable individual situations, this process imposes many different constraints on the narration of a story. This in turn means that even when a variety of such stories can be recognized as "essentially the same story," the variation itself is a controlled affair. In other words, the Purāṇas do not just provide a fixed type of immmutable information but transform their raw material in the process. At least indirectly the texts themselves acknowledge this by referring us, through sometimes very lengthy strings of narrators who tell what they heard from other previous narrators, to some primordial storytelling event, and by having different individuals pick up the same story. Moreover, the whole process is labelled *smṛti*—transmission through memory. However, *this* aspect of transformation will not be central to my discussion; instead, another aspect has to be unravelled upon which the emphasis will lie. The question-answer situation, which is assumed here as the primary context of Purāṇic narrative, tends to imply that he who provides the answer (by drawing on the primordial story material) is in some sense authoritative. This creates no problem as long as the information he provides refers to something that lies outside the questioner's own miniature cosmos. However, the question could well concern something known by, directly relevant to, and already in some form meaningful for, the person asking the question. Given the authoritative status of the narrator, it now becomes possible that the kind of answer given actually reinterprets, namely, transforms, the view of the world held by the questioner. In other words, Purāṇic narrative becomes ideological.

Let me summarize the program as it has emerged so far. I propose to look at the production of Purāṇic stories as a process aimed at providing information desired in specific contexts by means of a specific literary form. Provided that this process carries on as a live affair, it has a definite historical dimension, in that the story material undergoes transformation, and an ideological aspect, in that the specific story might transform a previously held worldview.

This now implies that what is presented here as the Purāṇic process has to be envisaged as operating on two levels. On the one hand we have a continuous production of literary texts—the fall-out products of the process—crystallizing in written form as the *x-Pur-*

āṇa. At this point the text may develop a history of its own (through interpolations and so forth) or may become totally ritualized.[14] On the other hand, the live process of narrating Purāṇic stories continues in accordance with its central premise: to provide continuously meaningful information for specific situations.

What is the purpose of this exercise? My intention in setting up this kind of conceptual framework under the banner of the two key ideas of information and transformation is to investigate to what extent it allows us to bring together disparate material in the enormous field of Purāṇic literature. The degree of insight it might yield into the nature of this literature will depend on the range that can be accommodated.

The two faces mentioned in the subtitle of this paper imply no exclusivity. The Indianist needs no reminding of Brahmā's four or five faces or of Skanda's six, or Rāvaṇa's ten! Thus I would not claim that the present exploration of the constraints upon individual Purāṇic narratives is essential in all contexts. To treat the stories in their own right, comparing different versions, listing various recurrent themes and motifs, exploring deeper levels of symbolism—all these are possible further faces. To provide entertainment or to allow the narrator to make a living similarly are further constraints not directly connected with the function of imbuing meaning. My aim here is to emphasize the rational, historical, and social dimensions, in order to counteract judgements and implicit assumptions that Purāṇic materials are "irrational," "contradictory," "meaningless," or "merely expressions of the subconscious" (or even, for that matter, ahistorical and immutable primordial mystical insights).[15]

Let me now apply my program to some concrete material. I shall start with fairly straightforward examples of Purāṇas providing information in particular situational contexts. Inevitably I choose as a starting point the area I am personally most familiar with, the South Indian Vaiṣṇava temples.[16] The pilgrim to a particular temple is faced with a great variety of specific features, which, by themselves or by comparison with similar items in other temples, arouse his curiosity: How did Viṣṇu get here? What are the special virtues of this locality? Why is milk used in the daily *pūjā?* Why is the god called "thief"? These and many more questions are in the minds of the curious, and the *pūjārī*s, as part of their job, along with the (Sanskrit) *sthalapurāṇa*s and the more modern Tamil adaptations of the latter, provide the answers. Inevitably this will be given in the form of a story referring to a past event. But at the same time, the information provided thereby is more than merely factual: it wants to imbue the present, in that particular situation and often with reference to other Vaiṣṇava or even Śaivite or Devī temples, with religious meaning and thereby to stimulate devotion. A randomly chosen example (from the *Nāthaṉ-kōvil-māhātmya*) may illustrate this.

When Indra was fighting with Vṛtra, Vṛtra began to win. Indra in despair approached King Śibi, who was famous for the protection he offered to those who sought refuge with him. Promptly Śibi set out to fight with Vṛtra and managed to kill him. The gods gratefully offered him a boon, but when he chose liberation, they had to confess that that was a gift they were unable to make. Instead they directed him to the town of Śrīnivāsa, where Viṣṇu was residing as Nandinātha. Under a pipal tree to the west of the temple, he engaged in worship. After a hundred years Viṣṇu indeed turned the temple round, so that he himself and the entrance door now faced west, to grant Śibi the fulfilment of his desire.

"Factually" this story explains why the statue is facing west (unusual by comparison with other Viṣṇu temples) and why Viṣṇu here is looking at Śibi (all temples have statues of one or more sages, kings, etc., who are looking at the main *arcā*). In addition, the past event is meant to illustrate that powerful grace abides here; consequently the text adds: "And looking at Nandinātha and circumambulating him, even sinners can find here freedom from their evil (*pāpa*)—how much more can the virtuous expect here!" (III, 52).

What it is that triggers off curiosity and questions varies enormously with the individual text and context. Essential in any case are: an explanation of which circumstances made Viṣṇu settle permanently in the place, how he acquired his local name, and whom he is facing (*pratyakṣam*). However, this mode of providing meaning for concrete features can go much further than commenting on isolated items. Sometimes very complex structures, incorporating dozens of such features in one overall coherent narrative, are created; in the case of large and famous temples like Śrīraṅgam and Veṅkaṭam, the items may be counted in the hundreds.

We may ask whether this is a way of understanding reality that is totally at variance with our own. We might pride ourselves that we would choose a "historical" explanation instead. So let us turn to the following example, namely, the *sthalapurāṇa* of TirukḰaṇṇamaṅkai. The actual narrative jumps backwards and forwards in time, through various emboxed stories. But when we plot the events narrated on a time scale, we realize that a logically coherent historical sequence of causes and effects is presented here.

In the Kṛta Age, the central lotus pond (*puṣkariṇī*) arose in the print left by Vāmana's big toe in the earth, filled with the water from

Brahmā's vessel. This lake then revealed its extraordinary powers by purifying Candra after he had committed adultery. It then attracted Brāhmī, the sage Markaṇḍeya, and Kāśinātha Śiva. After the churning of the ocean, when Lakṣmī had fallen desperately in love with Viṣṇu, she settled here to perform *tapas* in order to obtain him as her husband. Viṣṇu arrived here in his celestial chariot (*vimāna*) and gratified her desires by marrying her. Brahmā asked them to abide permanently in the place, and Śiva took on various forms to protect the territory (*kṣetra*). In the next Age, Purūravas performed a sacrifice here and recited Viṣṇu's names; Bhṛgu worshipped here during the following Age. Finally, in the last Age, King Caṇḍavarmā [and with him we might be dealing with resonances of history] bathed here and purified himself from the crime of drinking alcohol in a prostitute's house.

Thus, at least in principle, a historical mode of thought is also implied in this type of Purāṇic material. The ancient stories told are definitely perceived as referring to real historical events;[17] thus I prefer to use "story" here and not "myth." To use "myth" prejudges the whole issue, quite apart from the fact that this would force us into a scholastic discussion of how to define "myth." For our purposes it is sufficient to talk about information derived from past (that is, historically perceived) events for the present.

But it is not just the temple that appears as a situational constraint upon the story. When the merchant Samādhi and King Suratha had found refuge in a hermitage from the tribulations of their worldly lives, and the sage had offered them an interpretation of their personal situation by reference to the all-pervasive activities of Mahāmāyā (the Great Power of Illusion), the king asked: "Who is that goddess you call Mahāmāyā?"[18] This should be characterized as a theological question; yet the answer is provided through the three well-known stories in which she allows Viṣṇu to kill Madhu and Kaiṭabha and she herself kills Mahiṣa and Niśumbha. What the goddess did in the past defines her nature, and a religious world is opened for Samādhi and Suratha in which they find the fulfilment of their own ambitions.

How much further can we pursue this? It would obviously be highly interesting to see whether this Purāṇic mode of providing information is typically Hindu or not. Well, it is not. With only one small modification we can describe Jaina and Buddhist material within our present conceptual framework. This modification consists in a far greater emphasis on a series of past lives firmly concatenated through the rational laws of *karma*.

Such a Jaina participation in the Purāṇic process may serve

merely to interpret traditional Hindu material through a Jaina model. So we hear (in the Jaina *Kahakosu*) how Brahmā acquired his five heads: He was doing *tapas* in order to win worship among humans; an *apsaras* named Tilottamā was sent to destroy his store of energy, and while she was moving about in her dance, Brahmā grew heads in all directions—the one facing upwards being that of a donkey. This Hindu story is told to show "that even mighty beings like Brahmā are ruined by attachment to women"[19] (a point of view shared by Hindus and Jainas). Another story tells us how, as a result of the *tapas* performed by Rohinī, the Yamunā river chose a different course and is now flowing north of Mathura.[20]

A story[21] about Kartikeya, in the same corpus is more complicated. Disgusted at being the son of his own grandfather (Agni), he turned ascetic. Rain created a lake around him when he was performing *tapas,* and "anybody bathing in it has his diseases destroyed."[22] Later he met his sister and was suspected of incest with her by her husband, who wounded him mortally. Since he died with an attitude of forgiveness, "he who worships him gains merit (*puṇya*)."[23] His sister was thrown into a state of utter depression at the death of her brother. Her husband tried in various ways to console her but succeeded only when he had a folk-actor impersonate Kartikeya so that his wife could talk to him. "From that time originates the festival of *bhāuāi.*"[24] Thus three features are explained here: the origin of Kartikeya worship; the sanctity of a particular [unspecified] lake; and the custom of celebrating annually the festival (called *bhāiyādūj* or *bhāīdūj* in Hindi and *bhāubīj* in Marathi) to which a married woman invites her brother and treats him lavishly with food and presents. Now a comparison with a Sanskrit parallel version[25] reveals that these three specific explanations are absent there, which suggests that this particular reading of the story of Kartikeya is original to the author of the *Kahakosu.*

So far our examples have dealt with material of Hindu origin. But typically Jaina stories can be used equally well in this manner. Thus the *Karakaṇḍacariü* tells us that during a military expedition King Karakaṇḍu (a famous *pratyekabuddha* of Jaina legend) arrived at a particular Jaina temple. Various peculiarities aroused his curiosity, and a sage whom he questioned narrated to him past events about the place that can be regarded as a *sthalapurāṇa* of Terāpura.[26]

Buddhist literature also illustrates our Purāṇic process. To demonstrate this I turn to the *Mahāvastu,* a Mahāsāṅghika work from India that belongs to the Lokottara tradition. Its bulk deals with a partial life-story of the Buddha. Various incidents in his life aroused the curiosity of the disciples of the Buddha, and he narrated "past stories" (*jātakas*) to demonstrate how the present circumstances make perfect sense in view of former events. For example: Why is Yaśodharā so fastidious and difficult to satisfy? Now Jātakas are narrated to show how this is a consequence of events that transpired during past existences of Yaśodharā. A comparison of these Jātakas with the corresponding ones in the Pali tradition reveals that there they are told in a totally different context and have nothing to do with a former existence of the Bodhisattva's wife. Thus these stories represent raw material, which is utilized here in an original manner.[27] Moreover, it is possible to identify the actual constraint that motivates this specific reading of the stories. Māra, the god of lust and passion, is in this work the central antagonist[28] of Gautama, and Yaśodharā as a woman is logically drawn into this cosmic dialectic, to appear in a far less favorable light than in the corresponding Pali tradition.

Such references to past existences are by no means restricted to Jaina and Buddhist Purāṇic material. King Suratha worshipped the goddess and succeeded in being reborn as the eighth Manu Sāvarṇi;[29] and it is that life that motivates the inclusion of the *Devīmāhātmya* into the *Mārkaṇḍeya Purāṇa*. A more fully developed example can be found in the *sthalapurāṇa* of TiruNakari. Kardama, one of Brahmā's sons, was suffering from a curse: he was to be born on earth during the four Ages. He asked Viṣṇu for help, but Viṣṇu replied: "This curse you are suffering is due to your *karma,* and I cannot grant you liberation now in the Kṛta Age. But in the fourth Age I shall grant you liberation."[30] So he was reborn first as a Kṣatriya king named Vasu, then as a Vaiśya named Vairamegha (who also became a king).[31] Finally, in the Kali Age, he was born as a Śūdra—none other than the Vaiṣṇava saint TiruMaṅkai-Āḻvār, who is worshipped in a side shrine within the temple of TiruNakari, his home-town.[32]

This may suffice to illustrate initially how the concepts of "information", "situational control", and "rational constraint" could be applied to a variety of Purāṇic or quasi-Purāṇic material.

Let us turn now to a further Jaina example taken from the same *Kahakosu.*[33] The intention of the story is clear: it is meant to explain how the worship of Śiva's *liṅga* came about and what the Hindus are up to with this cult. The account is conceived of on a large scale, and we must follow our heroes through various past existences, as a *vidyādhara* couple happily married, as gods in the Saudharma heaven, and finally as Prince Sātyaki and Princess Jyeṣṭhā.

Two royal children were betrothed to each other, but due to a trick of the girl's younger sister, they never get married and become ascetics instead. One day the nun seeks shelter in a mountain cave during a shower and meets her Prince Sātyaki. Their brief union results in the birth of a boy, later to be called Svayambhū and then Rudra, "the vicious one."[34] Informed about his origin by his foster-mother, he becomes an ascetic. One day he sees the eight daughters of a *vidyādhara* king (who had been ousted from his rightful kingship by his own brother) bathing in a mountain pool. Rudra helps their father to reconquer his lost city, Tripura and, as a reward, is given the eight girls in marriage. Alas! His passion is so violent that none of the girls can bear it and they all die. Subsequently, many other girls are given to Rudra in marriage, but each suffers the same fate during her wedding night. In despair the king gives him Umā as wife. She is a widow whom unrestrained physical desires have made a libertine. But the passion of her second husband, Rudra, satisfies her. After this success, Rudra becomes very boisterous and travels the world shouting: "I am the creator and destroyer of the world."[35]

Then he composes the Śaivite scriptures in Bhāratavarṣa and, promulgating them, acquires many followers. His tyranical nature begins to trouble the *vidyādhara*s and they scheme to kill him. Through trickery they find out that only while engaged in making love with Umā is he defenseless. So on one such occasion they succeed in cutting his head off [and presumably that of Umā as well; see below]. But his *vidyās,* who have not been consulted beforehand, create terrible calamities in the whole land. A sage named Nandiṣeṇa knows the remedy: "Cut off Rudra's *liṅga* (penis) and place it upon Umā's *yoni* (vagina); then worship the *vidyās* with gifts, to propitiate them. If you do that, the calamities will cease."[36] The king follows this advice:

> He called all the people of his realm, and built a high platform of bricks. He cut out Umā's *yoni,* that singular mine of sexual delights, and placed it on the platform. Then with effort he placed in its center Śiva's *liṅga.* He bathed it and anointed it with sandal-paste and perfumed it with masses of fine-smelling substances. . . Then the *vidyās* resumed their attitude of forgiveness, and that was the end of the people's afflictions. From that day has originated the shameless worship of the *liṅga* by people.[37]

Our initial reaction might be to characterize this passage as a stark distortion of Hindu Purāṇic material and a rejection of Hindu religious practices. But why should we do this? If we did not possess the corresponding Hindu versions, and if we were to look at the passage summarized above without its Jaina ideological frame, we would be in no position to talk of "distortion." It is only because we are already familiar with the Hindu side that we can regard the Jaina version as a transformation.

From this we can derive a rather interesting question: are the Hindu versions of the Purāṇic material more "objective"? As long as we treat "Hinduism" as one undifferentiated whole, and, moreover, as long as we possess no material with which we can contrast it, this must remain a question without an answer. However, during recent years material has been discovered that can be used for such contrastive comparisons (alongside an increasing realisation that "Purāṇic Hinduism" ought to be differentiated from other forms of Hinduism). So I shall present a rather random selection of examples by means of which we may be able to grasp further facets of the transforming functions of the Purāṇic tradition.

Still remaining with the Jainas, let us look at the figure of the first *tīrthaṅkara,* Ṛṣabha. In Jinasena's *Ādi Purāṇa* this sage has been presented as the originator of many features found in the contemporary world of South India; he appears there as a kind of culture-hero.[38] Soon after Jinasena (who died ca. 845 C.E.), a Hindu Purāṇa, namely, the *Bhāgavata Purāṇa,* which was composed in the same South Indian environment, takes up the theme. Here (book 5, chapters 1 to 6) Ṛṣabha is presented on the one hand as a descendant (in the fifth generation) from Manu and, on the other hand, as an incarnation of Viṣṇu himself.[39] This example clearly illustrates an aspect of the transformatory function of the Purāṇic tradition.

The same *Bhāgavata Purāṇa* offers us further illustrations of this process. There is another South Indian tradition that has been preserved independently from this text, namely, the Tamil poetry of the Āḻvārs. I have shown in detail elsewhere[40] that in many instances this Purāṇa actually translates or paraphrases stanzas of that poetic corpus. Here I shall briefly single out two features where the transformation undergone in the text is perhaps particularly striking. There is, first of all, the figure of the deity who is the object of *bhakti.* With the Āḻvārs, it is perhaps best to name this deity Māyōṉ, "he of black complexion." This is a composite figure (in terms of the Sanskrit traditions), in so far as Māyōṉ combines aspects of Kṛṣṇa and of Viṣṇu. The *Bhāgavata* accepts this situation to some extent; thus its metaphysical position could well be described as a form of Kṛṣṇaite Advaita. On the other hand, the basic literary model for the Purāṇa is the *Viṣṇu Purāṇa.* Here we find Kṛṣṇa treated unequivocally as the avatār of Viṣṇu (a precise formula that is absent in the Āḻvārs). Given that Śrīvaiṣṇavism follows the *Viṣṇu Purāṇa* in its conception of Kṛṣṇa, we need not be surprised to find that the *Bhāgavata Purāṇa,* and even the Āḻvārs, were increasingly read in this sense. The *Bhāgavata*'s recourse to the classical *Viṣṇu Purāṇa* thus initiated a process of major theological transformation.

A second point concerns the specific type of *bhakti* cultivated by the Āḻvārs. This form of devotion, which I have styled *viraha-bhakti,* implied (in my reading of the poetry) some form of differentiation and autonomy of the full person experiencing it.[41] The *Bhāgavata Purāṇa,* which must be given credit for taking over this type of devotion and making it available to the rest of India, imposed on it a metaphysical framework that sees even in the most ardent separation of the *gopī*s ultimately no more than Kṛṣṇa's own play, "as a boy plays with his own mirror image."[42] Moreover, the *bhakti* of the Āḻvārs oriented itself very centrally according to poetic symbols (thereby keeping it within a specific, live cultural context); in the *Bhāgavata* it is totally mythologized, above all through the mythological symbol of the *gopī*s. However, this transformation of poetic into mythological symbols is a process noticeable already in the later Āḻvārs themselves.[43]

From Kṛṣṇa we may turn to the goddess. Here we find ample material to illustrate another form of transformation imposed on independent religious material through the Purāṇic process. Thus the *Devībhāgavata Purāṇa,* by an extraordinary *tour de force,* reinterprets material within the Purāṇic tradition itself. Relatively few new stories are told about the goddess; instead the Purāṇa tries to demonstrate how in the well-known events of Purāṇic mythology (which deals almost exclusively with the male *deva*s) the working of Devī (as egoism, delusion, craving, and so on) is hidden. Then in book 9 (which has a very close parallel in the *Brahmavaivarta Purāṇa*) the transformatory process is also applied to a large number of other *devī*s, at least some of whom, we may assume, figured in the actual religious life of the time as independent, autonomous objects of worship.

The *Devībhāgavata* is by no means unique with its reinterpretation of traditional Purāṇic material from the point of view of an autonomous Devī religion. Thus, for example, the *Bṛhaddharma Purāṇa* also offers us illustrations of this:

When Rāvaṇa was creating havoc from his island of Laṅkā, Brahmā approached Viṣṇu for help, suggesting that he be born as King Daśaratha's son. Then the two of them went to Pārvatī, who emitted from her body a goddess who had eighteen arms and was surrounded by eight further *devīs*. The two gods worshipped her and confessed that they had a problem: Rāvaṇa was her devout *bhakta* (devotee), and thus they would not be able to kill him. The Devī devised a scheme by which she would be able to withdraw herself from Laṅkā and thereby enable Viṣṇu (as Rāma) to kill the demon. The birth of Viṣṇu and the other gods on earth took place, and for a time the story follows traditional lines. Then Brahmā arrived on earth and discovered a young girl asleep on a leaf of a *bilva* tree. He sang a hymn in her praise: "You are the Śakti in Rāvaṇa and Rāghava, and you are the pure power in Rudra, Indra, the other gods, and in me, too."[44] But since he had awakened her "at the wrong time for the sake of Rāvaṇa's death and for favoring Rāma," he made another vow: "We shall worship you on the new-moon day in conjunction with the lunar mansion *ārdrā,* until you have killed Rāvaṇa. Then we shall dismiss you."[45] The goddess agreed to this and told them what she would be doing during the next fifteen days, while at the same time specifying what people should do—every year—during those same fifteen days. Rāma then performed her autumnal *pūjā,* which ended with him killing Rāvaṇa on the last day.[46]

The passage clearly wants to do more than just extoll the greatness and autonomy of the goddess: it wants to provide significance for an annual event, *Durgā-pūjā,* by means of the past events it talks about. The situational constraint on the narrative, which means the motive for the transformation of traditional material, is quite apparent here.

There are other aspects to this process of Purāṇic transformation. For the Jaina side we have already seen the example of a blatant distortion: the worship of the *liṅga* was explained in a definitely inimical, ideologically biased manner. Can we now find similar examples in the Hindu Purāṇas that document a loss of essence, of integrity, through such a transformation? If so, this would yield insights into the ideological function of the Purāṇic tradition. I shall suggest two cases here, where the availability of parallel but independent material allows us to highlight a particular aspect of that ideological bias.

For the first example we can remain in northeast India, where we find the cult of the *devī* Manasā. There are basically three independent traditions that provide us with information about her: some late, northeastern Purāṇas (the *Brahmavaivarta Purāṇa* and the *Devībhāgavata Purāṇa*); folktales narrated during the *Manasā-vrata;* and a literate tradition of *Manasā-maṅgal*s. The simplest case is that of the *vrata*-story.[47] Here the existence of the goddess Manasā is taken for granted, as is that of her eight sons; but there is no reference to a father or a husband, two characters who are pivotal in the literary tradition of the *Manasā-maṅgal*s. A large number of works in Bengali, Assamese, and Bihari, covering a period of at least three or four hundred years, have been produced on the basis of some kind of common core (which need not have been a written text and which is not available to us). Smith has compared a number of such *maṅgals*[48] and produced a kind of synopsis of the common, but individually developed, themes. Three such areas are worth mentioning.

The first theme, which is extremely fluid and variously developed, is that of creation. Smith comments: "Some of the Manasā poets, as well as many dealing with Caṇḍī and Śiva, regularly refer to their works as *Purāṇas* and, well aware of the Sanskrit parallels, made conscious efforts to pattern their work upon them. As a description of creation was one of the traditional components of a Sanskrit *Purāṇa,* an attempt was made to imitate them in this."[49]

Not much more common ground is found in the treatment of Manasā's father, the second theme. Śiva's seed is frequently made responsible for her birth, but there are other suggestions, too, in some authors. We may presume that this dependance of Manasā on Śiva is secondary, given the autonomous existence she displays in the *vrata*-story, and given that she is able to kill Śiva and bring him back to life at will! Smith comments: "By being assigned the role of Śiva's daughter Manasā was given a direct familial link with the central figure in the popular Bengali divine hierarchy. Śiva's enormous popularity, his status as both a textual deity and a powerful local agricultural god, made such a connection not only desirable, but inevitable."[50]

The third, and perhaps the most interesting, fluid area is that of Manasā's marriage. There are at least three totally different versions of this, but in any case the marriage does not work out. Her ex-husband plays no role in the main body of the *maṅgal* literature.[51]

What these three fluid complexes have illustrated is the fact that here the extant *maṅgal* literature approximates the Purāṇic tradition (using many Purāṇic figures and motifs in the process)—halfway between an autonomous Manasā figure and what we actually find in the Purāṇas. Here we are told that the sage Kāśyapa created her out of his mind (thus her name, "Manasā") to protect the world from serpents. By performing *tapas* towards Śiva and then worshipping Kṛṣṇa, she managed to acquire supernatural faculties. Married to the irascible sage Jaratkāru, her function was restricted to giving birth to a son, Āstika. Her husband abandoned her.[52] Nothing is left here of Manasā's rôle and dignity as it is found in the popular, vernacular religious traditions associated with her. Male gods and sages have taken over, producing or abandoning her at will: she has become a mere woman. . . In this context we can return to Smith's remarks: "The compilers of the Purāṇas must have been aware of the Bengali myth but chose to ignore it. Their accounts are almost totally purged of folk elements and are of little help for our understanding of the popular goddess and her cult. One of their greatest values is what they can tell us about the way in which the compilers transformed their materials when they incorporated them into the Purāṇas."[53]

For our second example we have to go to Maharashtra where we find the goddess Yellammā. Again our sources are threefold: poems in rural Marathi dialect, *sthalapurāṇas* from her two major temples, Māhūr and Saundatti, and—through the identification of Yellammā with Reṇukā—the Purāṇas. Here again we can distinguish three different attitudes (or historical stages?) towards the status of the Devī. Some of the popular Marathi poems suggest a totally autonomous goddess-figure: unmarried, childless, in full control over gods and demons. Even here she is indiscriminately called Yellammā or Reṇukā. Like the Goddess of the *Devīmāhātmya,* she makes her appearances in the world of man, to be challenged by the established authorities (even if this is merely a gardener or a British colonial officer) and to be given blatantly impossible tasks to fulfil. Naturally these stories end with Yellammā winning, taking her revenge on the opponents, and rewarding the faithful with her blessings. Sanskrit phrases which characterize Yellammā as "primordial power," "veil of delusion," and so on, are interspersed into the narrative poetry. Such language offers further pointers towards her perception as autonomous deity.[54]

We find other poems in which Yellammā has a son, called variously Parsu, Parśarām, Parśurām. It is this son who creates trouble for her and challenges her authority. One of the problems is that the son is "fatherless" (a swearword implying illegitimate birth). This is how she explains it in one poem: "When Śiva's daughters had gone to play, I gave my blessings to those six girls. For that I received you from them, without a husband, when I asked them for a child. Thus I have no husband, and you no father."[55]

Finally, there are poems[56] that treat the subject very much along the lines of the Purāṇas. Reṇukā was married to the irascible sage Jamadagni, who imposed an impossible task on her. Since she failed in it, the sage ordered Paraśurāma to cut off her head—which he did. (In an altogether different popular Marathi tradition it is the male god Kāḷ-Bhairav who manages to subdue her when she has treated all other male gods in the most humiliating manner.[57]) Here we have reached a situation identical to the Purāṇas' depiction of Reṇukā: a powerless female, married to a cruel and irascible sage, famous merely for her son Paraśurāma.

The sthalapurāṇa material introduces further interesting variations. In one poem on Saundatti,[58] after Reṇukā has killed the local demon, she asks her son for water: "'I am feeling so thirsty, my son! Before anything else, refresh me with water.' Parśarām shot an arrow and brought the Ganges up from the Pātāla (underworld). 'Drink this water, mother!'"

The *sthalapurāṇa* of Māhūr[59] begins with the conventional account of Reṇukā's marriage to Jamadagni, the birth of their son Paraśurāma, and the theft of the Wishing-cow. However, now a new story line begins. The sage is killed by the king, and Reṇukā is mortally wounded. After killing the Kṣatriyas, Paraśurāma places a yoke on his shoulder, with the corpse of his father in one of the containers hanging from it and his mother in the other one. He wanders through the country until he comes to the hermitage of Dattātreya. There he cremates his father, and his mother commits suttee. Later she rises from the ground there; this is the origin of the temple of Māhūr.

This whole process of transformation, controlled by the need to provide specific information, has revealed itself as possessing two dynamic directions. We may choose as our starting point classical standards, which means assuming that there are objective, fixed archetypes (like "the" story about Rāma). The various examples discussed so far would then suggest that the Purāṇic process constantly transforms these by localizing them. Whatever significance is asked for and perceived to exist in the classical models is applied to specific, local situations. The clearest example we have encountered so far is that of the *Durgā-pūjā* prevalent in northeast India. On the other hand, we may choose as our starting point the most restricted, localized milieu available. Now we find that the Purāṇic process is busy transforming this by providing much wider confines and by creating far larger contexts. This may be described as "integration," but could also be called "distortion," depending on what ideological yardstick one uses. It is a most versatile process, which may be illustrated somewhat further by focusing directly on the aspect of regionalization.

The visitor to a South Indian Vaiṣṇava temple is confronted with a stone sculpture (usually a figure in one of four standard poses: standing, seated, reclining, or walking) and a specific name given to the figure portrayed (say Padmanābhan̲ or Maṇavāḷan̲). To the superficial observer (and that includes the more popular books on India) this would signify no more than: a temple in which Viṣṇu, or one of his avatars like the Man-lion (Nṛsiṃha), is worshipped. But such a view does not do justice to the actual complexities of the perception of the Śrīvaiṣṇavas themselves. To them there is something unique here, already indicated by the name given to the deity. This uniqueness derives from a specific past event that took place in that particular spot. The conventional way of the *sthalapurāṇas* is to say that some sage who encountered Viṣṇu when the latter was busy executing a particular task asked him to abide permanently in that place. The stone image is no less than an externalized presence of Viṣṇu in that particular locality, deriving from a particular event in the past. Similarly, the specific name of the *arcā* in a given temple may at first glance be obvious, for example, when we find a lord of thieves (*coranātha*) or a milk thief (*kṣīracora*). O yes, we may say, that will be Kṛṣṇa in his aspect of butter thief, and we might leave it at that. But consulting the *sthalapurāṇa,* to our surprise we find that the name is derived from a totally different event, specific to that locality. It may be that Viṣṇu assisted a local band of pious brigands, turning "robber" himself (as in Śrīvaikuntam);[60] or it may be that Kṛṣṇa "stole" from the milk used in his daily *pūjā* so that the sage could taste it (as in Remuna, Orissa).[61] Maṇavāḷa inside the famous temple of Śrīraṅgam is not Vāsudeva reclining on the serpent in the milk-ocean, as the iconographic type of the *mūrti* might suggest. He is in fact the eternalised Rāma resting on his march towards Lanka and looking with longing towards the island where his Sītā is held captive.

This contrast between the classical or pan-Indian and the localized, incidentally, corresponds to an area of misunderstanding between the classical Indianist or philologist and the anthropologist—a disagreement that prevails even today.[62]

Having encountered minute local universes of meaning (an individual temple connected with unique events), we must turn round and follow another trend, namely, that into wider realms. In the Toṇṭai region of Tamil Nadu we find a large number of Nṛsiṃha shrines, which continue as far north as Ahobilam in Andhra. In a sense they are all discrete universes; yet when we read the *sthalapurāṇa* of (Vaiṣṇava) Kancipuram,[63] things are envisaged differently.

Once upon a time Nṛsiṃha and the demon Hiraṇyakaśipu were fighting with each other. While the demon produced replicas of himself from each drop of his blood, Nṛsiṃha did the same from the hairs of his mane. Thus a large area became filled with battling replicas of the main antagonists. The gods exclaimed, when witnessing this, ". . . *aho balam* [what strength!]" Finally Nṛsiṃha put the demon on his lap, tore up his body and killed him by drinking all his blood. This event has been eternalized in Ahobilam, where nine Nṛsiṃha shrines are scattered over the mountain.

Now, the demon had eight ministers, who fled towards the *Satyavrata-kṣetra* (Kancipuram). Nṛsiṃha raced after them; during his pursuit he had to rest for one second (*ghaṭikā*), and that produced the temple in Cōḷaciṅkapuram or Ghaṭikācala (ca. 100 km northwest of Madras). Meanwhile the demon ministers had hidden in a cave, but the Man-lion's roar made them flee deep into the Pātāla underworld. Nṛsiṃha decided to abide in the cave permanently, to prevent them from coming out again. (This is the shrine inside the Varadarājapperumāḷ temple complex in Kancipuram.) Now Brahmā arrived to perform a sacrifice in order to have a direct vision of Viṣṇu, but other demons tried to destroy his sacrifice. Nṛsiṃha in the cave took on a second live form and chased them away towards the west, settling there to keep them away from the sacrifice. (This is the Kāmāsikā shrine, still in Kancipuram.)

What we find here is an area stretching almost 250 km from north to south, which is provided here with a coherent explanation of the presence of twelve Nṛsiṃha shrines in it. What is particularly interesting is the conceptual mechanism by means of which this is carried out. While one would be inclined to describe the classical avatars of Viṣṇu theologically as manifestations of the eternal in space and time, here we would have to add that moments of this temporal manifestation are, in turn, eternalized in space and matter (the *arcā* in the temple). Behind this stands—in non-Purāṇic discourse—the Śrīvaiṣṇava theology of Viṣṇu's desire to be available to as many people as possible, in the here and now of the concrete world.

This supralocal integration that I have described for Nṛsiṃha may transform classical mythology about the Man-Lion but could not be regarded as a distortion of the significance of each of the temples involved. Let me briefly turn to another, well-known example where this is not the case. It seems legitimate to assume that many Devī temples constitute their own independent and autonomous universes of meaning. The famous story of the dismemberment of Satī serves as a supraregional construct, to integrate such local centers of Devī worship. Using this schema, for example, Maharashtra presents itself as possessing "three and a half" such *pīṭhas*. But obviously this type of interpretation is highly ideological: eternalized remnants of Satī's body are the center of worship of a married woman totally subservient to the grand male god Śiva. Thus it is not surprising to find that in the *sthalapurāṇas*[64] of such *pīṭhas* other past events are referred to that are less distorting to the local religious cosmos. For example, three different stories are connected with Kolhāpur. The first is the well-known myth about Devī killing Mahiṣa, an event localized directly in this place. The second talks about the demon Kolhāsur, who worshipped Mahālakṣmī (the name of the Devī in this temple) so that she would leave him alone for a hundred years. After this period, during which he committed endless crimes, the goddess returned and killed him. Finally we hear that Lakṣmī (Viṣṇu's wife in heaven) was cursed to turn into an elephant cow (in revenge for her jealous curse of a young girl). She descended to earth, performed penance at the *Garuḍeśvara-tīrtha* (part of the Kolhāpur temple complex), and was released from the curse. While we find here other features that distort the role of Mahālakṣmī in the Kolhāpur universe of meaning,[65] they are less obtrusive than the Satī myth.

I hope that by now enough material has been collected to attempt a more systematic assessment. The situational constraint has presented itself increasingly as the asking for and obtaining of information (the religious significance) with reference to very specific, local or regional, socially well defined contexts (the universes of meaning). Whatever may have been felt about the usefulness of our initial concepts of information and transformation, this further narrowing down may well appear very questionable. It might thus be objected that most of the material adduced so far is of a rather ephemeral, tangential nature when looked at in the context of Purāṇa studies. A more brutal objection might point out that by using primarily *sthalapurāṇa* material we can hardly be surprised when we end up again with locally oriented Purāṇic processes. I would like to make three observations here, in answer to such objections.

First, it appears possible to trace sthalapurāṇa feature also in the better-known Upa- and even Mahāpurāṇas. The *Kālikā Purāṇa* is certainly very much concerned with the worship of the Goddess in Kāmākhya.[66] The *Brahmāṇḍa Purāṇa* incorporates a very lengthy *Lalitā-māhātmya,* which concerns Kāmākṣī in Kancipuram. The *Devībhāgavata Purāṇa* is probably a product of Benares and localizes the Goddess in that town.[67] Even the famous *Devīmāhātmya* might have its regional focus.[68]

Second, I am not sure whether the relative antiquity of some of the *sthalapurāṇa*s is fully realized. There is evidence to suggest that (in some form, some of the) South Indian Sanskrit sthalapurāṇa are products of a period prior to the thirteenth century (though later than, say, the eighth).[69] But, in a sense, all of this is no more than window dressing, even if we can thereby make inroads into the classical Purāṇas. So, third, let me explore a more fundamental question.

Does it make any sense at all to ask what the original intention of the Purāṇic literature could have been? Well, at least a partial answer is suggested by the work of Kirfel. This scholar has suggested that three ancient repertoire pieces of the ancient Purāṇic bards can be isolated: the *purāṇa-pañcalakṣaṇa,* the *bhuvanavinyāsa* and the *śrāddhakalpa.*[70] In the extant Purāṇas, certainly the first two tend to be found together. Kirfel is by no means suggesting that he has reconstructed anything like an original core of Purāṇic literature; for the text he prints is differentiated into various recensions. In fact it would be a misunderstanding to read his material backwards, as it were. The whole layout looks forward in terms of textual history, pointing at an ever-increasing complexity of the Purāṇic literary process. Thus it is not surprising that other scholars have pursued this line of investigation further by tracing the process, for specific themes, in the direction of the present.[71]

It is perhaps no accident that the work of Kirfel and Hacker has been ignored by precisely the most vociferous advocates of an ahistorical approach to the Purāṇas. But something else is vital for our purposes. Not only does text-critical scholarship show itself capable of looking forward and describing organic religious processes; this is also the intention behind at least two of the repertoire pieces identified by Kirfel. The accounts of creation and the structure of the universe, of primordial world history and the Manus, lead up to what must have been the present at some time: the kings in the old Āryavārtā. The past is generally used to imbue the present with meaning and, besides, to provide very specific information. This is how I would venture to interpret the *lakṣaṇa* of *vaṃśa* (lineage). In the course of time those endless lists of kings and so on lost their relevance (since they do not seem to have been updated), and theism appropriated the now obsolete genre.[72] Where matters could be subjected to empirical tests, at least sometimes adjustments were made in the course of the transmission history—a remarkable testimony to the rationality of the tradition![73]

With this insight in mind we can now go much further. Thus it seems possible to interpret even the Buddhist text of the *Mahāvastu* as a Purāṇa in the sense stated. Primordial world history and cosmography leads to the Buddhas of the past, turns to the *rājavaṃśa* (lineage of kings) and culminates in the life of Śākyamuni, the culmination, as it were, of history. As we have seen above, the past is further appropriated, in the form of many *jātakas,* to interpret *this* life and, we can add, to read it in the light of contemporary questions and views.

Similarly with the Jainas. Here the texts present themselves as Purāṇas: *Ādi, Uttara, Mahā-, Śrī-* and so on. Spread out before us is a history of the world, culminating in the last of the Tīrthaṅkaras, the Mahāvīra. Sequences of rebirths overarch this history (particularly through Marīci, a contemporary of Ṛṣabha, who was reborn as Tripṛṣtha and then became the Mahāvīra). That this presentation occurred under specific circumstances has been pointed out above.[74]

I hope these considerations are sufficient to make my program less ephemeral than it might have appeared at a first glance. By looking first at concrete material that is close to us and that allows us to gain clearer insights into the Purāṇic process (catching it, as it were, in the act), it may well be possible to abstract more general principles that can then be applied to the study of the ancient texts.

Now it should be obvious that little more has been achieved so far than to suggest that our program might actually prove useful. Many tasks have to be left undone here that would be essential for a more substantial treatment of the subject. I shall simply list some of these.

1. To talk about a Purāṇic mode of providing meaning implies that there are other such modes. In the case of South Indian Śrīvaiṣṇava literature, it appears that the *sthalapurāṇa*s do indeed represent a tradition that differs from other types of discourse.[75] The theologian would justify the usage of Tamil by the Āḻvārs by saying that Viṣṇu wants to make himself available to as many people as possible. The Purāṇic justification involves a story about Agastya.[76] Or a pun might explain a particular iconographic peculiarity. Why is the *cakra* in the "wrong" (viz., right, instead of left) hand of the Viṣṇu of TirukKōvalūr? To demonstrate his *dakṣiṇa* (right, benevolent) attitude.[77] Or, in a modern setting, "Why does Kṛṣṇa have a blue complexion?" a lady at a conference asked an Indian *svāmi.* "To symbolize the infinity of the blue sky," was his prompt reply.

2. At least for South Indian *sthalapurāṇa*s, a differentiation in terms of symbolism and intention for the Vaiṣṇava and the Śaiva material seems likely.[78] This would probably have far wider ramifications, in the light of which a generic concept like 'Purāṇic process' might well reveal itself to be very naive.

3. The Purāṇic ideology has been treated here mainly with reference to the erosion of autonomous religions of the goddess. Surely there will be many further such ideological aspects.

4. Far more information ought to be gathered about the actual mechanics of transmitting the Purāṇic tradition. I am thinking here not just about the history of individual texts but also about the Paurāṇikas as a professional group in which learning is passed on to the next generation.

5. Practically no attention has been paid to the innumerable vernacular translations of the main Purāṇas. It would be interesting to explore similar situational constraints on the rewritten versions.

6. Finally, the history of the process itself ought to be investigated further. Are we dealing with major, recognizable periods and fashions? How long can we assume the process to have remained alive? On the latter question it seems possible to give a simple answer: the process is still continuing. In 1985 the Swaminarayan Hindu Mission celebrated a "Cultural Festival of India" on a grand scale in London. One of the highlights of the festival was an exhibition called "Cradle of Civilisation," which "portray[ed] the evolution of Indian culture, commencing with the Vedic era and concluding with the modern era, in 63 breathtaking tableaux."[79] The first scene showed the syllable *oṃ,* symbolizing the creation of the world. Then we moved through the ages of the Vedic sages, the *Rāmāyaṇa,* the *Mahābhārata,* and the *Bhāgavata Purāṇa* to arrive at scenes with famous medieval theologians and poets. At "No. 39," questions about the "meaning of life" were asked, and the remaining scenes provided the answer in the form of an account of the life of Swaminarayana (1781–1840) and his spiritual lineage. Scenes 41 and 42 were particularly interesting from the point of view of the Purāṇic process: as a child, the saint displayed superhuman powers by reviving a fisherman's catch of fish and throwing it back into the water; some time later, the boy was attacked by a demon named Kalidutta in the dark forests, but a mere flicker of his glance defeated the demon.

Let me sum up in a few words the suggestions that have been made here. A program for exploring the Purāṇas has been put forward that envisages a historical process of transmitting and imposing meaning, from the past into the present, through a particular mode of discourse (the Purāṇic) and operating within rational constraints. This process is indirectly documented in a series of texts (themselves of different degrees of solidification and fixation) and, more directly, in the very continuity of the process of producing such works. Behind this dynamic activity lies the acknowledgment of a need simultaneously to make localized concrete environments meaningful and to expand these limited horizons (integration, pan-Indianization). The meaning as derived from the past and presented through stories has ideological functions that may erode the autonomous situations upon which the stories comment. But this erosion is counterbalanced by the readiness of the Purāṇic tradition to transform its own premises constantly and not to insist on some absolute, objective account of the past.

III.

From Hindu to Jaina and Back Again

8

An Overview of the Jaina Purāṇas

John E. Cort

The Jainas have been prolific composers of Purāṇas, primarily in Maharastri Prakrit, Apabhramsa, Sanskrit, and Kannada. A list of all the known Jaina Purāṇas would total about several hundred. Within such a vast body of literature, there is of course a great range in quality and popularity, and over the centuries only a few of these Purāṇas have remained important for the Jaina tradition. Unlike the Brahminic Sanskrit Purāṇas, which are anonymous texts composed by many hands and mouths over many centuries, and for which sometimes there seem to be almost as many recensions as manuscripts, for the Jaina Purāṇas we can assign specific authors and dates of composition. This paper is intended to serve as an introduction into this vast literary corpus for those unfamiliar with Jaina literature, and to suggest some areas for fruitful future research. After first outlining the different subgenres within the body of Jaina Purāṇas, I will look at the distinctive features of the Jaina Purāṇas in order to present an internal definition of a Jaina Purāṇa. While this paper does not attempt an explicit overall comparison with the Hindu Purāṇas, a close look at the nature of the Jaina Purāṇas can shed light on much of what is distinctive about the Hindu Purāṇic tradition.

THE JAINA PURĀṆAS IN JAINA LITERATURE

The oldest stratum of the Jaina Āgama (their canon) consists of the eleven Aṅgas.[1] The Digambara Jainas claim that all of the canon was lost except for a small section of the *Dṛṣṭivāda,* the twelfth Aṅga, dealing with the doctrine of *karma,*[2] and so deny that the texts preserved by the Śvetāmbaras are the original texts with those names. The Śvetāmbara Mūrtipūjaka Jainas say that all of the *Dṛṣṭivāda* was lost but claim that their versions of the Aṅgas are the original versions.

The postcanonical texts of both the Śvetāmbara and Digambara traditions are called *anuyoga*s (expositions), although this term is used primarily by the Digambaras. The *anuyoga*s are divided into four categories. According to the Digambaras, these four are: *prathamānuyoga,* the exposition of the lives of famous and exemplary Jainas, intended for the laity; *karaṇānuyoga,* the exposition of technical matters such as metaphysics and cosmology; *caraṇānuyoga,* the exposition of mendicant discipline; and *dravyānuyoga,* the exposition on philosophical matters such as ontology, epistemology, and psychology. The Śvetāmbara terms for the same four categories are *dharmakathā, gaṇita, caraṇakaraṇa,* and *dravya.*

Both Padmanabh Jaini (1979:78) and H. R. Kapadia (1941:57) assign the Jaina Purāṇas to the *prathamānuyoga* (Śvetāmbara *dharmakathā*). Hīrālāl Jain (1962:127) adds that the *prathamānuyoga* was one of the five sections of the lost *Dṛṣṭivāda,* and so implies a quasi-canonical status for the Purāṇas. This tactic of claiming authoritative status for a text or class of texts by asserting that the text is the direct descendant of a lost canonical text is a common one in Indian religious traditions. Kapadia observes that while *anuyoga* was one of the five sections of the *Dṛṣṭivāda*[3] and the content of this *anuyoga* consisted of biographies, there is also the notion of the four *anuyoga*s "permeating the entire sphere of the Jaina scriptures" (Kapadia 1941:12). The Jaina Purāṇas thus can best be characterized as a post-Āgamic literary corpus based upon themes found in the Āgama.

An external categorization of the Jaina Purāṇas, in terms of their literary style, is provided by A. K. Warder (1972–83; 1975) and G. C. Caudharī (1973). Viewing the Jaina Purāṇas from the general perspective of Indian literature, they both describe the Purāṇas as *kāvya,* or epics in poetic style.

In terms of their contents, the Jaina Purāṇas can be described as biographies.[4] Whereas the Hindu Purāṇas are extensively preoccupied with the activities of the gods and goddesses on an often transcendent level, the Jaina Purāṇas are concerned with the lives of specific human beings who lived at specific times in Jaina history. Thus, many of the Jaina Purāṇas are called *caritras* (literally, "deeds" or "acts"), the Indian literary genre that most closely resembles the Western genre of biography. In general, the Digambaras called their works "Purāṇas" and the Śvetāmbaras called their works "Caritras," although in some cases both terms are applied to the same work; there is no difference in genre implied by the use of the different terms.

Unlike the Brahminic Sanskrit tradition, the Jaina tradition did not develop a distinction between the genres of Purāṇa and *itihāsa* (epic). In this respect the Jaina tradition is similar to many of the vernacular literary traditions, such as Oriya, wherein both the Oriya *Mahābhārata* and the Oriya *Bhāgavata Purāṇa* are sectarian tellings of the regional cult of Jagannātha. At the same time, the Jaina Purāṇas are less inclusive than the Hindu Purāṇas. The Jaina Purāṇas did not have the same all-absorbent capacity as their Hindu namesakes. We do not find the proliferation of *māhātmyas* of specific *tīrthas* that mark many Hindu Purāṇas (although pilgrimage has been as important a religious act in the Jaina tradition as in the Hindu), and so an important text such as Dhaneśvarasūri's *Śatruñjaya Māhātmya* (7th–8th c.)[5] was not incorporated into any Purāṇa, but remained an independent text. Nor did the Jaina Purāṇas absorb ritual, cultic, and sectarian texts as did the Hindu Purāṇas.

Jaina literature has been the major repository for the *kathā* (story) literature, the third major narrative tradition in India besides the Brahminic Purāṇas and Epics. This tradition of story literature is represented in the literatures of the Hindus, Buddhists, and Jainas, but most of what we possess today has been preserved by the Jainas. It not only permeates the Jaina Purāṇas but is also extensively represented in Jaina commentarial and homilitic literature.[6] The statement of Johannes Hertel (1922:11) that "during the middle ages down to our days the Jains . . . were the principle story tellers of India" is not as hyperbolic as it might at first seem, and the Jaina Purāṇas should be of central interest to scholars looking at story and oral traditions in India.

A general morphological definition of a Jaina Purāṇa is, therefore, that it is a postcanonical biographical *kāvya* that has much overlap with the genre of story. The Jaina Purāṇas can be divided into three major types in terms of content. These are: (1) the life of one of the twenty-four Tīrthaṅkaras or Jinas of the present age

(Jinacaritra); (2) the Jaina version of the story of Rāma (*Rāmāyaṇa* or *Padmacaritra*); and (3) the Jaina version of the story of Kṛṣṇa and the Bhārata war (*Harivaṁśa*). Covering all these topics are the Jaina Mahāpurāṇas, which give the biographies of all of the sixty-three heroes of the present age. These sixty-three heroes, known as *śalākā puruṣa*s or Eminent People (see below), are the twenty-four Tīrthaṅkaras or Jinas, twelve Cakravartins, and nine linked trios of heroes, the nine each Vāsudevas, Baladevas, and Prati-vāsudevas. They are not so much unique characters as they are archetypical characters who repeatedly act correctly and incorrectly according to the guiding principle of *karma* in the moral universe of the Jainas.

THE JINA CARITRA

The primary meaning of *caritra* (Prakrit *carita, cariya*) is "conduct, acts, deeds," and hence a secondary meaning of *caritra* is the literary genre equivalent to biography in English. The related *cāritra* is also a technical term in Jainism for religious conduct, and *samyakcāritra* (correct conduct) is one of the *ratnatraya,* the three gems,[7] which are the three foundations and prerequisites of *mokṣa* (liberation). Thus a Jinacaritra, a life story of a Tīrthaṅkara, is not just a biography but also a telling of the proper conduct on the *mokṣamārga,* the path to *mokṣa*. A *caritra* is not a biography in the modern sense of an investigation into what made a particular person either unique or representative of his or her time but rather a telling of how one soul (*ātman*) travelled along the predetermined correct path to *mokṣa*.

Relating the lives of the twenty-four Jinas of the present cycle of time has always been a popular topic for Jaina authors. One of the earliest extant Jaina texts, the *Kappa Sutta* (Sanskrit *Kalpa Sūtra*) attributed to Bhadrabāhu Svāmī (third century B.C.E.),[8] contains a lengthy biography of Vardhamāna Mahāvīra (the twenty-fourth Jina) and shorter biographies of Pārśvanātha (twenty-third), Neminātha/Ariṣṭanemi (twenty-second), and Ṛṣabhanātha/Ādinātha (first).[9] These early biographies covered only the human lives of the Tīrthaṅkaras, especially the five beneficial events (*kalyāṇaka*s) of conception (*cyavana*), birth (*janma*), renunciation (*dīkṣā*), enlightenment (*kaivalya*), and liberation (*mokṣa, nirvāṇa*).[10] With the passage of time authors of subsequent texts came to embellish the stories by describing many of the previous births of the Tīrthaṅkaras, as well as adding many incidents to the final incarna-

Table 8.1 Biographies of Tīrthaṅkaras

NAME OF TĪRTHAṄKARA	ORDER OF TĪRTHAṄKARA	NUMBER OF BIOGRAPHIES
Neminātha	22	34
Śāntinātha	16	29
Ṛṣabhanātha	1	24
Pārśvanātha	23	24
Mahāvīra	24	19
Candraprabha	17	17
Mallinātha	19	14
Munisuvrata	20	12

Source: H. D. Velankar, *Jinaratnakośa* (Poona: Bhandarkar Oriental Research Institute, 1944).

tions of the Tīrthaṅkaras. In this way the authors explained the effects of *karma* graphically and exhaustively, for the *karma* acquired in one action in one life might not ripen and fall away until many lives (and pages) later. The stories of opponents of the Tīrthaṅkaras, also described through many lives, were added to some of these stories. The authors could thereby trace the effects of bad as well as good actions; while the hero alternated a life as a human or an animal with a life in some heaven, the opponent alternated between earth and some hell. The mendicant authors were able to gratify an urge common to many moralistic authors and describe the torments of the residents of hell in great detail. While the individual authors may well have invented some of the stories to display their own creative imagination, presumably most of the stories were taken from the oral traditions of the time and were well known to the audience listening to the recitation. By applying Jaina theories of *karma* to the tales, the authors could both reinforce the understanding of the Jaina listeners and try to convince non-Jainas of the correctness of the Jaina teachings.

These biographies became very popular subjects for medieval Purāṇic authors, and eventually individual *caritra*s were written for each of the twenty-four Tīrthaṅkaras.[11] H. D. Velankar, in his catalogue of Jaina texts, listed more than two hundred Caritras and Purāṇas. The most popular Tīrthaṅkaras in terms of numbers of separate biographies are given in Table 8.1.

THE JAINA RĀMĀYAṆA

The Jaina versions of the story of Rāma (or Padma, as he is also known in the Jaina tradition) constitute what is probably the most-studied area of Jaina literature aside from the Āgamas.[12] The story of Rāma is an old one within the Jaina tradition; the earliest extant Jaina telling of the story is Vimalasūri's *Paümacariya*. Dated variously between 2 C.E. and 474 C.E., this is the earliest surviving Jaina Purāṇa.[13] It is primarily written in Maharastri, with a few sections in Sauraseni. There is wide disagreement among scholars as to the date of the *Paümacariya*. The earliness of the text can be seen in its occasional use of Sauraseni and in the lack of any clear sectarian preference on the part of Vimalasūri in his telling of the story.[14] Thus it was probably written before the Śvetāmbara-Digambara split was finalized and sectarian differences hardened, and certainly before the final redaction of the Śvetāmbara canon at the councils of Valabhi and Mathura in the fifth century C.E. Until there is a careful linguistic study of the text, the safest statement concerning the date of composition of the *Paümacariya* is that it was composed sometime in the first five centuries of the common era.[15]

Some scholars have viewed the differences in the Jaina versions of the Rāma story as attempts by Jaina authors to change the Vālmīki Rāma story into a Jaina moralizing tract.[16] While Vimalasūri pointedly disagrees with Vālmīki's rendering of many episodes, the antiquity of Vimalasūri's version may well mean that he had access to episodes and accounts still prevalent in the oral tradition of that time, which had either been left out or changed in the Vālmīki version and have since disappeared from the Hindu tradition due to the primacy of Vālmīki's version within Indian culture. It is just as likely that Vālmīki greatly changed the earlier oral heroic epic to make it into a Brahminic Hindu tract and that parts of Vimalasūri's version represent an older, pre-Hindu, non-Brahminic tradition. That Rāma and Rāvaṇa are characterized in the Jaina Rāma story as humans, whereas Vālmīki portrays them as a god and a demon, offers a case in point.[17] Neither version has clear and logical priority over the other. The way in which the contents of the Jaina Rāmāyaṇas and Mahābhāratas were thoroughly Jainized by Jaina authors suggests the extent to which the Hindu Rāmāyaṇas and Mahābhāratas were Hinduized and Brahminized by their Hindu Brahmin authors and redactors.[18]

THE JAINA HARIVAṀŚA

In contrast to the Jaina versions of the Rāma story, the Jaina versions of the story of Kṛṣṇa have been little studied. But this story is just as important as the Rāma story within the Jaina tradition; perhaps it is even more so, given the long-standing interaction between Jainas and the Vaiṣṇava Kṛṣṇa cult in Mathura and western India.

The Jaina versions of the Kṛṣṇa story are known as Harivaṃśa Purāṇas, in line with the oldest Hindu version of the Kṛṣṇa story.[19] Vimalasūri is said to be the author of the earliest Jaina version of the Kṛṣṇa story in his *Harivaṃśa Purāṇa*. But no manuscripts of this text have been found, and it is likely that authors of later Jaina Harivaṁśas wanted an antiquity and pedigree for their story as great as those of the Jaina Rāma story and so attributed a *Harivaṃśa Purāṇa* to Vimalasūri as the source for their own works. The oldest extant Jaina telling of the story of Kṛṣṇa is the Sanskrit *Harivaṃśa Purāṇa* of Jinasena (known as Punnāṭa Jinasena, after his lineage designation, to distinguish him from the later Digambara author of the same name), finished in 783 C.E. in Gujarat.

The Jaina version of the story of Kṛṣṇa, however, is found at earlier levels of Jaina literature, in the Śvetāmbara Āgama. The *Antagaḍa-dasāo,* one of the Aṅgas, contains a brief account of the life of Kṛṣṇa.[20] As with the Rāmāyaṇas, the Jaina tellings of the story of Kṛṣṇa are less violent and bloody than the Hindu versions. The Jaina versions also have different genealogies of the characters. The role of Kaṃsa is de-emphasized and that of Jarāsandha emphasized in comparison with the Hindu versions. Early Jaina tellings almost totally ignore the Pāṇḍavas, although a later tradition of Pāṇḍava Purāṇas filled out their story.[21] The Jaina story of Kṛṣṇa was a popular one for Digambara authors in Karnataka. Svayambhū told the story in conjunction with that of Neminātha in his Apabhramsa *Riṭṭhaṇemicariu.* Kannada[22] versions of the Kṛṣṇa story were composed by Guṇavarma[23] and Pampa[24] in the late ninth and early tenth centuries.

MAHĀPURĀṆA

Within the Hindu Purāṇic tradition, there is an undefined distinction between an Upapurāṇa, or Lesser Purāṇa, and a Mahāpurāṇa, or Great Purāṇa. This distinction appears to have been based on the breadth and nonsectarian nature of the material covered in a Mahāpurāṇa, but the distinction becomes practically unusable upon closer scrutiny of the Purāṇas themselves. A major problem is the accretive, composite nature of the Hindu Purāṇas, whereby works of different sectarian traditions could find niches for themselves within the Purāṇas. But the fact that the Jaina Purāṇas were written by individual authors and did not absorb other texts over time, meant that within the Jaina Purāṇic tradition there was a valid, usable distinction between a Purāṇa and a Mahāpurāṇa. A Jaina Purāṇa focused on the life story of one Jaina hero (or a cluster of heroes, as in the Rāmāyaṇas and Harivaṃśas), whereas a Jaina Mahāpurāṇa gave the life stories of the entire cycle of sixty-three *śalākā puruṣas*, or Jaina heroes (see below).

While the first Jaina Purāṇa, the *Paümacariya* of Vimalasūri, contains the stories of all sixty-three of the Jaina heroes, the first text explicitly to be called a Mahāpurāṇa is the Maharastri Prakrit *Caüppaṇṇamahāpurisacariya* of the Śvetāmbara Ācārya Śīlāṅka, composed in 868 C.E.[25] The greatest of the Mahāpurāṇas was the Sanskrit *Mahāpurāṇa* composed in Karnataka by the Digambaras Jinasena and Guṇabhadra slightly later in the same century.

Jinasena (not to be confused with his namesake, the slightly earlier Punnāṭa Jinasena, who lived in Gujarat) is considered to be the finest of the Jaina Purāṇa authors in terms of literary style. Jinasena was a Brahmin convert to Jainism who, along with his teacher Vīrasena, is credited with converting Amoghavarṣa, the Rāṣṭrakūṭa king, to Jainism (Upadhye 1968:728).[26]

Perhaps in competition with the Digambara *Mahāpurāṇa,* the great Gujarati Śvetāmbara Ācārya Hemacandra, between 1160 and 1172 C.E., wrote his *Triṣaṣṭiśalākāpuruṣacaritra,* covering in great detail the lives of all sixty-three heroes. Hemacandra was the preceptor and advisor of Kumārapāla, the Jaina Caulukya emperor of Gujarat, and was instrumental both in Kumārapāla's accession to the throne, when the previous Śaivite emperor Jayasiṃha Siddharāja died heirless, and in Kumārapāla's efforts to transform Gujarat into an ideal Jaina state. Hemacandra is also known for his important contributions to Sanskrit aesthetic theory, Sanskrit and Prakrit grammar and lexicography, and Jaina philosophy and ethics, and for the encyclopedic breadth of his scholarship.[27]

The *Triṣaṣṭiśalākāpuruṣacaritra* is the only Jaina Purāṇa to have been translated in its entirety into English or any other non-Indian language. This heroic six-volume translation, published in the Gaekwad's Oriental Series between 1931 and 1962, was the lifework of the American Sanskritist Helen M. Johnson. In part because of this translation, and in part because of the predominance of Śvetāmbara studies among Western scholarship of the Jainas,[28] Hemacandra's work has been the best known and most studied of all the Jaina Purāṇas. But in terms of social and historical importance and literary style, this is not Hemacandra's most important work, nor is it as important as a normative and influential Jaina text as Jinasena's *Ādi Purāṇa*. While Hemacandra's work is rightly praised as a storehouse of information on Jaina practice and belief in medieval Gujarat, one does not hear the same praises for the quality of Hemacandra's writing and poetry that one hears for Jinasena's work.

Another important Mahāpurāṇa is the Apabhramsa *Mahāpurāṇu* of Puṣpadanta. He came from a Brahmin family that had converted to Digambara Jainism. He was patronized by Bharata, an official in the Rāṣṭrakūṭa court, and at Bharata's request composed his *Mahāpurāṇu*. He finished it in 965 C.E., after six years of work. A. K. Warder (1975:191) and Nāthūrām Premī (1956:225) consider him to have been the finest of the Apabhramsa poets.

Soon after Puṣpadanta, a Kannada Mahāpurāṇa was composed by Cāmuṇḍarāya. He was a general in the waning years of the Gaṅga dynasty in the late tenth century C.E. who almost singlehandedly held the kingdom together. He was also a patron of the poet Ranna and arranged for the carving of the famous colossal fifty-seven-foot standing image of the Jaina hero Gommaṭeśvara/Bāhubali at Śravaṇa Beḷgoḷa. His *Triṣaṣṭilakṣaṇamahāpurāṇa* is the oldest Kannada work in continuous prose. This work became so identified with its author that it is generally known as the *Cāmuṇḍarāya Purāṇa*.[29]

JAINA PURĀṆAS: AN INTERNAL DEFINITION

We have seen above two ways in which the Jaina Purāṇas can be defined. One is that a Jaina Purāṇa is a post-Āgamic biographical *kāvya* that tells a *kathā*. The second is according to the four subgenres of Jinacaritra, Rāmāyaṇa, Harivaṁśa, and Mahāpurāṇa. To understand fully the distinctiveness of the Jaina Purāṇas, however, they need to be placed in the context of the Jaina universal history, which allows for a neat categorization of all the Jaina Purāṇas.

Within the Hindu Purāṇic tradition, the fivefold definition of a Purāṇa as given by Amarasiṃha in his *Amarakośa* was widely accepted as normative. These five attributes of a Purāṇa, the *purāṇapañcalakṣaṇa,* provided an agreed-upon conceptual framework within which the Hindu Purāṇas were located.

Shaktidhar Jha (1978:52–53) has attempted to find in Jinasena's *Ādi Purāṇa* an exact parallel for the *pañcalakṣaṇa* of Amarasiṃha. Padmanabh S. Jaini, in this volume, has similarly advanced the proposition that Vimalasūri used the *pañcalakṣaṇa* as guidelines for the Jaina Purāṇas, albeit under different names. Their arguments, however, remain unconvincing. Given that both Jaina and Hindu Purāṇas present their traditions as total worldviews and universal histories, and therefore of necessity discuss similar topics, one is not thereby justified in arguing that the Jainas borrowed the Hindu *pañcalakṣaṇa* scheme. The authors of the Jaina Purāṇas were not shy about explaining where the Brahmin authors were incorrect in other areas; but never do they say they are now presenting the correct understanding of the *pañcalakṣaṇa*s, which had been incorrectly stated by the Brahmins.

At the beginning of the *Ādi Purāṇa* Jinasena lists seven topics that are covered in the biography: the nature of the world at that time, the rise of the *kuladhara*s, the rise of the ruling dynasties, the rule of Ṛṣabha as king, the arhantship of Ṛṣabha, his liberation, and the end of that age.[30] Since Ṛṣabhanātha was the first Tīrthaṅkara in the present cycle of time, several elements found in his biography are not in the other Jinacaritras. The *kuladhara*s were the "lineage-heads," fourteen in number, who presided over humanity during the long time before Ṛṣabha, a time so pleasant that liberation was impossible. Ṛṣabha was the first king, and from his descendants the other ruling dynasties arose. With the *nirvāṇa* of Ṛṣabha, the third of the six time periods (*yuga*) in the present cycle of time came to an end. Ṛṣabha was also one of the few Tīrthaṅkaras actually to rule; while all Tīrthaṅkaras came from royal (*kṣatriya*) families, most renounced worldly life before sitting on the throne. The other three topics in this biography (the nature of the world, Ṛṣabha's arhantship, and his liberation) are common to all Jinacaritras.

Elsewhere in the *Ādi Purāṇa,* Jinasena gives other descriptions of the contents of a Jaina Purāṇa. In chapter 2 he says that a Jaina Purāṇa describes *kṣetra, kāla, tīrtha, satpuṃsa,* and *viceṣṭita.*[31] He then defines these terms.[32] *Kṣetra* refers to the arrangement of the three realms: the heavens, earth, and the hells. *Kāla* refers to the three times: past, present, and future. *Tīrtha* are the aids to liberation. *Satpuṃsa* are the people who work within the *tīrtha*s for the liberation of others (that is, the Tīrthaṅkaras and other Jaina heroes). *Viceṣṭita* is the conduct of these *satpuṃsa*s.[33] In the fourth chapter he lists eight topics covered in a Purāṇa: worlds, countries, cities, kingdoms, holy places, gifting, asceticism, and the natural order.[34] This is a totally human scheme, a description of the contents of the human universe rather than an attempt to situate the human universe within a vaster cosmic system. Finally, Jinasena also says simply that a Purāṇa is a history (*itihāsa*).[35] None of these various lists, however, adequately defines what is distinctive about a Jaina Purāṇa.[36] The contents could be found in a wide variety of Jaina texts, many of which make no claim to be Purāṇas. For the distinctive feature of a Jaina Purāṇa, what I call the "internal definition" of a Jaina Purāṇa, we must turn to the elaboration of the sixty-three heroes, the *śalākā puruṣa*s.

The stories of the sixty-three *śalākā puruṣa*s, or Great Men, formed the basis of what German scholars, such as Hermann Jacobi, Helmuth von Glasenapp, Walther Schubring, Ludwig Alsdorf, and Klaus Bruhn, and, following them in English, A. K. Warder have termed the Jaina *Universalgeschichte* (universal history). This universal history provided the contextual framework within which the Jaina Purāṇic tradition was located. Therefore, we can define a Jaina Purāṇa as a text dealing with the life story of one or more of the sixty-three Jaina heroes, and a Mahāpurāṇa as a text dealing with the entire universal history. But before discussing the details of this universal history, it will be useful briefly to trace its beginnings with the Jaina tradition.

The Śvetāmbara Mūrtipūjaka *Kappa Sutta* (Sanskrit *Kalpa Sūtra*) gives the biographies of the Jinas of the present time-cycle and when they lived. It does not mention any of the other *śalākā puruṣa*s by name, nor does it use the word *śalākā puruṣa* itself, but it does mention the categories of Arhats (Tīrthaṅkaras), Cakravartins, Baladevas, and Vāsudevas as always being born in royal (*kṣatriya*) families, thus foreshadowing fifty-four of the sixty-three *śalākā puruṣa*s.[37]

There are other references to the *śalākā puruṣa*s in the Śvetāmbara Āgamas, in particular the *Ṭhāṇāṅga*[38] and the *Samavāyāṅga*. The latter text in different places gives descriptions of sixty-three and fifty-four *śalākā puruṣa*s.[39] An early description of the developing Jaina universal history is found in the Digambara *Ṣaṭkhaṇḍāgama*.[40]

The tradition of there being only fifty-four *śalākā puruṣa*s continued until at least the mid-ninth century C.E., when the Śvetāmbara Śīlāṅka composed his *Caüppaṇṇamahāpurisacariya* (The Deeds of the Fifty-four Great Heroes). But with the composition by Jinasena and Guṇabhadra of the *Mahāpurāṇa,* also known as the *Triṣaṣṭilakṣaṇamahāpurāṇa* (The Great Purāṇa Describing the Sixty-three Heroes), the number of *śalākā puruṣa*s became fixed at sixty-three. Velankar (1944) in his *Jinaratnakośa* does not give any texts after Śīlāṅka's in which the title refers to only fifty-four *śalākā puruṣa*s.

Vimalasūri framed his telling of the story of Rāma within the context of the sixty-three *śalākā puruṣa*s, so the tradition of sixty-three *śalākā puruṣa*s is at least as old as the fifth century C.E. Vimalasūri claimed that he was transmitting a tradition handed down from the time of Mahāvīra and that the stories of the *śalākā puruṣa*s were to be found in the lost category of ancient texts known as Pūrvas. A. K. Warder (1972–83:2:227) has stressed the importance of the *Paümacariya* in the development of the Jaina universal history, from the brief outlines given in the earlier Ardha-Magadhi texts to the later massive works in which the history is laid out in full detail:

> Vimala established in literature the entire structure of Jaina universal history . . . it was his genius to create and give life to this grandiose conception out of the abstract sketch offered in the Jaina canon. His work is to be appreciated as a whole . . . Its study is also necessary to understand the many later *kāvyas* by Jaina authors which move within its literary universe. Vimala's influence . . . consists in his being followed in detail by so many Jaina writers, though hardly any of them acknowledge their source.

Before discussing the different categories of heroes within the *śalākā puruṣa* scheme, I want to touch briefly upon the significance of the number 63. Many people have noted that the number of Tamil Śaivite Nāyaṉār singer-saints also was 63.[41] This number appears to have been artificially imposed upon the tradition, much as we often find lists of 108 objects in India. It appears that the numbering of the Nāyaṉārs as 63 was in direct imitation of the earlier Jaina tradition, as the number is not found in the Śaiva tradition until centuries after it appears in the Jaina tradition. The Nāyaṉārs lived during the period from the seventh to the tenth centuries, by which time the Jaina tradition of the 63 *śalākā puruṣa*s was well established. The unanswered (and quite likely unanswerable) question is: Why 63? Also unanswered is whether this was a Jaina internal development or something the Jainas picked up from a South Indian folk tradition that also fed into the Nāyaṉār tradition.

An argument for a possible non-Jaina source for the importance of the number 63 is the arbitrariness of the number within the Jaina tradition. As mentioned above, there was within the Jaina tradition a tension as to whether there were 54 or 63 *śalākā pur-*

uṣas. During the eleventh and twelfth centuries C.E., Bhadreśvara in his *Kahāvalī* raised the number to 72 by adding the 9 Nāradas to the list (Parekh 1974:152). Jagmanderlal Jaini (1916:5, 127–28) gives a list of 106 other important people in the Jaina universal history: the 24 mothers and 24 fathers of the Tīrthaṅkaras, 9 Nāradas, 11 Rudras, 24 Kāmadevas, and 14 Kulakaras. Similar information is found in a late fifth to early seventh century Digambara cosmographical text, the *Tiloya Paṇṇatti* (4.510–1472) of Yativṛṣabha. This text gives descriptions of other Jaina heroes such as the 11 Rudras, 9 Nāradas, and 24 Kāmadevas, but specifically says that there are only 63 *śalākā puruṣas*.[42] Yativṛṣabha explains that the 9 Nāradas are anti-Rudras who are fond of war and thus go to hell, while the 24 Kāmadevas (of whom Ṛṣabha's son Bāhubali was the first) are heroes with especially lovely bodies who attain liberation, and one of whom lives during the time of each Tīrthaṅkara.

The use of the term *śalākā* in the context of the *śalākā puruṣa* scheme is a somewhat unusual one. Its primary meaning, in Sanskrit as *śalākā,* in Pali as *salākā,* and in Prakrit as *salāgā* and *salāyā,* is "stick." Within a Buddhist context it acquired a specialized meaning as "a ticket consisting of slips of wood used in voting and distributing food" (Rhys Davids and Stede 1975:699). This meaning, however, is not found in the Jaina tradition. Prakrit *salāgā/salāyā* has three definitions: (1) a stick; (2) a special kind of measurement; and (3), joined with *purisa,* to denote the great heroes (Sheth 1963:881).

S. D. Parekh (1974:152–53) quotes Hemacandra as saying that the sixty-three heroes are *śalākā*s who have become especially marked among men.[43] Parekh goes on to emphasize that it is as though the names of the *śalākā puruṣa*s were underlined or especially significant. Parekh also discusses the use of *śalākā*s as voting tickets among the non-Aryan people of ancient Magadha, such as the Śākyas, Licchavīs, and Vaidehas. From this he concludes that a *śalākā puruṣa* is a great person whose greatness has been accepted by the general public—who has won a popularity contest or general election, as it were.

For the present, Parekh's conclusions will be accepted. It would be useful, however, to know if *śalākā* is used in early Jaina writings in contexts other than *śalākā puruṣa*. The medieval and modern usage of *śalākā* in *añjana śalākā,* the "eye-opening" rite by which a *sādhu* enlivens a *mūrti* (image for worship), is a totally separate usage of the word, derived from its primary meaning as a stick. In an interview, one contemporary Śvetāmbara Mūrtipūjaka *ācārya* defined *śalākā* in *śalākā puruṣa* as meaning *śaktiśālī,* "imbued with power." While this folk definition is etymologically untenable, it does convey accurately the sense of the Jaina attitude towards the *śalākā puruṣa*s. The extent to which *śalākā* can also be taken as simply a synonym for great (*mahā*) is seen in Śīlāṅka's Purāṇa being entitled the *Caritra of the Fifty-four Mahāpuruṣas*.

A list of the names and temporal relationships of the sixty-three *śalākā puruṣa*s is appended to this paper. The sixty-three heroes appear during every cycle of time, although the names of the individuals are different in each cycle.

The Tīrthaṅkaras or Jinas are the twenty-four teachers or saviors who establish or reestablish the Jaina teachings on earth. *Tīrtha* means "ford," and *kara* means "maker," so a Tīrthaṅkara (or Tīrthakara) is a "maker of a ford," that is, one who helps people across the ocean of worldly sorrows and suffering to liberation. Jainas also define *tīrtha* as the *caturvidha saṅgha,* the fourfold religious congregation of *sādhu*s, *sādhvī*s, *śrāvaka*s, and *śrāvikā*s (male mendicants, female mendicants, laymen, and laywomen), which is established by each Tīrthaṅkara (Sheth 1963:437). The twenty-four Tīrthaṅkaras of the present time cycle are the central figures in both Jaina universal history and Jaina cult practice.

The relationship between great religious teachers and Cakravartins, world conquerors, was a strong one in the non-Vedic religious traditions. The Buddha would have become a Cakravartin if he had chosen a worldly path.[44] Of the twelve Jaina Cakravartins, three of them (Śāntinātha, Kunthunātha, and Aranātha) later became Tīrthaṅkaras. The closeness between the Tīrthaṅkara and the Cakravartin is seen in that the alternative word more commonly used for Tīrthaṅkara is Jina, "Victor," here meaning one who is victorious in the spiritual as opposed to political realm. Before the birth of either a Tīrthaṅkara or a Cakravartin, his mother sees the same number of auspicious dreams.[45]

Only three of the twelve Cakravartins (Bharata, Sagara, and Sanatkumāra) are found also in the Hindu tradition, and the twelfth Cakravartin, Brahmadatta, is very popular in the Buddhist Jātakas. Although the Jaina Rāma/Padma does not become a Cakravartin (or even a king, for that matter), we do find a Padma listed among the Cakravartins, perhaps representing another strand of the Rāma story within Jainism. The Cakravartins, in addition to being world conquerors, are also devout patrons and followers of Jainism. At the end of their lives, they renounce their thrones, become *sādhu*s, and eventually attain liberation.

The biographies of the remaining twenty-seven *śalākā puruṣa*s are all closely interrelated. The nine Baladevas are righteous Jainas who stick firmly to the central Jaina ethical principle of *ahiṃsā,* nonviolence. They are represented by Rāma in the Rāma story and by Balabhadra in the *Harivaṃśa.* Because of their adherence to *ahiṃsā,* after renouncing the world at the end of their lives they attain liberation.

The Vāsudevas are half-brothers (same father, different mothers) of the Baladevas. They are also half-Cakravartins, with half the status and power of full Cakravartins. They are represented by Lakṣmaṇa and Kṛṣṇa in the two main cycles. They engage in war and kill their enemies, the Prati-vāsudevas, for which they are reborn in hell. But befitting their status as *śalākā puruṣas*, the Vāsudevas will be reborn in the next time cycle as Tīrthaṅkaras. The Prati-vāsudevas (represented by Rāvaṇa and Jarāsandha) are Jaina kings who, through the powers of asceticism and devotion to the Jinas, have become powerful wizards. They misuse their powers and ultimately are slain by the Vāsudevas and reborn in hell.

Padmanabh Jaini, in his essay in this volume, has hypothesized that the twenty-seven Vāsudevas, Baladevas, and Prati-vāsudevas are an addition to the earlier list of twenty-four Tīrthaṅkaras and twelve Cakravartins and that the later figures were included within the Jaina tradition as a result of its interaction with the popular Bhāgavata cult and its two brother-deities, Balarāma and Kṛṣṇa, in the area around Mathura in the Maurya and Śuṅga periods. However, as mentioned above, the categories of the Vāsudevas and the Baladevas are found in the *Kappa Sutta* and quite possibly predate the Jaina-Vaiṣṇava interaction at Mathurā.

The Vāsudeva represents the ideal Jaina king, who protects the Jaina society but, unlike the Cakravartin, is not so perfect as to be able to attain liberation in this life. The Baladeva, on the other hand, represents the detached layman who does not participate in the violence inherent in the broader society. Perhaps these two represent ideal types for the two elements that made up early and medieval Jaina society, the Kṣatriyas and the Vaiśyas. While the Kṣatriyas sacrificed their own chances of liberation in this lifetime in order to maintain and further Jaina society, the Vaiśyas stayed aloof from politics and warfare and sought to further both their own spiritual well-being and that of Jaina society in general through strict adherence to *ahiṃsā.* While today the Jainas are almost all of merchant castes, it is important to remember that many generals and other royal advisors in Karnataka and Gujarat were Jainas during the time when the Jaina Purāṇas describing the *śalākā pur-*

*uṣa*s were being composed, and many Jaina castes, such as the Osavālas of Gujarat and Rajasthan, that today are of Vaiśya status claim that they were originally Kṣatriyas.

While the mother of a Tīrthaṅkara or Cakravartin sees fourteen or sixteen auspicious dreams[46] when the embryo enters her womb, the mother of a Vāsudeva sees seven,[47] and the mother of a Baladeva only four.[48] The mother of a Prati-vāsudeva sees no dreams. The Tīrthaṅkaras and Cakravartins, on the one hand, and the Vāsudevas and Baladevas, on the other, represent two different planes of activity. The Baladevas, the devout laymen who attain liberation, correspond to the Tīrthaṅkaras, the perfect heroes who become world teachers. The Vāsudevas, the imperfect half-Cakravartins and half-brothers of the Baladevas, correspond to the Cakravartins, the perfect kings who become world rulers and then attain liberation. The vertical rank between these two planes is represented by the number of dreams seen by the hero's mother. Horizontally, the superiority of the Tīrthaṅkaras can be seen in that they are the supreme teachers of the Jaina tradition, whereas the Cakravartins, although they attain liberation, rank only among the Siddhas, the other liberated and perfected souls besides the Tīrthaṅkaras. The precedence of the Tīrthaṅkaras over the Siddhas can also be seen in the *namaskāra mantra* that is chanted daily by all Jainas as a "confession of faith" in which obeisance is expressed first to the Tīrthaṅkaras and then to the Siddhas. The horizontal superiority of the Baladevas over the Vāsudevas is seen in that they attain liberation, whereas the latter, although they will attain liberation in a future life, must first be reborn in hell. We therefore have a fourfold division of the *śalākā puruṣa*s, which can be read both top-to-bottom and left-to-right in terms of superior rank (fig. 8.1). This fourfold division of the *śalākā puruṣa*s also corresponds to both the fourfold division of the Jaina congregation into *sādhu*s, *sādhvī*s, *śrāvaka*s, and *śrāvikā*s, and the fourfold division of saṁsāric existence into gods (*devatā*), humans (*manuṣya*), animals and plants (*tiryañc*), and hell-beings (*nāraka*).

In sum, the scheme of the *śalākā puruṣa*s represents a conceptual framework within which the Jainas elaborated their own view of history. As such, it can be juxtaposed with the Hindu *pañcalakṣaṇa* definition as providing a self-definition of the Jaina Purānas. V. Narayana Rao has argued, in this volume, that the *pañcalakṣaṇa* provide the framework within which the Hindu Purāṇas are located, that is, that the events described in a Hindu Purāṇa fall within a specific *sarga, pratisarga,* and *manvantara*. The *śalākā puruṣa* scheme provides a roughly similar framework, for the events in a Jaina Purāṇa are circumscribed by the *śalākā puruṣa*s.

Tīrthaṅkaras	Cakravartins
Baladevas	Vāsudevas

Figure 8.1

A. K. Warder has rightly observed the importance of the framework of the Jaina universal history for a work such as Vimalasūri's *Paümacariya*. What seems irrelevant from a Western perspective concerned with plot is essential from a Jaina perspective in order to establish the larger context within which the story occurs (Warder 1972–83:2:225):

> The setting of universal history is not simply an introduction, certainly not an irrelevant digression from the story; it is an essential part of the narrative because it tells us what the universe is like, as the author understands it, and it is the nature of the universe which explains the life of the hero. The Life of Padma [*Paümacariya*] is an artistic presentation of the Jaina view of the universe, a universe in which everything is alive and in which assault on life is the ultimate evil.

It is important to remember, however, that this is a conceptual framework, operating on the level of educated, literate discourse. It is not a framework that can be applied to actual Jaina cult practice. Except for the Tīrthaṅkaras, the *śalākā puruṣa*s are not cult figures for the Jainas, and important cult figures such as the *yakṣa*s, *yakṣī*s, goddesses, *vīra*s, and Bāhubali, who are important on the level of ritual action, find no place directly within the *śalākā puruṣa* scheme. In this way it is similar to some of the Hindu avatars, which also incorporate heroes who are important on a mythic, universal historical, or conceptual level, such as Matsya, Kūrma, or Paraśurāma, but who are not necessarily popular cult figures. This comparison is doubly appropriate, for authors such as Kirfel (1959:40) and Bruhn (1961:8) have argued that the Hindu avatars evolved in part in reaction to the non-Hindu, and especially Jaina, universal histories. In the same way that the Tīrthaṅkaras repeatedly revitalize the Jaina teachings, the Vaiṣṇavite avatars repeatedly revive the Hindu *dharma*.

Both the Jainas and Buddhists developed universal histories that differed greatly from that of the Brahmins and other Hindus.

The significant differences between the Jaina and Buddhist universal histories may well help explain why Jainism has survived in India for more than twenty-five hundred years, whereas Buddhism gradually disappeared. The Buddhist universal history tended towards a syncretistic relationship with Hinduism, wherein, for example, the Buddhist Bodhisattva Avalokiteśvara could be seen as the Hindu Śiva Lokeśvara (P. S. Jaini 1980:87). It also resulted in such cults as the Dharma cult in Bengal, and texts such as the *Śūnya Saṃhitā* of Oriya Vaiṣṇavism. Hindu authors adopted the Buddha into the avatars, against which the Buddhists did not adequately fight back.

The Jainas, on the other hand, vigorously opposed Hindu attempts at absorption. Padmanabh Jaini (1977) has shown how the Jainas successfully resisted the Hindu attempts to incorporate Ṛṣabhanātha into the avatars. Rather than ignore popular Hindu cult figures such as Kṛṣṇa and Rāma as the Buddhists did, the Jainas, through the *śalākā puruṣa* framework, were able to portray them as Jainas, presenting the Jaina laity with alternative identifications for these figures.

The Jaina Purāṇas differ from much of the early Hindu mythic material, resembling rather the later sectarian rewritings of the Hindu myths. The Jaina Purāṇas are works in which the hand of the author is ever present, shaping his material in the light of his own purposes and beliefs. The Jaina authors were interested in telling good stories, but they were always more interested in communicating to their audience an argument for Jaina religion and morality. Thus, the Jaina Purāṇas were *caritras,* biographies, tales of the famous heroes: they were written to provide role models for the Jaina laity to emulate.

JAINA PURĀṆAS IN A PERFORMATIVE CONTEXT

Jaina Purāṇas, like their counterparts in the Hindu tradition, were not intended to be read silently at home by an individual the way a contemporary American reads a novel (or an academic article). The Purāṇas were (and are) performance texts and need to be seen in a performative context for their place within the Jaina tradition to be fully understood.[49]

One of the major ways in which Jaina laity interact with the *sādhus* is through the sermons (*pravacana, vyākhyāna*) given by the latter.[50] The main time of the year when *sādhus* give sermons is during the *cāturmāsa,* the four-month period during the rainy season, from the full moon of Āṣāḍha (June–July) through the full moon of Kārttika (October–November), when all *sādhus* and *sādhvīs* must cease their travelling (*vihāra*) and remain in one place. Every morning during the *cāturmāsa* the *sādhus* give public sermons for all the local laity in the monastic residence (*upāśraya*). These sermons last for at least one, and usually two, periods of forty-eight minutes, as many of the attending laity take the temporary vow (*vrata*) of *sāmāyika,* in which they remain seated on a cloth, mendicant's broom in hand, and perform spiritual practices for these periods. The practices may consist of counting a special *mantra* on a 108- or 54-bead rosary, or it may consist merely in listening to the discourse of the *sādhu.*

Sādhus also give sermons at other times during the eight months of their travelling. Often a *sādhu* who is especially renowned for his sermons is invited by a local congregation to give a series of sermons on one text, lasting one or two weeks. The Jaina *Rāmāyaṇa* and Jaina *Mahābhārata*[51] are favorite topics for these special sermons, which are often advertized in the local newspapers.

At the beginning of the *cāturmāsa,* most *sādhus* announce one or two texts that they will read aloud and expound upon in their sermons. These are usually texts which the *sādhu* has previously studied, usually with his own guru. Sometimes the text is a Jaina Purāṇa, but usually it is another collection of religiously edifying stories similar in form and style to a Jaina Purāṇa. Only rarely, in the case of a more scholarly *sādhu,* is the text chosen a philosophically oriented text, and even that is accompanied by a commentary that provides stories to demonstrate the philosophical point under discussion. But the bulk of the sermon almost always consists of stories of ideal Jainas of the past. As one *sādhu* said to me, "These are simple people. They are just merchants and businessmen. They cannot understand philosophy. But if we tell them the philosophy in the form of stories, then they can understand it."

The texts read in the sermons are usually either in Sanskrit or Prakrit, generally with a vernacular translation/summary and commentary (*sārtha* or *artha sahita*). The *sādhu* often also has handwritten notes on the text, written either when he studied the text with his guru, or during a previous *cāturmāsa* when as a junior *sādhu* he listened to his guru's sermons on the text. *Sādhus* who are renowned for their sermons are able to discourse at length without the aid of notes, and the ability of a *sādhu* to give interesting and inspiring sermons is an important factor in establishing his fame (*kīrti, yaśas*) among the laity.

When giving a sermon, the *sādhu* has a copy of the text on a bookstand in front of him. Nowadays the text is in printed form (although usually still in the traditional *poṭhī* shape, of unbound pages about five inches by ten inches, rather than in modern bound-book shape). In earlier times, a wealthy layman would pay to have a handwritten copy of the text prepared for the *sādhu* as an act of devotion (*bhakti*) and gifting (*dāna*) within the field of scripture (*āgamakṣetra*), one of the seven fields of suitable gifting. For certain texts there was also a tradition of painted illustration,[52] and the illustrated pages were held up for the audience to view as the *sādhu* read the text. A very wealthy patron might arrange for all or part of the text to be written in gold paint, a practice especially popular for the *Kalpa Sūtra*.

The *sādhu* first reads from the root text, translates it into the vernacular, and then expounds upon the text, giving homilitic examples and quoting from other texts from memory as suits the occasion. *Sādhu*s less skilled in giving sermons often just recite the vernacular commentary as printed, rushing along in a singsong voice that lulls some (or many) of the audience to sleep. Because of the need for detailed vernacular expositions on texts to be read by less capable *sādhu*s, the expositions of some famous *sādhu*s have been copied down and published either to be read aloud verbatim or to be studied by a *sādhu* in preparing for his own sermon. In former times, some tellings of texts by famous *sādhu*s were written down at the request of a patron, either a wealthy merchant or a king, and preserved in the local manuscript storehouse (*bhaṇḍāra*). Thus in many texts, such as the *Triṣaṣṭiśalākāpuruṣacaritra,* the colophon will mention not only the author (Ācārya Hemacandra) but also the patron of the text (in this example, Kumārapāla of Aṇahillavāḍa Paṭṭaṇa, the Caulukya Emperor), as well as the patron who paid for the copying of the manuscript. This practice explains the proliferation of retellings of the same stories by different authors over the centuries, so that there exist today in manuscript form dozens of different versions of different Jinacaritras and other Jaina Purāṇas that show very little variation from one composition to another.

But in almost all cases the authors were *sādhu*s, and the Purāṇas have been largely an orthodox, *mokṣamārga* literature aimed at guiding the laity in proper religious conduct in the wider social world. This conduct is informed by the principles of Jaina ethics and ideally results in formal initiation (*dīkṣā*) as a mendicant and eventually, after lifetimes spent wearing away accumulated *karma* through asceticism, in liberation.

CONCLUSION

In this paper, we have looked at various ways to characterize and define the Jaina Purāṇas. From an external perspective, they are post-canonical biographical stories in *kāvya* form. From an interval perspective, they can be divided into the three genres of the Jinacaritra, the Jaina *Rāmāyaṇa,* and the Jaina *Harivaṃśa,* with the fourth genre of the Mahāpurāṇa encompassing all of them. Thus, a Jaina Purāṇa is a *kāvya* that narrates the biography of one or more of the sixty-three Great Heroes of the Jaina universal history. The lives of these heroes demonstrate the central negative and positive values of the Jaina tradition, and it is in significant part through the hearing and reading of these biographies as contained in the Purāṇas and similar texts that the Jainas have and continue to understand and internalize the values and karmic principles of the Jaina worldview.

Appendix 1 Principal Jaina Purāṇas

CENTURY (ALL C.E.)	PADMA PURĀṆA	HARIVAṂŚA PURĀṆA	MAHĀPURĀṆA
1			
2			
3	Vimalasūri (Maharastri)	Vimalasūri (Maharastri) (lost)	
4			
5			
6			
7	Raviṣeṇa (Sanskrit)		
8		Punnāṭa Jinasena (Sanskrit)	
	Svayambhū (Apabhramsa)	Svayambhū (Apabhramsa)	
9			Śīlāṅka (Maharastri)
			Jinasena/Guṇabhadra (Sanskrit)
10		Pampa (Kannada)	Puṣpadanta (Apabhramsa)
			Cāmuṇḍarāya (Kannada)
11			
12	Nāgacandra (Kannada)		Hemacandra (Sanskrit)

Appendix 2 The Sixty-three Śalākā Puruṣas

	TĪRTHAṄKARA		CAKRAVARTIN		BALADEVA/VĀSUDEVA/ PRATI-VĀSUDEVA
1	Ṛṣabha (Ādi)	1	Bharata		
2	Ajita	2	Sagara		
3	Saṃbhava				
4	Abhinandana				
5	Sumati				
6	Padmaprabha				
7	Supārśva				
8	Candraprabha				
9	Suvidhi/Puṣpadanta				
10	Śītala			1	Vijaya/Tripṛṣṭha/Aśvagrīva
11	Sreyāṁsa			2	Acala/Dvipṛṣṭha/Tāraka
12	Vāsupūjya			3	Dharma/Svayambhū/Madhu
13	Vimala			4	Suprabha/Puruṣottama/ Madhusūdana
14	Ananta				
15	Dharma				
		3	Maghavan	5	Sudarśana/Puruṣasiṃha/ Madhukrīḍa
		4	Sanatkumāra		
16	Śānti	5	Śānti		
17	Kunthu	6	Kunthu		
18	Ara	7	Ara		
		8	Subhauma	6	Nandiṣeṇa/Puṇḍarīka/ Niśumbha
				7	Nandimitra/Datta/Bali
19	Malli				
				8	Rāma (Padma)/Lakṣmaṇa/ Rāvaṇa
20	Munisuvrata	9	Padma		
21	Nami	10	Hariṣeṇa		
		11	Jayasena		
22	Nemi			9	Balabhadra/Kṛṣṇa/ Jarāsandha
		12	Brahmadatta		
23	Pārśva				
24	Mahāvīra				

Based on Hemacandra, *Triṣaṣṭiśalākāpuruṣacaritra*.

9

Jaina Purāṇas: A Purāṇic Counter Tradition

Padmanabh S. Jaini

When discussing the Jaina Purāṇas and their relationship to the Brahminic Purāṇas, one is immediately struck by a metaphor that is readily understood by readers of Indological studies published in the early twentieth century. With rare exceptions, these works contain a large number of additions and corrections, which in turn need further additions and corrections, ad infinitum. Even a cursory glance at the Jaina Purāṇas makes it clear that the Jaina authors who composed them knew the Hindu Epics and Purāṇas well, studied them with the attention worthy of a board of censors examining the offensive portions of a story, and finally decided to rewrite the script in conformity with their own doctrines and sensibilities. To the credit of the Jainas, it must be said that they did not accomplish this project by any surreptitious means but instead, as will be seen below, achieved their goal by declaring openly that they were setting the record straight. For they alleged that certain narratives of these texts had been deliberately falsified by their adversaries, the Brahmins, proponents of the Vedic rituals and worshippers of such divinities as Brahmā, Viṣṇu, and Śiva. For the Jainas who did not believe in a creator God, who rejected the efficacy of the Vedic and Tantric rituals, and who questioned the power of the Deity to grant salvation, the Purāṇic descriptions of the sport of these divinities was of no value whatsoever. Indeed, one might surmise that if the Purāṇas had been content only to extoll the virtues of these gods, the Jainas probably would have ignored them as literature unfit for study by devout followers of the Jina, and of little consequence for their own creed. For the Jainas too had their own texts, called the Jinacaritas (biographies of their celebrated Tīrthaṅkaras), which could be expanded into popular narratives that could compete with the heretical Purāṇas.

What made the Jaina writers view these Hindu Purāṇas with hostility was the Brahminic attempt to appropriate such worldly heroes as Rāma and Kṛṣṇa, sanctify their secular lives, and set them up as divine incarnations of their god Viṣṇu. The devotional movements that grew up around these so-called avatars threatened to overwhelm the Jaina laity, who mostly belonged to the affluent merchant castes, and there was the increasing danger that they might return to the Brahminic fold from which they had earlier been converted. Rāma and Kṛṣṇa originally figured as human heroes even in the Brahminic Epics, which extolled their righteous rulership or heroic victories and thus were acceptable to all Indians, regardless of religion or creed. But once the proponents of Vedic religion identified them with the Vedic god Viṣṇu, the Jaina teachers seemed to have been faced with a difficult choice: either to accept the Brahminic version of history and forego their own identity as upholders of a different faith or to set forth a new version of these tales in which these two heroes would be integrated into the Jaina tradition and their magnificent lives would be made subservient to the holy careers of the Tīrthaṅkaras, the last of whom, namely, Vardhamāna, was appropriately hailed as Mahāvīra, the Great Hero!

The legends of the Tīrthaṅkaras are as foreign to the Brahminic traditions as are the stories of the Vedic and Purāṇic divinities to the Jainas. But both traditions must have found something that could be profitably exploited to present their own worldviews and ethical teachings in the historical accounts of Rāma and Kṛṣṇa, their mildly virtuous brothers Lakṣmaṇa and Balarāma, and their valorous adversaries, Rāvaṇa and Jarāsandha, respectively. The Jaina authors, who may well have preserved a different recension of these accounts than the one handed down in the Brahminic tradition, might have then decided to portray these heroes in such a manner as would be consistent with their peculiar doctrines of *karma* and salvation. This probably explains both the complete absence of the category known as *itihāsa* (Epic) in the Jaina literature and the presence of such unusual narrative texts as *Paümacariya* and *Pāṇḍava Purāṇa,* names conspicuously absent from the traditional list of Brahminic Purāṇas. The Jaina Purāṇas are thus distinguished from their Brahminic counterparts by their integration of the pan-Indian *itihāsas* with the exclusively Jaina legends of the Tīrthaṅkaras, which span more than an entire eon (*kalpa*).

How and when this process of Jainizing the accounts of the Epic heroes began is a question that, strangely enough, has not yet been raised. But a glance at the beginnings of the Jaina Purāṇic literature[1] indicates that this trend towards assimilation could have begun only after the elevation of Kṛṣṇa as an avatar of Viṣṇu in the Brahminic Epics and Purāṇas. This hypothesis is based on the fact that in the Jaina texts the names Baladeva and Vāsudeva are not restricted to the brothers otherwise known as Balarāma and Kṛṣṇa, the two Purāṇic avatars of Viṣṇu; instead, they serve as names of two distinct classes of mighty brothers, who appear nine times in each half of the time cycles of the Jaina cosmology and jointly rule half the earth as half-Cakrins! The texts give us no clue as to how the Jainas arrived at such an extraordinary class of beings, conspicuously absent from the Brahminic mythology as well as the earlier strata of the Jaina canonical literature. But it is possible to trace their origin to certain earlier lists of *śalākā puruṣas,* "Illustrious Beings," appearing in the Jinacarita of the pontiff Bhadrabāhu, who is said to have been a contemporary (and teacher) of Candragupta, the Mauryan emperor (ca. 330 B.C.E.). Incorporated in the famous *Kalpa Sūtra*[2] since very ancient times, this text contains a list of twenty-four Tīrthaṅkaras, beginning with Ṛṣabha and ending with Vardhamāna Mahāvīra, and contains a skeletal biography of these Supreme Teachers, with special emphasis on the five *kalyāṇas* or auspicious moments of their holy career, namely, conception (*garbha*), birth (*janma*), renunciation (*dīkṣā*), enlightenment (*kevalajñāna*) and death (*nirvāṇa*).

The Therevāda list of the twenty-five Buddhas (with Siddhārtha Gautama as the last), given in the *Buddhavaṃsa,*[3] was also probably formulated in the post-Mauryan period. Both of these Śramaṇic lists predate the lists of the Daśāvatāras and the still larger lists of the Aṃśāvatāras found in the later Purāṇas.[4] At some time soon after the compilation of the Jinacarita, the Jaina teachers seem to have drawn up a similar list of Cakravartins, next only to their Tīrthaṅkaras in glory, as is suggested by the example of Bharata, the eldest son of the first Tīrthaṅkara Ṛṣabha. Bharata appears in the Jaina canon as an ideal layman and a king, upholder of the Jaina law of nonviolence or noninjury (*ahiṃsā*), the first Cakravartin of this eon, from whom was derived the name *Bhāratavarṣa,* the continent of India. The list contained the following names of twelve such

Cakravartins, appropriately, half the number of the Tīrthaṅkaras, who claimed to be the Lords of Six Continents (*ṣaṭkhaṇḍa-adhipati*),[5] of which only the first two can be traced to the Brahminic Purāṇas: (1) Bharata, (2) Sagara, (3) Maghavan, (4) Sanatkumāra, (5) Śānti, (6) Kunthu, (7) Ara, (8) Subhauma (9) Mahāpadma, (10) Hariṣeṇa, (11) Jayasena, and (12) Brahmadatta.

It is said that three of these twelve Cakravartins, namely, Śānti, Kunthu and Ara, played the role of a Cakravartin as well as that of a Tīrthaṅkara, thus effectively reducing the number of Cakravartins to nine, a figure that will serve as a model in preparing other categories of the Illustrious Beings as well. Of the remaining nine, six Cakravartins, following the example of Bharata, renounced the world to become Jaina mendicants and attained release (*mokṣa*) after their death. Two, however, Subhauma and Brahmadatta, ruled unrighteously and were reborn in hell. It is evident that the Jaina list of Cakravartins made provision for bringing into the Jaina fold both virtuous heroes and villainous tyrants, in order to illustrate the Jaina doctrine of karmic justice as well as the path of salvation.

The hero as a spiritual victor, or Jina (an epithet claimed in ancient times for both the Buddha and Mahāvīra), and as a supreme ruler, or Cakravartin, were categories that originated in the Śramaṇic traditions of the Gangetic valley. In compiling the lists of these two kinds of "heroes," therefore, the Jainas were not influenced by Brahminic mythology or literary models. But the categories of Baladevas and Vāsudevas are unknown to the Buddhist tradition and, as noted earlier, cannot be traced to the earlier strata of the Jaina canon. The introduction of these novel categories in the Jaina tradition, therefore, cannot be explained without reference to the myths surrounding the two popular cultic figures of the Vaiṣṇava tradition, namely, Balarāma and his younger brother, Kṛṣṇa of Mathura.

Archeological remains found in the region of Mathura and literary references appearing in such works as that of the grammarian Patañjali support the fact that the popularity of these two cultic figures had reached its zenith in the Mauryan and the Śuṅga period and that the Bhāgavata religion had become widespread in Mathura and the Western India. This period coincides with the large scale migration of Jainas from Magadha to Mathura, where they flourished for several centuries, and their subsequent journeys to Punjab, Rajasthan, and Gujarat, and thence to the Deccan. It seems probable that close contact of their laypeople with the votaries of these cultic figures might have induced the Jaina *ācārya*s to devise means of integrating them with the Jaina tradition. There probably existed a canonical tradition that their twenty-second Tīrthaṅkara, Nemi, was a prince of the Yādava clan and that he was a cousin of Balarāma and Kṛṣṇa.[6] By accepting the Brahminic myths associated with these two heroes, albeit modified to suit the Jaina sensibilities, and by making them subservient to the Tīrthaṅkara Nemi, the Jainas could claim that these two popular heroes had actually once been members of the Jaina community and had, in these degenerate times, been falsely claimed by the Brahmins as incarnations of their god Viṣṇu. Several ancient (probably Kuśāṇa) images depicting the Tīrthaṅkara Nemi on a high pedestal flanked by the figures of Balarāma and Kṛṣṇa, now preserved in the Mathura Museum, attest to the credibility of our hypotheses.[7]

But Balarāma and Kṛṣṇa were not the only human avatars of Viṣṇu: long before them another pair of illustrious brothers had flourished; these brothers, Rāma and Lakṣmaṇa, also had been appropriated by the Brahmins as incarnations of the same deity appearing on earth to vanquish the demon Rāvaṇa. The coincidence of finding two such pairs of brothers, deeply attached to each other and fighting the same enemy, must have played some part in suggesting to the Jaina authors the possibility of devising newer categories of Illustrious Beings as a supplement to their lists of the Tīrthaṅkaras and Cakravartins.

The designations of these new categories of heroes, the Baladevas and Vāsudevas, are clearly adaptations of the personal names of the two Yādava brothers, Balarāma and Kṛṣṇa, respectively. The Jaina texts are ambiguous in defining their precise roles, but the intention of the *ācārya*s seems to be to depict the one (the Baladeva) as leading the life of an ideal Jaina layman, subsequently renouncing the world to become a Jaina monk, and to portray the other (the Vāsudeva) as the hero's companion, who is capable of carrying out terrible destruction regardless of the evil consequences that may ensue. They are often described as the joint sovereigns of half the earth (half-Cakrins), who play out their respective roles only during those long intervals when a Cakravartin, the ruler of the whole earth, may not appear. They are nine pairs of brothers born of the same father but different mothers; the elder brothers are the Baladevas and the younger are the Vāsudevas. All of the Baladevas fit the stereotype of Balarāma: like him they are white in complexion and can be recognized because they carry the weapon that characterized him, the plough (*aparājita-hala*). Because of this, they are also known as "Halabhṛts."[8] The following names appear in the list of Baladevas: Vijaya, Acala, Dharma, Suprabha, Sudarśana, Nandiṣeṇa, Nandimitra, Rāma (also called Padma), and Balarāma.

It should be noted here that Rāma, the hero of the *Rāmāyaṇa,* is reckoned as a Baladeva and, hence, is referred to by the Jaina Purāṇas as Halabhṛt, although no Brahminic account designates him as such.

All of the Vāsudevas are modeled after the descriptions of Kṛṣṇa found in the Brahminic Purāṇas. They are blue-black (*nīla*) in complexion and are designated by several names applied exclusively to Kṛṣṇa in the Brahminic tradition, for example, Keśava, Mādhava, Govinda, Viṣṇu, Janārdana, and, most importantly, Nārāyaṇa, which is used regularly as a synonym for the generic name Vāsudeva. The Vāsudevas are said to remain young forever, without growing facial hair, and come to possess the following seven gems (*ratna*s): the wheel (*sudarśana-cakra*), the mace (*kaumudī-gadā*), the sword (*saunandaka-asi*), the missile (*amogha-śakti*), the bow (*śārṅga-dhanu*), the conch (*pañcajanya-śaṅkha*), and the diamond (*kaustubha-maṇi*).[9] The following names appear in the list of Vāsudevas: Tripṛṣṭha, Dvipṛṣṭha, Svayambhū, Puruṣottama, Puruṣasiṃha, Puruṣapuṇḍarīka, Datta, Lakṣmaṇa, and Kṛṣṇa. The noteworthy feature of this list is that it includes Lakṣmaṇa; the son of Daśaratha thus gets the appellation Vāsudeva (literally, "son of Vasudeva"), a title never applied to him in the Brahminic texts.

The two lists above are accompanied by a complementary list of the Prati-vāsudevas, or Prati-nārāyaṇas, the deadly adversaries of the Vāsudevas.[10] This list includes: Aśvagrīva, Tāraka, Madhu, Madhusūdana, Madhukrīḍa, Niśumbha, Bali, Rāvaṇa, and Jarāsandha. Rāvaṇa and Jarāsandha are, of course, immediately recognizable; and the other Prati-vāsudevas, unlike the members of the other two categories of heroes, are not altogether unfamiliar. Some of them are names of demons (*asura*s) destroyed by Viṣṇu in his various avatars. In the Jaina Purāṇas, however, they are presented as *vidyādhara*s, men possessing great magic powers but given to excessive forms of greed, lust (as in the case of Rāvaṇa), or envy (as in the case of Jarāsandha). It is said that a Prati-vāsudeva has nursed a deep enmity against a Vāsudeva in previous lives and that the accumulated hatred culminates in a tremendous battle of cosmic proportions during his present incarnation. Further, it is believed that the wheel-gem called "*sudarśana*" first appears miraculously in the armory of the Prati-vāsudeva, tempting him to challenge the Vāsudeva, his predestined enemy, to battle. However, partly because of the Baladeva's power of merit, but mainly because of the invincible valor of the Vāsudeva, the wheel-gem fails to kill him when hurled by the Prati-vāsudeva in his direction. Instead, it comes of its own accord into the hands of the Vāsudeva, who throws it at the Prati-vāsudeva and beheads him; thereupon the Vāsudeva is hailed by gods and men as a half-Cakrin, the Lord of the Three Continents (Trikhaṇḍādhipati). Pursued by his evil *karma,* the Prati-vāsudeva is reborn in hell but, in due course, becomes a human being, follows the Jaina path, and attains *mokṣa.*

As was also the case with the Prati-vāsudevas, the class names Baladeva and Vāsudeva, the epithets used in describing the gods, and their personal names leave no room for doubting that the Jaina authors had deliberately embarked upon a project of producing grand narratives that would run parallel to those popularized by the Vaiṣṇavites. However, in retelling their versions the Jaina authors shrewdly made a major change that was to accomplish at a single stroke both the elevation of Rāma to the status of a Jaina saint and the consignment of Kṛṣṇa to hell. Both of these incarnations of Viṣṇu should have been accorded equal status, since both had successful vanquished demonic forces and thereby had accomplished the avowed purpose of an avatar. Yet, employing their discriminatory wisdom, the Jainas raised Rāma to the benevolent category of a Baladeva by freeing him from the dreadful task of killing Rāvaṇa. Instead, the Jainas chose to have this destruction occur at the hands of Lakṣmaṇa and thus cast him, together with Kṛṣṇa, in the role of the brave but malevolent Vāsudeva. They were then free to declare quite candidly that in accordance with the inscrutable laws of *karma,* all Baladevas had attained *mokṣa* (with the exception of Balarāma, who had been reborn in heaven), while their brothers the Vāsudevas were condemned to hell for having violently killed their archenemies, the Prati-vāsudevas, in fulfillment of a long-cherished evil aspiration (*nidāna*) from past lives.[11]

This would appear to be the process by which the "corrections" introduced by the Jainas into the Brahminic accounts of the Epic heroes occurred. In the course of time, even these Jainized versions would receive further modifications at the hands of zealous sectarian authors. Additional lists, such as that of the nine Nāradas[12] (Jaina counterparts of the Brahminic sage of that name, they were the instigators of strife between the Vāsudevas and the Prati-vāsudevas) and that of the eleven Rudras[13] (apostate Jaina mendicants who would misuse their occult powers) appeared, making the narratives as edifying and entertaining as those of their rivals. Thus is explained the origin of the sixty-three Illustrious Beings[14] (*śalākā puruṣas*: twenty-four Tīrthaṅkaras, twelve Cakravartins, nine Baladevas, nine Vāsudevas, and nine Prati-vāsudevas), who comprised the subject matter of the Jaina versions of the *itihāsas* and Purāṇas, an amalgamation of narratives pertaining to both the Spiritual Victors (Jinas) and the worldly heroes of the land of Bhāratavarṣa.

Just as the traditional eighteen Purāṇas, together with the Epics, are considered *smṛtis*, which were subservient in their authority to the *śrutis*, or Vedic literature, the Jaina Purāṇic literature is also relegated to a position secondary to that of the Jaina canon, known as the Pūrvas and Aṅgas. These latter two are said to have proceeded from the mouth of the Tīrthaṅkara Mahāvīra and to have been handed down in the oral tradition through the lineage of the Gaṇadharas, the immediate mendicant disciples of Mahāvīra, and, in a subsequent period, the *ācāryas*. According to Jaina tradition, the subject matter of the Purāṇas, namely, the sixty-three Illustrious Beings, was included in the section called the "Pūrvas" (Ancient Ones), which seems to be a Jaina synonym for the Purāṇa itself. However, the Pūrva became extinct soon after the death of Mahāvīra; according to unanimous Jaina tradition, the last person to retain the memory of a portion of it was the mendicant Bhadrabāhu, the chief pontiff of the Jaina mendicant community prior to the emergence of the Digambaras and the Śvetāmbaras, two rival sects. Both traditions agree that he was a contemporary of Candragupta, the first Mauryan king, who flourished around 330 B.C.E.

After the death of Bhadrabāhu the split between the two sects was so severe that each of them refused to acknowledge the authenticity of the scriptures that had been received in the other's tradition; and each eventually set up its own canonical, commentarial, and narrative literature in conformity with its own sectarian beliefs. Therefore, despite the fact that the contents of the Jaina Purāṇas are traced to the now extinct Pūrvas, the literature that has grown through the ages is a development that began several centuries after the death of Mahāvīra and was imbued with a sectarian spirit from its very inception. Both the Digambaras, who claimed that the entire Aṅga canon was also lost, and the Śvetāmbaras, who asserted that a great deal of it was preserved in their tradition, devised a new category of scripture, *anuyoga* (literally, "Additional Questions" [asked of Mahāvīra]), which was in four parts. The first of these, simply called the *prathamānuyoga,* was devoted to the biographies of the twenty-four Jinas of the present half of the Jaina time cycle (the Avasarpiṇī, or "Descending" half), to which were added, as we saw above, the narratives of the remaining *śalākā puruṣas,* forming the present-day Purāṇas of the Jaina community. Thus what we have available under the rubric of the Jaina Purāṇas are two sets of sectarian narratives, each purporting to describe accurately a single set of the lives of the sixty-three Illustrious Beings.

Unlike the Brahminic Purāṇas, most of which are of unknown authorship and in Sanskrit, all of the Jaina Purāṇas have well-known authors and are available in Sanskrit, Prakrit, and Apabhramsa as well. As a matter of fact, the earliest extant Jaina Purāṇa is in Maharashtri Prakrit, composed probably in conformity with the Jaina belief that Prakrit was the sacred language in which the words of Mahāvīra were preserved. However, this earliest narrative work is neither labelled as a "Purāṇa" nor named after a Tīrthaṅkara. Instead, as the title *Paümacariya*[15] would indicate, it is a *cariya* (Sanskrit *carita*), a "biography," a term rather close to the designation *itihāsa,* and celebrates the life of Padma, a Jaina name for Rāma, the eighth Vāsudeva of Jaina mythology, who was none other than the hero of Vālmīki's *Rāmāyaṇa*. The author of this work, Vimalasūri, is said to have been a mendicant of the Digambara sect. According to the colophon preserved in the text, the work was completed in the year 530 after the death of Mahāvīra; this corresponds to the fourth year of the common era. However, the linguistic study of the text has led scholars such as Hermann Jacobi and K. R. Chandra to place it in the third or fourth century C.E. The entire work is divided into 118 sections and consists of 8,651 *gāthā*s, which can be considered equivalent to about twelve thousand *śloka*s in extent; it is probably the earliest and longest poetical work extant in Prakrit.

There is probably no connection between the title *Paumacariya,* and the *Padma Purāṇa,* one of the eighteen Brahminic Purāṇas. The word *padma* in the title of latter work does not refer to Rāma, as it does in the Jaina work, but rather to the lotus shape of the earth after its recreation at the beginning of a new evolutionary cycle (*sarga*).[16] Vimalasūri's choice of the name *Padma* over the more familiar *Rāma* and *Rāghava* (names that were not unknown to him) may be considered an attempt to assert a Jaina identity for a work on the hero of the *Rāmāyaṇa*. This should not, however, mislead us into believing that the *Paümacariya* is merely a Jaina story of Rāma, for the work essentially covers all of the *śalākā puruṣas,* who flourished from the time of Ṛṣabha, the first Tīrthaṅkara, up to that of the twentieth Tīrthaṅkara, Munisuvrata, in whose regime (*tīrtha* or *śāsana*), roughly corresponding to the second Brahminic *yuga,* the actual story of Rāma took place. This becomes evident when we analyze the contents of the book's 118 chapters. The first 24 describe the Illustrious Beings who flourished before the time of Rāma; the next 61 chapters are devoted to the exploits of the brothers Rāma and Lakṣmaṇa, the eighth Baladeva and Vāsudeva, respectively, and end the account with their coronation in Ayodhyā after the destruction of Rāvaṇa, the eighth Prati-vāsudeva. In the remaining 33 chapters the poet describes the events following the banishment of Sītā; these events lead up to the death of Lakṣmaṇa and Rāma's renunciation and attainment of *mokṣa*.

The introductory portions of the *Paümacariya* reveal quite openly the purpose of writing the story: the presentation of a Jaina account of the tale of Rāma that should be seen as a deliberate rejection of the Brahminic version of the same story. The *Cariya* opens with a scene depicting Śreṇika, the king of Magadha, approaching Lord Mahāvīra in the holy assembly and asking him questions about the veracity of the accounts of Rāma and Rāvaṇa that he has heard from "*kuśāstra-vādins*" (expounders of false scriptures), a reference undoubtedly to the Brahminic version of that story. It should be remembered that Śreṇika was a recent convert to Jainism through his wife Cellanā, an aunt of Mahāvīra. The king is therefore an excellent instrument for the Jainas to use as an interlocutor, especially where there was an occasion to point out the beliefs of the heretics that needed to be examined. It is not surprising, therefore, that the king reaffirms his faith in Jainism by showing his disbelief in accounts he heard formerly, in which Rāvaṇa and his brothers were demons (*rākṣasas*) or given to the eating of flesh or in which Rāvaṇa defeated Indra, the king of gods, and yet had his powerful armies defeated by a bunch of monkeys (*vānaras*)! Śreṇika is specific in pointing his finger at the source of this travesty as he sees it: "The poets have composed the *Rāmāyaṇa* with perverse contents, like the killing of a lion by a deer or like the destruction of an elephant by a dog . . . All this appears to me to be lies, contrary to reasoning, and not worthy of belief by wise men."[17]

These and other similar questions raised by Śreṇika provide an opportunity for the Jaina author to put forth a new story of Rāma as it was originally narrated by the Omniscient Jina to the king, and as the author had received it in the tradition of the *ācāryas*. But the story proper will not begin until the king is given a detailed account of the lineage (*vaṃśa*) in which the hero Rāma was born, and that tale is closely connected with the origin of civilization at the start of a new time cycle. Thus a full discourse on the Jaina concept of time and space or the universe, known as *saṃsāra,* is required to be unfolded for the king to appreciate properly the place of Rāma in the Jaina history of the world. It is by this circuitous method that Vimalasūri introduces the Purāṇa topics known to us as creation, destruction, ancient dynasties, epochs of the Manus, and later dynasties. These *pañcalakṣaṇas*, the five characteristics of the Brahminic Purāṇas, thus become guidelines for the Jaina Purāṇas as well, albeit under different headings. They provide the Jainas with a new opportunity to expound their worldview, especially in the contexts of their independent cosmology, the beginning of civilization in our epoch, and the founding of the Jaina order of monks, from which would rise the most holy of the Illustrious Beings, the Tīrthaṅkaras and their eminent lay devotees.

Having thus provided a brief but essential outline of the Jaina doctrine pertaining to time, space, and the movement of souls therein, and having narrated in brief form the narratives of the twenty Tīrthaṅkaras, the nine Cakravartins, and the seven previous sets of the Baladevas, Vāsudevas, and Prati-vāsudevas, Vimalasūri launches the story of Padma, the Jaina version of Rāma, the son of Daśaratha. The story itself does not differ significantly from the version given in the Vālmīki *Rāmāyaṇa;*[18] the changes are more in the details of the plot or in the incredible descriptions of the secondary characters that had so confused the king (and, no doubt, many others who had heard it)! Rāvaṇa, in the Jaina version, is not a demon but a Jaina layman who has mastered certain magic powers (*vidyās*), is hailed as a *vidyādhara,* and has at his command a large host of other such beings to help him in his ambition to rule the world. Even the monkeys of the *Rāmāyaṇa,* namely, Bali and Sugrīva, are here declared to be *vidyādharas*, with Hanumān enjoying the additional distinction of being a God of Love (Kāmadeva), possessing a large harem of most beautiful women, yet destined to become a Jaina monk and attain *mokṣa* in that very life.

Vimalasūri also very cleverly employs the Jaina motif of renunciation in order to rectify some of the wrongs done to certain eminent heroines of the Epic. Kaikeyī, for example, has been portrayed by Vālmīki as a selfish woman wantonly demanding the kingdom for her son Bharata; in the Jaina version she is made to appear rather more like a concerned mother anxious to keep her son with her. In the Jaina story, Daśaratha seriously contemplates renouncing the world to become a Jaina monk; when the young Bharata hears of this, he becomes determined to follow his father into the forest and to assume the vows of a Jaina mendicant. Kaikeyī cannot bear the loss of both husband and son and believes that Bharata could be lured back to household life if he were offered the kingdom. Daśaratha readily agrees to this—in payment of the boon he has previously promised her—and informs Rāma of his decision, whereupon the noble Rāma obeys his father's will and proceeds to the forest of his own accord, accompanied by Sītā and Lakṣmaṇa.

The motif of renunciation becomes even more appropriate in the treatment of Sītā: in the Brahminic version, Sītā ends her life by what is euphemistically called "entering the earth," that is, committing suicide by falling into a pit. In Jainism, retribution for such a death is instantaneous rebirth in hell. The Jainas probably were determined not to make her suffer beyond what she had already undergone; in the Jaina version she renounces the world to become a Jaina nun as soon as her sons have been united with their estranged father. We have already alluded to the story of the death of Rāvaṇa, the Prati-vāsudeva, at the hands of Lakṣmaṇa the Vāsudeva, and their rebirth in hell as a consequence of their violent activities. We are told that Sītā, after performing great austerities, is reborn in heaven as a male god; having discovered by means of her supernatural knowledge the fallen state of these two heroes, she visits them in their hell and admonishes them to give up their long-cherished enmity. As for Rāma, the supreme hero of the *Paümacariya,* he transcends both heaven and hell by renouncing worldly life to become a Jaina mendicant and becomes a Siddha, a Perfected and Omniscient Being, at the end of his mortal life.

It may be pertinent to ask whether indeed Vimalasūri was influenced in his depiction of the story of Rāma and Lakṣmaṇa by the Purāṇic narratives of Balarāma and Kṛṣṇa, who, as we have suggested, were the models for the Jaina categories of Baladeva and Vāsudeva, respectively. Since the story of Rāma ends long before the advent of the twenty-second Tīrthaṅkara, Nemi (a cousin of Balarāma and Kṛṣṇa in the Jaina tradition), Vimalasūri's story does not include these latter heroes, but there is a rather insignificant detail in the *Paümacariya* that does betray such an influence. It is well known that in the Purāṇic texts Kṛṣṇa is said to have had sixteen thousand wives; this tradition is very much a part of the folklore surrounding the Kṛṣṇa myth even to this day. As we have seen earlier, Kṛṣṇa and Lakṣmaṇa are both called "Vāsudevas" (or "Nārāyaṇas") in Jaina mythology. Since the descriptions of these two heroes have been almost identical in many respects, one would expect that Lakṣmaṇa in the Jaina tradition would be found to have had a similar number of wives. One is therefore not surprised to find that the *Paümacariya* and the subsequent Jaina narratives about Lakṣmaṇa do indeed describe him as having sixteen thousand wives, with Rāma and Balarāma having only half as many wives as their younger brothers, the Vāsudevas![19]

Obviously the Jaina authors did not think much of Rāma's alleged virtue of monogamy as extolled in the Brahminic *Rāmāyaṇa.* Or, most probably, they found it expedient to make this change in order to establish uniformity with regard to the descriptions of these two pairs of Baladevas and Vāsudevas; this principle would be extended later to all of the remaining pairs of these two classes of heroes. Rāma's single wife certainly would have looked extraordinary in contrast to his brother's thousands of spouses. The excessive number of wives attributed to Rāma might also serve better to emphasize the greater degree of his detachment when the time of his renunciation would arrive. In the case of Lakṣmaṇa, however, as a Vāsudeva he was destined to be reborn in hell; hence his excessive indulgence in carnal pleasures would only contribute to his inevitable fate.

Vimala's Prakrit *Paümacariya* became the standard text for a great many Jaina compositions on the life of Rāma. Most noteworthy of these is the Sanskrit *Padma-Carita* in eighteen thousand *śloka*s, completed in 676 C.E. by the Digambara mendicant Raviṣeṇa.[20] Raviṣeṇa's Sanskrit rendering with added embellishments inspired the composition of Sanskrit Purāṇa works by a large number of Jaina poets, in both the Digambara and Śvetāmbara sects, as well as two Purāṇas in Apabhramsa by two Digambara laymen, one the eighth-century Svayambhū[21] and another the eleventh-century Puṣpadanta.[22]

The *Paümacariya* bore the name of Padma, that is, Rāma, because this hero flourished at a time when there was no living Tīrthaṅkara; hence a Baladeva, a *śalākā puruṣa* of a lesser order, could be elevated to the position of the supreme hero of this text. In the case of Kṛṣṇa and Balarāma, however, a similar elevation could not be effected, because the Yādava brothers were contemporaries, indeed, cousins of the twenty-second Tīrthaṅkara, Nemi (also called Ariṣṭanemi or Neminātha). The second stage in the development of the Jaina Purāṇas, therefore, begins ostensibly as a description of the advent of this Jina Nemi and only secondarily as that of the Epic heroes Balarāma and Kṛṣṇa. Since all three of these heroes were born in the great Hari dynasty (of which the Yadus were a prominent branch), a Purāṇa named after that lineage could readily encompass the narratives of a Tīrthaṅkara and of the two lesser Epic heroes as well. It is therefore fitting that the Prakrit *Paümacariya* should be succeeded by a text entitled *Harivaṃśa Purāṇa,* composed in 783 C.E., in Saurashtra—a Vaiṣṇavite stronghold—by a Digambara mendicant, [Punnāṭa] Jinasena.[23]

Whether the Jaina author owed his title to the *Harivaṃśa Parva,*[24] an appendix to the *Mahābhārata,* is a question that cannot be answered with certainty. There is no doubt, however, that both narratives share a great many common episodes, especially ones that concern the life of Kṛṣṇa and that of his sister Ekanāsā. Even so, there are a great many other characters in the Hari lineage who do not come under the purview of the *Harivaṃśa Parva*. One notable example is Kṛṣṇa's father, Vasudeva, whom the Jainas consider to be one of the twenty-four Kāmadevas of our time cycle.[25] For reasons that are not clear to us, the Jainas of Jinasena's time were more fascinated by this old character than by his more charismatic adolescent son, who wandered the pastures of Mathura! A great work called *Vasudeva-hiṇḍī* (Travels of Vasudeva), in two parts of eleven thousand and eighteen thousand verses, respectively, was composed as early as the fifth century C.E. in Maharashtri Prakrit by the two Śvetāmbara mendicant authors Sanghadāsagaṇi and Dharmadāsagaṇi.[26] The entire work was devoted to narratives concerning the amorous exploits of its hero, Vāsudeva, who wandered all over India for a hundred years and won the hands of numerous women in marriage. Such a work, however, could not qualify as a Purāṇa, since Vāsudeva was only a Kāmadeva and, as such, could not be a part of the traditional list of the *śalākā puruṣas*. Jinasena's *Harivaṃśa Purāṇa,* therefore, affords him a fresh opportunity to bring together a great many such related episodes (*ākhyānas*) and to weave them into the more prominent narratives of the officially accepted heroes. In this manner, the *Harivaṃśa Purāṇa* grew to be a treasure-house of information on such miscellaneous items as music (Saṅgīta-śāstra), dance (Sāmudrika-śāstra), and art (Śilpaśāstra), to mention only a few—a Jaina encyclopedia, as it were, in the manner of the Brahminic Purāṇas.

With regard to form, however, Jinasena closely follows the pattern established earlier by Vimalasūri. His work also begins with King Śreṇika's visit to the assembly of Mahāvīra, where the king asks a question about a contemporary, King Jitaśatru, a scion of the Hari's clan who had recently died as a Jaina saint. In response, Mahāvīra, through his interlocutor Gautama, narrates the origin of the Hari dynasty, preceded by a description of other illustrious dynasties, notably the Ikṣvāku and the Kuru, in which had been born a great many Tīrthaṅkaras and other *śalākā puruṣa*s. The first seventeen chapters of the *Harivaṃśa Purāṇa* are thus devoted to the description of the notable events that took place during the regimes of the first twenty-one Tīrthaṅkaras, culminating with that of Nemi, during whose time the Yādava branch of the Hari dynasty came into being.

In the eighteenth chapter the author sets forth the family tree of the ten Yādava brothers, the Vṛṣṇis, of whom King Samudravijaya, the father of Tīrthaṅkara Nemi, was the oldest, and Vasudeva, the father of Balarāma and Kṛṣṇa, the youngest. One might expect the Purāṇa to proceed at this point with the narrative of the Jina Nemi, yet the author finds it necessary to devote a full twelve chapters to describing the amorous pursuits of Vasudeva. The poetic accounts of Kṛṣṇa's rapturous amorous activities with the *gopīs* and other women is well known to us through the *Harivaṃśa Parva* and the *Bhāgavata Purāṇa*. One wonders if the Jainas, in portraying the father rather than the son in this manner, were not attempting to deflect attention away from Kṛṣṇa, the popular god of medieval India. Perhaps freeing Kṛṣṇa from the debaucheries otherwise attributed to him in the Brahminic Purāṇas made it possible for the Jainas to accept him as one of their own heroes, dignified enough to share the company of other *śalākā puruṣas*! Be that as it may, the actual story of Nemi, Kṛṣṇa, and Balarāma thus begins only in the thirty-third chapter, almost exactly at the midpoint of the *Harivaṃśa Purāṇa*.

The narrative pertaining to Kṛṣṇa gives the Jaina authors an excellent opportunity to introduce the episode of the *Mahābhārata* war between the Pāṇḍavas and their cousins, the Kauravas. The Pāṇḍavas were maternal cousins of Kṛṣṇa (sons of his aunts Kuntī and Mādrī), and their family strife made Kṛṣṇa's participation necessary for their victory in the war against the faction of Duryodhana. Here, too, the Jainas have effected a great many changes in the *Mahābhārata* story: excising entirely those parts that were offensive to them (such as Vyāsa's begetting children by Levirate appointment [*niyoga*] on the widows Ambikā and Ambālikā) or modifying other stories, such as that of Kuntī's obtaining children by the help of gods or the polyandry of Draupadī.[27] Nor did the Jainas have Kṛṣṇa appear in the great war as a charioteer for Arjuna preaching his Divine Song, the *Bhagavad Gītā,* but instead only as an instigator and an advocate of bravery in warfare.

The narrative pertaining to the untimely renunciation of Nemi (on the eve of his marriage) and his attainment of Jinahood dominates the rest of the work. The Purāṇa concludes with the description of Kṛṣṇa's death at the hands of his step-brother Jarākumāra (as in the *Bhāgavata* story); the renunciation of Balarāma and the five Pāṇḍava brothers, together with their innumerable spouses, including Satyabhāmā and Draupadī; their rigorous austerities; and the attainment of heaven by everyone except Kṛṣṇa, who, alas, being a Vāsudeva, was born in the same hell where his archenemy Jarāsandha, the last Prati-vāsudeva, had been dispatched by him earlier in the great war!

There are five principal characters who stand out in Jinasena's rendering of the Kṛṣṇa narrative. Of these, Nemi is an entirely Jaina character and does not figure in the Brahminic accounts. We have already remarked on the relatively excessive amount of attention paid by the Jainas to Vasudeva, the father of Kṛṣṇa and Balarāma. Before we turn to further modifications made by the Jainas in the stories of the latter two heroes, we may pause here to take into account a very important Jaina narrative pertaining to Kṛṣṇa's sister. She does not play a major role in the Brahminic narratives, either in the *Harivaṃśa Parva* or in the *Bhāgavata Purāṇa*. But Jinasena's version, for reasons that will become evident, devotes an entire chapter to the unfolding of her rather tragic life. This sister of Kṛṣṇa, Ekānaṃśā, who is worshipped as a personification of Durgā, appears probably for the first time in the *Harivaṃśa Parva* in connection with the birth of Kṛṣṇa.[28]

According to this account, Lord Viṣṇu asked his Yogamāyā to be born as a daughter to the cowherd couple Nanda and Yaśodā at the time when he himself was to be born to Devakī as Kṛṣṇa. It was foreseen that this daughter of Yaśodā would be exchanged for Devakī's son, Kṛṣṇa. Accordingly, she was brought home to Mathura by Vasudeva and placed by the side of Devakī, who did not know of the exchange and believed that she had given birth to a daughter. Kaṃsa, expecting the birth of Kṛṣṇa as foretold by the sage Nārada, went to Devakī's side; when he realized that the baby was a female, he grabbed it and, out of spite, smashed it to pieces by hurling it against a rock. Of course, this was no ordinary infant; she rose immediately into the sky, appeared in the fully divine form of a goddess and warned Kaṃsa of his impending doom. She made her abode in the Vindhya mountains and was known as Devī Ekānaṃśā, an epiphany of Durgā, a guardian deity of hunters and other hill-dwelling tribals, from whom she received offerings of flesh and blood.[29] The author of the *Harivaṃśa Parva* does not explain explicitly why she had to be the chosen deity of hunters, but probably it was not considered an inappropriate role for a woman who had, after all, been born into a lower-caste cowherd family.

The Jainas probably could have chosen to ignore this story entirely or could have dismissed it with only a brief account of her death at the hands of Kaṃsa, similar to the earlier accounts of Kaṃsa killing Kṛṣṇa's six brothers, born to Devakī before him. But the Jainas must have seen here an excellent opportunity to educate at least their own devotees, if not also the Vaiṣṇavites (who believed this story to be literally true), about the error of the Brahminic accounts of her becoming a bloodthirsty goddess. The name Ekānaṃśā is rarely used elsewhere but is attested for the first time in the *Harivaṃśa Parva,* where it is used as a synonym for such epithets of Durgā as Kātyāyanī, Pārvatī, Nārāyaṇī, Vindhyavāsinī, and so on, and where she is depicted as favoring devotees who propitiate her with flesh and blood. Yet in this same text she is also called an "Āryā,"[30] a term that is used among the Jainas for a nun (*sādhvī*), a circumstance that probably explains the peculiarly Jaina ending of her story.

The word Ekānaṃśā, literally meaning "the single portionless one," itself does not appear in Jinasena's work, but there can be no doubt that this obscure name must have inspired the Jaina story of Kṛṣṇa's sister called, instead, "Ekanāsā." Ekanāsā literally means "one having a single nose," (that is, nostril) and sounds a great deal like Ekānaṃśā; and it is not unlikely that by the time of Jinasena this goddess had come to be known by that name, at least among the lower classes of her worshippers, and was not therefore a purely Jaina invention. Jinasena very ingeniously utilizes this name to construct a counter story to that of the *Harivaṃśa Parva.*

According to his version, adopted by all succeeding Jaina writers, Ekanāsā was not a goddess but the daughter of the herdsman Nanda and his wife Yaśodā. As in the Brahminic story she was brought to Mathura in exchange for Kṛṣṇa. In the Jaina story, however, Kaṃsa does not kill the female infant. At first, Kaṃsa thinks that a woman could be no threat to him, but later he reflects that her future husband might well become his enemy; therefore he disfigures her face by pounding on her nose. As a result of this she came to be known as Ekanāsā, "one with a single nostril," or Cippiṭa-nāsikā, "one with a crushed nose." This girl grew to become a voluptuous maiden, but because of her hideously deformed nose she was mocked by all and remained without a suitor. It is said that in the full prime of her youth, as she was admiring herself in a mirror, the young sons of Balarāma passed by her and ridiculed her nose, called her by the hated epithet Cippiṭa-nāsikā and ran away, laughing derisively at her.[31] Stung by this ridicule, Ekanāsā (whose real name is not given anywhere by Jinasena or other authors) went crying to a Jaina mendicant and begged him to reveal the past *karma* that had brought this misfortune upon her. Perceiving her past life, the monk told her that in a previous birth she had been a very handsome man, proud of his looks and heedless and cruel. Feeling disgust for a Jaina monk seated in meditation, he drove his cart against him and caused him to fall and break his nose. The misfortunes in her present life were retributions for her act of willful mischief against a holy man.

Moved deeply by this story of her past life, Ekanāsā, full of remorse, renounced the world while still a maiden and became a Jaina nun under the guidance of Suvratā, a nun superior. Wandering from place to place with her teacher, she traveled far from Mathura and entered the forests of Vindhya. There she dedicated herself entirely to the most extreme forms of austerities and sat day and night in meditation in isolated forests and on mountaintops. One day, while she was seated rapt in meditation, an army of hunters from that forest who were marching forth together to rob a caravan happened to see her in that position under a tree. Thinking her to be the deity of the forest (*vanadevatā*), they greeted her, asked a boon of protection from her, and pledged to be her slaves and devotees if they were to be successful in their venture. While they were gone, a lion attacked her; the nun Ekanāsā quietly suffered the terrible violence, died peacefully, and was reborn in heaven. When the hunters returned to the site after their successful expedition, they found only a great deal of blood on the place where she had been seated and not a trace of her body, other than three pieces of her fingers. The hunters, who were not instructed in the true religion of nonviolence (*ahiṃsā*), believed that the goddess had disappeared but that she must take delight in blood, since it was in evidence everywhere. Worshipping the three pieces of fingers as emblems of the goddess, they offered her sacrifices of their domestic animals, such as goats and buffaloes.

Thus began, according to the Jaina *Harivaṃśa Purāṇa,* the horrible worship of this goddess Vindhyavāsinī, the cruel "guardian deity" of the heretics! Having narrated this account, entitled "Durgotpatti-varṇana," Jinasena warns the Jaina laymen of the dangers of listening to false scriptures, worshipping the wrong gods, and indulging in the manifold stupidities of the world (*loka-mūḍhatā*) practiced in the name of *dharma!*[32] Ekanāsā does not appear again in Jinasena's narrative, but her depiction here as a cruelly deformed woman sitting in unshakable meditation even at the moment of her death makes her probably a unique example of a heroine (*vīrā*) among the many Purāṇic accounts of male heroes.

Returning to the main hero of the *Harivaṃśa Purāṇa,* the "Vāsudeva" Kṛṣṇa, one finds that Jinasena retains a great many of the accounts of his childhood as narrated in the *Harivaṃśa Parva,* the only major modification being that his numerous enemies are not demons (*asuras*), but animals or human beings endowed with magical powers. For the Jainas these stories had no great religious significance. What distinguishes the Jaina account from the Brahminic narrative is Kṛṣṇa's relationship to his cousin Nemi, the

Tīrthaṅkara, on the one hand, and to his elder brother Balarāma, the "Baladeva," on the other.

Jinasena's narrative of Kṛṣṇa does not begin with his present life but looks back to several of his former lives and extends for at least two lives beyond his death as a "Vāsudeva." It is customary for Jaina authors to begin the life story of a major character with a significant event in one of his or her past lives that may hold the seed that bears fruit in the events of the present life of that person. The story of Kṛṣṇa thus begins in the seventh life prior to his current incarnation.[33] During that lifetime, the person now known as Kṛṣṇa was employed as a cook in the household of a king and gained a great reputation for preparing the most delicious meat dishes; he earned the title of Amṛta-rasāyana, as well as the lordship of ten villages. When the king died and his son succeeded to the throne, the new king came under the influence of a Jaina monk and gave up eating meat altogether. The cook was thus left without a job and also lost the revenue of nine of his ten villages. Realizing that a Jaina monk, the preceptor of the new king, was the cause of his loss, he fed the monk a poisonous bitter gourd; as a result the monk died. Because of this evil act, this cook was reborn in hell; eventually he emerged from that abode and, after various travails in succeeding births as a human being and once as a heavenly being, he was born as Kṛṣṇa, the ninth Vāsudeva. The significance of Jinasena's narration of this story of Kṛṣṇa's past life as a cook of meat dishes does not become clear until we examine his relationship to Jina Nemi, his cousin.

As noted above, Nemi was the youngest son of Samudra-vijaya, the eldest brother of Vasudeva, the father of Kṛṣṇa and Balarāma. Nemi must have been quite young, probably an adolescent, during Kṛṣṇa's war with Jarāsandha. He enters the Kṛṣṇa narrative when the latter was already married to several of his wives, including Satyabhāmā, Rukmiṇī, and Jāmbavatī. To these ladies Nemi was a younger brother-in-law (*devara*). It is well known even to this day in Rajasthan and Gujarat that a platonic romantic relationship often takes place between younger brothers and their elder brothers' wives. All of the Jaina accounts are unanimous in depicting Nemi as a very handsome but shy young man, one having little inclination towards the amorous sports in which the wives of Kṛṣṇa and Balarāma constantly tried to engage him. On one day, the story goes, they all enticed Nemi to sport with them in a pond; and when he left to dry himself he playfully asked Satyabhāmā, Kṛṣṇa's chief queen, to wash his wet clothes, a request that only a husband should properly make. Satyabhāmā pretended to be offended by this slight and taunted Nemi by asking if by making such a request he meant to set himself equal to her husband, the Lord of the Pāñcajanya conch. His pride hurt, Nemi walked away in anger and entered the armory of Kṛṣṇa, in which the conch, Pāñcajanya, was in safekeeping. It was believed that no one but Kṛṣṇa could lift this "jewel" of a conch, let alone blow it. Nemi marched inside and amazed the guardians of the conch by lifting it up and blowing it; the reverberations of the sound of the conch reached all over the city and even caused elephants to break their chains in agitation.

When Kṛṣṇa discovered that Nemi had ventured to blow the Pāñcajanya, he realized that his younger cousin was a serious potential rival for his wives' affections as well as for his kingdom, and he resolved to test Nemi's strength. Therefore, in a friendly manner, he asked Nemi to engage in an arm-wrestling contest. Nemi simply extended his arm for Kṛṣṇa to bend it down, but his arm stood like an iron crossbar and Kṛṣṇa was unable to shake it by even a hair's breadth. Several Jaina manuscripts illustrating this scene in the life of Nemi show Kṛṣṇa swinging like a monkey from Nemi's arm, unable to bend it.[34] Kṛṣṇa took the defeat gracefully and embraced Nemi; suggesting that it was time for him to get settled as a married man, he arranged for Nemi's alliance with princess Rājimati.

However, the threat of Nemi's superior might haunted Kṛṣṇa, and he was determined to remove this thorn in his side. He devised a plan for creating a situation that would result in Nemi's going to the forest as a monk. The fateful subconscious impression of his past life as a cook of meat dishes must have in some way led him to forge a plan to gather in the public park of Dvārakā a large herd of animals made ready for the butcher's knife, apparently for the wedding feast of Nemi and Rājimati.[35] Thus, as the bridegroom's procession made the rounds of the city on the day of the wedding, heading towards the home of the bride, Nemi's chariot passed by this park, and he was moved by the pitiable sight of these miserable animals bleating and crying. When Nemi learned from his charioteer that the animals had been brought there for those of his guests who ate meat, his heart was overcome with remorse, and he immediately left the wedding procession and turned toward the forest, with the determination to become a monk. Neither the wailings of Rājimati nor the pleas of Kṛṣṇa and Balarāma were able to dissuade him from his purpose.

It is well known that even in the most ancient times the Jainas have been—as attested by the evidence of Buddhist texts[36]—very scrupulous in the observance of a vegetarian diet for both laymen and monks and have never been known to serve any meat dishes under any circumstances whatsoever. In the entire narrative literature of the Jainas, there is no parallel to this story of a Jaina household, especially one so distinguished as to have given birth to a Tīrthaṅkara, preparing to slaughter animals to feed their guests. One might not be off the mark in suggesting that the purpose of this Jaina story was to defame Kṛṣṇa by making him capable of so heinous an act, calculated to sabotage his cousin's marriage and royal career. That the Jaina authors felt compelled even to allow such a story in their narrative of Kṛṣṇa is a sure indication of the fact that they had very serious problems in assimilating into their fold this divinity of a heretic faith, who was notorious for his unethical conduct. As noted above, Kṛṣṇa was to be reborn in hell—it would be his second time in that dismal abode since we began to trace his past lives—as a consequence, at least in Jaina minds, not so much of his acts of violence against his enemies in the great war as of his perpetration of this particular act of intended animal slaughter. Nevertheless, once Nemi had become a mendicant, Kṛṣṇa seems to have been a fervent devotee of the Jina Nemi and engaged in such pious acts as the occasional fasting required of a devout Jaina layman.

The Jaina account of the succeeding events in the lives of Kṛṣṇa and Balarāma, culminating in the destruction of Dvārakā by the curse of the sage Dvaipāyana, are related in much the same manner in the Jaina Purāṇas as they appear in the Brahminic texts, but they make a sudden departure from these texts when they come to describe the scene of the deaths of these two brothers. In the *Bhāgavata Purāṇa,* for example, the Yādavas killed each other under the influence of liquor, and even Balarāma and Kṛṣṇa got into a fistfight. When all of the remaining members of the Yādava clan perished in this manner, Balarāma, it is said, approached a rock beside the sea, sat down upon it, and peacefully breathed his last. Kṛṣṇa, we are told, lay resting all alone under a tree with one leg raised across his knee. A hunter named Jarā (old age), thinking it was a deer, shot an arrow at Kṛṣṇa and pierced his heel, wounding him mortally. As the hunter approached the body he realized his terrible mistake, but Kṛṣṇa reassured him and asked him to convey the news of the destruction of Dvārakā to the Pāṇḍavas. Then, by his yogic power Kṛṣṇa ascended to his divine abode, leaving behind no mortal remains.[37]

The Jaina account of this concluding event in the lives of these two brothers is markedly different, calculated to remove once and for all any doubt about their being anything but ordinary human beings! According to Jinasena, the sage Dvaipāyana was not a heretical ascetic but a Jaina monk given to extreme austerities, one who had amassed great yogic powers, which, if misused, were capable of burning anything at will. It is said that while drunk with liquor, some of the young Yādava princes, notably some of the sons of Balarāma and Kṛṣṇa, insulted the haughty sage and then assaulted him, thereby provoking his anger and the resulting destruction of Dvārakā by fire. Kṛṣṇa and Balarāma begged the sage to spare the lives of their children but were barely able to escape from the city themselves. The two brothers then wandered all alone, shorn of their royal insignia, barefoot in the sands of the desert of Kutch.

There Kṛṣṇa, suffering from great thirst and unable to walk even one step further, begged Balarāma to fetch water. While Balarāma was away, Jarākumāra, an older step-brother of Kṛṣṇa who had left his parental home in his youth and had somehow survived in the desert by hunting, saw him from a distance; thinking him to be an animal, he shot an arrow at him and wounded him fatally. He realized his mistake as he approached Kṛṣṇa, and, full of remorse, confessed to him that he had left his home precisely to avoid such an occurrence, which had been predicted for him by a soothsayer, and that the inevitable had at last happened. Kṛṣṇa recognized him and asked him to go to tell the Pāṇḍavas about the destruction of Dvārakā and also of his death, and, seeing no sign of Balarāma, gave his Kaustubha jewel as a token for him to reclaim the Yādava kingdom. As Jarākumāra departed, Kṛṣṇa covered himself completely with his upper garment and lay there thinking of all those among his relatives who had renounced the world, following the noble example of Nemi. He lamented the fact that he was not able to engage in any such holy act due to the heavy burden of his karmic deeds. Yet he reaffirmed his faith in the teachings of the Jina, chanted Pañcanamaskāra-*mantra* (a holy Jaina litany) and greeted Lord Nemi as he breathed his last. He was reborn instantaneously in [the third] hell.[38]

As in the case of Lakṣmaṇa, Kṛṣṇa's descent to hell as a result of his being a Vāsudeva need not come as a surprise to those who know the Jaina laws of *karma*. Yet what is greatly astonishing is that simultaneously with his statement of Kṛṣṇa's rebirth in hell, Jinasena declares that Kṛṣṇa was destined to be a future Tīrthaṅkara.[39] It should be remembered that, although it is required for a Vāsudeva to be reborn in hell, it is certainly not a Jaina rule that a Vāsudeva must become a Tīrthaṅkara. Jinasena must have had some scriptural authority for making such a claim for Kṛṣṇa, but he does not reveal any specific actions of Kṛṣṇa that might have earned for him such a unique status, either before or during his life as a Vāsudeva. Nor does Jinasena indicate how distant this future will be; but subsequent Jaina writers agree that Kṛṣṇa will be the sixteenth Tīrthaṅkara in the next time cycle,[40] which gives him a fairly long period of time to spend in his present abode. There is also unanimous agreement that Kṛṣṇa's birth as a human being will take place immediately as he emerges from hell and that it will be his last birth, the birth as a Tīrthaṅkara. If this were the case, then one must wonder when Kṛṣṇa could have accumulated those sixteen meritorious acts that are considered prerequisites for birth as a Tīrthaṅkara.[41] It seems that Kṛṣṇa's destination to become so exalted a person as a Tīrthaṅkara was the result of an exceptional concession made by the Jaina *ācāryas* in an effort to rehabilitate Kṛṣṇa and make this assimilation irrevocable.

Returning to the scene of Kṛṣṇa's death, we find that Balarāma returned after a long time and did not realize that Kṛṣṇa was dead but thought that he was asleep and let him rest. After several hours without seeing any sign of movement, Balarāma suspected that Kṛṣṇa might have died, but so deep was his attachment to Kṛṣṇa that he refused to believe it. For six months, we are told, he carried Kṛṣṇa around, bathing his body and taking care of it and crying over his silent brother. Eventually the Pāṇḍavas, accompanied by Jarākumāra, arrived in the desert and found him in that miserable condition. Even they could not persuade Balarāma to believe that Kṛṣṇa indeed was dead. A god named Siddhārtha, the soul of Kṛṣṇa's former charioteer, saw Balarāma in this state and by magical means created in front of him a scene in which someone was planting a lotus on a rock. When Balarāma laughed at the foolishness of the god's act, the celestial being in turn pointed out the stupidity of Balarāma in carrying a dead body around with the hope of reviving it! That finally opened his eyes, and the Pāṇḍavas brought the corpse of Kṛṣṇa to Tungi, a hill top, where it was cremated.[42] Both Balarāma and the Pāṇḍavas handed over their kingdoms to Jarākumāra and renounced the world to become Jaina monks. Then, leading the holy life of yogis, they one by one died peacefully in meditation. Of the five Pāṇḍavas, Yudhiṣṭhira, Bhīma, and Arjuna attained *mokṣa*[43] at the end of their lives, while Nakula and Sahadeva were reborn in heaven.

Balarāma could not overcome his attachment to Kṛṣṇa and hence was not yet ready to attain *mokṣa*.[44] He therefore was reborn in heaven and started immediately to seek his lamented brother. His grief knew no bounds when, with his extrasensory perception, he saw that Kṛṣṇa was nowhere to be found in heaven but had been consigned to hell. Using his supernatural powers, Balarāma then descended into hell and approached Kṛṣṇa and asked him to ascend to heaven with him. But as soon as Kṛṣṇa made an effort to rise, his limbs began to drip as if they were made of butter. Kṛṣṇa then realized the force of the inexorable laws of *karma,* and asked his brother to return to heaven. He then resolved to be reborn as a human being and to strive to attain *mokṣa.*[45]

This Jaina account of the deaths of the two *śalākā puruṣas* and their passing into the destinies of heaven and hell, respectively, are truly remarkable. The Jaina tradition that Kṛṣṇa died before Balarāma and that Balarāma carried Kṛṣṇa's dead body around for six months was probably intended to counter the Vaiṣṇavite belief that Kṛṣṇa, being an avatar, was transported to his divine abode in his physical body (*sadehamukti*). As for Balarāma, who also was considered a minor avatar in the Brahminic stories, his lack of fortitude in the face of his brother's death belied any such claim of a divine portion in him. It should be remembered that Balarāma's counterpart in the Jaina *Rāmāyaṇa,* namely Rāma, also survived his younger brother Lakṣmaṇa and mourned over his death for a long time; and yet Rāma, unlike Balarāma, was deemed virtuous enough to attain *mokṣa* in that very life.

Balarāma's visit to hell to raise Kṛṣṇa follows the example of Sītā, who, after having been born in heaven, visited Lakṣmaṇa in hell to admonish him to abide by the Jaina faith. The Jainas probably saw in these visits merely an affection for a former brother and brother-in-law and hence considered them fitting conclusions to their stories. Jinasena's *Harivaṃśa Purāṇa,* however, goes a step further and describes an extraordinary scene showing the weakness of the brothers Kṛṣṇa and Balarāma, a weakness that appears inappropriate in a soul who was, as noted earlier, destined to become a Tīrthaṅkara upon his immediate rebirth as a human being. Incredible as it may seem, Jinasena's account tells us that when the god Balarāma took leave of Kṛṣṇa in hell, the latter implored him to popularize the cult of Viṣṇu by uttering the following words:

> O Brother, return to heaven, and enjoy the fruits of your meritorious deeds. I, too, at the end of my life here, shall attain human birth for the sake of *mokṣa.* We shall together then perform austerities by taking refuge in the teachings of the Jina and will together destroy the bonds of *karma* and attain the bliss of *mokṣa.* But in the meantime, please, for the sake of increasing my glory, fill the whole land of Bharata with temples containing images of me bearing the conch and the wheel

and the mace in my hands. Fill the minds of the people of Bhāratavarṣa with astonishment by displaying [scenes depicting] the two of us, accompanied by our sons, and so forth [that is, spouses], and endowed with great riches.[46]

Jinasena's account concludes with the following words:

> Hearing these words of Kṛṣṇa, Balarāma, that King of Gods, came to the land of the Bharatas and, constrained by love for his brother, did as he was enjoined by Viṣṇu. He created representations of Kṛṣṇa and Balarāma holding the wheel and the ploughshare, respectively, standing in celestial mansions [*vimāna*s, that is, *ratha*s?], and had their images enshrined in a great many temples dedicated to Lord Vāsudeva which were located in large cities. He thus made the entire world fall under the spell of Viṣṇu and returned to his abode in heaven.[47]

Having narrated this extraordinary story, which probably had no other purpose than to explain to the Jainas how a pair of Jaina heroes, one of whom was a would-be Tīrthaṅkara at that, came to be worshipped as the deities of the heretics, Jinasena closes his narration by drily observing: "Alas! What will not be done by those who are given to such [foolish] affection!"[48]

Vimalasūri's *Paümacariya* took us up to the twentieth Tīrthaṅkara and Punnāṭa Jinasena's *Harivaṃśa Purāṇa* brought us to the narrative of the twenty-second Tīrthaṅkara Nemi. In both texts the emphasis was more on the Baladeva-Vāsudeva pairs of heroes than on the Tīrthaṅkaras themselves. It is for this reason that these two narrative works, although commonly considered to be Purāṇas, do not qualify as Mahāpurāṇas, the characteristic Jaina designation for the comprehensive biographies of all the sixty-three *śalākā puruṣas*. This honor truly belongs to the ninth-century narrative work *Triṣaṣṭi-lakṣaṇa-śrī-mahāpurāṇa-saṅgraha,* or, in brief, *Mahāpurāṇa.* This monumental work of some twenty thousand *śloka*s, written in two parts (*Ādi Purāṇa*[49] and *Uttara Purāṇa,*[50] respectively), was initiated by the Digambara mendicant Jinasena, who is said to have been a teacher of the Rāṣṭrakūṭa King Amoghavarṣa I, who ruled from Mānyakheṭa in the ninth century (814–77 C.E.). This Jinasena was probably unaware of the *Harivaṃśa Purāṇa* written by his predecessor of the same name, who is, hence, differentiated by his ecclesiastical lineage name, Punnāṭa. It is stated in the text that (the second) Jinasena died after having completed the first section, *Ādi Purāṇa,* comprising forty-six chapters and dedicated entirely to the story of the first Tīrthaṅkara Ṛṣabha, and the first two chapters of the second section. The remainder of the work, extending to the seventy-sixth chapter and containing the biographies of all the remaining Tīrthaṅkaras and the other Illustrious beings, was completed by Jinasena's immediate disciple, Guṇabhadra.

Hitherto Jaina authors appeared to have been preoccupied with the narratives of "historical" figures, the Epic heroes of the *itihāsa* literature. Jinasena was to arrest this trend and to concentrate attention not only on the Tīrthaṅkaras, the true heroes of the Jainas, but especially on the life stories of the first Tīrthaṅkara Ṛṣabha and his son, Bharata, the first Cakravartin. Although adopted at some stage by the Brahminic Purāṇas as their own minor characters, as will be seen below, both Ṛṣabha and Bharata were truly Jaina characters, and their assimilation required no special effort. Since their advent in the Jaina mythology took place at the very beginning of the present cycle of time, they could be hailed by the Jainas as the founding fathers of our civilization, lawgivers for secular welfare as well as for the spiritual path of salvation.

In his introductory chapter of the *Ādi Purāṇa,* Jinasena rightly claims that his work is a *Mahāpurāṇa* because it deals with all the sixty-three *śalākā puruṣas,* but it can also be considered an *itihāsa,* as well as a *dharmaśāstra*. Although he makes specific references to creation and the other *pañcalakṣaṇa*s, he chooses a novel characterization for his Purāṇa, consisting of such items as space (*kṣetra,* that is, Jaina cosmology), time (*kāla,* that is, the infinite cycles of time divided into ascending and descending halves), the fourfold organization of a community as monks, nuns, laymen, and laywomen (*tīrtha*), the Great Beings (*sat-puruṣa*s, that is, the *śalākā puruṣa*s), and finally their conduct (*carita*).[51]

The narrative of the first Tīrthaṅkara Ṛṣabha thus begins with a description of the present half of the Jaina time cycle, the *avasarpiṇī* (Descending). It is said that this period began billions of years ago when human beings lived in the paradise that was earth and were sustained by wish-fulfilling trees (*kalpavṛkṣa*s) and had no form of government whatsoever. As time passed, the magic trees disappeared, the population increased, and there arose a need to organize a society with leaders able to teach farming and other means of producing food, preserving it for storage and distribution, and protecting it from the depredations of greedy people. Thus began the first social structure, the heads of which were called "Kulakaras" or "Manus." The first of these was Pratiśruti, in whose line was born Nābhi, the fourteenth Kulakara. Ṛṣabha, the first Tīrthaṅkara and the fifteenth Kulakara, was born to Nābhi's wife,

Marudevī. Jinasena devotes a great many verses to the conception and birth of this first *śalākā puruṣa,* the founder of Jainism in our epoch.

According to Jinasena's narrative, gods appeared on earth to celebrate these two auspicious events in the career of the new Tīrthaṅkara, calling him the "first lord," the "Ādideva." At this time all men were equal, and as yet society was not divided into the four classes (*varṇa*s). Indeed, it may be said that such a division came into existence quite inadvertently, when Ṛṣabha, as he grew to be a young man, bore arms and assumed the role of a king and gave the title of Kṣatriya to those who were assigned the duty of protecting the people and enforcing the law. Eventually, as he discovered different means of livelihood, such as the sword (*asi*, that is, government), ink (*masi*, that is, reading and writing), agriculture (*kṛṣi*), the arts (*vidyā*), crafts (*śilpa*), and commerce (*vāṇijya*), there came into existence groups of people engaging in one or another of these occupations, who came to be called "Kṣatriyas," "Vaiśyas," and "Śūdras." The Brahmin class had not yet come into being, and the path of renunciation also was as yet unknown.

Kulakara Ṛṣabha led a fruitful life as a householder and fathered one hundred sons and two daughters. The eldest of his sons, Bharata, became the first of the twelve Cakravartins of the Jaina Purāṇic tradition. Eventually, Ṛṣabha renounced the world to become a Jaina mendicant; divested of all his possessions including his clothing, he wandered about "sky-clad," a fact agreed upon both by Digambara and Śvetāmbara traditions alike. Thus he had the distinction of being the first renouncer of our epoch. It is said that a great many of his friends, sons, and even grandsons, at first joined him in assuming the holy vows of homelessness and celibacy but soon left him due to their inability to withstand the rigors of his discipline. Ashamed to return to their homes, these proud men became wanderers, calling themselves *parivrājakas,* the founders of what the Jainas consider to be heretical schools of mendicants, such as the Ājīvakas, Ekadaṇḍins, Tridaṇḍins, Vaikhānasas, and so forth.[52]

Ṛṣabha, however, remained firm in his austerities and became the omniscient Jina, the first initiator of a new Tīrtha, an institution that had been extinct for countless years. A great many of his former subjects, including many of his sons and two daughters, called "Brāhmī" and "Sundarī," became members of the order of monks and nuns. The Jina Ṛṣabha then laid down rules for the guidance of lay people also, whereby they could progressively refrain from worldly activities and gradually reach the stage of mendicancy.

Thus there came into being an ideal society predominantly consisting of these four sections, collectively called the "Tīrtha," with groups of apostates subsisting on its fringes and professing their heresies.

One would expect that the Lord of this Tīrtha would be described merely as a saint rapt in meditation and living for the most part in seclusion in a forest. But such is not the case; the Ādi, that is, the First Tīrthaṅkara, after whom Jinasena's Purāṇa is named, is portrayed as possessing such majesty and grandeur that it would surpass any description of the great Trinity of Purāṇic mythology: Brahmā, Viṣṇu, and Śiva. Jina Ṛṣabha is a sky-clad (*digambara*) mendicant, and yet in Jinasena's account we find him seated in the midst of a palatial assembly especially prepared for his sermons by Indra the king of gods and flanked by gods who hold raised parasols and proclaim his lordship over the three worlds. He has a human body, and yet it is so pure that its luster can outshine the divine bodies of the heavenly beings assembled there. By an extraordinary miraculous power he can be seen facing all four directions at once, a feature claimed by the Brahminic Purāṇas for Brahmā, the creator.

The Jainization of Rāma and Kṛṣṇa having been completed by his predecessors, Jinasena seems to have set his sights on claiming the functions of the Purāṇic holy trinity for the founder of Jainism. He employs the most characteristic adjectives traditionally reserved for Brahmā to describe his chosen Deity, Lord Ṛṣabha.[53] Thus Ṛṣabha is called "womb of gold" (*hiraṇyagarbha*), as there was a shower of gold when he was born! He is hailed as "lord of creatures" (Prajāpati) and "ordainer" (*vidhātṛ*), for he was the first king and the first to invent fire and other means of livelihood. He is called "self-existent" (*svayambhū*) because he was self-taught and hence had a spiritual rebirth independent of a teacher. Being the first to realize perfection in our epoch he is called "primordial man" (*purāṇa-puruṣa*), and because of his omniscience he can be described by the [*Puruṣa-sūkta*] term "all-seeing" (*viśvataścakṣuḥ*)! In short, he is to be called the "first lord," the "Ādideva," the "very Brahmā himself."

Ṛṣabha may be called "Viṣṇu" as well, since his knowledge is all pervasive. And he is truly "unfallen" (*acyuta*), as he has reached the most sublime state, which is unshakable and eternal. Being the most auspicious, he deserves to be called "Śiva," and he is "the end of being" (*bhavāntaka*), for he has freed himself from the bonds of *saṃsāra*. And above all he is lord of yogis (*yogīśvara*), for he has reached *kaivalya* solely by the path of meditation (that is, without the aid of an external agency). Such investment of Ṛṣabha with the divinity of the Purāṇic trinity without, of course, making him the creator, sustainer or destroyer, allows Jinasena to deify his human Jina and to claim for him both the antiquity and the spiritual authority that will be required to challenge the validity of the Vedic and Purāṇic teachings on creation and dissolution, the false claim of divinity for their gods and avatars, and, above all, their doctrine of the divine origin of the caste system and the alleged supremacy of the Brahmin within it.

The examination of the Brahminic doctrines of creation and secondary creation provides Jinasena with an excellent opportunity to engage in a debate on the validity of a theistic creation, and to propound the Jaina doctrines of the plurality of souls and their transmigration and possible release from the regions of Jaina cosmology, all without the benefit of a superior being—the Creator God. As for the epochs of the Manus, Ṛṣabha himself was a Manu and himself laid down the duties of the various sections of society; these can never be found in the false scriptures that enjoin animal sacrifices in the name of *dharma* but only in the Jaina scriptures. The same holds true for the knowledge of royal dynasties (*vaṃśa*s), for the best of these lineages, such as the Ikṣvāku, Kuru, and Hari lineages, also originated from Ṛṣabha and his son Bharata, the first Cakravartin. Having thus contested the right of the Brahminic Purāṇas to instruct on the proposed goals of a scripture, Jinasena expounds the Jaina teachings pertaining to all those areas considered to be essential for the true realization of the four goals of human life (*puruṣārthas*).

The differences between the Brahminic and Jaina cosmologies as expounded by Jinasena need not detain us here, but the Jaina challenge to the alleged superiority of the Brahmin class, a major theme of the *Ādi Purāṇa,* surely merits discussion. As has been pointed out earlier, there were no caste distinctions at the beginning of our epoch, since all mankind was a single caste (*manuṣyajātir ekaiva*), according to Jinasena.[54] Divisions arose, however, not because of any premeditated design, but as a result of the discovery of new means of livelihood. It is also significant that Ṛṣabha was portrayed as a householder, and not as the holy Jina, at the time when the Kṣatriya, Vaiśya, and the Śūdra classes evolved; this would deny any sacredness to their origins through a holy injunction, as in the case of the Vedic *Puruṣa-sūkta* in the Brahminic tradition. What is, however, far more significant is the fact that in the Jaina narrative the class of the Brahmins was promulgated, not by the omniscient Jina, but by his householder son Bharata; this deprives that class of any sanctity whatsoever.

There are two Jaina narratives that explain the origin of the

Brahmin class, one appearing in the commentarial and Purāṇic literature of the Śvetāmbaras and the other in the *Ādi Purāṇa* of Jinasena. A fanciful derivation of the Sanskrit word *brāhmaṇa* from the Prakrit form *māhaṇa* provides the context for the Śvetāmbara story. It is said that Bharata, after his conquest of the world, returned with a large amount of booty and wanted to share it with his ninety-nine brothers, who had become Jaina monks in the monastic order established by Jina Ṛṣabha. He approached them with a cartload of food and other gifts, but this was rejected on the grounds that Jaina monks may not accept food specially prepared for them (*uddiṣṭa*). Indra, the king of gods, then suggested to Bharata that the food might be offered to those lay people who had assumed the minor vows (*aṇuvrata*s) prescribed by Ṛṣabha for householders and had thus been initiated as lay people (*upāsakas*). Bharata offered them food and other gifts and invited them to have their meals at his palace forever. Not only were they to be permanent guests of his household but also to forsake all means of livelihood that involved violence (*hiṃsā*) and devote their lives to the study and teaching of the scriptures and the worship of the Jina. Their most important task, however, was to keep a vigil over the Cakravartin's conduct by admonishing him, "Do not kill, do not kill" (*mā hana, mā hana*): thus they came to be called *māhaṇa*s, that is, Brahmins! Fanciful as this derivation of the word *brāhmaṇa* through its Prakrit form might be, it was endorsed by the great Jaina grammarian Hemacandra.[55] It is the Jaina way of explaining not only the origin of the Brahmin class but also the beginning of the pan-Indian rite of feeding Brahmins, a practice not unknown even to the orthodox Jainas of our day; it is claimed that the Jainas started this good practice in order to promote *ahiṃsā,* but, alas, it has now degenerated into an adjunct to the common household rituals!

Jinasena ignores both the Prakrit *māhaṇa* and the Sanskrit *brāhmaṇa* and concentrates on the word *dvija* (twice-born) for his explanation of the origin of the Brahmin class under the patronage of Bharata. According to his narrative, a large number of laymen, headed by Bharata himself, had been initiated into the vows (*aṇuvrata*s), which had been enunciated by Jina Ṛṣabha for householders. Bharata wished to reward the true initiates and devised a way of testing their adherence to the vows. He had the courtyard of his residence strewn with fresh flowers and sprouting grain and invited the citizens to a feast on a sacred day. Those who were careless crossed the courtyard without regard for the vegetable life, but those who were virtous did not enter lest they trample on it and thus break their vows against harming living beings. Bharata then invited those virtuous people to enter by a suitable path, and he honored them. He also encouraged them to assume further restraints on their conduct so as to make progress on one or more of the eleven stages of spiritual progress (*śrāvaka-pratimā*)[56] as laid down by the Jina Ṛṣabha, which would prepare them for mendicant life. Those who accepted this new status (*varṇa-lābha*) he designated as the "Twice-born" (*dvija*s) in the discipline of the Jina. He confirmed their advancement by investing them with sacred threads (*yajñopavīta*), the number of which indicated the number of stages (*pratimā*s) they had assumed. Thus began the ritual known as initiation (*upanayana*) and the practice of wearing sacred threads, as well as the formation of a special class of people (*dvijas*), the first "divine Brahmins" (*deva-brāhmaṇa*s) of our epoch.[57]

A long time was to elapse before Bharata began to have doubts about the wisdom of his instituting a class of "Twice-born" without first obtaining the permission of Lord Ṛṣabha. He therefore approached Ṛṣabha and described the manner in which he had established the "Twice-born" and begged the Lord to declare to him both the consequence of his presumptuous act as well as the virtues and vices of this class.

Jinasena's strictures concerning this class, as will be seen presently, match in spirit and letter the invective and prophecies that appear in the Brahminic Purāṇas against the followers of Ṛṣabha. This portion of the *Ādi Purāṇa* therefore deserves to be reproduced fully here:

> O son, that which has been done is good indeed, and moreover, the worship of pious Brahmins is good, too. However, there will be some harmful consequences about which you must be informed. You have created the Brahmin class, who will be righteous teachers as long as the Kṛta Age endures, but when the Kali Age draws near there will be backsliding teachers who, out of pride in their high birth, will embrace the very opposite of the right path. These people, full of the arrogance of their rank, will claim to be most excellent among men, and soon, greedy for wealth, they will delude the world with their false scriptures. The favored treatment that they will enjoy will increase their presumptuousness and make them puffed up with a false pride, so that they will lead men astray as they themselves fashion false religious treatises.
>
> They will be so short sighted that they will promote changes for the worse at the end of the Age, and, their minds clouded by evil, they will become the enemies of religion. As they delight

> in injury to life and relish eating honey and meat, these wicked people will, alas, promote the *dharma* of action and, full of evil hopes, corrupt the *dharma* of nonviolence in favor of the *dharma* of injunctions (*codanā*). As the Age progresses, rogues will blasphemously wear the sacred thread and engage eagerly in the killing of life, thereby obstructing the right path.
>
> Therefore, although the creation of the Brahmin class is not of itself harmful today, it does contain the seed of harm as yet buried in the future, because impious heretics will come forth. Nevertheless, although this seed of harm is truly there for the end of the Age, there is no cause for removing it at present, for you have not transgressed against the nature of *dharma*.[58]

Jinasena was apparently not content with his suggestion that the present-day Brahmins were descendants of apostates from the original groups of devout Jaina laymen, the first to be designated as "Twice-born" by Cakravarti Bharata. His prophecy that in degenerate times these so-called Brahmins would compose their own scriptures disregarding the doctrine of *ahiṃsā* had come true; the Jaina authors had studied them with great care and had noted several portions that openly enjoined animal sacrifices. Still, these texts by themselves did not explain how the Brahmins came to adopt as their means of livelihood the performances of sacrifices and other rituals. In his zeal to establish a community of Jainas parallel to that of Brahminic society, Jinasena put forth a new lawbook (*dharmaśāstra*), a Jaina lawbook, as it were, to serve both as a manual of ritual, complete with litany, and as a code of civil law as well. In this manner the third distinguishing mark of the Jaina Purāṇas, namely, reigns (*tīrtha*), corresponding to the epochs of the Manus of the Brahminic Purāṇas, would be fulfilled for the first time by a Jaina Purāṇa.

The ritual of initiation, for example, as described above, was carried out by Bharata himself and needed neither a priest nor the sacred fire. Indeed, the notion that fire is sacred is alien to Jaina doctrine, since for them the four basic elements, earth, water, air, and fire, belong to the species of life that has only the tactile sense and therefore ranks lowest in the classification of sentient beings. For the Brahminic tradition, fire was sacred because it was the embodiment of both Agni the fire god and Agni the domestic priest (*purohita*) of the gods. Jinasena therefore shows great courage of conviction when he declares that fire by itself has no inherent sacredness or divinity (*na svato 'gneḥ pavitratvaṃ devatārūpam eva vā*). Anticipating a question about the propriety of Jaina laymen lighting fires on such occasions as marriages and other rites of passage, Jinasena replies that fire can nevertheless be considered pure, on account of its contact with the body of the Tīrthaṅkara Ṛṣabha at the time of his cremation. Lest this association between the holy Jina and fire be taken as granting absolute sacredness to fire, Jinasena hastens to add that fire is to be considered suitable for worship only on a conventional level (*vyavahāranaya*); it is comparable to the worship of holy places and pilgrimage sites that become worthy of worship only because a Jina has attained enlightenment (*nirvāṇa*) in those places.[59]

Jinasena's explanation of the sacredness of fire seems to have gained acceptance by the learned sections of both the Digambara and the Śvetāmbara sects, as can be witnessed from similar explanations found in the works of the twelfth-century author Hemacandra. In his monumental work, the *Triṣaṣṭiśalākāpuruṣacaritra,* the *Mahāpurāṇa* of the Śvetāmbara tradition, Hemacandra goes even further and suggests that the ritual of the fire (*agnihotra*), the hallmark of the Brahmin class, is to be traced to the cremation ceremony of the Jina Ṛṣabha. The three different fires that came to be held sacred by the Vedic Brahmins had truly originated from those fires in which the bodies of the Jina Ṛṣabha, the sages born of the noble Ikṣvāku lineage, and those of the remaining saints (Arhats), had been respectively cremated.[60]

What was originally an act of piety, namely, keeping the holy flame alive, turned gradually into a means of livelihood in the hands of the Brahmins of degenerate times. They employed it even in the worship of demigods and goddesses who were given not only to false views, but also to the most unholy practice of receiving offerings of flesh and blood. It is clear from reading the *Ādi Purāṇa* that during the time of Jinasena a large number of the Jaina laity had come to accept the worship of these heretic gods and goddesses as a legitimate part of their worship of the Jinas and had probably installed their images in their own temples as well. Jinasena was waging an open war against the worship of these non-Jaina divinities and had to combat their influence by installing a new set of Jaina "guardian deities" somehow associated with the lives of the Tīrthaṅkaras and thus worthy of occupying a place of honor near the pedestal of the Jina and sharing in the devotions offered by the laity. Through his Purāṇa, which he characterized as a *dharmaśāstra,* Jinasena demanded that a true Jaina should remove the images of the heretic gods (*mithyā-devatā*) from his residence, and added: "He should in a public manner (*prakāśam*) take them away somewhere else and abandon them, saying: 'Until now, out of ignorance we have worshipped you with respect. However, now the time has come for us to worship our own guardian deities (*śāsana-devatā*). Pray do not be angry; you may go wherever you please.'"[61]

Jinasena's *Ādi Purāṇa* thus discharged the function of a lawbook, containing recommendations and prohibitions addressed to the followers of a Jina. Prior to his time, the Jaina books of discipline concerned themselves with the conduct of monks and nuns alone. There were guide books (*Śrāvakācāras*) to instruct the laity in keeping the vows prescribed and to set forth the procedures for their observation. But the Jainas lacked the type of lawbook comparable to the *Manusmṛti,* for example, in the Brahminic tradition. Jinasena's *Ādi Purāṇa* fills this need and carries with it the kind of authority one associates with the *dharmaśāstra* literature pertaining to the duties of the castes, rites of passage, and so forth. In writing the *Ādi Purāṇa,* Jinasena thus introduced a new function for the Jaina Purāṇas, namely, educating the Jaina community to preserve its identity as a community separate from that of the Brahmins, a task that they perceived was necessary in the face of the Brahminic attempts to absorb them.

Jinasena did not live to complete his work; the lives of the remaining sixty-one *śalākā puruṣa*s were therefore compressed into a single volume, the *Uttara Purāṇa,* by his disciple Guṇabhadra. The reader is immediately aware of his stereotyped descriptions of the warfare conducted by the Cakravartins and other heroes. Once again Guṇabhadra returns to the narratives of Rāma and Lakṣmaṇa or of Kṛṣṇa and Balarāma. These show further modifications of the versions of Vimala or of Punnāṭa Jinasena, modifications that strive even further to remove certain aspects of these stories that the medieval Jainas found offensive to their moral sensibilities. In Guṇabhadra's narrative of the *Rāmāyaṇa,* for example, Rāma is not asked to abdicate in favor of Bharata, as he is in Vimalasūri's *Paümacariya,* but instead leaves Ayodhya of his own volition, together with Sītā and Lakṣmaṇa, and sets out to found a kingdom of his own. Similar changes in the stories of the Kṛṣṇa legend also appear in other Purāṇas by subsequent authors, most notably in the writings of the Śvetāmbara *ācārya*s, especially in Hemacandra's work referred to above. The works hitherto examined in some detail all happen to be the works of Digambara writers, for whom the Purāṇas were the only surviving scriptures. The Śvetāmbaras, however, had such canonical narratives as the *Nāyādhammakahāo*[62] or the *Uvāsagadasāo,*[63] which relate the stories of some of the *śalākā puruṣa*s, including Kṛṣṇa. Their narratives, therefore, often differ from those found in the Digambara tradition.

A fine example of this is provided by the story of Draupadī as narrated in the literature of these two sects. No Jaina writer has been comfortable with the *Mahābhārata* account of Draupadī's polyandrous marriage to all five Pāṇḍava brothers. Digambara writers have tended to treat this as a slander of the Brahmins against the character of Draupadī and the Pāṇḍavas, and have devised means of explaining the event away as a gross misrepresentation of an accidental falling of the garland, thrown by Draupadī to Arjuna, on the heads of all five brothers at the time of her self-choice (*svayaṃvara*) marriage.[64] The author of the *Harivaṃśa Purāṇa,* who explains this event in the above manner, takes the heretical Brahmins to task for suggesting that she had actually married all five brothers and wonders why their tongues do not split into a hundred pieces for uttering such slanderous words against so pure a woman and against the brothers of Arjuna, who treated her as their sister![65]

Hemacandra, on the other hand, in his *Triṣaṣṭi,* allows the polyandrous marriage to stand as something that had indeed happened, but he explains it by recourse to a story of Draupadī's past as given in the Śvetāmbara scripture *Nāyādhammakahāo* and its ancient commentaries. According to this story, Draupadī in one of her former lives was a beautiful woman called Nāgaśrī, who out of disgust towards a Jaina monk had fed him poisonous food that caused great burning in his body. As a result she suffered for long periods in hell and in animal existences and eventually was reborn as a beautiful woman—but one with a peculiar defect: anyone who touched her carnally would experience the great pain of being burned by fire. Although she attracted a large number of suitors, no one dared to approach her; when finally she was married to a man of her liking he screamed in anguish at her first touch and ran away from the bridal chamber. Nāgaśrī was then abandoned by her husband's household as well as by her own parents and wandered alone from place to place for several years. Eventually she became a Jaina nun and threw herself wholeheartedly into severe austerities hoping thereby to get rid of her ailment. One day, it is said, she saw five handsome young men pursuing a beautiful courtesan, and Nāgaśrī, having been deprived of her conjugal happiness, felt a forceful longing (*nidāna*) that as a result of her severe penances she might enjoy similar pleasure in her next life. She died instantly at that moment and in the course of time was reborn as Draupadī. Her polyandrous marriage to the Pāṇḍavas was therefore predestined by her *nidāna,*[66] a theme all too familiar to us from the stories of Kṛṣṇa, Ekanāsā, and others; it had to be endured and could be overcome only by an act of renunciation demanding an equal force of will by her and all of her husbands, which did eventually occur.

The brief survey of the major trends in the Jaina Purāṇic literature given above supports our contention that the Jaina writers, in addition to their primary purpose of expounding Jaina doctrine, used this medium to combat Brahminic influences emanating from their Epics and Purāṇas. One must ask here whether the Jainas in fact had any reason to believe that they were under attack from their perceived adversaries, and also whether indeed the authors of the Brahminic Purāṇas were even aware of these Jaina appropriations of their heroes, the two avatars of Viṣṇu, as well as their attempt to Jainize, as it were, the god Brahmā-Prajāpati through the character of Jina Ṛṣabha.

An answer to these questions cannot be truly given without first establishing the chronological order in which the Brahminic Purāṇas were committed to writing. No Jaina Purāṇa has ever been mentioned in any of the traditional eighteen Mahāpurāṇas or the Upapurāṇas, and, with the exception of Ṛṣabha and his son Bharata, no other character of the Jaina Purāṇas has figured in their narratives. The Jainas, on the other hand, show a remarkable familiarity with the Brahminic Purāṇas, although only one late Jaina Purāṇa, namely, the seventeenth-century *Pāṇḍava Purāṇa,* explicitly mentions the *Śiva Purāṇa* in criticizing the latter's alleged misrepresentation of the Pāṇḍava story.[67] But such a lack of cross-references does not tell us the whole story of the mutual impact between these two literary traditions, which were probably competing for the patronage of a common audience, namely, the mostly urban and affluent sections of the Indian community.

Nothing for example is known about the process by which Gautama, the Buddha, came to be assimilated into the Vaiṣṇava tradition to make him worthy of being declared a full avatar of Viṣṇu. One would expect the Brahminic authors to devote at least an episode or an entire chapter, if not an independent Purāṇa, to explain this momentous event in the history of the Vaiṣṇava religion. Yet all that one finds are a few lines here and there, often copies of what are probably the original verses of the *Viṣṇu Purāṇa,* which tell us nothing more than that Lord Viṣṇu employed his power called "Yogamāyā" and was thereby born as Buddha, the son of Śuddhodana in the land of Kīkaṭas (district of Gayā), to delude the demons, lead them astray into non-Vedic creeds, and thus bring about their destruction.[68] The Buddhist records are even more silent on this fateful co-option of their supreme teacher by a heretical cult. We do not know if the Buddhists were even aware that he was hailed as an avatar of a god, a truly blasphemous act against one whose atheistic doctrines were no secret to anyone. Indeed, it has been suggested that the Buddhists lost ground in the land of their birth precisely because they remained oblivious to the dangers inherent in such assimilation: first, that of the Buddha being represented as an avatar of Viṣṇu, and second, that of their heavenly Bodhisattvas (such as Mañjuśrī and Avalokiteśvara) being regarded as emanations of Śiva.[69]

Only two short Jākata tales about Rāma and Kṛṣṇa[70] are known to have been written in the Buddhist tradition, in marked contrast to the Jaina's voluminous Purāṇic and other narratives devoted entirely to these Epic characters, which survive to this day. It is very much to the credit of the Jainas, therefore, that they were vigilant about what was being said in the "heretic" Purāṇas and took vigorous steps not only to correct the "errors" perpetrated by their adversaries but even to confound them by producing revised versions of the events that claimed to be the authentic ones! We will never know the reasons why the Brahminic authors chose to favor the Buddha over his contemporary Jaina teacher Mahāvīra for the role of the avatar of Viṣṇu, especially when it is realized that there are far more numerous, albeit oblique, references in their Purāṇas to Jaina heroes and their religion than to Buddhism and its heroes. Two examples of such references can be noted here, an earlier one from the *Bhāgavata Purāṇa* and a later one from the *Śiva Purāṇa*.

The *Bhāgavata Purāṇa* betrays its knowledge of Jainism by its use of the word *Arhat,* a characteristic epithet of the Jina, in conection with its narrative pertaining to one of Viṣṇu's twenty-two minor (*aṃśa*) avatars, namely, Ṛṣabha, who appears there in the company of such Brahminic sages as Kapila, Nārada, and Veda-Vyāsa. According to the author of the *Bhāgavata Purāṇa,* the purpose of the Ṛṣabha-avatar was to establish the *śramaṇa dharma* of the naked ascetics (*vātaraśanānāṃ śramaṇānām ṛṣīṇām*).[71] As in the Jaina tradition, the Ṛṣabha of the *Bhāgavata Purāṇa* was also born to Marudevī and Nābhi, one of the Manus; his story in the *Bhāgavata Purāṇa* is different in that Nābhi is said to have performed a great Vedic sacrifice that so pleased Viṣṇu that he himself consented to be born as his son Ṛṣabha. This Ṛṣabha too begot a hundred sons, the eldest of whom was Bharata, the first Cakravartin, after whom the land of Ṛṣabha was named Bhāratavarṣa. Unlike his counterpart in the Jaina accounts, this Ṛṣabha himself as well as his sons became great devotees of the Brahmins and propitiated Viṣṇu with many sacrifices. In fulfillment of his function as an avatar, this Ṛṣabha then renounced the world to become a naked ascetic, a celibate *avadhūta;* after spending a great many years in severe austerities, he died in a forest fire while fasting to death and became one with Vāsudeva.

Although the Jainas would strongly repudiate many of the details that appear in the *Bhāgavata Purāṇa* account of Ṛṣabha, most importantly the claims that he was associated with Vedic sacrifices and devoted to the Brahmins and to Viṣṇu, as well as the account of the manner of his death, there could be no objection to his being described as someone who taught the yogis the ascetic path of nudity. What is most offensive to them, however, is the great hostility to their religion shown openly in the following invective, which is presented as a prophecy by the *Bhāgavata Purāṇa* in its conclusion of the story of the Ṛṣabha-avatar:

> When Arhat, the king of Koṅka, Veṅka, and Kuṭaka, comes to hear of this conduct of the divine Ṛṣabhadeva, he too will give himself over to it. Indeed, since irreligion will thrive in the Kali Age, the king, confounded by inevitable fate, will abandon the security of his own religion and in consequence of his deluded understanding will promote the heretical and evil ways of the heretics (*pākhaṇḍas*).
>
> It is for this reason that villainous people, confounded by the illusion-provoking powers of God (*devamāyāmohitāḥ*), will forsake the duties of purity and good conduct that are enjoined upon them and take up at will wicked vows that mock the gods, such as not bathing, not rinsing their mouths, not maintaining purity, and pulling out their hair. With their understanding thus corrupted by the irreligious Kali Age, they will forever deride *brahman*, the Brahmins, the Lord of the sacrifice, and other people. Then, trusting in the maintenance of their own world by upstart non-Vedic rites, like a blind man leading the blind, they will themselves fall into the blind darkness of hell.[72]

I have examined elsewhere[73] the many allusions to the practices of Jaina monks and the historical significance of the references made to "King Arhat" in the above quotation: it must be taken as referring to a king of the Deccan newly converted to the Jaina faith, and could well refer to Amoghavarṣa I (814–77 C.E.), the Rāṣṭrakūṭa king who was claimed as a patron of the Jaina *ācārya* Jinasena, the author of the *Ādi Purāṇa*. The old idea found in the *Viṣṇu Purāṇa* that Viṣṇu became incarnate as the Buddha through the power of his Yogamāyā in order to delude the demons is now applied instead to the Jaina Tīrthaṅkara Ṛṣabha and to the contemporary royal houses whose members had once been staunch followers of the Vedic religion but had since embraced the heretical religion.

The account in the *Śiva Purāṇa* also contains the word *Arhat,* although no Jaina character such as Ṛṣabha is mentioned there by name. According to this account, Lord Śiva instigated Lord Viṣṇu to create a man, "illusion personified" (*māyāmayaṃ puruṣam*), with the sole purpose of teaching *dharma* to the demons, who by adhering to his false teaching would be consigned to the lower worlds (Pātāla). Viṣṇu then created such a man, Arhat, who became a mendicant and produced false scriptures in Apabhramsa that were opposed to the teachings of the *śruti* and *smṛti* and contrary to the *dharma* of class and stage of life. He was able to initiate the demon Tripura and others into the mendicant order of the Jainas, and brought about their destruction as desired by the gods Viṣṇu and Śiva. While this story agrees substantially with the *Viṣṇu Purāṇa* account of the Buddha avatar of Viṣṇu, the author of the *Śiva Purāṇa* goes a step further and brings the narrative of this Arhat up to date by placing him in the Rajasthan desert, a stronghold of the Jaina community. In the Kali Age, he says, this Arhat (the *māyāmaya puruṣa*) will settle in Marusthalī and initiate into the Jaina mendicancy a large number of men who will go about wearing rags, holding pieces of cloth in front of their mouths, and constantly uttering the words, "*Dharma, dharma!*" The description is certainly meant to be a mockery of the Jaina monks of Rajasthan called "Sthānakavāsis," an offshoot of the Śvetāmbara sect, who are recognized even to this day by their *muhpatti* (a piece of white cloth held like a surgical mask over the mouth).[74]

The specific reference to place names like Koṅka, Veṅka, and Kuṭaka in the *Bhāgavata Purāṇa,* and to Marusthalī in the *Śiva Purāṇa,* in connection with the depiction of the "heresy" called "Jainism" proves abundantly that the Brahminic authors of the Purāṇas were well acquainted with the Digambara and the Śvetāmbara mendicant communities of Karnataka/Maharashtra and Gujarat/Rajasthan, respectively, where they flourished during medieval times.

The passages from the *Bhāgavata Purāṇa* and the *Śiva Purāṇa* quoted above, which openly use invective against Jaina holy men and their teachings, were probably a response of the Brahminic tradition to the persistent and sustained attack on their gods and teachings made in the Jaina Purāṇas. Yet the converse is also not impossible: should it be proved that these Brahminic imprecations predate the works of Vimalasūri or even of the two Jinsenas, which seems unlikely, it is conceivable that the Jainas decided to play the same game as the Brahmins and went them one better by undertaking a wholesale appropriation not only of the most popular avatars of the god Viṣṇu, but even of the god Brahmā-Prajāpati, the creator god of the Brahminic Purāṇas. Whereas we have enough evidence to show that the Jainas had indeed studied the Brahminic Purāṇas, there is very little indication that their works were studied by the authors of the Brahminic Purāṇas, for had the Brahmins indeed seen what the author of the *Harivaṃśa Purāṇa* or the *Pāṇḍva Purāṇa* had said about them, they would certainly have made some angry rejoinders. Unfortunately, no record of such literary retaliation has become available to us. In view of the kind of religious and sectarian segregation that exists between various communities of India, it is more than likely that non-Jainas ceased to have any contact with the Jaina material; and hence Jaina works enjoyed a very limited readership, probably confined only to a few Jaina monks and still fewer members of the learned laity.

Fortunately for us, a single piece of literary evidence from the time of Hemacandra, the twelfth-century *ācārya,* has survived, and it sheds unprecedented light on the way in which those of the Brahminic tradition did indeed react when confronted publicly with Jaina stories about their Purāṇic heroes. It is well known that Hemecandra, the renowned author of the *Triṣaṣṭi,* had been the celebrated teacher of Kumārapāla, the Śaivite king who had converted to the Jaina faith. Hemacandra was on many occasions hailed as a court pandit, an upholder of the Jaina faith in what was once a fortress of Śaivism and Vaiṣṇavism. Prabhācandra, the author of the *Prabhāvakacarita,* who made a compilation of the biographies of several Śvetāmbara *ācārya*s, has given the following account of one of Hemacandra's sermons on the life of the Pāṇḍavas, and how it led to a great scuffle between the Brahmins and the Jainas that was finally resolved by the royal preceptor Hemacandra himself:[75]

> One day during the rainy season, when Ācārya Hemacandra was in residence at a Jaina temple called "Caturmukha," he narrated the life of the Tīrthaṅkara Nemi in front of the fourfold assembly. The whole city, attracted by his most excellent speech, came there to listen to him and to have his *darśana.* Now, one day, in the course of this narration of Lord Nemi's life, he described in detail the episode pertaining to the renunciation of the Pāṇḍava brothers and their becoming Jaina monks.
>
> The Brahmins who heard it were extremely jealous of his growing popularity and went to the king and complained to him, saying, "Lord, in the far distant past the great sage Vyāsa Kṛṣṇadvaipāyana had narrated the extraordinary life of Yudhiṣṭhira and his brothers, having known it by means of his

supernatural knowledge of future events. There in his work [the *Mahābhārata*] it is said that towards the end of their lives the sons of Pāṇḍu went wandering among the snow-filled Himālayas and, having performed there the ritual bathing and the proper rites, they propitiated Lord Śiva [that is, the *śivaliṅga*] established at the holy Kedāra. Their minds thus filled with devotion to Lord Śiva, they then met their death. But these Śvetāmbaras, who are actually Śūdras since they have abandoned the true words of the Purāṇas, babble things about the Pāṇḍavas in their own assemblies, things which are contrary to the *smṛti*s. Because of this conduct, which is absolutely inappropriate, there is great calamity in store for you in the future. It is only proper that when your subjects are given to wrong conduct they must be restrained by the king. Therefore, O king, think deeply in your heart about what should be done in this matter, and do it." Having spoken thus, the group of Brahmins, who had been so extremely bold in their speech, fell silent.

The king replied, "The protectors of the earth do not act without contemplation and must not show disrespect to any particular faith without due consideration. Therefore these Śvetāmbara monks should be questioned further [on this matter]. If they give us a truthful answer, then they are to be honored by us, for that is just. For our friend here, the venerable Ācārya Hemacandra, is a great sage who has renounced all attachment and is free from all possessions. How could he ever speak anything untruthful? This matter therefore needs much contemplation."

The learned Brahmins also agreed and said, "So be it." Then the king had Hemacandra, the lord of the sages, summoned and questioned him, saying, "A king belongs to all and is impartial in this matter. Is it true that, according to the scriptures, the Pāṇḍavas renounced the world according to Jaina rules [that is, they became Jaina monks]?" The venerable *ācārya* said, "This has been said by our ancient *ācārya*s in our scriptures, and it is [equally] true that their sojourn in the Himālayas is described in the *Mahābhārata*. But we do not know whether those [Pāṇḍavas] who are described in our scriptures are the same as those who are described in the work [*Mahābhārata*] of sage Vyāsa, or yet by still other authors in different works."

To this the king said, "But then, O sage, were there more

than one of these persons, and were they all born in ancient times?" Then the teacher said, "O king, listen to my answer. In the narrative of Vyāsa itself there is the following episode about Bhīṣma the grandfather, who is also known as the descendant of the Ganges. At the time of entering the battlefield he told his attendants, 'At my death cremate my body only on a piece of earth which has always been pure, a place where no one has ever been cremated.' After acquitting himself justly in the war, Bhīṣma died. His attendants remembered his words and, lifting his body, took it to a hill. There on its top, which had never been visited by any man, they readied it [for cremation]. At that time a divine voice spoke:

> A hundred Bhīṣmas have been cremated here,
> and three-hundred Pāṇḍavas,
> and a thousand Droṇācāryas;
> As for Karṇas (cremated here),
> their number is beyond counting!"[76]

[Having quoted this verse from the *Mahābhārata*] Hemacandra said: "Hearing this [verse], in our minds we believe that among the hundreds of Pāṇḍavas mentioned here it is possible that some may have been Jainas. Moreover, on the Śatruñjaya hilltop their images can be seen, and also in the temple dedicated to Jina Candraprabha in the city of Nāsika, as well as in the great pilgrimage spot of Kedāra. We have gained our knowledge of *dharma* from various sources. Let the Brahmins who are experts in the Vedas and who believe in the *smṛtis* [that is, the *Mahābhārata*] also be questioned now about this matter [namely, the plurality of the Pāṇḍavas]. Knowledge can be obtained from any source. Like the River Ganges it cannot be claimed by anybody as his paternal property!"

Having heard this speech, the king addressed the Brahmins, "Is what the Jaina sage says true? Give me your reply, if indeed there is truth on your side. Surely in this matter you should give only a truthful answer, since the lord of the earth must act only after due consideration. In settling this matter, mine will be the last word, since I am impartial regarding all schools of philosophy, and also because I have erected temples in honor of gods of all faiths." Not knowing what to answer, the Brahmins remained silent. The king too honored the *ācārya* and said, "No fault attaches to you, not even the slightest, while you speak the truth."[77] Honored thus by the king, the teacher Hemacandra shone in the sky of Jaina teaching like the light of the midday sun.

The Brahmins lost their case precisely because they did not have a complete edition of the *Mahābhārata,* one with a verse-index! I assumed that the verse quoted by Hemacandra must be found in the modern critical edition of the great Epic, and took the trouble to look it up on behalf of the defeated Brahmins. But, to my utter suprise, there was no trace of it anywhere, not even in a marginal note. Is it possible that Hemacandra composed this verse on the spot and confounded the Brahmins? If so, then he himself played, as it were, the final role of that Arhat of the Brahminic Purāṇas, the strange emanation of Viṣṇu!

Notes

INTRODUCTION

1. Rajendra Chandra Hazra, *Studies in the Purāṇic Records on Hindu Rites and Customs* (Dacca, 1948) and *Studies in the Upapurāṇas,* 2 vols. (Calcutta, 1958 and 1963).

2. Ludo Rocher, *The Purāṇas,* vol. 2, fasc. 3 of *A History of Indian Literature,* ed. Jan Gonda (Wiesbaden: Otto Harrassowitz, 1986).

CHAPTER 1

1. As pointed out most recently by Jan Gonda, *The Indra Hymns of the* Ṛg Veda (Leiden: E. J. Brill), 1989.

2. Alf Hiltebeitel, "Hinduism," *The Encyclopedia of Religion,* vol. 6, edited by Mircea Eliade (New York: Macmillan, 1987), 342.

3. Wendy Doniger O'Flaherty, *Tales of Sex and Violence* (Chicago: University of Chicago Press, 1985), 118.

4. See *Nirukta* 1.15ff. Yāska refutes Kautsa, an opponent who questions the authority of the Vedas and asserts that Vedic *mantras* are meaningless.

5. See *Pūrva Mīmāṃsā Sūtras* 1.5, denoting the eternal relationship between words and their meaning; 1.26 for an assertion of the everyday quality of Vedic language; and 2.1–23 for a discussion of the significance of *arthavāda*—explanatory passages that are subordinate to *codana,* or ritual injunctions, but nonetheless meaningful as passages that provide incentives to and augments of sacrificial action. The substance of Kautsa's criticisms of Yāska and Yāska's rejoinder are discussed and amplified in the first

chapter of Jaimini's *Mīmāṃsa Sūtras*. See also Francis X. Clooney, *Thinking Ritually* (Vienna: de Nobili, 1990.)

6. Rājendralāla Mitra attempted a critical edition in 1892: Bṛhaddevatā, *or an Index to the Gods of the* Rig Veda *by Śaunaka, to which have been added* Ārṣānukramaṇī, Chandonukramaṇī and Anuvākānukramaṇī *in the Form of Appendices,* Bibliotheca Indica Sanskrit Series, n.s., nos. 722, 760, 794, 819 (Calcutta: Baptist Mission Press, 1893). This edition was quickly eclipsed by Macdonell's edition in 1907; in his introduction, Macdonell roundly criticized Mitra's editorial principles. (See his *Bṛhaddevatā,* 2 vols. Harvard Oriental Series. Cambridge: Harvard University Press, 1904.) The new edition, however, was well received. Moriz Winternitz's generally favorable review (*Wiener Zeitschrift für die Kunde des Morgenlande* 19 [1905]: 422–26) made only the slight demur that Macdonell may have included a larger number of redundant or superfluous lines than necessary. Isidore Scheftelowitz, who reviewed the work mainly with an interest in the *khila* portion of the *Ṛg Veda,* agreed with this idea and removed some lines from the text as later interpolations. (See Isidore Scheftelowitz, review of Arthur A. Macdonell's *The Bṛhaddevatā, Zeitscrift der Deutschen Morgenländischen Gesellschaft* 56: 420–27. See also his *Die Apokryphen des* Ṛgveda, pt. 1 of *Indische Forschungen* [Breslau: Verlag von M. & H. Marcus, 1906.])

7. See Lakṣman Sarup, Introduction to The Nighaṇṭu *and* the Nirukta: *The Oldest Indian treatise on Etymology, Philology, and Semantics* (Oxford: Oxford University Press, 1920); *Sanskrit Text, with an Appendix Showing the Relation of the* Nirukta *with other Sanskrit Works* (Lahore: University of the Panjab, 1927); *Indices and Appendices to the* Nirukta *with an Introduction* (Lahore: University of the Panjab, 1929); *The* Nighaṇṭu *and the* Nirukta, reprint ed. (Delhi: Motilal Banarsidass, 1967), 54.

8. See A. A. Macdonell, *The Bṛhaddevatā* vol. 1, xxii, and the introduction to his edition of the *Sarvānukramaṇī* (Oxford: Clarendon Press, 1886), viii, for a full discussion.

9. Muneo Tokunaga, "On the Recensions of the *Bṛhaddevatā,*" *Journal of the American Oriental Society* 101 no. 3 (1981): 275–86; "The Text and Legends of the *Bṛhaddevatā*" (Ph.D. diss., Harvard University, 1979).

10. See Laurie L. Patton, "Beyond the Myth of Origins: Types of Tale-telling in Vedic Commentary," in *Myths and Fictions: Their Place in Philosophy and Religion,* ed. Shlomo Biderman (Leiden: E. J. Brill, forthcoming).

11. Ernst Windisch, in a study of Irish literature, made a conjecture that the song of Purūravas and Urvaśī might well be a poem detached from its narrative context. (See Windisch, "Ueber die altirische Sage der *Táin Bó Cúalnge,*" *Verhandlung der 33. Philologenversammlung in Gera* [1879]: 15ff.) Hermann Oldenberg picked up on this possibility in his study of the Suparṇa legend and, later, in his "*Ākhyāna*-Hymnen im *Ṛg Veda*" in 1885.

(See "Das altindische *Ākhyāna,* mit besonderer Rücksicht auf das *Suparṇākhyāna,*" *Zeitschrift der Deutschen Morgenlandischen Gesellschaft* 37 [1883]: 54–86; and "*Ākhyāna* Hymnen im Ṛg Veda," *Zeitschrift der Deutschen Morgenlandischen Gesellschaft* 39 [1885]: 52–83.) Basing his theory on the literary style of the Pali Jātaka tales, he argued that the dialogue hymns of the *Ṛg Veda* postulate a prose narrative as the connecting medium of the metrical parts. This resulted in a combination of prose and poetry, in which poetic verse was the high point of emotion. The older portion of the *Mahābhārata* and later Vedic texts, such as the *Suparṇākhyāna,* also preserved this pattern. Yet Oldenberg saw the later *itihāsas* as useless historically, the fanciful creations of the commentators to describe and rationalize the hymns of the *Ṛg Veda* that were embarrassing or puzzling to them. Karl Geldner, in his important study of Purūravas and Urvaśī, argued against Oldenberg's denegration of later *itihāsas.* (See Geldner, "Purūravas und Urvaśī," *Vedische Studien,* Vol. 1 [Stuttgart: Verlag von W. Dohlhammer, 1889], 243–95.) Following his teacher Geldner, Emil Sieg's *Die Sagenstoffe des* Ṛg Veda *und die indische Itihāsa-tradition* (Stuttgart: W. Kolhammer, 1902) is still regarded as the most thorough treatment of Ṛg Vedic legends available.

12. The ensuing twenty years resulted in specific studies of those particular stories for which Sāyaṇa gives no ritual employment (*viniyoga*), such as the Vṛṣākapi hymn (*Ṛg Veda* [hereafter cited as *RV*] 10.86), Saramā and the Paṇis (*RV* 10.108), the recovery of Agni (*RV* 10.51–53), Mudgala's race (*RV* 10.102), the dialogue between Purūravas and Urvaśī (*RV* 10.95), Lopāmudrā and Agastya (*RV* 10.179), and Indra, the Maruts, and Agastya (*RV* 10.165, 170, 171). Bloomfield's "Contributions to the Interpretation of the Veda" treated the stories of Indra and Namuci, the two dogs of Yama, and the marriage of Saraṇyū, as well as Trita. (See Bloomfield, "Contributions to the Interpretation of the Veda 3. 1. The Story of Indra and Namuci. 2. The Two Dogs of Yama in a New Role. 3. The Marriage of Saraṇyū, Tvaṣṭar's Daughter." *Journal of the American Oriental Society* 15 [1898]: 143–88; "Contributions to the Interpretation of the Veda 7. 6. Trita, the Scape-goat of the Gods, in Relation to *Atharva Veda* 6.112 and 113." *American Journal of Philology* 17 [1896]: 430–37.) Albrecht Weber contributed an important study, "Episches im vedischen Ritual," (*Sitzerberichte der Preussischen Akademie der Wissenschaft,* 38 [1891]: 769–819), which focused on the ritual use of Vedic legends and the relationship between the legends in ritual literature and in the *Mahābhārata.*

13. Not surprisingly, in the first part of the twentieth-century scholars reacted against this theory about the origins of Vedic hymns, in all of its variations. The "anti-*ākhyāna*" reaction believed that the Ṛg Vedic hymns were coherent enough on their own. Sylvain Lévi, in his work, *Le Théâtre Indien,* held that these legends represented some sort of cohesive dramatic scene, independent of any supporting prose apparatus. (See Lévi, *Le Théâtre Indien,* 2 vols. [Paris: College de France, Libraire Honore Champion, 1963.], translated by N. Mukherji as *The Theatre of India,* 2 vols. [Calcutta:

Writers' Workshop, 1980].) In addition to Lévi's work, various other scholars took positions in various degrees of extremity against the *ākhyāna* theory. In *Mysterium und Mimus im* Ṛg Veda (Leipzig: H. Haessel Verlag, 1908), Leopold von Schroeder went further than Lévi and asserted that they were ritual dramas. Later, Jarl Charpentier joined the debate by rejecting both the drama as well as the *ākhyāna* theory, stating that, with the exception of four hymns, the Ṛg Vedic hymns could be read as epic poetry without the addition of prose. (Jarl Charpentier, *Die Suparṇasage: Untersuchungen zur Altindischen Literatur und Sagengeschichte* [Uppsala: A.-b. Akademiska Bokhandeln i Kommission, 1922].) J. Hertel, working independently of Lévi, rejected the *ākhyāna* theory in several articles. Moriz Winternitz tried to reconcile the idea by postulating that some of the *samvāda* hymns were ballads, in which everything is told in versified speeches, some were *ākhyāna,* poetic fragments that did have the nonsurviving prose element, and some were strophes that belonged to ritual dramas. (See "Dialog, Ākhyāna, und Drama in der Indischen Literatur," *Wiener Zeitschrift für die Kunde des Morgenlandes* 23 [1909].) In a similar vein, A. B. Keith, in "The Vedic *ākhyāna* and the Indian Drama" (*Journal of the Royal Asiatic Society,* pt. 2. [1911]: 979–1009), in one great sweep rejects both the *ākhyāna* and the drama theory, stating that there is not enough evidence for either. The debate about the *ākhyāna* theory died down in the early twenties, and the fourth period is marked by a notable silence on the subject of Vedic legends. Interestingly, in the later sixties there do exist attempts to reconsider and reaffirm the *ākhyāna* theory. Ludwig Alsdorf attempted to vindicate the *ākhyāna* theory from the perspective of Jaina literature. (See Ludwig Alsdorf, "The *Ākhyāna* Theory Reconsidered," *Journal of the Oriental Institute of Baroda* 13, no. 3 [1964]: 195–207.)

14. For a full account of this legend, see Ṣaḍguruśiṣya on the *Sarvānukramaṇī,* 155–58; Sāyaṇa in his introduction to *Ṛg Veda* 10.95; *Śatapatha Brāhmaṇa* 5.68ff.; 11.5.1.1; 3.4.1.22. The legend is called an *ākhyāna* in the *Nirukta* 5.13 (s.v. "Urvaśī"), 10.46, 47 (sv. "Purūravas"), and 11.36 (s.v. "Urvaśī"). Also see *Kathaka Saṃhitā* 8.10. For secondary literature, see Albrecht Weber, *Indische Studien* vol. 1 (Berlin: F. Dummler, 1850–63; Leipzig: F. A. Brockhaus, 1865–98), 196; Hermann Oldenberg, *Vedic Hymns,* Sacred Books of the East (Delhi: Motilal Banarsidass, 1964) vol. 46; 28,323. Ernst Geldner, in *Vedische Studien* treats the whole story historically (see Richard Pischel, and Karl F. Geldner, *Vedische Studien* (Stuttgart: W. Kohlhammer. vol. 1 [1889]: 243–84.)

15. See the *Viṣṇu Purāṇa* (4.6.35–93), where, instead of being instructed, Purūravas himself discovers that he must use the wood of the *aśvattha* tree and recite the correct *mantras* in order to become a *gandharva.*

16. The word used by the *Bṛhaddevatā* is *abhirūpa,* "lovely," but in the context of the use of *sarasi* and *iva* in the verse, and in the context of the *Śatapatha Brāhmaṇa* story, it is more likely the earlier reading was *āti-*

rūpa, "the form of a swan." The *Bṛhaddevatā* (*BD*) implies that she is in some other form, although it does not specifically mention the swan.

17. The story of Purūravas is told in the *Viṣṇu Purāṇa* 4.6.35–93. It is also mentioned in the *Vāyu, Matsya, Vāmana, Padma,* and *Bhāgavata Purāṇas*, as well as in the *Mahābhārata.*

18. 9.18–42. This Purāṇa recounts that Īlā is originally a woman, who because of a boon had been turned into a man, Sudyumna. Sudyumna then roams the forest, interrupts Śiva and Parvatī, and is turned back into a woman. Upon the intercession of Vasiṣṭha on Sudyumna's behalf, Śiva decides that every year Sudyumna will spend six months as a man, and six months as a woman.

19. Geldner is of the opinion that it is the close relationship between Indra and the *apsaras*es in the Epic literature that brought Indra into this episode. (*Vedische Studien* 1: 256 n. 2) Yet if one looks at the stories in terms of their thematic emphases, one might well argue as above, that the story is given a newly theological thrust as a result of the more Purāṇic perspective of the *itihāsa* interpolations.

20. The *Tāṇḍya Brāhmaṇa* (1.8.2.5), among others, does underscore this association of the *ṛṣi*s with the gods: "The seminal fluid of Indra, having his characteristic power, was discharged threefold. The third born was Bhṛgu." Durga, commenting on the *Nirukta,* writes, "Prajāpati took his own seminal fluid and sacrificed. From the blazing fire Bhṛgu was born; Aṅgiras rose from the ashes. Then the two just born said, 'Seek the third also here;' thus the *ṛṣi* who sprang up was called 'Atri.' Not yet satisfied, they began to dig and the seer thus produced was called 'Vaikhānasa.'" (Cf. the story of Trita, "the third" in *BD* 3.132–7.) The *Aitareya Brāhmaṇa* story builds a complete cosmogony out of this motif. The seed of Prajāpati was surrounded with Agni, and the Maruts blew upon it, but Agni could not make it move. It was then surrounded with Agni Vaiśvānara, and then the Maruts blew upon it, and it moved. The text goes on:

> The first part of the seed that was kindled became Āditya, the second became Bhṛgu, which Varuṇa took for himself. The third was brilliant [*adidet*] and became the Ādityas. The coals became the Aṅgirases, born from the coals. Bṛhaspati came forth from the coals, which, after being quenched, blazed up again; and from the extinguished coals emerged black cattle, from the reddened earth came the ruddy cattle. The ash there crept about in diverse forms—buffalo, the cow, the antelope, camel and the donkey, and these ruddy ones. (3.34)

21. Other texts, such as the *Nirukta,* attest to Bhṛgu's unusual birth, although they do not directly associate him with a god. The *Nirukta* (3.17) tells this story:

> Bhṛgu is produced in flames, that is, one who, although being roasted, was not burnt. Aṅgiras [was born] from live coals. Live coals [are so called because] they leave a mark, or they are bright. They said, "Seek

the third in this very place." Thus Atri [not three] is so called, Vaikhānasa is so called from being dug out, the root *khan*. Bharadvāja is so called from being brought up, the root *bhṛ*. Virūpa [is so called] from being multiform.

22. See Sieg, *Sagenstoffe,* pp. 105–8 on the birth of Agastya. Also see *Sarvānukramaṇī* 1.166 and Sāyaṇa on *RV* 7.33.11. The *Nirukta* tale is also similar to its counterpart above. It tells how, upon seeing the *apsaras,* the seminal fluid of Mitra and Varuṇa fell down, and it is to this event that *Ṛg Veda* 7.33.1 refers: "O Vasiṣṭha, you are the son of Mitra and Varuṇa."

23. That is, *kumbha* is a unit of measure, like an English bushel.

24. This phrase could mean that the fish, or Matsya, mentioned above, turned into Vasiṣṭha. Since they are named as two separate sages, however, this is unlikely.

25. *Śraiṣṭyakarmaṇaḥ,* "to be expressive of excellence."

26. *Karmaṇi.* See *RV* 7.33.11 and *Taittirīya Saṃhitā* 3.5.2 for similar usages.

27. *Mahābhārata* 3.101.14; 12.291.7ff.; 13.143.18; 13.102.1ff. This passage's relationship with the *Mahābhārata* is close in another respect. In *Mahābhārata* 1.7.59–60, the same list of the daughters of Dakṣa appears, with Pradhā and Kapilā substituted for Variṣṭhā and Surabhi.

28. *Agni Purāṇa* 206.1–12; *Bhāgavata Purāṇa* 6.18.5–6; *Matsya Purāṇa* 201.1–39; *Narasiṃha Purāṇa* 6.1.ff.; *Padma Purāṇa* 5.22.19–40; *Śiva Purāṇa* 45.23–26; *Viṣṇu Purāṇa* 4.5.1.ff.; *Viṣṇudharmottara Purāṇa* 1.117.1ff.

29. John E. Mitchiner, *Traditions of the Seven Ṛṣis* (Delhi: Motilal Banarsidass, 1982), 77.

30. Mitchiner, *Traditions of the Seven Ṛṣis,* 86–87.

31. *Rāmāyaṇa* 1.45.ff.; 1.69.17ff.; 2.102ff.; *Mahābhārata* 1.59; 1.9ff.; 1.60.33–35; 12.200.1–46; *Harivaṃśa* 3.45–49; 31.100–9; *Mārkaṇḍeya Purāṇa* 104.1–9; *Vāyu Purāṇa* 1.30.72–73; 2.3.1; 2.4.109ff.; 2.5.101; 2.6.43–44; 2.6.76; 2.8.334, etc.

32. So, too, in the main plot of the *Mahābhārata,* Satyavatī's daughter-in-law Kausalyā proves herself to be a lover of *dharma,* since she lies with the seer Vyāsa at her mother's command, thus giving birth to Dhṛtarāṣṭra, the Kaurava king and a principle character in the *Mahābhārata.*

33. For instance, the story of Trita, told by both the *Bṛhaddevatā* and the *Mahābhārata,* is used in the *Mahābhārata* to illustrate the *dharma* of the sage who, set upon and abandoned by his cruel brothers, can perform a sacrifice in his head and convince the gods to help him.

34. One might wonder why this *anukramaṇī* was chosen for expansion, and not others. Although nothing can be firmly concluded, some speculations are persuasive. The fact that the list of deities is chosen above the list of meters, *ṛṣis*, and others is not insignificant. If one assumes the *Bṛhaddevatā* to be from the early Purāṇa period, when the first Purāṇas were being collated and formed as specifically theological statements, it may well be no accident that the Vedic list of deities would be singled out as the most appropriate point of expansion. Gods, and not meters or *pādas,* are the most persuasive means of explaining the Veda.

35. Moreover, it must be noted that its expansion is largely narrative in nature. Unlike the core text of the *Devatānukramaṇī,* the ritual application of *mantra* is not the only motivation behind the new, expanded text, the *Bṛhaddevatānukramaṇī.* Narrative and commentary take on a more central role. One might put it another way: commentary on the Veda is no longer concerned exclusively with step-by-step details of the *mantra*'s ritual use but also with other forms of the explanation of *mantra.* To be sure, narratives are also part of the *Brāhmaṇas,* but they act more as handmaidens to the larger project of ritual philosophy and do not provide the kind of grounding and explanation which they do in the *Bṛhaddevatā.* And, unlike the *Sarvānukramaṇī,* where the *itihāsa*s are simply named or signaled, the *Bṛhaddevatā*'s *itihāsa*s are actually related. The *anukramaṇī,* the list, becomes embedded within narrative.

This "narrative" tendency of the *Bṛhaddevatā* is corroborated by statements within the text itself. Several parts of the shorter version of the text actually express divergences between Śaunaka and the writer of the *Bṛhaddevatā*—the interpretation of the *sūkta.* For instance, the *Bṛhaddevatā* author is more inclined to take the "elaborate" view as to who the deities are in any given *sūkta*—incorporating all the speakers of the scene portrayed. Thus, in its discussion of *RV* 8.96:13–15, the *Bṛhaddevatā* (6.116–17) believes that Indra, Agastya, and the Maruts are the deities of the triplet, whereas Śaunaka regards Indra alone as its deity. More importantly, the *Bṛhaddevatā* considers several hymns to be "narratives" or "stories," disagreeing with Śaunaka and appealing to other early Vedic authorities. For instance, the *Bṛhaddevatā* (8.11–12) considers *RV* 10.102, the story of the race of Mudgala, to be a narrative hymn, following the Vedic interpreter Śākaṭāyana, although Śaunaka says it is addressed to Viśvedevas. Moreover, the *Bṛhaddevatā* (6.107) seems to side with Vedic interpreters Yāska and Bāghuri, who call *Ṛg Veda* 8.91—the story of Apālā and Indra—an *itihāsa,* while Śaunaka believes it is addressed to Indra.

36. Wendy O'Flaherty, *The Origins of Evil in Hindu Mythology* (Berkeley and Los Angeles: University of California Press, 1976), 79.

37. O'Flaherty, *Origins of Evil,* 79.

38. O'Flaherty, *Origins of Evil,* 80.

39. O'Flaherty, *Origins of Evil,* 82.

40. See Laurie L. Patton, "Beyond the Myth of Origins: Types of Tales Telling in Vedic Commentary," forthcoming.

41. *Turaṣat,* "overpowering the mighty" or "overpowering quickly."

42. Literally, "touched the hand with the hand."

43. *Jaiminīya Brāhmaṇa* 1.228, cited in O'Flaherty, *Tales of Sex and Violence,* 75–76.

44. *Aitareya Brāhmaṇa* 6.20; *Jaiminīya Upaniṣad Brāhmaṇa* 3.3.7–10; *Mahābhārata* 1.165.135–145.

45. See, for example, the *Vāyu Purāṇa* 1.59.79–105; *Matsya Purāṇa* 145.81–91.

46. This and following *śloka* are quoted by Ṣaḍguruśiṣya on *RV* 2.43. See Macdonell's *Sarvānukramaṇī* on *RV* 2.43, 104. Also see *Ṛg Vidhāna* 1.31.3, 4.

47. The phrase "praised Indra" is taken from the following verse, *BD* 6.118.

48. Geldner posits that the dialogue is between Viṣṇu, who recites the first verse, and Indra, who recites the rest of the verses in reply (see his *Ṛg Veda,* 2: 428).

49. Cited in Cornelia Dimmitt and J. A. B. van Buitenen, *Classical Hindu Mythology* (Philadelphia: Temple University Press, 1978), 269–70.

50. Mitchiner, *Traditions,* 210.

51. Cited in Dimmitt and van Buitenen, *Classical Hindu Mythology* 174–76.

52. If read in this particular way, one might remark upon how the *anukramaṇī,* or indexical genre of the *Bṛhaddevatā* plays an important role in this development. One moves from the *Ṛg Veda,* where the *mantra*s are recited, to the Brāhmaṇas, where the *mantra*s are explained according to their sacrificial usage. In the Brāhmaṇa, one can detect the increased usage of *pratīka*s—the first syllables of a verse—to refer to particular *mantra*s; yet the discourse about *mantra*s remains fairly concretized in discussion of sacrificial procedures. In the *anukramaṇī*s, the *pratīka* is virtually the sole means of reference to *mantra*s. While the contents of the *mantra* are indeed implied by those *pratīka*s, they are nonetheless a shortened form of *mantra*. Indeed, if one is to take seriously the claim that *anukramaṇī*s too are transcendental knowledge, then they function metonymically. As parts, they symbolize the entire *mantra*—inaugurating the process whereby smaller and smaller parts can stand for the entire utterance. As sacrificial performance becomes less and less a concern, in texts like the early Purāṇas, the actual contents of the *mantra* are less necessary. Thus the simple references to "appropriate *mantra*s" or "*mantra*s praising Prajāpati" may be a later point in the process of abstraction that begins with the *pratīka*.

53. Jan Gonda, "The Hindu Trinity," in *Anthropos* 63 (1968): 212–26; also in *Selected Studies,* vol. 4, *History of Ancient Indian Religion* (Leiden: E. J. Brill, 1975), 27–41. See also H. Sh. Joshi, *Origin and Development of Dattareya Worship in Indra.* (Baroda: University of Baroda, 1965), chap. 1.

54. *Ṛg Veda* 5 3.6.9; 8.35.3; 1.139.11; *Atharva Veda* 10.7.13; 10.9.12.

55. *Taittirīya Saṃhitā* 6.6.8.2 and *Śatapatha Brāhmaṇa* 4.5.4.1.

56. *Śatapatha Brāhmaṇa* 2.17.5.32; 11.2.3; *Kauṣītaki Brāhmaṇa* 8.8; and *Nirukta* 7.5; 88. For Sūrya as part of the trinity conception, see D. P. Pandey, "Sūrya" (Ph.D. diss., University of Leiden, 1939), 84ff.

57. Gonda, "Hindu Trinity," 216.

58. The *RV* verses to Agni (3.26.7; 3.20.2; 1.146.1, among others) show the threefold division of this god. *Bṛhaddevatā* 1.90–96 follows a similar pattern.

59. *Śatapatha Brāhmaṇa* 6.1.1.5; 8.3.4.15; with the whole of *brahman* 7.3.1.42.

60. *Taittirīya Upaniṣad* 3.1.1; 2.8.1; also see *Muṇḍaka Upaniṣad* 1.1.1.

61. See, for instance, *Nirukta* 9.4–7 where, among other things, the word derivations for frogs, boards, rushes, and dice are given as deities of the earthly sphere, without particular reference to their "earthly" properties.

62. The citations of joint actions of the Purāṇic triad are myriad: *Agni Purāṇa* 61.27; 66.12; 78.31; 92.45; *Mārkaṇḍeya Purāṇa* 1.44; 16.89; 17.10; 20.34. Also see *Matsya Purāṇa* 265.4, where only the man who is friendlily disposed to all three gods is allowed to erect and consecrate a sanctuary.

63. *Kūrma Purāṇa* 1.14.4–97; see Dimmitt and van Buitenen, *Classical Hindu Mythology,* 174.

64. *Kūrma* 1.10.1–38.

65. Gonda, "Hindu Trinity," 220–21.

CHAPTER 2

1. See Bruce L. Sullivan, *Kṛṣṇa Dvaipāyana Vyāsa and the* Mahābhārata: *A New Interpretation* (Leiden: E. J. Brill, 1990); Wendy Doniger O'Flaherty, *Dreams, Illusion, and Other Realities* (Chicago: University of Chicago Press, 1984), chap. 4; Wendy Doniger O'Flaherty, *Other Peoples' Myths: The Cave of Echoes* (New York: Macmillan, 1988), chap. 3 and 7; and Wendy Doniger O'Flaherty, "Horses and Snakes in the *Ādi Parvan* of the

Mahābhārata," in *Aspects of India: Essays in Honor of Edward Cameron Dimock,* ed. Margaret Case and N. Gerald Barrier (New Delhi: American Institute of Indian Studies and Manohar, 1986), 16–44; A. K. Ramanujan, "Where Mirrors are Windows: Towards an Anthology of Reflections," *History of Religions* 28: 3 (February, 1989), 1–30.

2. *Bhāgavata Purāṇa,* with the commentary of Śrīdhara (Bombay: Sri Venkatesvara Steam Press, 1832). Henceforth cited as *BP.*

3. *Mahābhārata* (Poona: Bhandarkar Oriental Research Institute, 1933–69). Henceforth cited as *M.*

4. *Devībhāgavata Purāṇa* (Benares, 1960). Henceforth cited as *DBP.*

5. See Brian K. Smith, "Exorcising the Transcendent: Strategies for Defining Hinduism and Religion," *History of Religions* 27, no. 1 (August 1987): 32–55.

6. Though even the Upaniṣads, which are part of *śruti,* list the chain of their transmission *after* the divine revelation took place. See *Bṛhadāraṇyaka Upaniṣad* 2.6.1–3 for one of several very long lists of teachers.

7. See J. A. B. van Buitenen, "On the Archaism of the *Bhāgavata-Purāṇa,*" in *Krishna: Myths, Rites, and Attitudes,* ed. Milton Singer (Honolulu: East-West Center Press, 1966), 23–40.

8. But it might well be Vyāsa, who is often called the "great sage." Ganesh Vasudeo Tagare (*The Bhāgavata Purāṇa,* vol. 1, Ancient Indian Tradition and Mythology Series, vols. 7–10 [Delhi: Motilal Banarsidass, 1978], 6), identifies the "great sage" as Vyāsa.

9. The text calls him "Son of Romaharṣaṇa" (literally, "he who causes the hair to stand on end," a common epithet of great storytellers), and Śrīdhara further identifies him as Ugraśravas, a famous bard and a key figure in the transmission of the *Mahābhārata.*

10. Eric A. Huberman, "Language, Love, and Silence: Readings of Separation in the Sanskrit Epic, Poetic, and Puranic Traditions" (Ph.D. diss., Department of Middle East Languages and Cultures, Columbia University, 1990).

11. See O'Flaherty, "Horses and Snakes."

12. At the end of this episode (*BP* 1.18.9), the Sūta says to the sages, "Thus I have told you what you asked me, the story about Parikṣit, as it is connected with the story of Kṛṣṇa Vāsudeva."

13. Śuka is described as an *avadhūta,* one who has "shaken off" all social ties and social conventions; it is often used as a pejorative term for a yogi.

14. *BP* 12.5–6. There are a few further chapters of conversation between Śaunaka and Sūta involving a story about Markaṇḍeya and the child

Viṣṇu in the cosmic waters, and then the final praise and summing up of the *Bhāgavata Purāṇa.*

15. It is perhaps appropriate that my decision to write this essay about a story about pupils surpassing teachers was inspired by a suggestion from David Shulman, who was once my student.

16. See the birth of Skanda, *Mahābhārata* 3.213–16, 13.83–86, and so on. See Wendy Doniger O'Flaherty, *Śiva: The Erotic Ascetic* (Oxford and New York: Oxford University Press, 1973).

17. See Wendy Doniger O'Flaherty, *Women, Androgynes, and Other Mythical Beasts* (Chicago: University of Chicago Press, 1980), 267.

18. This syndrome, known from other myths as well, makes sense of what in our culture is a joke, the paradox of the man who says, "I'm a bachelor, and so was my father." The equivalent in Indian parlance is the paradox of "the son of a barren woman," a catchphrase that Śuka uses several times in the *Devībhāgavata* to characterize the meaninglessness of the householder life.

19. Janaka is often depicted as a learned king at whose court the great sages such as Yajñavalkya propounded their doctrines: *Bṛhadāraṇyaka Upaniṣad* 3.1.1, 4.1.1. Janaka himself is presented as a paradigm of knowledge in *Kauṣītaki Upaniṣad* 4.1.

20. William K. Mahony, "Flying Priests, Yogins, and Shamans in Early Hinduism and Buddhism" (Ph.D. diss., University of Chicago, 1982).

21. Cf. in Aśvaghosa's *Buddhacarita,* the description of Gautama Śākyamuni leaving the harem.

22. Cf. Nārada and the sons of Dakṣa: *Mahābhārata* 1.70; *Bhāgavata Purāṇa* 6.5. See Wendy Doniger O'Flaherty, *Hindu Myths* (Harmondsworth: Penguin, 1975), 46–48; and O'Flaherty, *Śiva,* 70–77.

23. *Chāṇḍogya Upaniṣad* 5.3–10; *Bṛhadāraṇyaka Upaniṣad* 6.2.1–15.

24. The three strands (*guṇas*) or components of matter (*prakṛti*) according to Sānkhya philosophy are darkness or entropy (*tamas*), energy or passion (*rajas*), and lucidity or goodness (*sattva*).

25. *Brahman,* the godhead.

26. See *Ṛg Veda* 10.95 (see Wendy Doniger O'Flaherty, *The Rig Veda: An Anthology,* [Harmondsworth: Penguin, 1981]), *Śatapatha Brāhmaṇa* 11.5.1; *Mahābhārata* 3, app. 1, 6.36–162; and Kālidāsa's play, *Vikramorvaśīya.*

27. Though this is a fairly normal thing to say to console a parent grieving for a lost child, it may here also be a pun on the name of Vyāsa's granddaughter, Kīrti (Fame).

28. See the discussion of shadow doubles in Wendy Doniger O'Flaherty, *Dreams, Illusion, and Other Realities.*

29. Ovid, *Metamorphoses,* trans. Frank Justus Miller (Cambridge, Mass.: Harvard University Press, 1974) 3.341–401.

30. Ovid, *Metamorphoses* 3.402–510.

31. See O'Flaherty, *Śiva,* 148–71.

32. *Krauñca* birds.

33. *Rāmāyaṇa* (Baroda: Oriental Institute, 1960–75) 1.1–2. Henceforth cited as *R.*

34. I cite here the summary by Sheldon Pollock on page 384 of his translation of vol. 2 *Ayodhyākaṇḍa* of *The Rāmāyaṇa of Vālmīki,* (Princeton: Princeton University Press, 1986). Pollock also cites folk variants of the theme discussed by Walter Ruben, "Vier Liebestragödien des Rāmāyaṇa," *Zeitschrift der Deutschen Morgenländischen Gesellschaft* 100 (1950), 287–355, 294 n. 1.

35. The story of the child Viṣṇu on the banyan leaf, floating in the cosmic waters, is not told in this Purāṇa. But another variant of it, the story of Markaṇḍeya stumbling upon the child Viṣṇu in the cosmic waters, is the main subject of the final chapters of the *Bhāgavata Purāṇa.*

36. *Ṛg Veda* 1.164.20; *Muṇḍaka Upaniṣad* 3.1.1; *Śvetāśvatara Upaniṣad* 4.6.

37. *Śvetāśvatara Upaniṣad* 4.4.

38. The image of the parrot as mimic appears in the translator's note to verse 1.1.4 of the *Devībhāgavata Purāṇa* (*The Sri Mad Devi Bhāgavatam,* vol. 26 of *The Sacred Books of the Hindus,* trans. Swami Vijnanananda [Allahabad 1921–23]). Where in the text the sage Śaunaka says to the Sūta, "You have learnt the eighteen Purāṇas from Vyāsa the son of Satyavatī," the translator remarks: "It is not that you have read them like a parrot; but you have thoroughly grasped the meaning of them all as you have learnt them from Vyāsa himself, the son of Satyavatī."

39. S. Sorensen, *Index to the Names in the Mahābhārata* (London: Ernest Benn, 1904), 219.

40. Cited by S. K. Belvalkar on page 2223 of the Poona edition of the *Śānti Parvan.*

CHAPTER 3

1. See Wendy Doniger O'Flaherty, *Other Peoples' Myths: The Cave of Echoes* (New York: Macmillan, 1988), chap. 3, for a discussion of the fluidity

of written texts in India. See also the essay by V. Narayana Rao in this volume.

2. See Wendy Doniger O'Flaherty, *The Origins of Evil in Hindu Mythology* (Berkeley and Los Angeles: University of California Press, 1976), 157 n. 98.

3. See Ludo Rocher, *The Purāṇas,* vol. 2, fasc. 3 of *A History of Indian Literature,* ed. Jan Gonda (Wiesbaden: Otto Harrassowitz, 1986), 230, for a discussion, without date, of the "Kedāra Khaṇḍa."

4. This, and much of the ensuing discussion of the role of the *Skanda Purāṇa* in Indian culture, I owe to a conversation with V. Narayana Rao, on May 24, 1991.

5. Velcheru Narayana Rao, "Epics and Ideologies: Six Telugu Folk Epics," in *Another Harmony: New Essays on the Folklore of India,* ed. Stuart H. Blackburn and A. K. Ramanujan (Berkeley and Los Angeles: University of California Press, 1986), 131–65.

6. For a similar, but far more detailed, argument for the integrity of the laws of Manu, see the introduction to Wendy Doniger and Brian K. Smith, trans. *The Laws of Manu* (Harmondsworth: Penguin, 1991).

7. Rather than tackle the *Skanda Purāṇa* as a whole in this brief article, let me confine myself to the "Kedāra Khaṇḍa." We are justified, I think, in taking this book as a self-contained literary work; Ludo Rocher confirms what has long been suspected, that the "Kedāra Khaṇḍa" was composed at a time and place distinct from the other Khaṇḍas of the *Skanda Purāṇa,* even from the other portions of the "Maheśvara Khaṇḍa." Another text, also called the "Kedāra Khaṇḍa" and said to be a part of the *Skanda Purāṇa* (but not of the "Maheśvara Khaṇḍa") was published by the same press (Bombay: Venkatesvara Steam Press, n.d.). This is an entirely different work, much longer than the text that I am using here (the one to which Ludo Rocher also refers).

8. This is particularly true of the so-called *sthala-purāṇas* of vernacular traditions (see David Dean Shulman, *Tamil Temple Myths* [Princeton, New Jersey: Princeton University Press, 1980]), but it also applies to several Sanskrit Purāṇas, or, more usually, sections of Sanskrit Purāṇas.

9. This way of organizing myths is already found in the *Mahābhārata,* which groups several cycles of stories around journeys to holy places.

10. There are the solar and lunar lineages of the great Purāṇas, but also the minor lineages of other Purāṇas.

11. Ludo Rocher, *Purāṇas,* 230, citing John D. Plott, *Bhakti at the Crossroads* (New York: Carlton Press, 1971), 85.

12. See the appendix for an outline of the plot of the "Kedāra Khaṇḍa."

13. *Padma Purāṇa* 1.1.

14. *Śivapurāṇa Māhātmya* (Benares, 1964), 2.1–40.

15. See O'Flaherty, *Origins of Evil,* 317–18.

16. *Bhāgavata Purāṇa* 12.8–10.

17. *Viṣṇudharmottara Purāṇa* 1.236.1–21.

18. *Liṅga Purāṇa* 1.30.1–25; *Kūrma Purāṇa* 2.35.12–38.

19. See O'Flaherty, *Origins of Evil,* for the confluence of Vedic and devotional ideas of reciprocal affection between gods and humans.

20. *Mahābhārata* 3.163.

21. Thus, for example, the identity of Kutsa and Indra, Kutsa's father, causes Indra's wife to sleep with Indra—until Indra mutilates Kutsa "so that she can tell them apart." See *Jaiminiya Brāhmaṇa* 3.199–200 (translated by Wendy Doniger O'Flaherty in *Tales of Sex and Violence* [Chicago: University of Chicago Press, 1985]), 74–76.

22. *Liṅga Purāṇa* 1.104–5; *Śiva Purāṇa* 2.4.13–20.

23. Bali does it in chap. 9; Nahuṣa, in chap. 15.

24. See the theme of the overcrowding of heaven, in O'Flaherty, *Origins of Evil,* chap. 9.

25. There is a pun here on twice-born (*dvi-ja*): birds reborn from the egg, and Brahmins reborn at initiation. (Teeth are also called "twice-born").

26. The leaves of the *bilva* tree are used in the worship of Śiva.

27. By eating the food, the dog, an unclean animal, inadvertently made the Kirāṭa and his wife participants in the act of giving food, a part of the *pūjā* prescribed for the Night of Śiva. This is not mentioned in the text itself, but the table of contents helpfully points it out.

28. *Mahābhārata* 1.16.39–40.

29. *Bhāgavata Purāṇa* 8.12.12–35; *Agni Purāṇa* 3.17–20; *Śiva Purāṇa* 3.20.3–7; *Brahmāṇḍa Purāṇa* 4.10.41–77). See Wendy Doniger O'Flaherty, *Women, Androgynes, and Other Mythical Beasts* (Chicago: University of Chicago Press, 1980), 320.

30. *Ṛg Veda* 10.95.15.

31. *The Laws of Manu* 9.17.

32. *Mahābhārata* 5.12–17.

33. *Mahābhārata* 1.98.1–5. For the *Bṛhaddevatā* version, see Laurie Patton's article in this volume.

34. But other texts do connect Bṛhaspati's rape of Utathya's wife, Mamatā, with his own cuckolding by Candra, his pupil. This occurs, for instance, in a Telugu text, the *Tarasasankavijayamu* by Samukhamu Venkata Krsnappa Nayaka; personal communication from David Shulman, July 22, 1991.

35. *Viṣṇu Purāṇa* 5.27; *Harivaṃśa* 99.1–49.

36. *Bhāgavata Pūraṇa* 10.55.7.

37. There is a significant double entendre here, both "I am looking for *my* husband" and "I am seeking *a* husband."

38. Another pun, on *guṇa* ("virtue" or "quality or characteristic"): "You are devoid of virtue" can also mean, applied to the supreme godhead, "You have no qualities" (*nirguṇa*).

39. T. A. Gopinatha Rao, *Elements of Hindu Iconography,* vol. 2, pt. 1 (Madras, 1916), 322–23.

40. *The Laws of Manu* 3.34.

41. Personal communication from David Shulman, June 17, 1991.

CHAPTER 4

1. Ganti Jogi Somayaji, ed., *Telugu Documents: Being Petitions Etc. in Telugu Preserved in the Oriental Collections in the National Archives of India* (Waltair: Andhra University Press, 1957), 63–9.

2. Allasani Peddanna, *Manucaritramu,* translated by Hank Heifetz and V. Narayana Rao (unpublished manuscript). 1.18–22.

3. Ludo Rocher, *The Purāṇas,* vol. 2, fasc. 3 of *A History of Indian Literature,* ed. Jan Gonda (Wiesbaden: Otto Harrassowitz, 1986), 24–30.

4. The verse reads: *sargaś ca pratisargaś ca vaṃśo manvantarāṇi ca/ vaṃśānucaritaṃ ceti purāṇaṃ pañcalakṣaṇam.* My translation follows the paradigmatic one given by Horace Hayman Wilson in his introduction to his translation of the *Viṣṇu Purāṇa* (1840), iv–v.

5. Vans Kennedy, *Researches into the Affinity of Ancient and Hindu Mythology* (London: Longmans, 1831), 153n.

6. Rocher, *Purāṇas,* 29.

7. Pandurang Vaman Kane, *History of Dharmaśāstra,* vol. 5.2 (Poona: Bhandarkar Oriental Research Institute, 1962), 841.

8. Rocher, *Purāṇas,* 30.

9. Rocher, *Purāṇas,* 30.

10. Pierre Macherey, *A Theory of Literary Production* (London: Routledge and Kegan Paul, 1978), 85–89.

11. *Śukranīti*. (Varanasi: Chowkhamba Sanskrit Series, 1968), 2.180. The verse reads: *sāhitya śāstra nipuṇaḥ sangītajñaś ca susvaraḥ/ sargādi pañcakajñātā ca sa vai paurāṇikaḥ smṛtaḥ.*

12. For a more detailed study of this story in its folk and Purāṇa versions, see Velcheru Narayana Rao, "Epics and Ideologies," in *Another Harmony*, ed. Stuart Blackburn and A. K. Ramanujan, (Berkeley and Los Angeles: University of California Press, 1986).

13. Vātsyāyana's commentary on Gautama's *Nyāyadarśana* (ed. Swami Dwarikadasa Sastri. Varanasi: Bharatiya Vidya Prakasan, 1966), 4.1.62.

14. This statement is often made in books on Sanskrit poetics, including Mammaṭa's *Kāvyaprakāśa.*

15. Velcheru Narayana Rao, "Texts Without Authors and Authors Without Texts" (Paper presented at the Annual Conference on South Asia, University of Wisconsin-Madison, 1985).

16. Quoted by Elūripati Anantarāmayya, Introduction to *Viṣṇupurāṇam* (Gunturu: Anantasahiti, 1979), 45. The verse reads: *vyāso vetti śuko vetti rājā vetti na vetti vā/ śrīdharaḥ śakalam vetti śrīnṛsiṃhaprasādataḥ.*

17. The saying goes: *itihāsapurāṇāni bhidyante lokagauravāt.*

18. A slightly different version of this oft cited verse appears in *The Mahābhārata* (Poona: Bhandarkar Oriental Research Institute, 1942), 3, Appendix 1, #32, lines 65–70.

19. *Nāradīya Purāṇa* 1.60–61: *purāṇam sarvaśāstrāṇāṃ prathamaṃ brahmaṇā smṛtaṃ/anantaraṃ ca vaktrebhyo vedās tasya viniśrutāḥ.*

20. *Mārkaṇḍeya Purāṇa* (ed. Satyavrata Simha. Sitapuri, 1984), 45.20.

21. Cornelia Dimmit and J. A. B. van Buitenen, *Classical Hindu Mythology: A Reader in the Sanskrit Purāṇas* (Philadelphia: Temple University Press, 1978), 5.

22. Bammera Potana, *Śrīmahābhāgavatamu* (Hyderabad: Andhra Pradesh Sahitya Akademi, 1964), 10.8–13.

CHAPTER 5

1. David Dean Shulman, *Tamil Temple Myths: Sacrifice and Divine marriage in the South Indian Śaiva tradition* (Princeton, N.J.: Princeton University Press, 1980).

2. U. Vē. Cāminātaiyar (1855–1942), *En Carittiram* (Cennai (Madras): U. Vē. Cā. Nūl Nilaiyam, 1982).

3. P. K. Rājaśēkhara (ed.), *Janapada Mahākāvya Maleya Mādēśvara* (two vols.) (Mysore: Samyukta Prakasana, 1973).

4. See "Two Realms of Kannada Folklore," in Stuart Blackburn and A. K. Ramanujan (eds.) *Another Harmony, New Essays in South Asian Folklore* (Berkeley: University of California Press, 1986).

5. Roland Barthes, "Theory of the Text," in Robert Young (ed.) *Untying the Text: a Post-structuralist Reader* (London: Routledge and Kegan Paul, 1981), 39.

6. See "Repetition in the Mahābhārata," in Arvind Sharma (ed.), *Essays on the Mahābhārata* (Leiden: E. J. Brill, 1991).

7. In these characterizations, I'm indebted to the researches of Jī. Sam. Paramaśivayya (especially in *Dakṣiṇa Karnāṭaka Janapada Kāvyaprakāaragaḷu,* Mysore: University of Mysore, 1979) and P. K. Rājaśēkhara (ibid., and his Ph.D. dissertation, *Dakṣiṇa Karnāṭakada Janapada Purāṇagaḷu,* University of Mysore, 1980).

CHAPTER 6

I wish to thank Velcheru Narayana Rao and Galit Hasan-Rokem for their wisdom, and to absolve them of responsibility for the instances when I stubbornly ignored it. This publication has been supported by the National Endowment for the Humanities.

1. On the *Bhāgavata* and the considerable scholarly literature devoted to it, see Ludo Rocher, *The Purāṇas,* vol. 2, fasc. 3 of *A History of Indian Literature,* ed. J. Gonda (Wiesbaden: Otto Harrassowitz, 1986), 138–51. On dating, see F. Hardy, *Viraha-bhakti: The Early History of Kṛṣṇa devotion in South India* (Delhi: Oxford University Press, 1983), 486–88. The composition of the text is studied in Hardy, *Viraha-bhakti,* 483–547; J. A. B. van Buitenen, "On the Archaism of the *Bhāgavata-Purāṇa,*" in *Krishna: Myths, Rites, and Attitudes,* ed. Milton Singer (Honolulu: East-West Press, 1966), 23–40. See also the recent study by D. Pocock, "Art and Theology in the *Bhāgavata Purāṇa,*" in *The Word and the World: Fantasy, Symbol and Record,* ed. Veena Das (New Delhi: Sage Publications, 1986), 9–40.

2. We may mention the well-known Tamil version by Cĕvvaiccūṭuvār (late fifteenth to early sixteenth century).

3. See the introduction to the Vāviḷḷa Rāmasvāmiśāstrulu and Sons edition of *Kucelopākhyānamu* (Madras, 1966), 4–5.

4. I have discussed this pattern at some length, with further examples, in "Sage, Poet, and Hidden Wisdom in Medieval India," in S. N.

Eisenstadt and I. F. Silver (eds.), *Cultural Traditions and Worlds of Knowledge: Explorations in the Sociology of Knowledge* (Greenwich, Conn., and London: JAI Press), 1988, 109–37.

5. See the afterward in V. Narayana Rao and Hank Heifetz, *For the Lord of the Animals—Poems from the Telugu: The Kāḷahastīśvaraśatakamu of Dhūrjaṭi* (Berkeley and Los Angeles: University of California Press, 1987).

6. Potana also informs us that it was Rāma who revealed himself to him and inspired him to compose the Telugu *Bhāgavatamu:* 1.14–16. (I have used the critical edition published by Telugu Viśvavidyālayam [Hyderabad, 1986.])

7. Note, for example, the founding of the famous Ahobilam Mutt in 1398; see N. Jagadeesan, *History of Sri Vaishnavism in the Tamil Country (Post-Ramanuja)* (Madurai: Koodal Publishers, 1977), 154–58. This is but one example of a much more widespread pattern of institutional growth, related in part to the migration northward of important Tamil Śrīvaiṣṇava families and their integration into the institutional structure of Andhra Vaiṣṇava shrines. Compare K. Sundaram, *The Simhachalam Temple,* 2d ed. (Simhachalam: Simhachalam Devasthanam, 1984), 78–79. We may also recall the emergence of Vaiṣṇava liturgical literature in Telugu, of a completely new type in Andhra, toward the end of the fifteenth century in the Tāḷḷapāka corpus from Tirupati.

8. See pages 91–92 and 146–49 in the introduction to the Telugu *Bhāgavatamu* (Telugu Viśvavidyālayam critical edition); in English, D. Venkatadhvani, *Pothana* (Delhi: Sahitya Akademi, 1983), 32–42, 77–78.

9. Cf. Velcheru Narayana Rao, *Tĕlugulo kavitā viplavāla svarūpam* (Vijayavada: Viśālāndhra Pracuraṇālayam, 1978), 29–49 (especially 46–47).

10. Examples are too numerous to require exposition, but we may cite by way of illustration the outstanding Telugu *kāvya* by Pĕddana, *Manucaritramu,* an adaptation of an episode from the *Mārkaṇḍeyapurāṇa.* In some cases the *prabandha* may follow upon a Telugu version of the Purāṇa as a whole. The same process occurs, of course, in Sanskrit, with the appearance of *mahākāvya*s based on selected episodes from *itihāsa-purāṇa.*

11. See the cogent remarks on the Purāṇa frame by V. Narayana Rao, "Poetics of a Purāṇa in Telugu: Potana's *Mahā Bhāgavata*" (manuscript, 1979).

12. See my paper "Toward a Historical Poetics of the Sanskrit Epics," *International Folklore Review,* 1991, pp. 9–12.

13. See Rocher, *Purāṇas,* 24–30, 53–59.

14. Technically, this frame is itself part of a wider one involving the Sūta's recitation to the sages of Vyāsa's text, which the Sūta had heard Śuka

recite to Parikṣit. The internal composition of the *Bhāgavata*'s frame-story and its linkages to the rest of the text represent important keys to the specific dynamics and vision of this text. See chapter 2 of the present volume.

15. See Gail, *Bhakti im Bhāgavatapurāṇa,* Münchener Indologische Studien, vol. 6 (Wiesbaden, 1969), 20–38; Hardy, *Viraha-bhakti,* 494–97, 538–41. Surendranath Dasgupta, *A History of Indian Philosophy,* vol. 4 (Cambridge: Cambridge University Press, 1961), aptly describes the philosophy of the *Bhāgavata* as a "monistic transformation of Sānkhya" (p. 33, highlighting the metaphysical passages of the eleventh *skandha*); "the monistic tendency which regards all worldly experiences as illusory is so remarkably stressed that it nearly destroys the realistic note which is a special feature of the Sānkhya schools of thought" (p. 32). Note the distinctiveness of the *Bhāgavata* in this respect from the later development of Tamil Śrīvaiṣṇavism in the direction of the anti-illusionistic Viśiṣṭādvaita.

16. Hardy, *Viraha-bhakti,* 541.

17. E.g., F. J. Meier, "Der Archaismus in der Sprache des *Bhāgavata-Purāṇa,*" *Zeitschrift für Indologie und Iranistik* 8 (1931): 33–79; see also Hardy, *Viraha-bhakti,* 489–90; van Buitenen, "Archaism of the *Bhāgavata-Purāṇa.*" T. S. Rukmani, *A Critical Study of the Bhāgavata Purāṇa (with special reference to bhakti)* (Chowkhamba Sanskrit Studies 77, Varanasi: 1970) offers an appendix containing a long list of the *Bhāgavata*'s Vedisms.

18. See G. N. Reddy, "Purāṇa Performance—A Case Study from Telugu," paper delivered at the Madison Purāṇa conference.

19. Hardy, *Viraha-bhakti,* 491.

20. Van Buitenen, "Archaism of the *Bhāgavata-Purāṇa.*"

21. Van Buitenen focuses on Pāñcarātra, citing Yāmuna's *Āgamaprāmāṇya;* but, as Gail has shown (4–9), the teachings of the Pāñcarātra, strictly speaking, are not represented in the *Bhāgavata Purāṇa.*

22. Cf. also W. G. Neevel, *Yāmuna's Vedānta and Pāñcarātra: Integrating the Classical and the Popular* (Missoula, Mo.: Scholar's Press, 1977).

23. See David Shulman, "The Dynamics of Sect Formation in Medieval South India," to appear (in German) in a volume on the "Axial-Age" civilizations edited by S. N. Eisenstadt.

24. *Vāmana Purāṇa* (Varanasi: All-India Kashiraj Trust, 1967) 58.2, 80; *Bhāgavatapūraṇa with the commentary of Śrīdhara* (Varanasi: Paṇḍita Pustakālaya, Samvat 2013) 8.4.14.

25. For another Purāṇic version, see *Vāmana Purāṇa* 58.1–84.

26. E.g., *Pĕriyāḻvār* 2.10.8; *Pĕriyatirumŏḻi* 3.8.2–3; cf. Hardy, *Viraha-bhakti,* 373 n. 1.

27. See Joanna Gottfried Williams, *The Art of Gupta India, Empire and Province* (Princeton: Princeton University Press, 1982), p. 33 and plate 24; but as there is no sign of Viṣṇu here, the carving may simply represent the motif of an elephant struggling with a serpent or crocodile.

28. Williams, *Art of Gupta India,* p. 134 and plate 205. The Gupta relief is copied, with a distinct change in spirit, on the Varāha Temple, also at Deogarh (eighth century?): Williams, *Art of Gupta India,* p. 179 and plate 268.

29. *Brahmavaivarta Purāṇa,* Ānandāsrama Sanskrit Series no. 102 (Poona, 1935), 3.12.9–22. It is interesting that this Purāṇa preserves the erotic theme present in the story as told in the *Bhāgavata:* Viṣṇu, seeing Pārvatī's distress after Śani had beheaded her son, went to look for another head for him; he found Gajendra, exhausted after making love, lying in the forest; Viṣṇu cut off Gajendra's head and transferred it to Pārvatī's child and, moved by the piteous cries of Gajendra's mate, he cut off another elephant's head and attached it to Gajendra's body, thus bringing him back to life. Compare the discussion by Paul B. Courtright, *Gaṇeśa: Lord of Obstacles, Lord of Beginnings* (New York and Oxford: Oxford University Press, 1985), 39–40.

30. K. V. Raman, *Sri Varadarajaswami Temple—Kanchi* (New Delhi: Abhinav Publications, 1975), 9; cf. *Kāñcippurāṇam of Civañāṉacuvāmikaḷ* (Kancipuram: Tiruvaḷḷuvar cĕntamiḻp pāṭacālai, 1964), 9.1–34. In the latter Śaiva rendering of the story, Gajendra enters the crocodile's pond to bring flowers to his master, Viṣṇu, for offering to Śiva. In other respects, Civañāṉacuvāmikaḷ's version is remarkably close to the main features of the *Bhāgavata.*

31. Timmavajjhala Kodandaramaiah, *The Telugu Poets of Madura and Tanjore* (Hyderabad: Andhra Pradesh Sahitya Akademi, 1975), appendix 4.

32. See *Pĕriya purāṇam* of Cekkiḻār (Tirunelveli: South India Saiva Siddhanta Works, 1970), 4232–42; Cuntaramūrttināyaṉār, *Tevāram* (Tarumapuram: Tarumaiyātīṉam, 1964), *patikam* 92, vol. 4 (but see remarks on this *patikam* in my translation of the *Cuntarar Tevāram: Songs of the Harsh Devotee* (Philadelphia: Department of South Asia Regional Studies, University of Pennsylvania, 1990). And compare MBh 1.123.68ff.

33. Compare *Kuriñcippāṭṭu* 61–95; Cuntaramūrtti, *Tevāram, patikam* 12; K. Zvelebil, *The Smile of Murugan* (Leiden: E. J. Brill, 1973), 58 n. 1.

34. On this key term in the Śrīvaiṣṇava tradition, see Robert C. Lester, "Rāmānuja and Śrī-Vaiṣṇavism: The Concept of Prapatti or Śaraṇāgati," *History of Religions* 5 (1966), 266–82.

35. Hardy, *Viraha-bhakti,* 25–29, 36–38.

36. Dasgupta, *History of Indian Philosophy,* 33; see n. 15 above.

37. Compare the opening verse of the *Bhāgavata,* discussed by Gail, 19.

38. Hardy, *Viraha-bhakti* 637, cites this as evidence of the *Bhāgavata*'s Tamil provenance.

39. Compare the emphasis on memory as the form of yogic meditation in Rāmānuja and his successors: Robert C. Lester, *Rāmānuja on the Yoga* (Adyar, Madras: Adyar Library and Research Centre, 1976), 135.

40. Velcheru Narayana Rao, personal communication.

41. Verse numbers refer to the consecutive numbering of *Bhāgavata Purāṇa, skandha* 8, in the edition cited above (which also, however, retains the Sanskrit adhyāya division).

42. See D. Shulman, "The Scent of Memory in Hindu South India," *Anthropology of Aesthetics* 3 (1987), pp. 123–33.

43. These statements, by inverting conventional comparisons (the woman's thigh to elephant's trunk, etc.), exemplify the figure *vyatireka.*

44. *Naṟṟiṇai* 202. Note that the *veṅkai* (kino tree) is homonymous with *veṅkai,* "tiger."

45. Compare *Kalittŏkai* 11; discussed in D. Shulman, "The Crossing of the Wilderness: Landscape and Myth in the Tamil Story of Rāma," *Acta Orientalia* 42 (1981), 26–27.

46. On *akam* poetics, see the afterword in A. K. Ramanujan, *Poems of Love and War* (New York: Columbia University Press, 1985), 231–97.

47. The root recurs in participial form in the phrase cited from 65, **padākrāntanirvakramai.* On *trivikrama,* see F. B. J. Kuiper, "The Three Strides of Viṣṇu," in *Indological Studies in Honor of W. Norman Brown,* ed. E. Bender (New Haven, 1962), 137–51.

48. Cf. D. Shulman, "Divine Order and Divine Evil in the Tamil Tale of Rāma," *Journal of Asian Studies* 38 (1979): 651–69.

49. A recorded *harikathā* version of our story (by Veeragandham Venkata Subba Rao, *Gajendra Moksham* [Oriental Records, n.p. 1980]) takes this colloquial soliloquy still farther: Gajendra asks himself, "The Lord—where is he? What's he like? I don't know what form he has, or his name, or what village he lives in."

50. The critical edition reads *kamalāpta,* "beloved of Kamalā/Śrī," which amounts to the same thing. We note in passing that the version of *Vāmana Purāṇa* 58 explicitly identifies Viṣṇu as the addressee of the *stotra* throughout.

51. Chāgaṇṭi Śeṣayya, *Śrī Āndhrakavitaraṅgiṇi,* vol. 6 (Kapileśvarapuramu, n.d.), 220 (my thanks to V. Narayana Rao for this refer-

ence). The author aptly remarks, "The remaining verses truly appear to have been composed by God."

52. I owe this term to Dmitri Segal.

53. *Mahābhāgavatamu* 7.80–384.

54. v. 1. *garinula maralan,* which reverses the direction of the caress. The verb *nivuru* is shared with v. 39 (see above).

55. See Margaret Egnor, "On the Meaning of Śakti to Women in Tamil Nadu," in *The Powers of Tamil Women,* ed. Susan S. Wadley (Syracuse: Syracuse University Press, 1980), 19–20.

56. One thinks, perhaps, of Mandelstam's attractive and idiosyncratic notion of Hellenism as "the conscious surrounding of man with domestic utensils, and the humanizing and warming of the surrounding world with the most delicate teleological warmth." Osip Mandelstam, "On the Nature of the Word," in *Modern Russian Poets on Poetry,* ed. Carl Proffer (Ann Arbor: Ardis, 1976), 45. (But in South India the appropriate thermal metaphor would be cooling rather than warmth.)

57. A. K. Ramanujan, "Two Realms of Kannada Folklore," in *Another Harmony: New Essays on the Folklore of India,* ed. Stuart H. Blackburn and A. K. Ramanujan (Berkeley and Los Angeles: University of California Press, 1986), 64–67; Stuart H. Blackburn, "Domesticating the Cosmos: History and Structure in a Folktale from India," *Journal of Asian Studies* 45 (1986), 527–43.

58. Ramanujan, "Two Realms of Kannada Folklore," 41–55.

59. Erich Auerbach, *Mimesis: The Representation of Reality in Western Literature* (New York: Anchor Books, 1957).

60. Tiruñāṉacampantar, *Tevāram* (Tarumapuram: Tarumaiyātīṉam, 1954), 2.98.9.

61. Hardy, op. cit., pp. 308–371.

62. Cf. ibid., pp. 520–22. The Bengal Vaiṣṇavas venerate this passage, based on the experience of separation, as an example of ecstatic love, superior to *mokṣa,* in the *mahānubhāva* stage. See the note by Ganesh Vasudeo Tagare in his translation of the *Bhāgavata* (Delhi: Motilal Banarsidass, 1979), 4:1540.

63. See the translation with introductory study by Velcheru Narayana Rao, *Śiva's Warriors* (Princeton University Press, 1990).

64. *Basavapurāṇamu* of Pālkuriki Somanātha (Madras: Vavilla Ramasvamisastrulu and Sons, 1952), 3 (pp. 151–60).

65. *Pěriya Purāṇam* of Cekkiḻār, 3664–3702.

66. For a survey of the literature, see R. V. Ramakoti Sastry, "Telugu Versions of the Purāṇas," *Purāṇa* 4 (1962), pp. 384–407. The features that have emerged from the above discussion are also applicable, with some important distinctions, to the large Nayak-period literature of Tamil Purāṇas, as I hope to show in a separate essay.

67. Compare the remarks by Don Handelman on a major Tamil Purāṇa, probably slightly later than Potana: "The *Kantapurāṇam* may be thought of as a dialogue, or multilogue, between various points of view, some opposed and some shading into one another, and of the consequences for cosmic order of their implementation. The text explicates alternative positions and the reasoning that underlies them. Although the text is slanted strongly toward the validity of the position it espouses, it still brings such order into question, and pursues its contradictions until their confluence or eradication." D. Handelman, "Myths of Murugan: Asymmetry and Hierarchy in a South-Indian Purāṇic Cosmology," *History of Religions* 27 (1987), p. 170. This process is, however, greatly moderated in Potana, under the constraining impact of his Sanskrit model.

67. Cf. Pocock, op. cit., pp. 10–15.

CHAPTER 7

I would like here to express my gratitude to the British Academy for two grants that allowed me in 1982 and 1988 to travel extensively in South India and visit many Śrīvaiṣṇava temples.

1. J. Wicki, ed., *Tratado do Pe. Gonçalo Fernandes Trancoso sobre o Hinduísmo (Maduré 1616)* (Lisbon: Centro de Estudos Históricos Ultramarinos, 1973), 155.

2. Wicki, *Tratado do Pe. Gonçalo Fernandes Trancoso,* 159: "Até aqui dos *pranas* de Juden."

3. Wicki, *Tratado do Pe. Gonçalo Fernandes Trancoso,* 160: "Bramanta-puranão."

4. He adds in chapter 30 what "Manu, son of Brahmā," has to say about it (Wicki, *Tratado do Pe. Gonçalo Fernandes Trancoso,* 167–74) and, in Chapter 31, an account said to be from an "Āraṇyaka of the Yajurveda" (Wicki, *Tratado do Pe. Gonçalo Fernandes Trancoso,* 175–82).

5. Wicki, *Tratado do Pe. Gonçalo Fernandes Trancoso,* 155f. The original has *iruxi* (for *ṛṣi*), *Viasen* (for Vyāsa) and *Romacuruguen.* For "sacrifice" we find *equiam,* which is Tamil *ekkiyam,* from Sanskrit *yajña.*

6. Wicki, *Tratado do Pe. Gonçalo Fernandes Trancoso,* 157. Vexnu, Urutiren (for Rudra).

7. Wicki, *Tratado do Pe. Gonçalo Fernandes Trancoso,* 157.

8. J. A. Dubois, *Hindu Manners, Customs, and Ceremonies,* 3d ed. (Oxford, Oxford University Press, 1906), 109.

9. Dubois, *Hindu Manners,* 542–45.

10. Dubois, *Hindu Manners,* 543.

11. J. Rösel, *Der Palast des Herrn des Welt: Entstehungsgeschichte und Organisation der indischen Tempel- und Pilgerstadt Puri* (Munich, 1980), 215f.

12. Rösel, *Palast der Herrn der Welt,* 216.

13. Similarly also T. B. Coburn, *Devī-māhātmya: The Crystallization of the Goddess Tradition* (Delhi, 1984), 48, speaks of the *Purāṇas'* "dynamic quality, for they are a process." Even when looking "merely" at the texts, this dynamism is apparent. Compare, for example, the evolution of the *Brahmāṇḍa* and *Vāyu Purāṇas* from a common archetype (see W. Kirfel, *Das Purāṇa Pañcalakṣaṇa: Versuch einer Textgeschichte* (Bonn, 1927), x–xviii) or the story of Kṛṣṇa in the parallel recensions of the *Brahma* and *Viṣṇu Purāṇas* (see F. Hardy, *Viraha-bhakti: The Early History of Kṛṣṇa Devotion in South India* (Delhi: Oxford University Press, 1983), 86–91), or the influence of the *Bhāgavata Purāṇa* on the *Devībhāgavata Purāṇa* and the *Mahābhāgavata Purāṇa.*

14. See, for example, chapter 12 of the *Devīmāhātmya* where the recitation of the text itself is recommended as profitable religious act; compare L. Babb, *The Divine Hierarchy: Popular Hinduism in Central India* (New York, Columbia University Press 1975), (33–43, 218f) for a modern ritualized use of the same text. Or see the *Śiva-Purāṇa-Māhātmya* (derived from the *Skanda Purāṇa*), chapters 3 to 6, on ritual details for the recitation of this work and on the rewards arising from it (Shastri, trans. *Śiva-Purāṇa,* [Delhi, Motilal Banarsidass 1970], vol. 1, 9–30). This aspect of the "oral purāṇic tradition" (viz., the ritualised recitation of, and improvisation on, a textually fixed Purāṇa) will be ignored here.

15. For useful discussions of method with regards to the study of the Purāṇas see, for example, M. Biardeau, "Some Considerations About Textual Criticism," *Purāṇa* 10 (1968), C. M. Brown, *God as Mother: A Feminine Theology in India* (Hartford, Vt., 1974), 12–20, and, most detailed, Coburn, *Devī-māhātmya,* 19–50.

16. Further material of this kind has been discussed in F. Hardy, "Ideology and Cultural Contexts of the Śrīvaiṣṇava Temple," *The Indian Economic and Social History Review* 14, no. 1 (1977): 119–51; F. Hardy, "The Tamil Veda of a *Śūdra* Saint: The Śrīvaiṣṇava Interpretation of Nammālvār," in *Contributions to South Asian Studies,* ed. Gopal Krishna, vol. 1 (Delhi, 1978), 29–87; F. Hardy, review of *Tamil Temple Myths,* by D. D. Shulman," *JRAS* 1982, no. 2: 201ff.

17. "Historicity" appears as a problem in Biardeau, "Considerations about Textual Criticism."

18. See *Devīmāhātmya,* chap. 1.60.

19. *Kahakosu, sandhi* 39.11–16.

20. *Kahakosu, sandhi* 35.1–3.

21. *Kahakosu, sandhi* 48.15–21.

22. *Kahakosu, sandhi* 48, 17, 12.

23. *Kahakosu, sandhi* 20, 5.

24. *Kahakosu, sandhi* 21, 11.

25. *Bṛhatkathākoṣa,* no. 136.

26. *Karakaṇḍacariü, sandhi* 5. The editor offers in his introduction (pp. 56–60) a description of the actual cave-temple complex near the modern village Terā in the Osmanabad district of Mahārāṣṭra.

27. For details see Rahula, Bhikkhu Telwatte: *A Critical Study of the Mahāvastu,* (Delhi, 1978), 100–106.

28. See Rahula, *Bhikkhu Telwatte,* 108ff.

29. The final verses of the *Devīmāhātmya.*

30. *Bilvāraṇyakṣetra-māhātmyam,* 5.59f.

31. This reference to King Vairamegha may be a historical resonance; for a king of that name is actually mentioned in one of the poems by TiruMaṅkai-Āḻvār. See Hardy, *Viraha-bhakti,* 264f.

32. Further details on this mythology will be found in F. Hardy, "The Śrīvaiṣṇava Hagiography of Parkāla," in *Indian Narrative Literature,* ed. C. Shackle and R. Snell (forthcoming).

33. *Kahakosu, sandhi* 38.1–15.

34. *Kahakosu, sandhi* 38.5.9.

35. *Kahakosu, sandhi* 13.4.

36. *Kahakosu, sandhi* 15.1f.

37. *Kahakosu, sandhi* 15.3–10.

38. Details can be found in Padmanabh S. Jaini, *The Jaina Path of Purification* (Delhi, 1979), 288–304.

39. For further references to this Ṛṣabha avatar see, e.g., *Cēṭamalaippatiṟṟuppatt' Antāti* v. 87.

40. See Hardy, *Viraha-bhakti,* 511–26, 647–52.

41. See Hardy, *Viraha-bhakti,* 542–47.

42. *Bhāgavata Purāṇa* 10.33.17. Compare Hardy, *Viraha-bhakti,* 538–41.

43. Hardy, *Viraha-bhakti,* e.g., 445.

44. *Bṛhaddharma Purāṇa* 1.22.11.

45. *Bṛhaddharma Purāṇa* 1.22.14f.

46. *Bṛhaddharma Purāṇa* 1.17–22. For a similar story, with identical motivation, see the *Mahābhāgavata Purāṇa,* chap. 36–48 (also summarized in R. C. Hazra, *Studies in the Upapurāṇas,* vol. 2, *Śākta and Non-sectarian* [Calcutta, 1963], 265ff).

47. See Maity, *Historical Studies in the Cult of Manasā: A Socio-Cultural Study* (Calcutta, 1966), 300–302.

48. For a partial translation of one Bengali version see E. C. Dimock, trans., *The Thief of Love: Bengali Tales from Court and Village* (Chicago, 1963), 197–294.

49. W. L. Smith *The One-eyed Goddess: A Study of the Manasā Maṅgal* (Stockholm, 1980), 49.

50. Smith, *One-eyed Goddess,* 51.

51. Smith, *One-eyed Goddess,* 47f, 52ff.

52. *Devībhāgavata Purāṇa* 9.48; *Brahmavaivarta Purāṇa, Prakṛti-khaṇḍa* 46. Compare Maity, *Historical Studies,* 129f and Smith, *One-eyed Goddess,* 15ff.

53. Smith, *One-eyed Goddess,* 15.

54. The relevant poems are Sarojinī Bābar (ed.), *Ek hotā rājā,* pt. 1, *Yallammā-devīcī gāṇī* (N.p. 1965), nos. 1, 4 and 7.

55. Bābar, *Ek hotā rājā,* no. 8, verse 7. No. 3 mentions that the son was a miraculous gift from Śāmbhā (=Śiva).

56. Bābar, *Ek hotā rājā,* nos. 2 and 5.

57. See G.-D. Sontheimer, *Birobā, Mhaskobā und Khaṇḍobā: Ursprung, Geschichte und Umwelt von pastoralen Gottheiten in Mahārāṣṭra* (Wiesbaden, 1976), 55–58.

58. Bābar, *Ek hota rājā,* no. 6, verses 3f.

59. See *Devīkathā,* pp. 16–21. Sontheimer, *Birobā, Mhaskobā und Khaṇḍobā* is a detailed general study of the processes leading from "folk religion" to textual purāṇic forms in Maharastra.

60. See Hardy, "Ideology and Cultural Contexts of the Śrīvaiṣṇava Temple," *The Indian Economic and Social History Review* 14, no. 1 (1977): 147f.

61. See F. Hardy, "Mādhavendra Purī: A Link between Bengal Vaiṣṇavism and South Indian *Bhakti,*" *JRAS* 1974, no. 1: 36.

62. See, e.g., *JRAS* 1985, no. 1: 23–28. Höfer, an anthropologist of Nepal, replies here to a review by the Tibetologist Skorupski (in *JRAS* 1982, no. 2: 205ff). In his reply Höfer justifies his translation of words used in the Tamang language according to meanings provided by his own informants. Skorupski on the other hand had suggested that such meanings ought to be discarded in favor of classical, viz., textual Tibetan definitions.

63. See *Kāñcīmāhātmyam* and compare Marie-Claude Porcher, "La représentation de l'espace sacré dans le *Kāñcīmāhātmya,*" *Puruṣārtha* 8 (1985): 23–50.

64. *Devīkathā,* pp. 7–11.

65. Thus the version of the Mahiṣa episode, in *Devīkathā,* pp. 7–11, states that Śiva emitted fire from his eyes that turned into the goddess—a definite Śaivite twist to the intention of the *Devīmāhātmya.*

66. See in particular chapters 61 to 63, in K. R. van Kooij, *Worship of the Goddess according to the* Kālikāpurāṇa, pt. 1 (Leiden, 1972).

67. The Purāṇa tells a long love-story which explains how the Goddess settled in Benares. See 3.14–25.

68. The evidence is not very strong, but at least it might point us into a more definite direction. The figure of Dattātreya has enjoyed enormous popularity in Maharastra, and the long section on him in the *Mārkaṇḍeya Purāṇa* (16.37–44) is almost the only classical text on him. The *sthalapurāṇa* of Kolhāpur in Southern Mahārāṣṭra claims (see *Devīkathā,* pp. 7–11) that the killing of Mahiṣa took place there—could this be connected with the mysterious Kolas mentioned at the beginning of the *Devīmāhātmya?*

69. This issue would require a more detailed and technical discussion. Here I may just mention two considerations. Veṅkaṭanātha (thirteenth to fourteenth century) refers to the "*Brahmāṇḍa Purāṇa*" as the source of the story about Brahmā's sacrifice in Kancipuram. Thus at least the *sthalapurāṇa* of that temple must have been accepted by that date as established. The *sthalapurāṇa* of TirukKuṟuṅkuṭi mentions an encounter in a forest between a Brahmin, a demon and Viṣṇu in the guise of a boy. From the thirteenth century a *Kaiśika Purāṇa* is textually established (which serves as the basis for an annual drama-event in the same temple that is performed even today). Here however the demon threatens an Untouchable. Given the existence of the annual ritual in the temple, it seems very unlikely that the *sthalapurāṇa* could have been written *after* the introduction of

the *Kaiśika Purāṇa*. Since a number of Vaiṣṇava *sthalapurāṇas* mention the Āḻvārs, it seems plausible to assume that this marks their *terminus a quo*. Nevertheless in cases where the temple itself is older, one could argue that these hagiographic passages are later additions.

70. W. Kirfel, *Das Purāṇa Pañcalakṣaṇa: Versuch einer Textgeschichte* (Bonn, 1927); W. Kirfel, *Das Purāṇa vom Weltgebäude (Bhuvanavinyāsa)—Die kosmographischen Traktate der Purāṇa's: Versuch einer Textgeschichte* (Bonn, 1954).

71. Kirfel himself (1926) applied this direction of study to the figure of Kṛṣṇa; this was developed further by Hardy, *Viraha-bhakti*. Hacker focused on the figure of Prahlāda to establish a tentative "history of ideas" of medieval theistic Hinduism. P. Hacker, *Prahlāda: Werden und Wandlungen einer Idealgestalt—Beiträge zur Geschichte des Hinduismus,* 2 vols. Akademie der Wissenschaften und der Literatur, Abhandlungen der Geistes- und Sozialwissen-schaftlichen Klasse, no. 9. Wiesbaden, 1959.

72. Thus in the *Harivaṃśa,* history with its royal *vaṃśas* is presented as culminating in Kṛṣṇa; see Hardy, *Viraha-bhakti,* 67ff.

73. See Kirfel, *Purāṇa vom Weltgebäude,* 47f.

74. See note 38 above.

75. The life story of Nammāḻvār as narrated in the *sthalapurāṇa* of Āḻvār-TiruNakari differs in many important respects from that found in *sāmpradāyika* works of the Śrīvaiṣṇavas (for details see Hardy, "Tamil Veda of a Śūdra Saint," 56–61). Similarly the hagiography of Parakāla or TiruMaṅkai-Āḻvār found in the Purāṇa of his hometown TiruNakari presents a very different person, and reads a very different message out of his life, compared with traditions more centrally connected with Śrīvaiṣṇavism. Details will be found in Hardy, "Śrīvaiṣṇava Hagiography of Parakāla."

76. For details see Hardy, "Tamil Veda of a *Śūdra* Saint," 55f.

77. For details see F. Hardy, "The Philosopher as Poet: A Study of Vedantadeśika's *Dehalīśastuti,*" *Journal of Indian Philosophy,* 7 (1979): 288f.

78. My review of Shulman, *Tamil Temple Myths* (F. Hardy, review of *Tamil Temple Myths* by D. D. Shulman, *JRAS* 1982, no. 2: 201ff.) was published in a truncated form. Originally it contained a final section in which I summarized the *Tañjā-māhātmya* to demonstrate such differences between the Vaiṣṇava and Śaiva *sthalapurāṇa* traditions. "The Vaiṣṇava works share a considerable amount of the mythical idiom [analyzed by Shulman], but use it for a different ideological and theological purpose."

79. Quoted from one of the brochures of the festival. Also the description of various "tableaux" given below derives from such a brochure.

CHAPTER 8

In an earlier form, this article was written for the Pro-Seminar on the Purāṇas at the University of Wisconsin under David Knipe and V. Narayana Rao in 1981. It was extensively revised for publication after I participated in the Conference on the Purāṇas at the University of Wisconsin in August 1985, and after fieldwork on the contemporary Śvetāmbara Mūrtipūjaka Jainas of Gujarat from August 1985 through April 1987. Fieldwork was carried under a Fulbright-Hays Dissertation Grant.

1. For the problematic nature of the Western scholarly understanding of the Jaina "canon," see Folkert 1975:43–56 and 1989.

2. This preserved section is the *Ṣaṭkhaṇḍāgama* of Puṣpadanta and Bhūtabali.

3. J. C. Jain (1984: 34–38) argues that the *Dṛṣṭivāda* contained a catalogue of heretical, i.e., non-Jaina, perspectives on various philosophical matters. The safest comment on the *Dṛṣṭivāda* is probably that of Ludwig Alsdorf (1973: 5), who describes a "firmly established if somewhat naive belief that 'the Dṛṣṭivāda contains *everything*'—a belief obviously betraying complete ignorance of the real contents of the long-lost text and, on the other hand, conveniently permitting to derive from 'the Dṛṣṭivāda' . . . any text or subject which it is desired to invest with canonical dignity." For a review of the scholarly literature concerning the contents of the *Dṛṣṭivāda,* see Folkert 1975: 80–81 n. 1.

4. In this context I do not find it helpful to distinguish between the genres of biography and hagiography, and so characterize the Jaina Purāṇas as biographies.

5. See Weber 1858 and 1901.

6. See J. C. Jain 1970, 1977, and 1981. For examples of texts, see *Bṛhatkathākośa, Kahākosu, Kathākośa,* and *Vasudevahiṇḍī*. For a modern example of this genre, see Mahendra Kumārjī 1984.

7. The other two are *samyagdarśana* (correct faith) and *samyagjñāna* (correct knowledge), to which are often added *samyaktapas* (correct penance).

8. The authenticity of this text is denied by the Digambaras, as well as the Śvetāmbara sects of the Sthānakavāsīs and Terāpanthīs.

9. See appendix 2 for a list of all twenty-four Tīrthaṅkaras of the current cycle of time.

10. See Fischer and Jain 1978 for a length discussion of the *kalyāṇakas* in Jaina literature, art, and ritual.

11. See Bloomfield 1919 for a detailed English synopsis of a Jinacaritra, the Sanskrit *Pārśvanātha Caritra* of the Śvetāmbara Bhāvadevasūri, composed in 1256 C.E. in Gujarat.

12. On the different subtraditions within the Jaina Rāmāyaṇas, see V. M. Kulkarni 1959–60, 1962, and 1990; and U. P. Shah 1983.

13. For an English summary of the story as told by Vimalasūri, see Chandra 1970: 18–32.

14. See K. R. Chandra 1970: 4–9.

15. See K. R. Chandra 1964.

16. See, for example, Winternitz 1933: 489–90 and Jha 1978: 17–18.

17. This argument is also made by P. S. Jaini in this volume.

18. There are Rāmāyaṇas at the earliest levels of Jaina writings in several other languages. For Raviṣeṇa's *Padma Purāṇa,* the first Jaina Sanskrit Purāṇa, composed in 676 C.E., see Premī 1956: 87–108. The popularity of this theme for later authors can be seen in that there were at least thirteen more Jaina tellings of the Rāma story in Sanskrit alone (Caudharī 1973: 42–43).

The oldest extant Jaina Purāṇa in Apabhramsa, the *Paümacariu* of Svayambhū, is also a telling of the Rāma story. Unlike most Jaina authors, Svayambhū was a householder, not a mendicant. He lived sometime between the early eighth and early ninth centuries C.E., probably in Karnataka (Premī 1956: 209–11; J. P. Jain 1964: 201–2).

There is also an important Kannada version of the Rāma Caritra, by Nāgacandra, more generally known as Abhinava Pampa (New Pampa). He was a court poet of the Viṣṇuvardhana, the great Hoysaḷa emperor who reigned from 1104 to 1141 C.E. His most famous work is the *Rāmacandra Caritra Purāṇa,* more widely known as the *Pampa Rāmāyaṇa.* It is closely based on the *Paümacariya* of Vimalasūri.

19. For a detailed summary and discussion of Punnāṭa Jinasena's eighth-century C.E. Sanskrit *Harivaṃśa Purāṇa,* see P. S. Jaini in this volume. See also Warder 1972–83: 4.463–66. For a summary of the story of Kṛṣṇa as contained in Puṣpadanta's tenth-century C.E. Apabhramsa *Mahāpurāṇu,* see the introduction by the editor, P. L. Vaidya (vol. 3, pp. xxv–xxxi). For a German translation of part of the latter, see Alsdorf's 1936 edition.

20. For a short discussion of Jaina versions of one genre of child Kṛṣṇa stories, see Hawley 1983: 27–29.

21. On the Pāṇḍava Purāṇas, see Caudarī 1973: 52–55; H. Jain 1962: 166; P. S. Jaini 1984; and D. P. Mishra 1983–83: 43–44. See also *Pāṇḍavacarita* of Devaprabha, *Pāṇḍava Purāṇa* of Subhacandra, and *Pāṇḍava Purāṇa* of Vādicandra.

22. Kannada was the most important of the vernacular languages for Jaina Purāṇic composition, and in turn Jaina authors were instrumental in the development of Kannada as a literary language. The "Three Gems" of

Kannada literature, Pampa, Ponna, and Ranna, were all Jainas who wrote less than a century after the great Karnataka Sanskrit author Jinasena. But whereas Jinasena and his disciple Guṇabhadra were both mendicants, the Kannada authors were householders. The development of Jaina literature in the vernacular seems to have been a process similar to the development of Hindu literature in vernaculars such as Bengali, Hindi, Oriya, and Telugu. In both cases, educated laity wrote in a language accessible to the broader populace, in reaction to the elite, nonmother languages used by the religious professionals.

23. Guṇavarma's *Neminātha Purāṇa* (also known as the *Harivaṁśa Purāṇa*) is the earliest known Jaina Purāṇa in Kannada, but it is no longer extant. Guṇavarma was an author in the court of Ereyappa, the Gaṅga king who reigned from 886 to 913 C.E.. See Rice 1921: 30.

24. Pampa came from a family of Brahmins that had converted to Jainism one generation previously. He was both a court poet and a general under the Cāḷukya Arikesari, a tributary ruler of the Gaṅgas in the mid-tenth century C.E. His most famous work is the *Vikramārjunavijaya,* more popularly known as the *Pampa Bhārata,* in which he retells the Jaina *Mahābhārata.* See Rice 1921: 30–31.

25. See Bruhn 1954 and 1961.

26. The Digambara Jainas of the Karnataka region used Sanskrit in their writings probably from the time of the earliest penetrations of Jainism into the area in the early centuries of the Common Era. For parts of Karnataka, Jainism was the vehicle by which the North Indian Brahminic Sanskrit tradition was introduced. Jaina mendicants and laity were influential in the courts of the Gaṅga, Rāṣṭrakūṭa, and Hoysaḷa dynasties. Many of these royalty were strong patrons of the Jainas, and occasionally Jaina themselves. For several centuries Jainism and culture were nearly synonymous. The seventh through tenth centuries C.E. saw the flourishing of a Jaina Sanskrit literature, and Jaina Purāṇas were some of the more important works composed. The *Ādi Purāṇa* was also popular among the medieval Digambaras of North India and western India. Saryu Doshi (1985: 85–102) has published and analyzed illustrations from five illustrated manuscripts of the *Ādi Purāṇa* from Jaipur and Delhi, dated from ca. 1420 C.E. to 1606 C.E.

27. The best source on Hemacandra remains Bühler 1936, but a fuller study is needed. See also Jacobi 1914 and Sharma 1975, and the special issue of *Jain Journal* (2, no. 4 [1968]) devoted to Hemacandra.

28. On this, see P. S. Jaini 1976.

29. For a list of twenty-eight Mahāpurāṇas from the tenth to eighteenth centuries, see D. P. Mishra 1982–83: 44–45.

30. sthitiḥ kuladharotpattirvaṁśānāmatha nirgamaḥ/
puroḥ sāmrājyamārhantyaṁ nirvāṇaṁ yugavicchidā//

ete mahādhikārāḥ syuḥ purāṇe vṛṣabheśinaḥ/
yathāvasaramanyeṣu purāṇeṣvapi lakṣayet//
(Jinasena, *Ādipurāṇa* II.158–59)

31. sa ca dharmaḥ purāṇārthaḥ purāṇaṁ pañcadhāḥ viduḥ/
kṣetraṁ kālaśca tīrthañca satpuṁsastadviceṣṭitam//
(Jinasena, *Ādipurāṇa* II.38)

32. kṣetraṁ trailokyavinyāsaḥ kālastraikālyaviṣtaraḥ/
muktyupāyo bhavettīrthaṁ puruṣāstanniṣeviṇaḥ//
nyāyyamācaritaṁ teṣāṁ caritaṁ duritacchidām/
iti kṛtsnaḥ purāṇārthaḥ praśne saṁbhāvitastvayā//
(Jinasena, *Ādipurāṇa* II.39–40)

33. The earlier Digambara Punnāṭa Jinasena in his eighth-century C.E. *Harivaṃśa Purāṇa* (1.55a) seems to refer to a similar fivefold definition, when he mentions the fivefold "ends" or "meanings" (*artha*) of a Purāṇa as "*kṣetra,* etc." (*pañcadhāpravibhaktārthaṁ kṣetrādipravibhāgataḥ*). The use of "etc." (*ādi*) indicates that Punnāṭa Jinasena was referring to a well-known formula, which he does not feel necessary to spell out.

In a Digambara cosmographical text, the Sanskrit *Lokavibhāga* of Siṃhasūrarṣi, there is a similar fivefold definition of a Purāṇa as consisting of *kṣetra, kāla, tīrtha, mahatta* (the greatness of the Jaina heroes), and *carita* (their deeds). While the *Lokavibhāga* was written after the times of both Jinasenas, it claims to be the Sanskrit translation of a lost fourth-century C.E. Prakrit text written by Sarvanandi. This fivefold definition may have been in Sarvanandi's text, but considering the looseness of the notion of faithfulness to the original in Indian translations, and the tendency to increase a text's authority by claiming that it contains all or part of an earlier text, this definition may have been added (or an earlier definition changed) by Siṃhasūrarṣi. But regardless of the antiquity of this definition, it does not seem to have caught on explicitly, for it is not used by the many later authors of Jaina Purāṇas.

34. loko deśaḥ puraṁ rājyaṁ tīrthaṁ dānatapo'nvayam/
purāṇeṣvaṣṭadhakhyeyam gatayaḥ phalamityapi//
(Jinasena, *Ādipurāṇa* IV.3)

35. purāṇamitihāsākhyaṁ yatprovāca gaṇādhipaḥ/
(Jinasena, *Ādipurāṇa* I.26b)

36. One finds similar tables of contents in other Jaina Purāṇas. See, for example: Vimalasūri, *Paümacariya* 1.32; Raviṣeṇa, *Padma Purāṇa* 1.43–44; and Punnāṭa Jinasena, *Harivaṃśa Purāṇa* 1.71–72.

37. . . . arahaṅtā vā cakkavaṭṭī vā baladevā vā vāsudevā vā. . .
(*Kappa Sutta* 17)
See also *Kappa Sutta* 18, 21–22.

38. See A. K. Warder 1972–83: 2.221.

39. This text seems to have suffered excessively from later interpolations, and different manuscripts are of widely different lengths (see the introduction by the Sthānakavāsī editor Mīni Kanhaiyālāl to his 1966 edition of the text, page *ṅa*). The different lists may either or both be additions. For the description of the sixty-three *śalākā puruṣa*s, see vv. 246–75, Hīrālāl Jain 1962: 128, and G. C. Caudarī 1973: 67; for fifty-four *śalākā puruṣa*s, see vv. 54 and 132.

40. This Sauraseni Prakrit text is believed by the Digambaras to contain the only extant portion of the lost *Dṛṣṭivāda*. Padmanabh Jaini (1979: 50) dates the writing down of the text to the second century C.E., and it probably represents a fairly faithful oral transmission from the earliest days of the Jainas. *Sūtra* 1.1.2 (p. 113) of the *Ṣaṭkhaṇḍāgama* states that the *prathamānuyoga* of the *Dṛṣṭivāda,* also known as the *Purāṇa,* contained 5,000 verses (paḍamāṇiyogo pañcasahassapadehi 5000 purāṇaṁ vaṇṇedi). According to verses 77–80 of the *Dhavalāṭīkā* commentary on the *Ṣaṭkhaṇḍāgama,* written around 800 C.E. by Jinasena's teacher Vīrasena, these 5,000 verses describe the twelve lineages, those of the Tīrthaṅkaras, Cakravartins, Vidyādharas, Vāsudevas, Cāraṇas, Prajñāśramaṇas, Kurus, Haris, Ikṣvākus, Kāśyapas, Vādis, and Nāthas. The Tīrthaṅkaras, Cakravartins, and Vāsudevas constitute forty-five of the *śalākā puruṣa*s. The Vidyādharas might well here refer to the nine Baladevas, and possibly also the nine Prati-vāsudevas, in which case the list would include the whole of the fifty-four or sixty-three *śalākā puruṣa*s.

41. The best treatment of the Nāyaṉārs is Peterson 1989. Indira Peterson does not, however, discuss the genesis of the number sixty-three.

42. . . . etto salāyapurisā tesaṭṭhī . . .
(Yativṛṣabha, *Tiloya Paṇṇatti* 4.510)

43. jinaiḥ saha triṣaṣṭiḥ syuḥ śalākāpuruṣā amī/ (jinairṛṣabhādibhiścaturviṁśatyā sārdhamamī dvādaśa cakravartinaḥ nava vāsudevāḥ nava baladevāḥ nava prativāsudevāśceti triṣaṣṭiḥ śalākābhūtaḥ puruṣeṣu jātarekhā ityarthaḥ) (Hemacandra, *Abhidhānacintāmaṇi* 3.364a and *Svopajñavṛtti*)

44. For a detailed discussion of the Arhat-Cakravartin relationship in the Buddhist tradition, see Tambiah 1976.

45. According to the Śvetāmbara tradition she sees fourteen dreams, while according to the Digambara tradition she sees sixteen.

46. According to the Śvetāmbaras, these are: elephant, bull, lion, Gajalakṣmī, garland, moon, sun, banner, full pot, lotus lake, ship, heavenly vehicle, heap of jewels, and flame (see *Kappa Sutta* 34–47). The Digambaras add a throne and a pair of fish.

47. Lion, sun, fire, elephant, banner, heavenly vehicle, and lotus lake.

48. Elephant, ocean, lion, and moon.

49. The material in this section is based on fieldwork in Gujarat among the Śvetāmbara Mūrtipūjaka Jainas, and the comments are applicable only to this sect, not the other three. For another description of a Jaina sermon, see Cort 1989: 312–13.

50. It is a matter of custom (*māryadā*) in the Tapāgaccha, the major *gaccha* (subdivision) of the Mūrtipūjakas, that *sādhvīs* do not give sermons. This restriction does not apply to the other *gacchas* of the Mūrtipūjakas (Kharatara, Añcala, Vimala) or to the Sthānakavāsī or Terāpanthī sects.

51. For printed examples of modern tellings of these stories, see Candraśekharvijay Gaṇi 1977, 1985; Rāmcandrasūri 1941.

52. See Doshi 1985.

CHAPTER 9

1. For a brief survey of the Jaina Purāṇic literature, see M. Winternitz, *A History of Indian Literature,* vol. 2, trans. S. Ketkar and H. Kohn (University of Calcutta, 1933), section 4 479–520; Hiralal Jain, *Bhāratīya saṃskritimeñ Jain dharma kā yogadān* (in Hindi) (Bhopal: Madhyapradesha Shasana Sahitya Parishad, 1962); Gulabchandra Chaudhari, *Jain Sahitya kā bṛhad itihās,* pt. 6, (in Hindi), Parshvanatha Vidyashrama Granthamala, vol. 20, (Varanasi, 1973), 35–128.

2. *Jaina Sūtras,* translated from Prakrit by Hermann Jacobi, pt 1, (*Kalpa-Sūtra,* pp. 217–311 [*Jinacarita,* pp. 217–85]), The Sacred Books of the East, vol. 22, 1884.

3. *Buddhavaṃsa and Cariyāpiṭaka,* ed. N. A. Jayawickrama (London: Pali Text Society, 1968).

4. For a list of twenty-two *aṃśāvatāras,* see *Śrīmad-Bhāgavata,* Gītā Press Edition, vi, viii, 13–19.

5. For a scriptural description of the Cakravartins, see Jinendra Varni, *Jainendra-Siddhānta-Kośa,* 4 (Varanasi: Bharatiya Jnanapitha, 1944): 10–16.

6. See *Uttarādhyayana,* lecture 22, translated by Hermann Jacobi, in *Jaina Sūtras,* pt 2, The Sacred Books of the East, vol. 45 (1895).

7. See R. C. Sharma, "Jaina Sculptures of the Gupta Age in the State Museum, Lucknow," in *Shri Mahāvīra Jaina Vidyālaya Golden Jubilee Volume,* (Bombay, 1968), 142–53; U. P. Shah, "Evolution of Jaina Iconography & Symbolism," *Aspects of Jaina Art and Architecture,* ed. U. P. Shah and M. A. Dhaky, (Ahmedabad, 1975), 49–74.

8. See *Jainendra-Siddhānta-Kośa,* 4, pp. 16–17.

9. See *Jainendra-Siddhānata-Kośa,* 4, pp. 18–20.

10. See *Jainendra-Siddhānta-Kośa,* 4, pp. 20–21.

11. aṇidāṇagadā savve Baladevā Kesavā ṇidāṇagadā /
uddhaṃgāmī savve Baladevā Kesavā adhogāmī //
Tiloya-paṇṇatti 4.1436, quoted in the
Jainendra-Siddhānta-Kośa 4, p. 18.

12. kalahappiyā kadāyiṃ dhammaradā Vāsudevasamakālā /
bhavvā nirayagadiṃ te hiṃsādoseṇa gacchaṃti //
Trilokasāra 835, quoted in the *Jainendra-Siddhānta-Kośa* 4, p. 22.

13. savve dasame puvve Ruddā bhaṭṭā tavāu visayatthaṃ /
sammattarayaṇarahidā buḍḍā ghoresu ṇirayesuṃ //
(*Tiloya-paṇṇatti* 4.1442, quoted in the *Jainendra-Siddhānta-Kośa* 4, p. 22).

14. The inclusion of the Prati-vāsudevas in the list of the *śalākā puruṣas* has not escaped controversy. Śīlāṅka's (ca. 868) *Mahāpurāṇa,* for example, omits them from this list and hence is entitled *Caupaṇṇa-mahāpurisa-cariya.* See Winternitz, *History of Indian Literature,* vol. 2, 506 n. 1.

15. *Paümacariya* of Vimalasūri, (Varanasi: Prakrit Grantha Parishad, 1962).

16. padmākārā samutpannā pṛthivī saghanadrumā /
tad asya lokapadmasya vistareṇa prakāśitam //
Vāyu Purāṇa, adhyāya 45, quoted in Baladeva Upadhyaya, *Purāṇa-vimarsha* (in Hindi), (Varanasi, 1960).

17. sīho maeṇa nihao sāṇeṇa ya kuṃjaro jahā bhaggo /
taha vivarīyapayatthaṃ kaīhi Rāmāyaṇaṃ rahiyaṃ //
aliyaṃ pi savvaṃ eyaṃ uvavattiviruddhapaccayaguṇehiṃ /
na ya saddahaṃti purisā havaṃti je paṃḍiyā loe //
evaṃ ciṃtaṃto cciya saṃsayaparihārakāraṇaṃ rāyā /
jinadarisaṇussūyamaṇo gamaṇucchāho tao jāo //
(*Paümacariya* 2.116–18)

18. For the Jaina versions of the Rāma story, see Camille Bulche, *Ramakathā* (in Hindi) (Prayag, 1950).

19. Cf. Pṛthivīsundarīmukhyāḥ Keśavasya [i.e., Lakṣmaṇasya] manoramāḥ /
dviguṇāṣṭasahasrāṇi devyāḥ satyo 'bhavan śriyāḥ //
Sītādyaṣṭasahasrāṇi Rāmasya prāṇavallabhāḥ /. . .
halāyudhaṃ mahāratnam Aparājitanāmakam //
(*Uttara-Purāṇa* 68.666–67, quoted in the *Jainendra-Siddhānta-kośa,* 4, pp. 18–19).

20. *Padma-Carita* of Raviṣeṇa, 3 pts., (Varanasi: Bharatiya Jnanapitha, 1958–59).

21. *Paümacariu* of Svayambhū, ed. H. C. Bhayani 3 pts., (Bombay: Bharatiya Vidyabhavana, 1953 and 1960).

22. *Mahā-Purāṇa* of Puṣpadanta, ed. P. L. Vaidya 3 parts, (Bombay: Manikchandra Digambara Jaina Granthamala, 1937–47). See also sections 81–92 (pt. 3), entitled *Harivamśa-Purāṇa,* in a German translation by L. Alsdorf, (Hamburg, 1936).

23. *Harivaṃśa-Purāṇa* of [Punnāṭa] Jinasena, edited with Hindi translation by Pannalal Jain (Varanasi: Bharatiya Jnanapitha, 1962).

24. *The Harivaṃśa,* ed. P. L. Vaidya (Poona: Bhandarkar Oriental Research Institute, 1969), vol. 1.

25. kālesu jinavarāṇaṃ cauvīsānaṃ havaṃti cauvīsā /
te Bāhubalippamuhā kaṃdappā niruvamāyārā //
(*Tiloya-paṇṇatti* 4.1472, quoted in the
Jainendra-Siddhānta-kośa 4, p. 22).

26. *Vasudevahiṇḍī,* ed. Muni Caturavijaya and Muni Punyavijaya, 2 pts. (Bhavanagara: Jaina Atmananda Sabha, 1930–31); J. C. Jain, *Vasudeva-Hiṇḍī: Authentic Jaina Version of Bṛhatkathā:* (Ahmedabad: L. D. Institute of Indology, 1977).

27. For a brief survey, see Padmanabh S. Jaini, "*Mahābhārata* Motifs in the Jaina *Pāṇḍava-Purāṇa,*" *Bulletin of the School of Oriental and African Studies,* 47, no. 1 (1984), 108–15; Padmanabh S. Jaini, "Bhaṭṭāraka Śrībhūṣaṇa's *Pāṇḍava-Purāṇa:* a case of Jaina sectarian plagiarism?," *Panels of the VIIIth World Sanskrit Conference,* vol. VI and VII (Leiden: E. J. Brill, 1991), pp. 59–68.

28. For a discussion on the goddess Ekānaṃśā in the Purāṇas, see Vinapani Pande, *Harivaṃśa Purāṇa kā sāṃskritika vivecana* (in Hindi) (Uttar Pradesh: Hindi Samiti Granthamala, Publication Division, 1960). On the possible identity of Ekānaṃśā with the Tamil goddess Pinnai (a sister as well as a lover of Kṛṣṇa), see Dennis Hudson, "Pinnai, Krishna's Cowherd Wife," in *The Divine Consort,* ed. J. S. Hawley and D. M. Wulff (Berkeley: Berkeley Religious Studies Series, 1982), 256. Both accounts appear to be unfamiliar with the Jaina tradition discussed here.

29. tatas tvāṃ gṛhya caraṇe śilāyāṃ nirasiṣyati /
nirasyamānā gagane sthānaṃ prāpsyasi śāśvatam //. . .
kīrṇā bhūtagaṇair ghorair man nideśānuvarttinī /
kaumāraṃ vratam āsthāya tridivaṃ tvaṃ gamiṣyasi //. . .
tatraiva tvaṃ bhaginyarthe gṛhīṣyati sa Vāsavaḥ /
Kuśikasya tu gotreṇa Kauśikī tvaṃ bhaviṣyasi //. . .
sa te Vindhyanagaśreṣṭhe sthānaṃ dāsyati śāśvatam /
tataḥ sthānasahasrais tvaṃ pṛthivīṃ śobhayiṣyasi //. . .

kṛtānuyātrā bhūtais tvaṃ nityaṃ māṃsabalipriyā /
tithau navamyāṃ pūjāṃ tvaṃ prāpsyase sapaśukriyām //
(*Harivaṃśa, Viṣṇuparva, adhyāya* 58)

30. Āryāstavaṃ pravakṣyāmi yathoktaṃ ṛṣibhiḥ purā /
Nārāyaṇīṃ namasyāmi devīṃ tribhuvaneśvarīm //. . .
(*Harivaṃśa, Viṣṇuparva, adhyāya* 59.1)

31. (a) svasuḥ prasūtiṃ pratividya Kaṃsaḥ prasūtyagāraṃ vighṛṇaḥ praviśya /
vilokya bālām amalām amuṣyāḥ patiḥ kadācit prabhaved arir me //
vicintya śaṅkākulitas tadeti nirastakopo 'pi sa dīrghadarśī /
svayaṃ samādāya kareṇa tasyāḥ praṇudya nāsāṃ cipiṭīcakāra //
(*Harivaṃśa Purāṇa* 35.31–32)
(b) vasunibha Vasudevo Devakī cātmajasya
praśamitaripuvahner vīkṣya viśrabdham āsyam /
sukham atulam agātām Ekanāsā ca kanyā
bhuvi sutasahajānāṃ samprayogaḥ sukhāya //
(*Harivaṃśa Purāṇa* 36.50)
(c) iti samaye prayāti tu kadācid asau praṇatair
upahasitā prayādbhir avaśād Balarājasutaiḥ /
Vicipiṭanāsikaṃ rahasi darpaṇake svamukhaṃ
sphuṭam avalokya tadbhavavirāgam agāt trapitā //
(*Harivaṃasa Purāṇa* 49.13)

32. avitatham ity amī vitatham eva śaṭhā kavayaḥ
svaparamahārayo vidadhate vikathākathanam /
paravadhakāpatheṣu bhuvi teṣu tatheti janaḥ
suraravamūḍhadhīḥ patati gaḍḍarikākaṭavat //. . .
atinicitāgnivāyujalabhūmilatātarubhiḥ
kṣitir apacetanaiś ca gṛhakalpitadaivatakaiḥ /
ravividhutārakāgrahagaṇair jananetrapathair
gaganam ato 'stu mūḍhir iha kasya janasya na vā //
(*Harivaṃśa Purāṇa* 49.37, 47)

33. See *Harivaṃśa Purāṇa* 33.150–73.

34. Cf. ākuñcya caraṇau paścāt sārasarvābhisārataḥ/
lalambe Nemidoḥstambhe Kṛṣṇaḥ kapir iva drume //
na ca Nemibhujastambhaḥ sūtramātram api kvacit /
sthanāc cacāla kiṃ Meroś cūlī calati vātyayā //
(*Pāṇḍava-Caritam* of Maladhāri Devaprabha, Kāvyamālā Series no. 93 [Bombay, 1911], 16.54–55)

35. Cf. paredyuḥsamaye pāṇijalasekasya Madhavāḥ /
yiyāsur durgatiṃ lobhasutīvrānubhavodayāt //
durāśayaḥ surādhīśapūjyasyāpi mahātmanaḥ /

svarājyādānam āśaṅkya Nemer māyāvidāṃ varaḥ //
nirvedakaraṇaṃ kiñcin nirīkṣyaiṣa viraṃsyati /
bhogebhya iti saṃcintya tadupāyavidhitsayā //. . .
vyādhādhipair dhṛtānītaṃ nānāmṛgakadambakam /
vidhāyaikatra saṃkīrṇaṃ vṛtiṃ tatparito vyadhāt //
(*Uttara Purāṇa* of Guṇabhadra [Varanasi: Bharatiya Jnanapitha, 1954]. 71.152–55)

36. See, for example, the story of Sīha Senāpati, *Vinaya-Piṭaka,* vol. 1 (London: Pali Text Society, 1879–83), 233ff.

37. atha tāv api saṃkruddhāv udyamya Kurunandana /
erakāmuṣṭiparighau carantau jaghnatur yudhi //. . .
Rāmaḥ samudravelāyāṃ yogam āsthāya pauruṣam /
tatyāja lokaṃ mānuṣyaṃ samyojyātmānam ātmani //
Rāmaniryāṇam ālokya bhagavān Devakīsutaḥ /
niṣasāda dharopasthe tūṣṇīm āsādya pippalam //. . .
musalāvaśeṣāyaḥkhaṇḍakṛteṣur lubdhako Jarā /
mṛgasyākāraṃ tac caraṇaṃ vivyādha mṛgaśaṅkayā //
(*Śrīmad Bhāgavata* 11.30.23–33)

bhagavān pitāmahaṃ vīkṣya vibhūtīr ātmano vibhuḥ /
saṃyojyātmani cātmānaṃ padmanetre nyamīlayat //
lokābhirāmāṃ svatanuṃ dhāraṇādhyānamaṅgalam /
yogadhāraṇayā "gneyyā 'dagdhvā dhāmāviśat svakam //
(*Śrīmad Bhāgavata* 11.31.5–6)

38. puṇyodayāt purā prāptāv unnatiṃ yau janātigām /
cakrādiratnasampannau balinau BalaKeśavau //
puṇyakṣayāt tu tāv eva ratnabandhuvivarjitau /
prāṇamātraparīvārau śokabhāravaśīkṛtau //
prasthitau dakṣiṇām āśāṃ jīvitāśāvalambinau /
kṣutpipāsāpariśrāntau yātau satkāṃkṣiṇau pathi //. . .
tasmin gate Haris tīvravraṇavedanayārditaḥ /
uttarābhimukho bhūtvā kṛtapañcanamaskṛtiḥ //. . .
karmagauravadoṣeṇa mayā 'pi na kṛtaṃ tapaḥ /
ityādiśubhacintātmā bhaviṣyat tīrthakṛdd Hariḥ /
baddhāyuṣkatayā mṛtvā tṛtīyāṃ pṛthivīm itaḥ //
(*Harivaṃśa Purāṇa* 62.1–3, 58–63)

39. bhaviṣyat tīrthakṛdd Hariḥ (*Harivaṃśa Purāṇa* 62.62)

40. For a chart of the twenty-four future Tīrthaṅkaras, see *Jainendra-Siddhānta-Kośa,* 2, p. 376.

41. See "Tīrthaṅkara," *Jainendra-Siddhānta-Kośa,* 2, p. 372; P. S. Jaini, "Tīrthaṅkara-prakṛti and the Bodhisattva Path," *Journal of the Pali Text Society* (London) 9 (1981): 96–104.

42. Pāṇḍavaiḥ saha Jarāsutānvitais Tuṅgyabhikhyagirimastake tataḥ /

saṃvidhāya Haridehasaṃskriyāṃ Jāraseyasuvitīrṇarājyakaḥ //
(*Harivaṃśa Purāṇa* 63.72)

43. jñātvā bhagavataḥ siddhiṃ pañca Pāṇḍavasādhavaḥ /
Śatruñjayagirau dhīrāḥ pratimāyoginaḥ sthitāḥ //
śukladhyānasamāviṣṭā BhīmĀrjunaYudhiṣṭhirāḥ /
ḳrtvā 'ṣṭavidhakarmāntaṃ mokṣaṃ jagmus trayo 'kṣayam //
(*Harivaṃśa Purāṇa* 65.18–22)

44. ekaṃ varṣaśataṃ kṛtvā tapo Haladharo muniḥ /
samārādhya paripräpto brahmaloke sureśatām //
(*Harivaṃśa Purāṇa* 65.33)

45. avadhijñātaKṛṣṇaś ca gatvā 'sau Vālukāprabhām /
dṛṣṭvā 'nujaṃ nijaṃ devo duḥkhitaṃ duḥkhito 'bhavat //
ehy ehi Kṛṣṇa yo 'haṃ te bhrātā jyeṣṭho Halāyudhaḥ /
brahmalokādhipo bhūtvā tvatsamīpam ihāgataḥ //
ity uktvā taṃ samuddhṛtya svarlokaṃ netum udyate /
deve tasya vyalīyanta gātrāṇi navanītavat //
tataḥ Kṛṣṇo jagau deva bhrātaḥ kiṃ vyarthaceṣṭitaiḥ /. . .
bhrātar yāhi tataḥ svargaṃ bhuṅkṣva puṇyaphalaṃ nijam /
āyuso 'nte 'ham apy emi mokṣahetuṃ manuṣyatām //
āvāṃ tatra tapaḥ kṛtvā jinaśāsanasevayā /
mokṣasaukhyam avāpsyāvaḥ kṛtvā karmaparikṣayam //
(*Harivaṃśa Purāṇa* 65.43–51)

46. āvāṃ putrādisaṃyuktau mahāvibhavasaṅgatau /
Bhārate darśayānyeṣāṃ vismayavyāptacetasām //
śaṅkhacakragadāpāṇir madīyapratimāgṛhaiḥ /
Bhārataṃ vyāpaya kṣetraṃ matkīrtiparivṛddhaye //
(*Harivaṃśa Purāṇa* 65.52–53)

47. ityādi vacanaṃ tasya pratipadya sureśvaraḥ /
samyaktve śuddhim ākhyāpya Bhārataṃ kṣetram āgataḥ //
bhrātṛsnehavaśo devo yathoddiṣṭaṃ sa Viṣṇunā /
cakre divyavimānasthacakrilāṅgaladarśanam //
Vāsudevagṛhaiś cakre nagarādiniveśitaiḥ /
Viṣṇumohamayaṃ lokaṃ snehāt kiṃ vā na ceṣṭyate //
(*Harivaṃśa Purāṇa* 65.54–56)

48. Also: dhik dhik svarmokṣasaukhyapratigham
atighanasnehamohaṃ janānām //
(*Harivaṃśa Purāṇa* 65.58d.)

49. *Ādi-Purāṇa* of Jinasena, edited with Hindi translation by Pannalal Jain, 2 pts. Varanasi: Bharatiya Jnanapitha, 1944.

50. *Uttara-Purāṇa* of Jinasena and Guṇabhadra, edited with Hindi translation by Pannalal Jain (Varanasi: Bharataiya Jnanapitha, 1944).

51. sa ca dharmaḥ purāṇārthaḥ purāṇaṃ pañcadhāḥ viduḥ /
kṣetraṃ kālaś ca tīrthaṃ ca satpuṃsas tadviceṣṭitam //
(*Ādi Purāṇa* 2.38)

52. See *Ādi Purāṇa* 18.51–60.

53. See the stotra of 1008 names of Ṛṣabha in *Ādi Purāṇa* 25.99–217.

54. manuṣyajātir ekaiva jātinamodayodbhavā /
vṛttibhedāhitād bhedāc cāturvidhyam ihāśnute //
(*Ādi Purāṇa* 38.45)

55. *Triṣaṣṭiśalākāpuruṣacaritra* of Hemacandrasūri, trans. Helen M. Johnson, vol. 1, Gaekwad Oriental Series vol. 51, (1931), 343ff.

56. See P. S. Jaini, *The Jaina Path of Purification* (Berkeley and Los Angeles: University of California Press, 1979), chap. 4.

57. teṣāṃ kṛtāni cihnāni sūtraiḥ padmāvhayān nidheḥ /
upāttair brahmasūtrāhvair ekād ekādaśāntakaiḥ //
guṇabhūmikṛtād bhedāt kḷptayajñopavītinām /
satkāraḥ kriyate smaiṣām avratāś ca bahiḥ kṛtāḥ //
(*Ādi Purāṇa* 38.21–2)

58. sādhu vatsa kṛtaṃ sādhu dhārmikadvijapūjanam /
kintu doṣānuṣaṅgo 'tra ko 'py asti sa niśamyatām //. . .
tataḥ kaliyuge 'bhyarṇe jātivādāvalepataḥ /
bhraṣṭācārāḥ prapatsyante sanmārgapratyanīkatām //
te 'mi jātimadāviṣṭā vayaṃ lokādhikā iti /
purā durāgamair lokaṃ mohayanti dhanāśayā //
ahiṃsālakṣaṇaṃ dharmaṃ dūṣayitvā durāśayāḥ /
codanālakṣaṇaṃ dharmaṃ poṣayiṣyanty amī bata //
pāpasūtradharā dhūrtāḥ prāṇimāraṇatatparāḥ /
vartsyadyuge pravartsyanti sanmārgaparipanthinaḥ //
dvijātisarjanaṃ tasmān nādya yady api doṣakṛt /
syād doṣabījam āyatyāṃ kupākhaṇḍapravartanāt //
(*Ādi Purāṇa* 39.45–54)

59. na svato 'gneḥ pavitratvaṃ devatārūpam eva vā /
kintv arhaddivyamūrtījyāsambandhī pāvano 'nalaḥ //
tataḥ pūjāṅgatām asya matvā 'rcanti dvijottamāḥ /
nirvāṇakṣetrapūjāvat tatpūjā 'to na duṣyati //
vyavahāranayāpekṣā tasyeṣṭā pūjyatā dvijaiḥ /
Jainair adhyavahāryo 'yaṃ nayo 'dyatve 'grajanmanaḥ //
(*Ādi Purāṇa* 40.88–90)

60. *Triṣaṣṭiśalākāpuruṣacaritra* 1.6.546–56. See P. S. Jaini, "The Pure and the Auspicious in the Jaina Tradition," *Journal of Asian Perspectives* (Leiden) 1, no. 1 (1985): 69–76.

61. nirdiṣṭasthānalābhasya punar asya gaṇagrahaḥ /
syān mithyādevatāḥ svasmād viniḥsārayato gṛhāt //
iyantaṃ kālam ajñānāt pūjitāḥ sma kṛtādaram /
pūjyās tv idānīm asmābhir asmatsamayadevatāḥ //
tato 'pamṛṣitenālam anyatra svairam āsyatām /

iti prakāśam evaitān nītvā 'nyatra kvacit tyajet //
(*Ādi Purāṇa* 39.45–47)

62. See M. Winternitz, *A History of Indian Literature,* vol. 2, 445–49.

63. *Uvāsagadasāo* [i.e., *Upāsakadaśāḥ*], published in English as *The Religious Profession of an Uvāsaga,* trans. A. F. R. Hoernle, 2 vols., Calcutta: Bibliotheca Indica, 1888–90.

64. Draupadī ca drutaṃ mālāṃ kandhare 'bhyetya bandhure /
akarot karapadmābhyām Arjunasya varecchayā //
viprakīrṇā tadā mālā sahasā sahavartinām /
pañcānām api gātreṣu capalena nabhasvatā //
tataś capalalokasya tattvamūḍhasya kasyacit /
vāco vicerur ity uccair vṛtāḥ pañcānayety api //
(*Harivaṃśa Purāṇa* 45.135–37)

65. atyantaśuddhavṛtteṣu ye 'bhyākhyānaparāyaṇāḥ /
teṣāṃ tatprabhavaṃ pāpaṃ ko nivārayituṃ kṣamaḥ //
sadbhūtasyāpi doṣasya parakīyasya bhāṣaṇam /
pāpahetur amoghaḥ syād asadbhūtasya kiṃ punaḥ //
prākṛtānām api prītyā samānadhanatā dhane /
na strīṣu triṣu lokeṣu prasiddhānaṃ kim ucyate //
mahāpuruṣakoṭīsthakūṭadoṣavibhāṣiṇām /
asatāṃ katham āyāti na jivhā śatakhaṇḍatām //
(*Harivaṃśa Purāṇa* 45.152–55)

66. See *Triṣaṣṭiśalākāpuruṣacaritra,* vol. 5, G.O.S. vol. 139, 198–202.

67. Bhāṭṭāraka Vādicandra (ca. 1600) in his *Pāṇḍava Purāṇa* devotes the first sarga to describe the geneology of the Pāṇḍavas as allegedly found in the *Śiva Purāṇa:* Śiva-Purāṇābhimata-Pāṇḍavotpattivarṇano nāma prathamaḥ sargaḥ. See my article "The *Mahābhārata* Motifs in the Jaina *Pāṇḍava Purāṇa,*" referred to above in note 27.

68. For the Purāṇic passages dealing with the Buddhāvatāra, see R. C. Hazra, *Studies in the Upapurāṇas,* vol. 1, (Calcutta: Sanskrit College, 1958), 144ff.; Ramshankara Bhattacharya, *Itihāsa-Purāṇa kā anushīlan* (in Hindi) (Varanasi, 1963.), 280–86.

69. See P. S. Jaini, "The Disappearance of Buddhism and the Survival of Jainism: A Study in Contrast," *Studies in the History of Buddhism,* ed. A. K. Narain, (Delhi, 1980), 81–91.

70. The Dasaratha-Jātaka (Jātaka no. 461) and the Ghaṭa-Jātaka (Jātaka no. 454), respectively, refer to Rāma and Kaṇha. See *The Jātaka,* ed. V. Fausboll, (reprint; London: Pali Text Society, 1963).

71. . . . bhagavān paramarṣibhiḥ prasādito Nābheḥ priyacikīrṣayā tadavarodhāyane Merudevyāṃ dharmān darśayitukāmo vātaraśanānāṃ śramaṇānām ṛṣīṇām ūrdhvamanthināṃ śuklayā tanuvāvatatāra. *Śrīmad Bhāgavata* 5.3.20.

72. yasya kilānucaritam upākarṇya Koṅka-Veṅka-Kuṭakānāṃ rājā 'rhan nāmopaśikṣya kalāv adharma utkṛṣyamāṇe bhavitavyena vimohitaḥ svadharmapatham akutobhayam apahāya kupathapākhaṇḍam asamañjasaṃ nijamanīṣayā mandaḥ sampravartayiṣyate. yena ha vāva kalau manujāpasadā devamāyāmohitāḥ svavidhiniyogaśaucacāritravihīnā devahelanāny apavratāni nijanijecchayā gṛhṇānā asnānānācamanāśuacakeśolluñcanādīni kalinā 'dharmabahulenopahatadhiyo brahmabrāhmaṇyajñapuruṣalokavidūṣakāḥ prāyeṇa bhaviṣyanti. te ca hy arvāktanayā nijalokayātrayā 'ndhaparamparayā āśvastās tamasy andhe svayam eva prapatiṣyanti. *Śrīmad-Bhāgavata* 5.6.9–11.

73. P. S. Jaini, "Jina Ṛṣabha as an *Avatāra* of Viṣṇu," *Bulletin of the School of Oriental and African Studies* 40, no. 2, (1977): 321–337.

74. Sanatkumāra uvāca:
asṛjac ca mahātejāḥ puruṣaṃ svātmasambhavam /
ekaṃ māyāmayaṃ teṣāṃ dharmavighnārtham Acyutaḥ //
muṇḍinaṃ mlānavastraṃ ca gumphipātrasamanvitam /
dadhānaṃ puñjikāṃ haste cālayantaṃ pade pade //
vastrayuktaṃ tathā hastaṃ kṣīyamāṇaṃ mukhe sadā /
dharmeti vyāharantaṃ hi vācā viklavayā munim //
. . . Viṣṇuḥ . . . vacanaṃ cedam abravīt /
yad artham nirmito 'si tvaṃ nibodha kathayāmi te /
Arihaṃ nāma te syāt tu hy anyāni śubhāni ca /. . .
Apabhraṃśamayaṃ śāstraṃ karmavādamayaṃ tathā /
śrautasmārtaviruddhaṃ ca varṇāśramavivarjitam //
gantum arhasi nāśārthaṃ muṇḍas Tripuravāsinām /
tamodharmaṃ samprakāśya nāśayasva puratrayam //
tataś caiva punar gantvā Marusthalyāṃ tvayā vibho /
sthātavyaṃ ca svadharmeṇa kalir yāvat samāvrajet //
tataḥ sa muṇḍī paripālayan Harer
ājñāṃ tathā nirmitavāṃś ca śiṣyān /
yathāsvarūpaṃ caturas tadānīṃ
māyāmayaṃ śāstram apāṭhayat svayam //
Śiva Purāṇa ed. Ramateja Shastri Pandeya (Varanasi, Pandita Pustakalaya), 2 (Rudrasaṃhitā), 5 (Yuddhakāṇḍa), fourth *Adhyāya,* 1–24.

75. See *Prabhāvakacarita* of Prabhācandra, ed. Jinavijaya Muni, Singhi Jain Series, no. 13 (1940), 187–88.

76. Vyāsasandarbhitākhyāne śrīGāṅgeyaḥ pitāmahaḥ /
yuddhapraveśakāle 'sāv uvāca svaṃ paricchadam //
mama prāṇaparityāge tatra saṃskriyatāṃ tanuḥ /
na yatra ko 'pi dagdhaḥ prāg bhūmikhaṇḍe sadā śucau //
vidhāya nyāyyasaṅgrāmaṃ muktaprāṇe Pitāmahe /
vimṛṣya tadvacas te 'ṅgam utpāṭyāsya yayur girau //
amuñcan devatāvāṇī kvāpi tatrodyayau tadā //
tathā hi—

atra Bhīṣmaśataṃ dagdhaṃ Pāṇḍavānāṃ śatatrayam /
Droṇācāryyasahasraṃ tu Karṇasaṃkhyā na vidyate //
(*Prabhāvakacarita* 188, 159–62)

77. rājā śrutvāha tatsatyaṃ vakti Jainarṣir eṣa yat /
atra brutottaraṃ tathyaṃ yady asti bhavatāṃ mate //. . .
uttarānudayāt tatra maunam āśiśriyāṃs tadā /. . .
rājñā satkṛtya Sūriś cābhāsyata svāgamoditam /
vyākhyānaṃ kurvatāṃ samyag dūṣaṇaṃ nāsti vo 'ṇv api //
(*Prabhāvakacarita* 188, 167–71)

Bibliography

CHAPTER 1

Selected Sanskrit Texts

Agni Purāṇa. Edited by B. Upādhyāya. Kashi Sanskrit Series, no. 174. Benares: Sanskrit Series Office 1966.

______. Translated by M. N. Dutt. 2 vols. Benaras: Motilal Banarsidass, 1967.

Aitareya Brāhmaṇa. Translated by A. B. Keith. Harvard Oriental Series 25. Cambridge: Harvard University Press, 1920.

______. 2 vols. Ānandāśrama-saṃskṛta-granthāvaliḥ, granthānkḥa, no. 32. Poona: Ānandāśrama, 1931.

Atharva Veda Saṃhitā. Translated by W. D. Whitney. 2 vols. Harvard Oriental Series, vols. 7 and 8. Cambridge: Harvard University Press, 1905.

______. Edited by V. Bandhu. 4 vols. Hoshiarpur: Vishveshavaranand Vedic Research Institute, 1960–62.

Bhāgavata Purāṇa. Translated by J. L. Shastri. Ancient Indian Tradition and Mythology 7–11. Delhi: Motilal Banarsidass, 1976.

______. Edited by C. Śrīdhara and J. L. Shastri. Delhi: Motilal Banarsidass, 1983.

Brahma Purāṇa. Edited by H. N. Apte. Ānandāśrama Sanskrit Series 28. Poona: Ānandāśrama, 1895.

Brahmavaivarta Purāṇa. Translated by R. N. Sen. Sacred Books of the Hindus 24. 2 vols. Allahabad: Sudhindranāthat Vasu, 1912–22.

———. Edited by V. G. Apte. Ānandāśrama Sanskrit Series 102. 2 vols. Poona: Ānandāśrama, 1935.

Bṛhaddevatā, *or an Index to the Gods of the* Rig Veda *by Śaunaka, to which have been added* Ārsānukramaṇī, Chandonukramaṇī and Anuvākānukramaṇī *in the Form of Appendices,* Edited by Rājendrālala Mitra. Bibliotheca Indica Sanskrit Series, n.s. nos. 722, 760, 794, 819. Calcutta: Baptist Mission Press, 1893.

———. Edited and translated by Arthur Anthony Macdonnell. 2 vols. Harvard Oriental Series. Cambridge: Harvard University Press, 1904.

Jaiminīya Brāhmaṇa. Edited by R. Vira and L. Chandra. Sarasvati Vihara Series. Nagpur, 1954.

———. Incomplete translation by H. W. Bodewitz. *Jaiminīya Brāhmaṇa.* Vol. 1, 1–65. Leiden: E. J. Brill, 1973.

Kātyāyana Śrauta Sūtra. Edited by Albrecht Weber. Chowkhamba Sanskrit Series, no. 104. Reprint. Varanasi: Chowkhamba Sanskrit Series Office, 1972.

———. Translated by H. G. Ranade. Poona: Dr. H. G. Ranade and R. H. Ranade, n.d.

Kauṣītaki Brāhmaṇa. Edited by H. Bhattacharya. Calcutta Sanskrit College Research Series, no. 73. Calcutta: Sanskrit College, 1973.

Kūrma Purāṇa. Translated by Ahibhusan Bhattacharya. Edited by Anand Swarup Gupta. Varanasi: All-India Kashiraj Trust, 1972.

Liṅga Purāṇa. Edited by G. B. Nātu. Bombay: Veṅkaṭeśvara Press, 1924.

———. Translated by J. L. Shastri. Ancient Indian Tradition and Mythology 5–6. Delhi: Motilal Banarsidass, 1984.

The Mahābhārata. Edited by Visnu S. Sukthankar. 19 vols. Poona: Bhandarkar Oriental Research Institute, 1933–60.

———. Edited and translated by J. A. B. Van Buitenen. 3 vols. Chicago: University of Chicago Press, 1973–78.

Manu Smṛti. Translated by George Bühler. Sacred Books of the East. Oxford: Clarendon Press, 1886. Reprint. New York: Dover, 1969.

———. Edited by J. H. Dave. 5 vols. Bhāraitīya Vidyā Series. Bombay: Bhāratīya Vidyā Bhavan, 1972–82.

———. Translated by Wendy Doniger with Brian K. Smith. New York: Penguin, 1991.

Matsya Purāṇa. Translated by F. Eden Pargiter. Bibliotheca Indica Sanskrit Series. 2 vols. Calcutta: Baptist Mission Press, 1888–1904.

______. Edited by Ācārya Rāma Śarma. Bareli: Saṃskṛti Saṃsthāna, 1970.

Mārkaṇḍeya Purāṇa. Edited by K. M. Banerjea. Calcutta: Bishop's College Press, 1876.

Yāska's Nirukta *with Durga's Commentary*. Edited by H. M. Bhadkamkar. 2 vols. Bombay Sanskrit and Prakrit Series, nos. 73 and 85. Bombay: Government Central Press, 1918.

The Nighaṇṭu and the Nirukta. Edited from original manuscripts and translated by Lakṣman Sarup. London and New York: Oxford University Press, 1920–27.

Padma Purāṇa. 5 vols. Calcutta: Manusukharaya Mora, 1957–59.

Pañcaviṃśa Brāhmaṇa. Edited by P. A. Cinnaswami Sastri and P. Parrabhirama Sastri. 2 vols. Kashi Sanskrit Series, no. 105. Benares: Sanskrit Series Office, 1935.

Pūrva Mīmāṃsā Sūtras of Jaimini. In *Mīmāṃsā Sūtras of Jaimini,* Edited and translated by Mohan Lal Sandal. Delhi: Motilal Banarsidass, 1980.

Ṛg Veda Saṃhitā, *together with the* Commentary of Sāyaṇa Āchārya. Edited by F. Max Müller. 4 vols. Varanasi: Chowkhamba Sanskrit Series, 1966.

Sarvānumkramaṇī, *with Commentary with Ṣaḍguruśiṣya*. Edited by Arthur Anthony Macdonell. Oxford: Clarendon Press, 1886.

Śatapatha Brāhmaṇa. Translated by Julius Eggeling. Sacred Books of the East. Oxford, Clarendon Press, 1882–1900.

______. 5 vols. Bombay: Laxmi Venkateswar Steam Press, 1940.

Śiva Purāṇa. Edited by K. Śrīkṛṣṇadāsa. Bombay: Veṅkateśvara Press, 1929.

______. Translated by J. L. Shastri. Ancient Indian Tradition and Mythology 1–4. Delhi: Motilal Banarsidass, 1970.

Skanda Purāṇa. Edited by K. Śrīkṛṣṇadāsa. Bombay: Veṅkateśvara Press, 1910.

Vāmana Purāṇa. Edited and translated by A. S. Gupta et al. Banaras: All-India Kashiraj Trust, 1969.

Vāyu Purāṇa. Edited by Rájendralála Mitra. 2 vols. Calcutta: Kālikā Press, 1880–88. Reprint. Bibliotheca Indica Sanskrit Series no. 85. Calcutta: Baptist Mission Press, 1880.

Viṣṇu Purāṇa. Translated by H. H. Wilson. London: Oriental Translation Fund Committee, 1840.

———. Bombay: Veṅkateśvara Press, 1967.

Selected Secondary Texts

Alsdorf, Ludwig. "The *Ākhyāna* Theory Reconsidered." *Journal of the Oriental Institute of Baroda* 13, no. 3 (1964): 195–207.

———. "Ṣaḍguruśiṣya's Kommentar zur *Anukramaṇika*." *Indische Studien* 8 1856.

———. "die Sage von Apālā." *Indische Studien* 4 (1858): 1–8.

Bloomfield, Maurice. "Contributions to the Interpretation of the Veda 3. 1. The Story of Indra and Namuci. 2. The Two Dogs of Yama in a New Role. 3. The Marriage of Saraṇyū, Tvaṣṭar's Daughter." *Journal of the American Oriental Society* 15 (1898): 143–88.

———. "Contributions to the Interpretation of the Veda 7. 6. Trita, the Scape-goat of the Gods, in Relation to *Atharva Veda* 6.112 and 113." *American Journal of Philology,* 17 (1896): 430–37.

Böhtlingk, Otto, and Roth, Rudolph von. *Sanskrit-Wörterbuch*. 10 vols. St. Petersburg: Buchdruckerei der Kaiserlichen Akademie der Wissenschaften, 1875.

Brough, John. *Early Brāhmaṇical System of Gotra and Pravara*. Cambridge: Cambridge University Press, 1958.

Chakrabarti, S. K. "On the Transition of the Vedic Sacrificial Lore." *Indo-Iranian Journal* 21 (1979): 181–88.

Charpentier, Jarl. *Die Suparṇasage: Untersuchungen zur Altindischen Literatur und Sagen-geschichte*. Uppsala: A.-b. Akademiska Bokhandeln i Kommission, 1922.

Clooney, Francis X. *Thinking Ritually.* Vienna: de Nobili, 1990.

Dandekar, R. N. *Vedic Bibliography.* 4 vols. Bombay: Karnatak Publishing House, 1946.

Dange, Sadavshiv. *Cultural Sources from the Veda*. Bombay: Bharatīya Vidyā Bhavan, 1977.

———. *Legends in the* Mahābhārata, *With a Brief Survey of Folk-tales*. Delhi: Motilal Banarsidass, 1969.

Dikshitar, V. R. Ramachandra. *Some Aspects of the* Vāyu Purāṇa. Madras: University of Madras, 1933.

Dimmitt, Cornelia, and van Buitenen, J. A. B. *Classical Hindu Mythology: A Reader in the Sanskrit Purāṇas*. Philadelphia: Temple University Press, 1978.

Doniger, Wendy, trans. with Brain K. Smith *The Laws of Manu*. Harmondsworth: Penguin, 1991.

Geldner, Karl F. "Purūravas und Urvaśī." *Vedische Studien* 1 (1889): 243–95.

______. *Der Rigveda*. Göttingen: Vandenhoeck and Ruprecht, 1923.

Goldman, Robert. "Mortal Man and Immortal Woman: An Interpretation of Three *Ākhyāna* Hymns of the *Ṛg Veda*." *Journal of the Oriental Institute of Baroda* 18 (1969): 273–303.

Gonda, Jan. *Change and Continuity in Indian Religion*. The Hague: Mouton, 1965.

______. "Etymologies in the Ancient Indian *Brāhmaṇas*." *Lingua* 5 (1955): 61–85.

______. *A History of Indian Literature*. Vol. 1, fasc. 1, *Vedic Literature (Saṃhitās and Brāhmaṇas)*. Wiesbaden: Otto Harrassowitz, 1975.

______. *A History of Indian Literature*. Vol. 1, fasc. 2: *The Ritual Sūtras*. Wiesbaden: Otto Harrassowitz, 1977.

______. "The Indian *Mantra*." *Oriens* 16 (1963): 242–97.

______. *The Indra Hymns of the* Ṛg Veda. Leiden: E. J. Brill, 1989.

______. *Notes on Names and The Name of God in Ancient India*. Amsterdam: North-Holland Publishing, 1973.

______. *Selected Studies*. Vol. 4, *History of Ancient Indian Religion*. Leiden: E. J. Brill, 1975.

______. *Triads in the Veda*. Amsterdam: North-Holland Publishing, 1976.

Gopal, Ram. "Vedic Sources of the Śārṅgaka Legend in the *Mahābhārata*." *Journal of the Ganganath Jha Research Institute* 25 (1960): 37–401.

Hariyappa, H. L. *Ṛgvedic Legends Through the Ages*. Deccan College Dissertation Series, 9. Poona: S. M. Katre, 1953.

Hertel, Johannes. "Die Geburt des Purūravas." *Wiener Zeitschrift für die Kunde des Morgenlande* 25 (1911): 135–96.

______. "Der *Suparṇādhyāya*, ein Vedisches Mysterium." *Wiener Zeitschrift für die Kunde des Morgenlandes* 23 (1909): 273–346.

______. "Der Ursprung des Indischen Dramas und Epos." *Wiener Zeitschrift für die Kunde des Morgenlandes* 18 (1904): 59–83.

Hiltebeitel, Alf. "Hinduism." *The Encyclopedias of Religion,* edited by Mircea Eliade, vol. 6, 342. New York: Macmillan, 1987.

Hohenberger, Adam. *Die Indische Flutsage und das* Matsya Purāṇa. Leipzig: Otto Harrassowitz, 1930.

Horsch, Paul. *Die Vedische* Gāthā *und* Śloka *Literatur.* Bern: Francke Verlag, 1966.

Inden, Ronald. *Imagining India.* London: Basil Blackwell, 1990.

Iyengar, K. R. Srinivasa. "Urvaśī." *Sri Aurobindo Mandir Journal,* Jayanti 9 (1949): 46–84.

Jha, Ganganath. Pūrva Mīmāṃsā *in Its Sources.* Banaras: Banaras Hindu University Press, 1942.

Joshi, H. Sh. *Origin and Development of Dattātreya Worship in Indra.* Baroda: University of Baroda, 1965.

Kane, Pandurang Vaman. *History of Dharmaśāstra.* 2d ed. 5 vols. Poona: Bhandarkar Oriental Research Institute, 1968–75.

Kashikar, C. G. *A Survey of the* Śrauta Sūtra. Bombay: University of Bombay, 1968.

Keith, Arthur Berriedale. "The Birth of Purūravas." *Journal of the Royal Asiatic Society* January 1913: 412–17, 1913.

———. *Rigveda Brāhmaṇas: The Aitareya and Kauṣītaki Brāhmaṇas of the Rigveda.* Cambridge, Mass.: Harvard University Press, 1920.

Keith, Arthur Berriedale, and Macdonell, A. A., eds. *Vedic Index of Names and Subjects.* 2 vols. London: John Murray, 1912.

Kosambi, D. D. "Sociological Perspective on the Legend of Urvaśī and Purūravas." *Journal of the Bombay Branch of the Royal Asiatic Society* 27 (1950): 1–30.

Lévi, Sylvain. *Le Théâtre Indien.* 2 vols. Paris: Collège de France, Libraire Honore Champion, 1963.

Macdonell, A. A. Review *Die Sagenstoffe des* Ṛgveda *und die indische* Itihāsa-*tradition,* by Emil Sieg. *Deutsche Literatur-Zeitung* 38 (1903): 2302–3.

———. "Two Legends from the *Bṛhaddevatā* in an old MS of Ṣaḍguruśiṣya." *Journal of the Royal Asiatic Society* (1894): 11–28.

———. "Ueber die dem Śaunaka zugeschriebene *Ārṣānukramaṇī des Ṛgveda.*" In *Festgruss an Rudolf v. Roth,* 107–13. Stuttgart: W. Kohlhammer, 1893.

Mehta, M. "The Evolution of the *Suparṇa Sage* in the *Mahābhārata.*" *Journal of the Oriental Institute, of Baroda* 21, nos. 1–2 (1971): 41–65.

Mitchiner, John E. "The Concept of Emanation in Purāṇic Creation Accounts," *Viśva-Bharati Journal of Philosophy* 10, no. 1 (1973): 56–61.

______. *Traditions of the Seven Ṛṣis*. Delhi: Motilal Banarsidass, 1982.

Müller, Max. *Vedic Hymns*. Sacred Books of the East. Oxford: Oxford University Press, 1891. Reprint. Delhi: Motilal Banarsidass, 1964.

Nalin, Indira. "The Legend of Purāravas and Urvaśī." *Journal of Bombay University* 19, no. 2 (1950): 85–93.

Oertel, Hanns. "Contributions from the *Jaiminīya Brāhmaṇa* to the History of the *Brāhmaṇa* Literature." *Journal of the American Oriental Society* 18 (1897): 15–48.

______. "Contributions from the *Jaiminīya Brāhmaṇa* to the History of the *Brāhmaṇa* Literature." Second series, I. "Saramā and the Paṇis." *Journal of the American Oriental Society* 19, second half (1898): 97–103.

______. "Contributions from the *Jaiminīya Brāhmaṇa* to the History of the *Brahmaṇa* Literature." Fifth series, "Indra in the Guise of a Woman (JB. 2.78)." *Journal of the American Oriental Society* 26, first half (1905): 176–96.

O'Flaherty, Wendy Doniger. *The Origins of Evil in Hindu Mythology.* Berkeley and Los Angeles: University of California Press, 1976.

______. *The Rig Veda: An Anthology.* Harmondsworth: Penguin, 1981.

______. *Tales of Sex and Violence*. Chicago: University of Chicago Press, 1985.

Oldenberg, Hermann. "*Ākhyāna*-Hymnen im *Rigveda.*" *Zeitschrift der Deutschen Morgenlandischen Gesellschaft* 39 (1885): 52–83.

______. "Das altindische *Ākhyāna,* mit besonderer Rücksicht auf das *Suparṇākhyāna.*" *Zeitschrift der Deutschen Morgenlandischen Gesellschaft* 37 (1883): 54–86.

Pandey, D. P. "Sūrya." Ph.D. diss, University of Leiden, 1939.

Pargitar, F. E. *Ancient Indian Historical Tradition.* London: Oxford University Press, 1922.

Patton, Laurie. "Beyond the Myth of Origins: Types of Tale-Telling in Vedic Commentary," In *Myths and Fictions: their Place in Philosophy and Religion,* edited by Shlomo Biderman. Leiden: E. J. Brill. Forthcoming.

______. "Vāc: Myth or Philosophy?" In *Myth and Philosophy,* edited by Frank Reynolds and David Tracy, 183–214. Albany: State University of New York Press, 1991.

Pischel, Richard, and Geldner, Karl F. *Vedische Studien.* Stuttgart: W. Kohlhammer, 1889–1901.

Pollock, Sheldon. "*Mīmāṃsā* and the Problem of History in Traditional India." *Journal of American Oriental Society* 109, no. 4 (1989): 603–10.

Renou, Louis. *Bibliographie Védique.* Paris: Adrien-Maisonneuve, 1931.

______. *The Destiny of the Veda in India.* Delhi: Motilal Banarsidass, 1965.

______. *Etudes Védiques et Paninéènnes.* 17 vols. Paris: Publications de l'Institut de Civilisation Indienne, 1955–69.

Rocher, Ludo. *The Purāṇas.* Vol. 2, fasc. 3 of *A History of Indian Literature.* Edited by Jan Gonda. Wiesbaden: Otto Harrassowitz, 1986.

Said, Edward. *Orientalism.* New York: Vintage, 1978.

Scheftelowitz, Isidore. *Die Apokryphen des* Ṛgveda. Pt. 1 of *Indische Forschungen.* Breslau: Verlag von M. & H. Marcus, 1906.

______. Review of Arthur A. Macdonell's *The Bṛhaddevatā. Zeitschrift der Deutschen Morgenlandischen Gesellschaft* 56: 420–27.

von Schroeder, Leopold. 1908 *Mysterium und Mimus im* Rigveda. Leipzig: H. Haessel Verlag.

Sieg, Emil. 1902 *Die Sagenstoffe des* Ṛg Veda *und die indische* Itihāsa-*tradition.* Stuttgart: W. Kohlhammer.

Sinha, J. P. The Mahābhārata: *A Literary Study.* New Delhi: Meharchand Lachhmandas, 1977.

Smith, Brian K. *Reflections on Resemblance, Ritual and Religion.* New York: Oxford University Press, 1989.

Tokunaga, Muneo. "On the Recensions of the *Bṛhaddevatā.*" *Journal of the American Oriental Society* 101, no. 3 (1981): 275–86.

______. "The Text and Legends of the *Bṛhaddevatā.*" Ph.D. diss., Harvard University, 1979.

Weber, Albrecht. "Eine Legende des *Śatapatha Brāhmaṇa* über die Strafende Vergeltung nach dem Tode." *Zeitschrift der Deutschen Morgenlandischen Gesellschaft* 9 (1885): 237–43.

______. "Episches im vedischen Ritual." *Sitzungberichte der Preussischen Akademie der Wissenschaft* 38 (1891): 769–819.

Weber, Albrecht, ed.. *Indische Studien.* 18 vols. Berlin: F. Dummler, 1850–63; Leipzig: F. A. Brockhaus, 1865–98.

Windisch, Ernst. "Ueber die altirische Sage der *Táin Bó Cúalnge.*" *Verhandlung der 33 Philologenversammlung in Gera,* 15–30. N.p., 1879.

Winternitz, M. "*Bṛhaddevatā* und *Mahābhārata.*" *Wiener Zeitschrift für die Kunde des Morgenlandes* 20 (1906): 1–36.

———. Review of *The Bṛhaddevatā* by Macdonell. *Wiener Zeitschrift für die Kunde des Morgenlandes* 19 (1905): 422–26.

Wright, J. C. "Purūravas and Urvaśī." *Bulletin of the School of Oriental and African Studies* 30 (1967): 526–47.

CHAPTER 2

Primary Texts

Bhāgavata Purāṇa, with the commentary of Śrīdhara. Bombay: Sri Venkatesvara Steam Press, 1932. (*BP*).

Devībhāgavata Purāṇa. Benares, 1960. (*DBP*).

Mahābhārata. Edited by Visnu S. Sukthankar. 19 vols. Poona: Bhandarkar Oriental Research Institute, 1933–1960. (*M*).

Rāmāyaṇa. Baroda: Oriental Institute, 1960–75. (*R*).

Ovid, *Metamorphoses.* Trans. Frank Justus Miller. Cambridge, Mass.: Harvard University Press, 1974.

Secondary Texts

Huberman, Eric A. "Language, Love, and Silence: Readings of Separation in the Sanskrit Epic, Poetic, and Puranic Traditions." Ph.D. diss, Department of Middle East Languages and Cultures, Columbia University, 1990.

Mahony, William K. "Flying Priests, Yogins, and Shamans in Early Hinduism and Buddhism." Ph.D. diss, University of Chicago, 1982.

O'Flaherty, Wendy Doniger. *Dreams, Illusion, and Other Realities.* Chicago: University of Chicago Press, 1984.

———. *Hindu Myths.* Harmondsworth: Penguin, 1975.

———. "Horses and Snakes in the *Ādi Parvan* of the *Mahābhārata.*" In *Aspects of India: Essays in Honor of Edward Cameron Dimock,* edited by Margaret Case and N. Gerald Barrier, 16–44. New Delhi: American Institute of Indian Studies and Manohar, 1986.

______. *Other Peoples' Myths: The Cave of Echoes*. New York: Macmillan, 1988.

______. *The Rig Veda: An Anthology.* Harmondsworth: Penguin, 1981.

______. *Śiva: The Erotic Ascetic*. Oxford and New York: Oxford University Press, 1973.

______. *Women, Androgynes, and Other Mythical Beasts*. Chicago: University of Chicago Press, 1980.

Pollock, Sheldon, trans. Vol. 2, *Ayodhyākaṇḍa of The Rāmāyaṇa of Valmīki.* Princeton: Princeton University Press, 1986.

Ramanujan, A. K. "Where Mirrors are Windows: Towards an Anthology of Reflections." *History of Religions* 28:3 (February, 1989), 1–30.

Ruben, Walter. "Vier Liebestragödien des *Rāmāyaṇa," Zeitschrift der Deutschen Morganländischen Gesellschaft* 100: 287–355.

Sorensen, S. *Index to the Names in the Mahābhārata*. London: Ernest Benn, 1904.

Smith, Brian K. "Exorcising the Transcendent: Strategies for Defining Hinduism and Religion." *History of Religions* 27, no. 1 (1987), 32–55.

Sullivan, Bruce L. *Kṛṣṇa Dvaipāyana Vyāsa and the* Mahābhārata: *A New Interpretation*. Leiden: E. J. Brill, 1990.

Tagare, Ganesh Vasudeo, trans. *The Bhāgavata Purāṇa*. Ancient Indian Tradition and Mythology Series, vols. 7–10. Delhi: Motilal Banarsidass, 1978.

van Buitenen, J. A. B. "On the Archaism of the *Bhāgavata Purāṇa*." In *Krishna: Myths, Rites, and Attitudes,* edited by Milton Singer, 23–40. Honolulu: East-West Center Press, 1966.

Vijnanananda, Swami, trans. *The Śrī Mad Devī Bhāgavatam*. The Sacred Books of the Hindus, Vol. 26 Allahabad 1921–23.

CHAPTER 3

Primary Texts

Skanda Purāṇa. Bombay: Venkatesvara Press, 1867.

Secondary Texts

Dessigane, R., and Filiozat, Jean. *La légende des jeux de Çiva a Madurai.* [*Hālāsyamāhātmya*] Pondichery, 1960.

Doniger, Wendy, trans., with Brian K. Smith, *The Laws of Manu*. Harmondsworth: Penguin, 1991.

Dumézil, Georges. *The Destiny of the Warrior*. Translated by Alf Hiltebeitel. Chicago: University of Chicago Press, 1970.

———. *The Destiny of the King*. Translated by Alf Hiltebeitel. Chicago: University of Chicago Press, 1973.

Gopinatha Rao, T. A. *Elements of Hindu Iconography*. 2 vols., 4 parts. Madras, 1916.

O'Flaherty, Wendy Doniger. (See also Wendy Doniger.) *The Origins of Evil in Hindu Mythology*. (Berkeley and Los Angeles: University of California Press, 1976.

———. *Other Peoples' Myths: The Cave of Echoes*. New York: Macmillan, 1988.

———. *Women, Androgynes, and Other Mythical Beasts*. Chicago: University of Chicago Press, 1980.

Rocher, Ludo. *The Purāṇas*. Vol. 2, fasc. 3 of *A History of Indian Literature*. Edited by Jan Gonda. Wiesbaden: Otto Harrassowitz, 1986.

Shulman, David Dean. *Tamil Temple Myths: Sacrifice and Divine Marriage in the South Indian Śaiva tradition*. Princeton, 1980.

CHAPTER 7

Primary Texts

Bṛhaddharma-Purāṇa. Edited by Haraprasad Sastri. Bibliotheca Indica, n.s. 668. Calcutta, 1888.

Bṛhatkathākoṣa: by Hariṣeṇa (Sanskrit). Edited by A. N. Upadhye, Singhī Jaina granthamālā No. 17. Bombay, 1943.

"Cēṭamalaippatiṟṟuppatt' Antāti." In *Antāti-kkottu*. edited by T. Chandrasekharan, vol. 1, 27–47. Madras: Madras Government Oriental Manuscripts Series, 51. 1956.

Devīkathā. Locally published pamphlet (in Marāṭhī). No information available.

Devīmāhātmya. Sanskrit text and English translation by Swami Jagadisvarananda. Madras, 1972.

Kahakosu: by Siricandra (in Apabhraṃśa). Edited by Hiralal Jain. Prakrit Text Society Series, no. 13. Ahmedabad, 1969.

Kaiśika-Purāṇa: Sanskrit text (in Tamil script) with (Tamil) commentary by Parāśara Paṭṭar. Tirucci, 1973.

Karakaṇḍacariü: by Kanakāmara (in Apabhraṃśa). edited by Hiralal Jain, Bhāratīya Jñānapīṭha Mūrtideva Jaina granthamālā no. 4. Delhi, 1964.

Mahābhāgavata-Purāṇa. Edited by P. Kumar. Delhi, 1983.

South Indian *Sthalapurāṇas* (in Sanskrit)

Kāñcīmāhātmyam. Edited by P. B. Anantachariar (in Devanāgarī). Conjeevaram: Sri Sudarsana Press, 1907.

"Nāthaṉ-kōvil-māhātmya." Nos. 11315 and 11328 (Burnell) = Nos. 10024 and 10028 (descriptive); the first is in Grantha, the second in Telugu characters. Manuscripts. Tanjore Sarasvati Mahal Library.

"ŚrīVaikuntam" and "Āḻvār-TiruNakari." In *Navatirupathimāhātmyam,* edited by Śrīnivāsācārya (in Grantha characters). Śuṇḍappālayam, 1909.

"Tañjā-māhātmyam." No. 1886 (Burnell) = No. 10480 (descriptive); in Devanāgarī characters. Manuscript. Tanjore Sarasvati Mahal Library.

TirukKuruṅkuṭi-sthalapurāṇa. Locally published (1981) Sanskrit text (in Devanāgarī) edited and translated by A. Srinivasaraghavan. 1981.

"TiruNakari." Privately owned manuscript in Grantha characters, called *Bilvāraṇyakṣetra-māhātmyam.*

Information on other temples and *sthalapurāṇas* was derived from a series of articles in Tamil, by various authors, which appeared in the Śrīvaiṣṇava journal *Narasiṃhapriya.*

Secondary Texts

Bābar, Sarojinī, ed. *Ek hotā rājā.* Mahārāṣṭra rājya lokasāhitya mālā, *puṣpa* 10, Pt. 1, "Yallammā-devīcī gāṇī," 73–89. (In Marathi) N.p. 1965.

Babb, L. *The Divine Hierarchy: Popular Hinduism in Central India.* New York: Columbia University Press, 1975.

Biardeau, M. "Some Considerations about Textual Criticism." In *Purāṇa* (Benares: All-India Kashiraj Trust) 10 (1968): 286–91.

Brown, C. M., *God as Mother: a Feminine Theology in India—A Historical and Theological Study of the Brahmavaivarta Purāṇa,* Hartford, Vt.: C. Stark, 1974.

Coburn, T. B. *Devī-māhātmya: The Crystallization of the Goddess Tradition.* Delhi: Motilal Banarsidass, 1984.

Dimock, Edward Cameron, trans. *The Thief of Love: Bengali Tales from Court and Village.* Chicago: University of Chicago Press, 1963.

Dubois, J. A. *Hindu Manners, Customs and Ceremonies.* 3d ed., translated and edited by H. K. Beauchamp. Oxford: Oxford University Press, 1906.

Hacker, P. *Prahlāda: Werden und Wandlungen einer Idealgestalt—Beiträge zur Geschichte des Hinduismus.* 2 vols. Akademie der Wissenschaften und der Literatur, Abhandlungen der Geistes- und Sozialwissenschaftlichen Klasse, no. 9. Wiesbaden, 1959.

Hardy, F. "Ideology and Cultural Contexts of the Śrīvaiṣṇava Temple." *The Indian Economic and Social history Review* 14, no. 1 (1977): 119–51.

———. "Mādhavendra Purī: A Link between Bengal Vaiṣṇavism and South Indian *Bhakti.*" *JRAS* 1974, no. 1: 23–41.

———. "The Philosopher as Poet: A Study of Vedantadeśika's *Dehalīśastuti.*" *Journal of Indian Philosophy* 7 (1979): 277–325.

———. Review of *Tamil Temple Myths,* by D. D. Shulman. *Journal of the Royal Asiatic Society* 1982, no. 2: 201ff.

———. "The Śrīvaiṣṇava Hagiography of Parakāla." In *Indian Narrative Literature,* edited by C. Shackle and R. Snell. Forthcoming.

———. "The Tamil Veda of a *Śūdra* Saint: The Śrīvaiṣṇava Interpretation of Nammālvār." In *Contributions to South Asian Studies,* edited by Gopal Krishna, vol. 1, 29–87. Delhi: Oxford University Press, 1978.

———. *Viraha-bhakti: The Early History of Kṛṣṇa Devotion in South India.* Oxford University South Asian Studies Series. Delhi: Oxford University Press, 1983.

Hazra, R. C. *Studies in the Upapurāṇas.* Vol. 2, *Śākta and Non-sectarian.* Calcutta Sanskrit College Research Series, no. 22, Studies no. 10. Calcutta, 1963.

Jaini, Padmanabh S. *The Jaina Path of Purification.* Berkeley, CA: University of California Press, 1979.

Jones, J. J., trans. *The Mahāvastu.* 3 vols. Sacred Books of the Buddhists, vols. 16, 18, 19. London, 1949–56.

Kirfel, W. "Kṛṣṇa's Jugendgeschichte in den Purāṇa." In *Festgabe H. Jacobi,* edited by W. Kirfel, 298–316. Beiträge zur Literaturwissenschaft und Geistesgeschichte Indiens. Bonn, 1926.

———. *Das Purāṇa Pañcalakṣaṇa: Versuch einer Textgeschichte.* Bonn, 1927.

———. *Das Purāṇa vom Weltgebäude (Bhuvanavinyāsa)—Die kosmographischen Traktate der Purāṇa's: Versuch einer Textgeschichte.* Bonner Orientalistische Studien, n.s., vol. 1. Bonn, 1954.

Maity, Pradyot Kumar. *Historical Studies in the Cult of Manasā: A Sociocultural Study.* Calcutta, 1966.

Porcher, Marie-Claude. "La représentation de l'espace sacré dans le *Kāñcīmāhātmya.*" *Puruṣārtha* 8 (1985): 23–50.

Rahula, Bhikkhu Telwatte. *A Critical Study of the Mahāvastu.* Delhi, 1978.

Rösel, J. *Der Palast des Herrn der Welt: Entstehungsgeschichte und Organisation der indischen Tempel- und Pilgerstadt Puri.* Arnold-Bergstraesser-Institut, Materialien zu Entwicklung und Politik, vol. 18. Munich, 1980.

Shastri, J. L. trans. *Śiva-Purāṇa* (in English). Delhi, Motilal Banarsidass, 1970.

Shulman, D. D. *Tamil Temple Myths: Sacrifice and Divine Marriage in the South Indian Śaiva Tradition.* Princeton, Princeton University Press, 1980.

Smith, W. L. *The One-eyed Goddess: A Study of the Manasā Maṅgal.* Acta Universitatis Stockholmiensis, vol. 12. Stockholm, 1980.

Sontheimer, G.-D. *Birobā, Mhaskobā und Khaṇḍobā: Ursprung, Geschichte und Umwelt von pastoralen Gottheiten in Mahārāṣṭra.* Schriftenreihe des Südasien-Instituts der Universität Heidelberg, no. 21. Wiesbaden, 1976.

van Kooij, K. R. *Worship of the Goddess according to the* Kālikāpurāṇa, pt. 1 (contains chapters 54–69). Leiden, E. J. Brill, 1972.

Wicki, J., ed. *Tratado do Pe. Gonçalo Fernandes Trancoso sobre o Hinduísmo (Maduré 1616).* Centro de Estudos Históricos Ultramarinos. Lisbon, 1973.

CHAPTER 8

Note: While this bibliography is extensive, perhaps excessively so for a paper of this length, it is by no means exhaustive. It is intended merely to provide a starting point for any person interested in pursuing research on the Jaina Purāṇas. I have included none of the extensive secondary literature in Kannada, Tamil, or Marathi, as I have no means of assessing its quality. There are also many Ph.D. dissertations that have been done over the past twenty years in India devoted to studies of one or more Jaina

Purāṇas; for a large but incomplete list of these, see S. Jain and A. P. Singh (1983).

Abbreviations

BJP Bhāratīya Jñānapīṭha Prakāśana
JOI *Journal of the Oriental Institute* (Baroda)
JSSS Jaina Saṁskṛti Saṁrakṣaka Saṅgha
MDJG Maṇikacanda Digaṁbara Jaina Granthamālā
PTS Prakrit Text Society

Primary Texts

Ādipurāṇa of Jinasena. 2 vols. Sanskrit text with Hindi translation by Pannālāl Jain. Varanasi: BJP, 1951.

______. Sanskrit text with Marathi translation by Jindās Pārśvanāth Phaḍkule. Sholapur: Jīvarāja Jaina Granthamālā, n.d.

Amarakośa of Amarasiṃha, with *Amarapadavivṛti* of Liṅgayasūrin and *Amarapadapārijāta* of Mallinātha. Sanskrit text edited by A. R. Ramanathan. Adyar, Madras: Adyar Library and Research Centre, 1971.

Antagaḍa-dasāo. English translation by L. D. Barnett. London: Royal Asiatic Society, 1907.

Bṛhatkathākośa of Hariṣeṇa. Sanskrit text edited by A. N. Upadhye. Bombay: Siṅghī Jaina Granthamālā, 1943.

Caüppaṇṇamahāpurisacariya of Śīlāṅka. Maharashtri text edited by Amritlal Mohanlal Bhojak. Ahmedabad and Varanasi: PTS, 1961.

Harivaṃśa Purāṇa of (Punnāṭa) Jinasena. Sanskrit text edited by Pt. Darbārīlāl. 2 vols. Bombay: MDJG, 1930–31.

______. Sanskrit text with Hindi translation by Pannālāl Jain. Varanasi: BJP, 1962.

Kahākosu of Siricandra. Prakrit text edited by Hiralal Jain. Prakrit Text Society Series, no. 13. Ahmedabad: PTS, 1961.

Kappa Sutta (*Kalpa Sūtra*) of Bhadrabāhu. Ardha-Magadhi text edited by Hermann Jacobi. Leipzig: F. A. Brockhaus, 1879.

______. English translation by Hermann Jacobi in *Jaina Sūtras*. Vol. I. Sacred Books of the East, vol. 22. Oxford: Clarendon Press, 1884. Reprint. Delhi: Motilal Banarsidass, 1964; and New York: Dover, 1968.

———. Ardha-Magadhi text edited and Hindi translation by Mahopādhyāy Vinay Sāgar, English translation by Mukund Lath. Jaipur: Prakrit Bharati, 1977.

Kathākośa of Prabhācandra. Sanskrit text edited by A. N. Upadhye. Bombay: MDJG, 1938.

———. English translation by C. H. Tawney. London: Royal Asiatic Society, 1895. Reprint. New Delhi: Oriental Books Reprint Corp., 1975.

Lokavibhāga of Siṃhasūrarṣi. Sanskrit text with Hindi translation by Bālacandra Siddhāntaśāstrī. Sholapur: JSSS, 1962.

Mahāpurāṇa of Jinasena and Guṇabhadra. Sanskrit text with Kannada translation by A. Shantirajasastry. 4 vols. Bangalore: Kannada Sahitya Parisat, 1933.

———. See *Ādipurāṇa* of Jinasena and *Uttarapurāṇa* of Guṇabhadra.

Mahāpurāṇu of Puṣpadanta. Apabhramsa text edited by P. L. Vaidya. 3 vols. Bombay: MDJG, 1937–41.

———. Apabhramsa text and German translation of chapters 81–92 by Ludwig Alsdorf. Jamburg: Friedrichsen, De Gruyter, 1936.

Vīrajiṇinda Cariu. Apabhramsa text and Hindi translation of chaps. 95–108 by Hīrālāl Jain. New Delhi: BJP, 1974.

Padma Purāṇa of Raviṣena. Sanskrit text edited by Pt. Darbārīlāl. 3 vols. Bombay: MDJG, 1928–29.

———. Sanskrit text and Hindi translation by Pannālāl Jain. Varanasi: BJP, 1958–59.

———. Sanskrit text and Marathi translation by Jindās Pārśvanāth Phaḍkule. Sholapur: Rāmāyaṇ Prakāśan Samiti, 1965.

Pāṇḍavacarita Mahākāvya of Devaprabha. Sanskrit text edited by Kedarnath and Panshikar. Kāvyamālā Series 93. Bombay, 1911.

———. Hindi translation by Panyās Padma Vijay. Delhi: Nirgranth Sāhitya Prakāśan Saṅgh, 1983.

Pāṇḍava Purāṇa of Śubhacandra. Sanskrit text edited and Hindi translation by J. P. Śāstrī. Sholapur: JSSS, 1954.

Pāṇḍava Purāṇa of Vādicandra. Sanskrit text edited by P. S. Jaini. Forthcoming.

Pārśvanātha Caritra of Bhāvadevasūri. Sanskrit text edited by Pt. Hargovinddās and Pt. Becardās. Varanasi: Yaśovijaya Jaina Granthamālā, 1912.

———. English synopsis, see Bloomfield 1919.

Paümacariu of Svayaṃbhū. Apabhramsa text edited by H. C. Bhayani. 3 vols. Bombay: Siṅghī Jaina Śāstra Śikṣāpīṭha and Bhāratīya Vidyā Bhavan, 1953–60.

______. Apabhramsa text edited by H. C. Bhayani and Hindi translation by Devendrakumār Jain. 5 vols. Varanasi: BJP, 1957–1970.

______. Extremely abridged English trans. in *Jain Journal* 4, no. 1 (1969), 6, no. 2 (1971).

Paümacariya of Vimalasūri. 2d ed. Maharashtri text edited by Hermann Jacobi and revised by Muni Puṇyavijaya, with Hindi translation by Shantilal M. Vora. Varanasi: PTS, 1962.

Samavāyāṇga. Ardha-Magadhi text edited by Ṛṣi Nānakacandra, with Sanskrit *Ṭīkā* of Abhayadeva, and Gujarati *Bhāṣā Ṭīkā* by Megharājagaṇi. Benares: Rāya Dhanapatisiṁha Bahādūra Āgamasaṁgraha, 1880.

______. Ardha-Magadhi text, with Sanskrit *Ṭīkā* of Abhayadevasūri, and with Hindi and Gujarati translation by Paṇḍitamuni Kanhaiyālāl. Rajkot: Jaina Śāstroddhar Samiti, 1962.

______. Ardha-Magadhi text and Hindi translation by Muni Kanhaiyālāl. Delhi: Āgam Anuyog Prakāśan, 1966.

______ and *Sthāṇānga*. Ardha-Magadhi text, with Sanskrit *Ṭīkā* by Abhayadevasūri, edited by Sāgarānandsūri, Puṇyavijaya, and Jambūvijaya. Delhi: Motilal Banarsidass, 1985.

Ṣaṭkhaṇḍāgama of Puṣpadanta and Bhūtabali. 2 vols. Sauraseni text edited, with Sanskrit and Prakrit *Dhavalāṭīkā* of Vīrasena, and Hindi translation, by Hīrālāl Jain and A. N. Upadhye. Sholapur: JSSS, 1973–76.

Śatruñjaya Mahātīrtha Māhātmya of Dhaneśvarasūri. Sanskrit text and Gujarati translation by Ācārya Vijaya Kanakacandrasūri. Patan: Viśvamaṅgala Prakāśana Mandira. n.d.

Ṭhāṇāṅga. See *Samavāyāṅga*.

Tiloya Paṇṇatti of Yativṛṣabha. Sauraseni text edited by A. N. Upadhye and Hīrālāl Jain, and Hindi translation by Pt. Bālcandra. 2 vols. Sholapur: JSSS, 1943–1951.

Triṣaṣṭiśalākāpuruṣacaritra of Hemacandrasūri. Sanskrit text. 6 vols. Bhavnagar: Jaina Dharma Prasāraka Sabhā, 1906–1913.

______. English translation by Helen M. Johnson. 6 vols. Gaekwad's Oriental Series. Baroda: Oriental Institute, 1931–62.

______. *Jaina Jatakas*. English translation of canto 1 by Amulyacharan Vidyabhushana, edited by Banarsi Das Jain. Lahore: M. L. B. Das, 1925.

Uttarapurāṇa of Guṇabhadra. Sanskrit text and Hindi translation by Pannālāl Jain. Varanasi: BJP, 1954.

———. "The Story of Jīvandhara." English translation by E. Hultzsch. *Quarterly Journal of the Mythic Society* 12 (1922): 317–48.

———. "Life of Mahavira (Mahapurana)." English translation by K. C. Lalwani. *Jain Journal* 7 (1973): 199–218.

Vasudevahiṇḍī of Saṅghadāsagaṇi and Dharmadāsagaṇi. Maharashtri text edited by Muni Caturavijaya and Muni Puṇyavijaya. 2 vols. Bhavnagar: Jaina Ātmānanda Sabhā, 1930–31.

———. See J. C. Jain, *Vasudevahiṇḍī,* under "Secondary Sources."

Secondary Texts

Alsdorf, Ludwig. "What Were the Contents of the Dṛṣṭivāda?" In *German Scholars on India,* vol. 1, 1–5. Varanasi: The Chowkhamba Sanskrit Series Office, 1973.

Bloomfield, Maurice. *The Life and Stories of the Jaina Savior Pārçvanātha.* Baltimore: Johns Hopkins University Press, 1919. Reprint. Delhi: Gian Publishing House, 1985.

Bruhn, Klaus. Introduction to Śīlāṅka's *Caüppaṇṇamahāpurisacariya.* Ahmedabad and Varanasi: PTS, 1961.

———. *Sīlānkas Caüppaṇṇamahāpurisacariya: ein Beitrag zur Kenntnis der Jaina-Universalgeschichte.* Hamburg: Cram, De Gruyter & Co., 1954.

Bühler, G. *The Life of Hemacandracarya.* Vienna, 1889. Translated by M. L. Patel. Santiniketan: Singhi Jaina Jnanapith, 1936.

Candraśekharvijay Gaṇi, Paṁnyās. *Jain Mahābhārat.* 2 vols. Ahmedabad: Kamal Prakāśan Trust, 1985.

———. *Rāmāyaṇ mā Saṁskṛti no Sandeś.* 2 vols. Ahmedabad: Kamal Prakāśan Trust, 1977.

Caudharī, Gulāb Candra. *Jain Sāhitya kā Bṛhad Itihās.* Vol. 6, *Kāvya-Sāhitya.* Varanasi: P. V. Research Institute, 1973.

Chandra, K. R. *A Critical Study of the Paumacariya.* Muzaffarpur: Vaishali Research Institute of Prakrit, Jainology & Ahimsa, 1970.

———. "New Light on the Date of the *Paümacariyam.*" *Journal of the Oriental Institute* 13 (1964): 378–86.

Cort, John E. "Liberation and Wellbeing: A Study of the Śvetāmbar Mūrtipujak Jains of North Gujarat." Ph.D. diss., Harvard University, 1989.

Doshi, Saryu. *Masterpieces of Jain Painting*. Bombay: Marg Publications, 1985.

Dundas, Paul. "Food and Freedom: the Jaina Sectarian Debate on the Nature of the Kevalin." *Religion* 15 (1985): 161–98.

Fischer, Eberhard, and Jain, Jyotindra. *Jaina Iconography*. Leiden: E. J. Brill, 1978.

Folkert, Kendall W. "The 'Canons' of 'Scripture.'" In *Rethinking Scripture*, edited by Miriam Levering, 170–79. Albany: State University of New York Press, 1989.

______. "Two Jaina Approaches to Non-Jainas: Patterns and Implications." Ph.D. diss., Harvard University, 1975.

Hawley, John Stratton. *Krishna, the Butter Thief*. Princeton: Princeton University Press, 1983.

Hertel, Johannes. *On the Literature of the Shvetambaras of Gujarat*. Leipzig: Sächsiche Forschungsinstitute, 1922.

Jacobi, Hermann. 1914 "Hemacandra," in *Encyclopaedia of Religion and Ethics*, Vol. VI, 591. New York: Charles Scribner's Sons.

Jain, Hīrālāl. *Bhāratīya Saṁskṛti mẽ Jain Dharm kā Yogadān*. Bhopal: Madhyapradeś Śāsan Sāhitya Pariṣad, 1962.

Jain, Jadgish Chandra. "The Importance of the Vasudevahiṇḍī." *Wiener Zeitschrift für die Kunde Südasiens* 19 (1975): 103–16.

______. "Is Vasudevahiṇḍī a Jain Version of Bṛhatkathā?" *Journal of the Oriental Institute* 23 (1973): 59–63.

______. *Life in Ancient India as Depicted in the Jain Canon and Commentaries*. 2d ed. New Delhi: Munshiram Manoharlal, 1984.

______. *Prakrit Narrative Literature: Origin and Growth*. New Delhi: Munshiram Manoharlal, 1981.

______. *Prākṛt Jain Kathā Sāhitya*. Ahmedabad: L. D. Institute of Indology, 1970.

______. *The Vasudevahiṇḍī: An Authentic Jain Version of the Bṛhatkathā*. Ahmedabad: L. D. Institute of Indology, 1977.

Jain, Jyoti Prasad. *The Jaina Sources of the History of Ancient India (100 B.C.–A.D. 900)*. Delhi: Munshiram Manoharlal, 1964.

Jain, Sagarmal, and Singh, Arun Pratap. *Doctoral Dissertations in Jaina and Buddhist Studies*. Varanasi: P. V. Research Institute, 1983.

Jaini, Jagmanderlal. *Outlines of Jainism*. Edited by F. W. Thomas. 1916. Reprint. Indore: J. L. Jaini Trust, 1979.

Jaini, Padmanabh S. "The Disappearance of Buddhism and the Survival of Jainism: A Study in Contrast." In *Studies in History of Buddhism,* edited by A. K. Narain, 81–91. Delhi: B. R. Publishing, 1980.

———. "Jaina Debates on the Salvation of a Nun (Strīmokṣa)." Paper presented at Workshop on Women in Indian Religion, Centre for Cross-Cultural Research on Women, Oxford, June 1987.

———. *The Jaina Path of Purification.* Berkeley and Los Angeles: University of California Press, 1979.

———. "The Jainas and the Western Scholar." *Sambodhi* 5 (1976): 121–31.

———. "Jina Ṛṣabha as an Avatāra of Viṣṇu." *Bulletin of the School of Oriental and African Studies* 40, no. 2 (1977): 321–37.

———. "*Mahābhārata* Motifs in the Jaina *Pāṇḍava-Purāṇa.*" *Bulletin of the School of Oriental and African Studies* 47, no. 1 (1984): 108–115.

Jha, Shaktidhar. *Aspects of Brahmanical Influence on the Jaina Mythology.* Delhi: Bharat Bharati Bhandar, 1978.

Kapadia, H. R. *A History of the Canonical Literature of the Jainas.* Surat: H. R. Kapadia, 1941.

Kirfel, Willibald. *Symbolik des Hinduismus und des Jinismus.* Stuttgart: Anton Hiersemann, 1959.

Kulkarni, V. M. "Introduction to *Paümacariya*". In *Paümacariya* of Vimalqsūri. Varanasi: PTS. 2d. ed. 1962.

———. "Origin and Development of the Rāma Story in Jaina Literature." *Journal of the Oriental Institute* 9 (1959–60): 189–204, 284–304.

———. *The Story of Rāma in Jain Literature.* Ahmedabad: Saraswati Pustak Bhandar, 1990.

Mahendar Kumārjī "Pratham," Muni. *Jaina Stories.* Translated from Hindi by K. C. Lalwani. Calcutta: Arhat Prakashan, 1984.

Mishra, D. P. "Critical Study of the Jaina Puranas." *Sambodhi* 11 (1982–83): 39–47.

Parekh, S. D. "The Meaning of 'Śalākāpuruṣa'". *JOI* 24 (1974): 152–54.

Peterson, Indira Viswanathan. *Poems to Śiva: The Hymns of the Tamil Saints.* Princeton: Princeton University Press, 1989.

Premī, Nāthūrām. *Jain Sāhitya aur Itihās.* 2d ed. Bombay: Hindī Granth Ratnākar, 1956.

Rāmcandrasūri, Ācārya Vijay. *Jain Rāmāyaṇ.* Ahmedabad: Śāh Premcand Haṭhīsing, 1941.

Rhys Davids, T. W., and Stede, William. *Pali-English Dictionary.* 1921–25. Reprint. New Delhi: Oriental Books Reprint Corp., 1975.

Rice, Edward P. *A History of Kanarese Literature*. 2nd ed. Calcutta: Association Press, 1921.

Shah, U. P. "Ramayana in Jaina Tradition." In *Asian Variations in Ramayana,* edited by K. R. Srinivasa Iyengar, 57–76. New Delhi: Sahitya Akademi, 1983.

Sharma, Jagdish P. "Hemacandra: The Life and Scholarship of a Jaina Monk." *Asian Profile* 3 (1975): 195–215.

Sheth, Pandit Hargovinddas T. *Pāia-Sadda-Mahaṇṇavo*. Varanasi: PTS, 1928. Reprint. Delhi: Motilal Banarsidass, 1986.

Strohl, G. Ralph. "The Image of the Hero in Jainism: Ṛṣabha, Bharata and Bāhubali in the *Ādipurāṇa* of Jinasena. Ph.D. diss., University of Chicago, 1984.

Tambiah, S. J. *World Conqueror and World Renouncer.* Cambridge: Cambridge University Press, 1976.

Upadhye, A. N. "Jinasena and his Works." In *Mélanges d'Indianisme a la Mémoire de Louis Renou,* 727–32. Paris: Éditions E. de Bocard, 1968.

Velankar, H. D. *Jinaratnakośa*. Poona: Bhandarkar Oriental Research Institute, 1944.

Warder, A. K. "Classical Literature." In *A Cultural History of India,* edited by A. L. Basham. Oxford: Clarendon, 1975.

———. *Indian Kāvya Literature*. 4 vols. Delhi: Motilal Banarsidass, 1972–83.

Weber, Albrecht F. "The Satrunjaya Māhātmya." Translated by K. S. Godbole. *Indian Antiquary* 30 (1901): 239–51, 288–308.

———. *Über das Çatrunjaya Māhātmyam: Ein Beitrag zur Geschichte der Jaina*. Leipzig: F. A. Brockhaus, 1858.

Winternitz, Maurice. *History of Indian Literature*. Vol. 2, *Buddhist and Jaina Literature*. Translated by S. Ketkar and H. Kohn. Calcutta: University of Calcutta, 1933.

Contributors

John E. Cort is assistant professor in the Department of Religion at Denison University, author of several articles on the Jainas and of *Liberation and Wellbeing: A Study of the Svetambar Murtipujak Jains of North Gujarat* (Ph.D. diss., Harvard University, 1989), and translator of *Bhartṛhari, An Old Tree Living by the River* (Calcutta: Writers Workshop, 1983).

Wendy Doniger is the Mircea Eliade Professor of the History of Religions at the University of Chicago and author of many books and articles on the Purāṇas, including (under the name of Wendy Doniger O'Flaherty) *Śiva: The Erotic Ascetic, Hindu Myths, The Origins of Evil in Hindu Mythology,* and (under the name of Wendy Doniger) *Textual Sources for the Study of Hinduism.*

Friedhelm Hardy is Reader in Indian Religions at the University of London, King's College. Apart from a number of articles, he is the author of *Viraha-Bhakti: The Early History of Kṛṣṇa Devotion in South India* (Delhi: Oxford University Press). His Wilde Lectures in comparative religion at the University of Oxford will be published in 1993 as *Power, Love and Wisdom in the Religious Culture of India.*

Padmanabh S. Jaini is professor of Buddhist Studies in the Department of South Asian Studies at the University of California at Berkeley, and author of many books and articles, including *The Jaina Path of Purification* and *Gender and Salvation: Jaina Debates on the Spiritual Liberation of Women.*

Laurie L. Patton is assistant professor of Asian Religion at Bard College, and the author of several articles on Indian religions, Celtic studies, and interpretive issues in the study of religion. She is the editor of *Authority and Anxiety in the Vedas* and *Myth as Argument: Tales from the Bṛhaddevatā* (forthcoming).

A. K. Ramanujan is William E. Colvin Professor at the University of Chicago, and author of many books and articles, including *The Interior Landscape, Speaking of Śiva, Poems of Love and War,* and *Hymns for the Drowning.*

Velcheru Narayana Rao is professor of South Asian Studies at the University of Wisconsin, Madison, and the author of *Śiva's Warriors: The Basava Purāṇa of Palkuriki Somanatha* and (with Hank Heifetz) *For the Lord of Animals: Poems from the Telugu.*

David Shulman is Professor in the Dept. of Indian, Iranian, and Armenian Studies at the Hebrew University, Jerusalem, and author of many books and articles, including *Tamil Temple Myths, The King and the Clown in South Indian Myth and Poetry,* and *Songs of the Harsh Devotee* (all published by Princeton University Press).

Index

Acala ("immovable," a Jaina Baladeva), 211
Ācārya (teacher), 210, 214, 229, 246–48
action. *See karma*
Ādi Purāṇa, 170, 180, 193–94, 231, 236–40, 244
Adideva ("the first Lord," the first Jaina Tīrthaṅkara), 232–34. *See also* Ṛṣabha
Ādiśakti (a goddess), 107, 110–15
Ādiśeṣa (the primeval serpent), 91
Aditi (a goddess), 11
Ādityas (solar gods), 24, 26
Advaita (non-dualism, a philosophy), 125–26, 144–45, 154, 157, 170
Āgama (a type of text), 131, 186, 190–95
Agastya (a sage), 7, 9, 11, 13, 133, 180
Agni (the god of fire), 9, 24–28, 56, 167, 238
Agni Purāṇa, 21
Agnihotra (the fire sacrifice), 239
Ahiṃsā (non-injury), 199, 209, 224, 236, 238
Ahobilam (a temple center), 123, 176–77
Aitareya Brāhmaṇa, 19
Ājīvakas (an ancient Jaina sect), 233
akam (a genre of Tamil poetry), 136–37, 153
ākhyāna ("story," a narrative genre), 14, 220
Alsdorf, Ludwig, 195
Āḻvār (a type of Tamil poet saint), 121, 127, 154, 170–71
Amarakośa (a dictionary), 193
Amarasiṃha (an author), 193–94
Amarāvatī (a city), 68
Ambalikā (a princess), 221
Ambikā (a princess), 221
Amoghavarṣa (a king), 192, 231, 244
Aṃśa (son of the goddess Aditi), 11
aṃśāvatāras (partial incarnations), 209
Andhaka (a demon), 76, 79
Aṅgas (the oldest texts in the Jaina canon), 185, 214
Aṅgiras (a sage), 8, 10–13
Antagada-dasāo (a Jaina Aṅga), 191
Anti-god. *See asura*
Anuha (son-in-law of Śuka), 46
anukramaṇī (index), 15
anuyoga (exposition), 186, 214
apsaras (a celestial nymph), xi, 8, 11, 39, 44–48, 50, 167, 224
Ara (a Cakravartin), 210
Aranātha (a Jaina Cakravartin), 198

yogin, 139, 234
yoni (vagina), 72, 80–81, 169. *See also piṇḍa*
Yudhiṣṭhira (a king in the *Mahābhārata*), 57, 91, 247
yuga (one of the four ages), 89. *See also* Kali Age, Kṛta Age

Zodiac, 136